Annual Editions:
Education, 43/e

Rebecca B. Evers

http://create.mheducation.com

ISBN-10: 1259392260   ISBN-13: 9781259392269

Contents

Preface

The public conversation on the purposes and future direction of education is as lively as ever. Alternative visions and voices regarding the broad social aims of schools and the preparation of teachers continue to be presented. *Annual Editions: Education* reflects current mainstream as well as alternative visions as to what education ought to be. This year's articles contain research, opinion, and practical ideas regarding important issues facing educators such as educational reforms; effective teaching practices in literacy, using technology to teach all students while teaching all students in communities of caring learners, with an emphasis on students who live in poverty, are ELL, or are among the sexual minority.

We face a myriad of quandaries in our schools today, not unfamiliar to our history as a nation, which are not easily resolved. Issues regarding the purposes of education, as well as the appropriate methods of educating, have been debated throughout the generations of literate human culture. Today, we are asking ourselves and others to provide our children a *quality education* for the twenty-first century. But first we must answer the questions: What is a quality education? How do we provide such an education for all children? There will always be debates over the purposes and the ends of "education," as it depends on what the term means at a given place or time. Each generation must construct the definition of "education" based on its understanding of "justice," "fairness," and "equity" in human relations. Each generation must establish its understanding of social justice and personal responsibility for our children and youth.

All of this is occurring as the United States continues to experience important demographic shifts in its cultural makeup. Furthermore, our ability to absorb children from many cultures into our schools challenges our creativity to find new ways to teach. Teachers in large cities have worked with immigrant populations since this nation began, but now schools in mid-sized cities and rural towns are experiencing increasing numbers of children who speak a language other than English. Several topics in this edition address teaching methods for English Language Learners throughout as we look at diversity, caring communities, and collaboration. We explore the larger issues of literacy and the integration of new technologies in our teaching practices.

Technological breakthroughs in information sciences have an impact on how people learn. The articles in this edition address how technology can change the fundamental delivery of content and expand options for personalizing learning.

There are those who advocate increased collaboration among teachers across grades and content areas as well as with families and the communities that are served by the schools. This edition includes information on how collaboration can help support teachers, parents, and students to engage more effectively to improve learning and school climates.

School climate and the safety of our school is never far from the minds of educators, parents, and the community at large. School shootings, bullying, and sexual harassment must be acknowledged as ever-present dangers. We need to understand why and how these events occur and plan for prevention and recovery when they do. Issues surround how students who are in the sexual minority are treated and educated in public schools. This can be an extremely personal hot button issue that educators must face. We do not intend to inflame, but rather, to begin the conversation about our responsibilities and the decisions we must make. Finally, bullying, it just does not go away. The problems of bullying are still as difficult for schools to address as they were when I was a preteen. Educators must understand what bullying is and which students are most likely to be bullied; those who are different in some way from an unclear standard regarding gender identity, sexual orientation, ability, or race and ethnicity.

In assembling this volume, we make every effort to stay in touch with the important research in educational studies and with the social forces at work in schools. Members of the advisory board contribute valuable insights, and the production and editorial staffs at the publisher, McGraw-Hill Contemporary Learning Series, coordinate our efforts. The readings in *Annual Editions: Education* explore the social and academic goals of education, the current conditions of the nation's educational system, the teaching profession, and the future of American education. In addition, these selections address the issues of change and the moral and ethical foundations of schooling.

Editor

Dr. Rebecca Barr Evers
Winthrop University

Dr. Rebecca Evers, a professor in Counseling, Leadership, and Educational Studies at the Richard W. Riley College of Education, attended Illinois College to earn a BA in English education in 1966, an MA in the Rehabilitation Teaching of the Adult Blind from Western Michigan University in 1969, and an EdD in special education at Northern Illinois University in 1994. She was a secondary special educator in the Chicago Public Schools for 25 years. At Winthrop, she teaches courses in classroom management, inclusion of students with disabilities and other special needs, and assistive technology at both graduate and undergraduate levels. Her primary area of interest is in inclusion of students with disabilities and special needs, such as ELL and LGBTQ. She has published and presented her collaborative research on methods to determine and assess the quality of teacher candidate's dispositions.

Academic Advisory Board

Members of the Academic Advisory Board are instrumental in the final selection of articles for Annual Editions books and ExpressBooks. Their review of the articles for content, level, and appropriateness provides critical direction to the editor and staff. We think that you will find their careful consideration reflected here.

Christopher Boe
Pfeiffer University

Beverly Bohn
Park University

Saran Donahoo
Southern Illinois University

La Vonne Fedynich
Texas A&M University—Kingsville

Kathleen E. Fite
Texas State University—San Marcos

Jason Helfer
Knox College

John Janowiak
Appalachian State University

Tammy Ladwig
University of Wisconsin

Leigh Neier
University of Missouri

Jessie Panko
Saint Xavier University

Stephen T. Schroth
Knox College

John R. Shoup
California Baptist University

Susan Studer
California Baptist University

Thomas Walsh
Kean University

Unit 1

UNIT

Prepared by: Rebecca B. Evers, *Winthrop University*

School Reform in the Twenty-first Century

We are a democratic society, committed to the free education of all our children, but are we accomplishing that goal? There has been a deep divide about this question which has resulted in much discussion of school reform and several attempts to find the perfect reform solution for our schools.

In an attempt to give direction to the reform movement, the Clinton administration established Goals 2000 under the *Educate America Act.* One of these goals continues to be important to the discussion of what constitutes a well-educated citizen.

Goal 2 states that "The high school graduation rate will increase to at least 90%." (U.S. Department of Education, n.d.) To date, data indicate that we have not reached this goal and are far from achieving it. Educators have acknowledged that high school graduates get more satisfactory jobs, are happier in their job choices, and earn higher salaries than non-graduates. Heckman and LaFontaine (2010) note the decline in high school graduation since 1970 (for cohorts born after 1950) has flattened growth in the skill level of the U.S. workforce. We must confront the drop-out problem to increase the skill levels of the future workforce. We must also consider how high schools that respond only to higher education demands may be ignoring the needs of the nation at-large for a skilled workforce that can compete in a global market. Bridgeland, Dilulio, and Morrison (2006) found in a survey of dropouts that 47 percent reported a major reason why they left school was the classes were not interesting and did not prepare them for their adulthood goals and the life they wished. We should consider that by simply preparing students to attend traditional four-year institutions, we may be ignoring their interests and desires, thus alienating them.

Next we had the No Child Left Behind legislation which placed emphasis on the specific student subgroups—requiring schools to be accountable for the progress of minority students and students with disabilities and quantifying achievement gaps. The fundamental philosophy underlying the legislation is that all children can learn and schools must demonstrate that their students have made progress. Schools are issued annual report cards based on standardized assessments and must demonstrate *adequate yearly progress* (AYP). In their latest report, the Center on Educational Policy (2012) stated

An estimated 48% of the nation's public schools failed to make adequate yearly progress based on 2010–11 test results. This marks the highest national percentage of schools ever to fall short and an increase of 9 percentage points from the previous year (p. 9).

In 2009, the Secretary of Education issued a call to action by stating that education is the civil rights issue of this generation and the fight for education is about much more than just education; it is about social justice (Duncan, 2009). In 2009, President Obama's *Race to the Top* was passed and established new goals for schools, teachers, and students. However, is it realistic to expect that schools will make greater strides now than in the past? Boyle and Burns ask an important question: "Why do we ask citizens rather than education professionals to govern public schools?" Their concerns are centered on the responsibility of schools to socialize children into society. We transmit our collective knowledge and shared values via the public schools. Therefore, we must have public debate about the purpose of public education. Part of that debate may well include discussion of trust and accountability. Do we, as a nation, trust our teachers to do what they should or must we regulate every topic in the curriculum and hold them accountable via standardized assessments? This is a primary question that has political parties, teachers and their associations, and parents taking sides for and against Common Core and high-stakes standardized testing.

As we consider the educational system of the United States, we must engage in an intensively reflective and analytical effort. Further, we must give considerable contemplation and forethought to the consequences, because our actions will shape not only the students' futures, but also the future of our country in the global community. Prospective teachers are encouraged to question their own individual educational experiences as they read the articles presented in this section. All of us must acknowledge that our values affect both our ideas about curriculum and what we believe is the purpose of educating others. The economic and demographic changes in the last decade and those that will occur in the future necessitate a fundamental reconceptualization of how schools ought to respond to the social and economic environments in which they are located. There are additional articles in the next unit on poverty that, with the articles in this unit, will offer practical ideas to help answer the following question. How can schools reflect the needs of, and respond to, the diverse group of students they serve while meeting the needs of our democratic society?

References

Bridgeland, J. M., Dilulio, J. J., & Morrison, K. B. 2006. "The Silent Epidemic: Perspectives of High School Dropouts." Bill & Melinda Gates Foundation. Retrieved on 28 May 2008 from www.gatesfoundation.org/Pages/home.aspx.

Article

Prepared by: Rebecca B. Evers, *Winthrop University*

Warning: the Common Core Standards May Be Harmful to Children

The language arts standards of the Common Core in too many places are simply too difficult and/or irrelevant for elementary grade students.

JOANNE YATVIN

Learning Outcomes

After reading this article, you will be able to:

- Analyze the data presented about student achievement in your state as it measures up to the rest of the United States.

When I first read the Common Core English/language arts standards for grades K-5, my visceral reaction was that they represented an unrealistic view of what young children should know and be able to do. As an elementary teacher and principal for most of my life, I could not imagine children between the ages of 5 and 11 responding meaningfully to the standards' expectations. But clearly I was in the minority. Forty-five states have adopted the standards without a murmur of complaint; writers and publishers are racing to produce materials for teaching them, and the teachers quoted in news articles or advertisements speak of the standards as if they are the silver bullet they have been waiting for.

Since then, I have read the English/language arts (ELA) standards many times; each time, they are more troubling. Some standards call on young children to behave like high school seniors, making fine distinctions between words or literary devices, carrying on multiple processes simultaneously, and expressing their understandings in precise academic language. Others expect them to have a strong literary background after only two or three years of schooling. Some standards are so blind to the diversity in American classrooms that they require children of different abilities, backgrounds, and native languages to manipulate linguistic forms and concepts before they have full control of their own home language. And, sadly, a few standards serve only to massage the egos of education elitists, but are of no use in college courses, careers, or everyday life.

To give you just an inkling of the problems in applying the ELA standards to young children, I offer a scenario of what might happen in a 1st-grade classroom when the following language standard is approached:

(L.1.1) *Use the most frequently occurring inflections and affixes (e.g., -ed, -s, re-, un-, pre-, -ful, -less) as a clue to the meaning of an unknown word.*

While reading aloud from a 1st-grade book, Zach stumbled over the word "recheck" and, although he eventually pronounced it correctly, his teacher felt that he did not fully grasp its meaning in the sentence. It seemed like a good time to make the class aware of the prefix "re" and how it works. So, she stopped the lesson and wrote these words on the white board: remake, rewrite, and retell. Then she asked the children to explain what each word meant. Several students raised their hands and answered correctly.

"What does the 're' part of each word tell us?" she then asked. The first student called on said "re" means to do something again. Nodding in approval, the teacher wrote "recheck" on the board leaving a space between "re" and "check." Then she asked, "So, what does 'recheck' mean?"

"To check something again," answered the class in chorus.

Since things were going well, the teacher decided to continue by asking students to name other words that worked the same way. Various class members confidently suggested, re-eat, re-dance, re-sleep, re-win, and others were waving their hands when she stopped them.

"Those aren't real words," she said. "We don't say, 'I'm going to resleep tonight.' Let's try to think of real words or look for them in our books." After giving the class a few minutes, she asked again for examples.

This time, the words were real enough: repeat, renew, reason, remove, return, read, and reveal, but none of them fit the principle being taught. Since it seemed futile to explain all that to 1st graders, the teacher did the best thing she could think of: "You reminded (uh-oh) me of 'recess,'" she said. "So, let's go out right now."

As they left the room, the children chatted happily among themselves: "We're going to 'cess' again!" "We'll 're-see' our friends." "I want to 're-play' dodge ball."

"Next time," thought the teacher, "I'd better try a different prefix." But then "un-smart" and "un-listen" popped into her head, and she decided to leave that particular standard for later in the year.

Although I could write scenarios for several other standards, they would make this paper much longer and not be as amusing as this one. Instead, I will present just a few standards that I find inappropriate for K-5 students along with brief explanations of their problems.

A Reading/Literature standard for 4th grade calls on students to:

> **(RL.4.4)** *Determine the meaning of words and phrases as they are used in a text, including those that allude to significant characters found in mythology (e.g., Herculean).*

I can't help wondering how 9- and 10-year-olds are supposed to do their "determining." Competent, engaged readers of any age do not stop to puzzle out unknown words in a text. Mostly, they rely on the surrounding context to explain them. But, if that doesn't work, they skip them, figuring that somewhere down the page they will be made clear.

Should students regularly consult a dictionary or thesaurus while reading? I don't think so. That's a surefire way to destroy the continuity of meaning. Nor would I expect them to recall an explanatory reference from the field of classic literature at this early stage of their education. Moreover, for each "Herculean" word that matches a literary character, there would be several like "cupidity" and "pander" that have strayed far from their original meanings.

In the Reading/Information category, I quickly found a standard with expectations far beyond the knowledge backgrounds of the children for whom it is intended:

> **(RI.2.3)** *Describe the connection between a series of historical events, scientific ideas or concepts, or steps in technical procedures in a text.*

Just assuming that 2nd graders are familiar with "a series" of historical events, etc., is simply unrealistic. But expecting them to "describe the connection between (sic) them" is delusional. Is there only one simple connection among a series of "scientific ideas"? How would you, as an adult, describe the connections among the steps in building a robot or even baking a pie?

In most of the Reading/Information standards, the same expectations for describing complex relationships among multiple items appear:

> **(RI.5.5)** *Compare and contrast the overall structure (e.g., chronology, comparison, cause/effect, problem/solution) of events, ideas, concepts, or information in two or more texts.*

For 5th graders, this standard would be even more difficult to meet than the previous one because it asks them to carry out two different operations on two or more texts that almost certainly differ in content, style, and organization

In the Writing and Speaking/Listening categories, there are fewer standards altogether. Yet, some of these standards also make unrealistic demands. One asks 1st graders to:

> **(W.1.7)** *Participate in shared research and writing projects (e.g., explore a number of "how-to" books on a given topic and use them to write a sequence of instructions).*

Since this standard does not mention "adult guidance and support," as many others do, I assume that a group of 1st graders is expected to work on its own to digest the content of several books, prune it to the essentials, and then devise a well-ordered list of instructions. This would be a complicated assignment even for students much older, requiring not only analysis and synthesis, but also self-regulation and compromise. I cannot see 1st graders carrying it out without a teacher guiding them every step of the way.

Of all the ELA standards, the ones in the Language (i.e., grammar) category are the most unrealistic. I could cite almost all of them as unreasonable for the grades designated and a few as pointless for any grade. Here is part of a kindergarten standard that fits both descriptions:

> **(L.K.1).** *(When speaking) Produce and expand complete sentences in shared language activities.*

Most of the kindergartners I know have no idea what the term "complete sentence" means. Children and adults commonly speak short phrases and single words to each other. I can't imagine any kindergarten teacher insisting during a group language activity that children speak in "complete sentences" or that they "expand" their sentences. Those directions would in all likelihood end the activity quickly as most children fell silent.

Here is another unrealistic standard, this time designated for 3rd grade:

> **(L.3.1)** *Explain the function of nouns, pronouns, verbs, adjectives, and adverbs in general and their functions in particular sentences.*

Aside from the unreasonableness of expecting 7- and 8-year-olds to explain the use of grammatical terms, this standard has no applications in reading, speaking, or writing. Research has shown unequivocally that being able to name parts of speech or diagram sentences has no positive effect on students' writing. This standard wastes instructional time on a useless skill.

I cannot leave this critique of the ELA Standards without taking one more swipe at the Language category. Standard **(L.4.1)** asks 4th graders to:

> *Use relative pronouns (who, whose, whom, which, that) and correctly use frequently confused words (e.g., to, too, two; there, their) in speech and writing.*

Several of these words are ones that many educated adults use incorrectly all the time. In fact "who" is so often used in place of "whom" that it is widely recognized as correct. Why not hold adults accountable for meeting this standard before expecting 4th graders to do so?

In finding fault with so many of the K-5 ELA standards, my familiarity with children's abilities and educational needs have guided me. Standards advocates may well argue that I have offered no evidence and scant research to support my views. In rebuttal, I would argue that they are in the same position and that much of what they propose for children flies in the face of established learning theory and brain development research. The reality is that the standards' creators have laid out a set of expectations for America's children that are grounded only in an antiquated conception of education and their personal preferences. And their followers, bedazzled by the standards length and breadth, illusion of depth, and elitist aura, have fallen into line as if lured by the Pied Piper of Hamelin.

Critical Thinking

1. Yatvin presents examples of Common Core State Standards (CCSS) that she believes to be inappropriate for the developmental level of the students in elementary school grades. Do you agree with her? Are you able to recall research or educational psychology theories that would support her ideas? If you disagree with her, are you able to recall research or educational psychology theories that would refute her ideas?

2. If you are a middle-level or high school teacher, do you believe that here are problems with the CCSS at your grade level? Which standards trouble you?

3. If you believe that the CCSS are harmful to students, how do we account for the fact that so many states have adopted these standards? Think back to the first two articles in this unit. How might the ideas in them apply to the issues discussed by Yatvin?

Create Central

www.mhhe.com/createcentral

Internet References

What Works Clearinghouse
www.ies.ed.gov/ncee/wwc
The Center for Comprehensive School Reform and Improvement
www.centerforcsri.org

JOANNE YATVIN (jyatvin@comcast.net) is an adjunct professor and supervisor of student teachers at the Portland State University Graduate School of Education, Portland, Ore., and is a past president of the National Council of Teachers of English (NCTE).

Yatvin, Joanne. From *Phi Delta Kappan*, March 2013, pp. 42–44. Reprinted with permission of Phi Delta Kappa International. All rights reserved. www.pdkintl.org

Article   Prepared by: Rebecca B. Evers, *Winthrop University*

The Common Core "State" Standards: The Arts and Education Reform

ALICE WEXLER

Learning Outcomes

After reading this article, you will be able to:

- Explain the primary concerns about the standards for the Arts.

- Argue for or against the idea that, as now written, the standards marginalize persons who live in poverty, are members of minority cultures, or have disabilities.

- Present solutions or changes that would make the standards appropriate for all students in public schools.

As the Common Core "State" Standards (CCSS)[1] become reality, teachers have reason for concern. Their autonomy and intellectual freedom to craft curriculum, tests, and assessments are relinquished and put in the hands of "experts" and testing companies such as Pearson. This reform to public education has consequently marginalized the arts and exacerbated the inequities of people in poverty and with disabilities. These populations flourish when engaged in autonomous acts of discovery, experimentation, and hypothetical thinking, all antithetical to the new reform.

Published in 2010, the Common Core State Standards initiative for school reform has been intended to replace the current state standards. The initiative has been funded by the richest private foundations—primarily the Bill and Melinda Gates Foundation and Broad Foundation—wielding their influence on Obama's and Arne Duncan's polices. It has been backed by the most powerful federal agencies in education: the National Governors Association (NGA) Center for Best Practices, Achieve Inc., the Council of Chief State School Officers (CCSSO), and the United States Department of Education (Chapman, 2011).

As of January 27, 2013, 45 states, four territories, and the District of Columbia[2] have adopted the CCSS in English Language Arts (ELA) and mathematics, which will replace current state standards. States that accepted federal money have committed their schools to the most prescriptive and formalized curriculum we have seen in this country. The Common Core "State" Standards have aligned national curriculum and standardized testing to the effect that testing inexorably drives curriculum. Teachers, principals and, ultimately, schools are accountable for student test scores. Consistently low performing schools face corrective action, restructuring, or closure. Most at stake are the arts, faced with elimination if test scores are not raised in ELA and mathematics (Kohn, 2013). The curriculum materials of CCSS will be fully implemented by most states in 2013–2014.[3]

National Core Arts Standards

In January 2013, the National Coalition for Core Arts Standards (NCCAS) released *National Core Arts Standards: A Conceptual Framework for the Arts,* the revision of the National Arts Standards. Its purpose is to place the arts in the curriculum beyond their "integration" into ELA and mathematics.[4] Members of the coalition intend to dispel any doubt that the arts have a meritorious place within the curriculum. Inspiration for the arts framework came from McTighe and Wiggins (2005), authors of *Understanding by Design.* Among their foci are essential questions that promote engaged and provocative dialogue. The arts framework invites rhizomatic and hypertexual learning in contrast to the CCSS's linear processes of transmitting knowledge, although the authors must make clear that NCCAS standards conform in direct and meaningful ways to the CCSS. The arts framework is about to undergo a second review at the College Board[5] to align the goals of NCCAS with

CCSS and to determine whether the standards will or will not be framed to coordinate with CCSS.

The Arts According to David Coleman

David Coleman, a prominent architect of CCSS and the recently appointed president of the College Board, has taken the podium at several satellite organizations of CCSS to clarify his philosophy, often to soothe the nerves of educators and administrators who have taken offense at a clumsy comment. Coleman's presence at a panel given at the Common Core headquarters in Washington, DC, is an example of a strategic event. The Common Core is a non-profit organization based in Washington, DC, and founded in 2007 to conduct research and advocacy in K-12 education. The Common Core is unrelated to CCSS but has since become its partner, providing CCSS with tools such as curriculum maps. Common Core has co-opted CCSS's language of content-rich reform, and the knowledge that "students need to learn." Lynne Munson, president and executive director of the Common Core, led a symposium in Washington, DC, on March 15, 2012, provocatively called "Truant from School: History, Science, and the Arts." Its visual centerpiece was a poster of what Munson called the "missing icons": George Washington, Albert Einstein, and the Mona Lisa. The panel consisted of Steve Farkas, Carol Jago, Lewis Hoffman, and David Coleman. Munson (2012) introduced the subjects of the panelists as the cutting edge of social studies, art, music, and foreign language: "the question before us today is, how can we use the levers of change available to educators right now to bring some of these key subjects back into the curriculum?" (Coleman, 2012a). The purpose of this panel was to reassure the audience that CCSS content would be painted in deep and broad strokes to avoid the pitfall of a narrowed curriculum.

David Coleman approached the lectern to tell the audience that learning to read in the early grades must be built on dense knowledge that drives vocabulary. Coleman aggressively stabbed the air with his pen to drive home the point that "there is no such thing as doing the nuts and bolts of reading from Kindergarten to 5th grade without coherently developing knowledge in science, history, the arts—period—it is false." (Coleman, 2012a). This research is not entirely his own, he says. He stands on the shoulders of giants in the field: E. D. Hirsch and David Pearson.

> What is a catastrophe is the seeming focus in reading in the early grades was mirrored by a focus of reading stories and, often, much worse than stories. Not necessarily the high quality, to be clear, but that total focus on reading only stories in K-5. Then, expanding the literacy block to meet reading standards had the catastrophic

effect of crowding out history, the arts and social science in the elementary school . . . by cutting off the knowledge that is the foundation of reading itself, period. (Coleman, 2012a)

Coleman built on E. D. Hirsch's confidence that academic content will fix the economy and finally resolve the scourge of poverty. The core content that Hirsch speaks of is information based on memorization with little evidence of critical and analytical thinking or discussion. The teaching of facts transfers easily and efficiently to standardized tests and assessment. Coleman has inherited this conservative and single solution for a single national culture to the public school system, and ultimately the social context that has produced it. The ironic terminology of reform was used then as it is now. The shared background information and literacy that would put children on the same playing field and reduce the gap between the social classes, is not unlike traditional textbook knowledge in which cultural perspectives of American history go unquestioned.

Let us return to Coleman (2012a) as he paused for "a word about the arts." After what must be innumerable hours of writing curriculum, ("which was a rather exhausting time, you might imagine") (Coleman, 2012a), Coleman gathered 40 art teachers from all areas of the US to study CCSS's implications for the arts. What they discovered was that the arts should not be the handmaiden to ELA, but rather that English teachers should learn what the arts are better at that might inform literacy. I infer that the arts are not ordinary handmaidens; they are very good at what they do. Coleman went on to explain the two ways that art is significant: (1) students will need to read the new texts carefully and with repeated observation and (2) "every artist loves observation . . . vigorous and repeated" (Coleman, 2012a). The arts have multiple interpretations that enrich the reading of Shakespeare or listening to musical scores. In an effort to elicit more confidence from his listeners, and to shore up fears about the recent controversy of fiction versus informational texts, Coleman read the following:

> Beginning in Elementary, to move beyond the phrase 50/50 . . . more informational texts . . . the line that has resonated with teachers so beautifully around the controversy is that the CCSS restores the rightful place of elementary school teachers as the *guide to the world*. (Coleman, 2012a)

Guiding Principles for the Arts

Our public school system, although inching bravely into the twenty-first century, has made a sharp right turn back to early Modernism. David Coleman's (2012b) *Guiding Principles for the Arts Grades K-12* has suggested what is in store. Rather than a new vision, the new standards—with their recommendations of works of art that every child should see and know—appear to be closer to an early version of Disciplined Based Art Education (DBAE) centered on the study of "magnificent works of art" (Coleman, 2012b, p. 1). Coleman's vision, it could be argued, is elitist in his assumptions that all children should learn the same content. The document abounds with hyperbole, such as *magnificent works of art* and judgments thereof, or *art as transcendent and beautiful.* These notions are of course benign and even suggest enrichment, but my question is: Who decides what is magnificent, transcendent, and beautiful? What will happen to street art, public art, activist art as well as the rough, tattered, unguided, self-taught, and intuitive works of art traditionally made by the isolated, neglected, and disabled among us? Who will protect these often considered unattractive works that by their very unattractiveness compel us to look long and close, an activity Coleman advocates? But observation is only for the "magnificent works of art that are worthy of prolonged focus" (p. 1). Coleman's ideology reflects the meta-narrative of Western culture, the constructed image of the ideal and normal (white) human form and the rejection of the strange, the atypical, and all variation therein.

But Coleman is not interested in polemics. Rather, he suggests that students need to find evidence—to "follow the details" (Coleman 2012b, p. 3)—from the artworks to support their understandings, a modernist notion that meaning is inherent within. The postmodern movement challenges this notion; interpretations of works of art are filtered through diverse ways of knowing and that artists make art for multiple reasons: as protest, social equity, and cultural justice—not aesthetic alone. According to Coleman (2012b), students observe carefully so that they might imitate and apply their observations to their own work by "taking a great work of art as a model, and trying to make something that looks or sounds like it" (p. 4). Imitation, then, is the greatest accomplishment that can be expected from students in the K-12 public school system. The implication is that students have nothing to say. Coleman views the visual arts in CCSS as a set of texts that all children need to know and learn regardless of context, absent of nuance, interpretation, or internalization.

A declaration against the betrayal of children's potential is underway. Communities resisting CCSS are gaining momentum around the country by creating coalitions of educators, academics, administrators, and parents. For example, Reclaiming the Conversation on Education (http://reclaimingconversation.blogspot.com) hosts conferences and marches, strategizing actions that oppose reliance on quantitative outcomes, standardization of curriculum, high stakes testing, and new teacher education requirements. Another example is United Opt Out National: The Movement to End Corporate Education Reform (http://unitedoptout.com/ the-official-schedule-for-occupy-doe-

2-0-the-battle-for-public-schools). The homepage features women and men holding paper headstones engraved with somber and defiant warnings: "In Remembrance of Caring"; "In Loving Memory of Critical"; "Here Lies Art and Music"; "Here Lies the Future of Public Education"; "RIP Individuality"; and "In Memory of Cooperation Killed by High-Stakes Testing." The homepage posts news of events, such as their march to the White House in honor of Martin Luther King's birthday and the simultaneous launching of Occupy DOE 2.0: The Battle for Public Schools.

The removal of affect from the already emotionally flattened public school system will leave children unprepared to find what they are good at, to use their imaginations, to make school relevant in a critical period of transition into a technological world—thus, wasting precious human resources. I argue that CCSS[6] has overlooked the most fundamental growth that children are entitled: to imagine and shape their future.

References

Chapman, L.H. (2011, March). Report cards from hell on the near horizon: High stakes and ridiculous expectations. Paper presented at the 2011 National Art Education Association Convention, Seattle, WA.

Coleman, D. (2012a, March 15). Panel discussion at The Common Core's Truant from School: History, Science and Art, Washington, DC. Retrieved from www.americansforthearts.org/networks/arts_education/arts_education_015.asp

Coleman D. (2012b). *Guiding principles of the arts K-12.* Retrieved from http://usny.nysed.gov/rttt/docs/guidingprinciples-arts.pdf

Kohn, A. (2013, May). Asking core questions about common core standards: The latest version of top-down reform. Presented at the State University of New York at New Paltz.

McTighe, G. & Wiggins, J. (2005). *Understanding by design.* New York, NY: Pearson.

Munson, L. (2012, March 15). Panel discussion at The Common Core's Truant from School: History, Science and Art, Washington, DC. Retrieved from www.americansforthearts.org/networks/arts_education/arts_education_015.asp

Endnotes

1. "State" is a misnomer. The Common Core is a state standard in name only. In a recent paper. Chapman (2011) said, "all content must fit the aim of transcending state lines aligned with standardized tests" (p. 3). In other words, state standards function as federal mandates.

2. See www.corestandards.org/in-the-states

3. Arne Duncan sent a mass e-mail to teachers dated June 18, 2013. He presented a belated response to the concerns of teachers and administrators nationwide, entitled "What We

Need to Do to Get This Transition Right." He beseeched us to e-mail our voices through a new initiative driven by teachers, ironically called "RESPECT." Find out more about RESPECT at www.ed.gov/teaching

4. "Although the Standards mention arts-related skills and a few books about art and music appear on the list of Exemplary readings, these entries are entirely instrumental to learning in mathematics and ELA" (Chapman, 2011, p. 1).

5. The College Board provides college readiness initiatives such as the SAT subject tests and helps students earn credit for Advanced Placement (AP) courses and the Credit by Examination Program (CLEP) which tests mastery of college-level material.

6. See http://nccas.wikispaces.com/Conceptual+Framework

Critical Thinking

1. By virtue of their title, Common Core Standards imply that all students should learn the same content and further recommends the study of "magnificent works of arts." Why are some persons opposed to this recommendation?

2. Some critics of these standards note that if teachers use these standards that require students to view and observe great works of arts in order to replicate those works, then we have denied students their own voice and freedom of expression. Do you agree or disagree? Explain your response.

3. Coleman states that learning to read must be built on dense knowledge driven by vocabulary and knowledge of science, history, and the arts. How is this possible from Kindergarten to fifth grade?

4. The last paragraph of the article presents an argument to allow affective education to remain in the schools. Have you observed an "emotionally flattened public school system" in your area? Is this a concern worthy of our consideration?

Internet References

Achieve the Core
http://achievethecore.org

Arts Education Partnership
http://www.aep-arts.org

Common Core State Standards
http://www.corestandards.org

National Core Arts Standards
http://www.nationalartsstandards.org

Why Don't Students Like School? Willingham, Perkins, and a Comprehensive Model of School Reform by Jennifer Jones et al.

13

Article

Prepared by: Rebecca B. Evers, *Winthrop University*

Why Don't Students Like School? Willingham, Perkins, and a Comprehensive Model of School Reform

JENNIFER L. JONES, KARRIE A. JONES, AND PAUL J. VERMETTE

Learning Outcomes

After reading this article, you will be able to:

- List the reasons why students do not like school.
- Explain the core principles of educational reform.
- Apply the principles to your understanding of students and teaching practices.

One of the keys to school success is diversity (Harris, Rutledge, Ingle, & Thompson, 2006; Stanley, 2001). In staffing a school, balancing staff who have "seen it all" with those who are willing to "try it all" creates a learning environment where great educational reform can occur (Fullan, 2009). Both the analytic realist, who believes in working within the existing structures to make necessary sustainable changes, and the global idealist, who has extraordinary vision of how systemic change can transform educational systems, can be successful in achieving the same goal of improving education. Analogous to this staffing situation are the educational reform perspectives of Daniel Willingham and David Perkins in their respective 2009 texts *Why Don't Students Like School?* and *Making Learning Whole: How Seven Principles of Teaching Can Transform Education.*

Willingham, the pragmatic, is analogous to the veteran teacher whose actions are based upon observable facts, cognitive science, and the daily challenges of motivating students. Using an in-depth analysis of students' "cognitive equipment,"

Willingham provides educators with a means of using research on the biological basis of learning. His writing shows how to teach lessons that are compatible with the way the brain operates. In *Why Don't Students Like School?,* Willingham employs nine guiding questions:

1. Why don't students like school?
2. How can I teach students the skills they need when standardized tests require only facts?
3. Why do students remember everything that's on television and forget everything I say?
4. Why is it so hard for students to understand abstract ideas?
5. Is drilling worth it?
6. What's the secret to getting students to think like real scientists, mathematicians, and historians?
7. How should I adjust my teaching for different types of learners?
8. How can I help slow learners?
9. What about my mind?

Each chapter begins with a principle of cognitive psychology and systematically explores its implications for educators. In its entirety, Willingham's text explains how learning works, and how teachers can get students to do more of it.

Perkins, the idealist, is analogous to the forward-thinker whose holistic approach to schooling seeks to challenge the very structure of traditional education. In *Making Learning Whole,* Perkins' message is intertwined with the analogy of learning to play baseball. Using seven principles, he explains how the intricacies of the game are revealed over time, as difficult parts are identified and then improved through meaningful practice. By extending the analogy from a baseball game's beginning to end, he described why many students will work hard at sports and other activities, such as after school clubs and part time jobs, but give up so easily in school. As his guiding thesis, Perkins urges teachers to make instructional decisions based on understanding, expectations, choice, challenge, and imagination—even when these challenge the status quo. While Willingham seeks to use cognitive science to work within the system, Perkins seeks to use his holistic approach to transform the system, calling for a comprehensive reconsideration of effective schooling.

This article features a set of fundamental commonalities between these two thinkers—a synthesis of the components of teaching and learning common to both the Perkins and Willingham texts. These core principles, viewed in light of the latest educational research, are synthesized into specific teaching strategies. Through the exploration of both theory and practice, the work of such theorists has immediate classroom applicability.

Need for fun. Create learning experiences that allow students to feel some pleasure in learning as they "play" with ideas. For example: A teacher could help students understand how the body systems work by completing a role/audience/format/topic (RAFT) activity. Students could choose a body system and write an owner's manual to a human explaining how to maintain homeostasis.

Need for freedom. Provide students with choices in deciding when and how they will accomplish mandatory classroom assignments. For example: A teacher could have a list of choices from which students create their own project to demonstrate their understanding.

Need for power/confidence. Allow students to exercise their influence over something or someone by assigning roles such as timekeeper, attendance taker, or peer tutor. For example: A teacher could create a group assignment in which students decide amongst themselves who will be the timekeeper, facilitator, recorder, and encourager before they begin the task.

Need to belong. Design activities such as partner interviews and human scavenger hunts to promote class building and the development of peer relationships. For example: On the first day of school a teacher could have students interview their team mates about their strengths and potential contributions to the team. Then they could use that information to write a letter introducing their teams to the class.

Principle 2: *Learning is a complex cognitive process that requires more skills and competencies than educators may typically recognize or use.*

To explore this principle, we begin by looking into a classroom. Suppose students in Mr. Wright's 8th grade mathematics class have been assigned to classify each of the 10 geometric shapes (supplied on index cards) as examples of figures with reflection, rotational symmetry, or translational symmetry. What are the skills and/or competencies that are embedded into this assignment? What will students need to know and be able to do to be successful at this activity?

While considering the components of this task, both Perkins and Willingham would agree that this activity demands three fundamental things of the learner: (a) conceptual understanding (Bruner, Goodnow, & Austin, 1967; DiSessa & Sherin, 1998; Gunstone & White, 2000), (b) content-specific facts such as the properties of specific geometric shapes (Erickson, 2007), and (c) metacognitive skills (Darling-Hammond, 2008; Dewey, 1938). First, consider the plethora of conceptual knowledge needed to attempt this activity. To begin, students must have a flexible understanding of the concept of symmetry, including the differences among reflection, rotation, and translation. Students must understand the concept of geometric shapes, as well as the idea of classification. In this case, there is little value in even attempting this task without a schema for understanding the "big picture."

Second, though this specific case was a mathematics example, Perkins and Willingham agree that no matter the task, students cannot attempt to demonstrate mastery of a skill without a sufficient number of accessible facts in short-term memory. A reoccurring transfer of learning occurs, and many teachers are ill-equipped with strategies to promote such conceptual understanding (Haskell, 2001; Jones et al., 2009a; Jones et al., 2009b).

Using both cognitive science and decades of research, Willingham and Perkins provide several suggestions for creating conditions to facilitate transfer. Their suggestions range from the use of mnemonics and storytelling to the use of graphic organizers and reflection. Noting that students need to be doing and reflecting rather than listening and restating (Dewey, 1938), the notion that memory is the result of thought is strongly emphasized in both texts. (For further detail on student engagement and reflection, see Vermette, 2009.)

Jones et al. (2009a) compiled dozens of intentional transfer techniques that can be used to promote the cognitive and affective growth of students. Some of these additional suggestions (adapted from Fogarty, Perkins, & Barell, 1992), include the following: setting expectations to inform students that they will

Why Don't Students Like School? Willingham, Perkins, and a Comprehensive Model of School Reform by Jennifer Jones et al.

15

use the concept in future situations, anticipating applications to allow students to predict possible applications for the skills they have just learned, encouraging connections by adapting the learning experience to resemble an authentic application, and using analogies to force connections between the topic students are currently studying and their prior knowledge.

Principle 4: *Practice is worthwhile for students, but only if the practice is meaningful and engages the students in the learning.*

The idea of practice has long been a hotbed of contention among educators. Questions such as "How much practice is necessary?," "What type of understandings require practice?," and "What should practice 'look like'?" have inundated recent educational research (Darling-Hammond, 2008; Kohn, 2006; Vermette, 2009). This notion is addressed in the Perkins and Willingham books through a distinction between engaged and meaningful practice and process repetition practice. Both authors agree that practice *is* necessary, but only on certain facets of understanding and for a very specific purpose. Willingham identifies necessary practice as replication of the processes which must become automatic (Willingham, 2009, p. 84), and Perkins discusses them as replication and feedback on the hard parts of learning (Perkins, 2009, p. 217) but both concede that practice must be engaging and meaningful to be beneficial. Effective practice requires students to make connections around concepts, apply their understandings in new ways, extend their learning to new concepts, and gain useful feedback from the teacher and/or peers.

Conclusion

While Willingham's recipe for educational reform included cognitive science and adaptation of existing structures, and Perkins's view of educational reform called for a comprehensive overhaul in the way understanding is recognized in American schools, these seemingly diverse approaches are driven by a common vision of effective teaching and learning. The four core principles common to both Perkins and Willingham—and supported by dozens of other educational theorists—result in specific teaching strategies that can be used in an effort to bridge educational theory with actual classroom practice.

References

Jones, J., Jones, K., & Vermette, P. (2009a). Teaching mathematics understandings for transfer. *Teaching Mathematics and its Applications, 28*(3), 145–149.

Jones, J., Jones, K., & Vermette, P. (2009b). Using social and emotional learning to foster academic achievement in secondary mathematics. *American Secondary Education, 37*(3), 4–9.

Jones, K., Jones, J., & Vermette, P. (2009c). Using intentional transfer techniques to promote the cognitive and affective growth of middle level learners. *In the Middle, 28*(1), 9–13.

Kohn, A. (2006). *The homework myth: Why our kids get too much of a bad thing.* Cambridge, MA: Da Capo Press.

Miller, L., & Silvernail, D. L. (1994). Wells Junior High School: Evolution of a professional development school. In L. Darling-Hammond (Ed.), *Professional development schools: Schools for developing a profession* (pp. 28–49). New York: Teachers College Press.

Perkins, D. (2009). *Making learning whole: How seven principles of teaching can transform education.* San Francisco, CA: Jossey-Bass.

Perkins, D. N., & Salomon, G. (1988). Teaching for transfer. *Educational Leadership, 46*(1), 22–32.

Reeves, D. B. (2009). *Leading change in your school: How to conquer myths, build commitment, and get results.* Alexandria, VA: ASCD.

Stanley, C. (2001). A review of the pipeline: The value of diversity in staffing teaching and learning centers in the new millennium. *Journal of Faculty Development, 18*(2), 75–86.

Vermette, P. J. (2009). *ENGAGING teens in their own learning: 8 keys to student success.* Larchmont, NY: Eye On Education.

Whitaker, T. (2010). *Leading school change: 9 strategies to bring everybody on board.* Larchmont, NY: Eye on Education.

Willingham, D. T. (2009). *Why don't students like school? A cognitive scientist answers questions about how the mind works and what it means for your classroom.* San Francisco, CA: Jossey-Bass.

Critical Thinking

1. Do you think that students' general and inherent dislike of school is a contributing factor to the past failures of school reform? Support your answer with examples.

2. Thinking about your own time as a K-12 student, what did you dislike about school? Was that issue mentioned in this article?

3. Which principle in this article has changed your thinking about teaching? Explain your answer. If none, provide a rationale for that answer.

Internet References

Education Reform
http://www.ed.gov/p-12-reform
Education Reform Now
https://edreformnow.org/
Instructional Design
http://www.instructionaldesign.org/

Jones, Jennifer; Jones, Karrie; Vermette, Paul, "Why Don't Students Like School? Willingham, Perkins, and a Comprehensive Model of School Reform", *The Educational Forum,* vol. 77, 2013, pp. 199–206. Copyright © 2013 by Kappa Delta Pi. Used with permission of Taylor & Francis.

Unit 2

UNIT

Prepared by: Rebecca B. Evers, *Winthrop University*

Understanding Poverty

The problem of high levels of poverty in our country is of great concern to American educators. One in four American children do not have all of his/her basic needs met and lives under conditions of poverty. Almost one in three lives in a single-parent home, which in itself is no disadvantage, but under conditions of poverty it may become one. Children living in poverty are in crisis if their basic health and social needs are not adequately met and their educational development can be affected by crises in their personal lives. We must teach and support these students and their families, even when it appears that they are not fully invested in their education. As a teacher, you may not have much control over the factors that shape the lives of our students, but hopefully with these readings you will begin to see how you can help students in other ways.

What is poverty? Jensen (2009) defines poverty as "a chronic and debilitating condition that results from multiple adverse synergistic risk factors and affects the mind, body and soul" (p. 6). Some of the risk factors frequently mentioned in the literature on poverty include (1) violence in the community; (2) stress and distress felt by the adults in the child's life; (3) a disorganized family situation, including physical and substance abuse; (4) negative interactions between parents and children; and (5) parents' lack of understanding of developmental needs. Rawlinson (2007) grew up in poverty and later wrote about her experiences in *A Mind Shaped by Poverty: Ten Things Educators Should Know*. These words give us a peek into the mind of the children we teach.

> When I entered school, I took all the pain, anger, frustration, resentment, shame, low self-esteem, debilitating worldview, and dehumanizing effects of poverty with me. I had a poverty mind-set (p. 1).

After looking at the list of risk factors and Rawlinson's admitted poverty mindset, what are teachers to do? Can teachers ignore these concerns to treat and teach all students as NCLB requires? Smiley and Helfenbein (2011) found that how teachers see themselves, their students, and the larger community plays a powerful role in planning and instructing students from poverty. That study leaves us with new questions. So what can we do about our beliefs? If a majority of teachers in the United States are non-minority, middle-class, and female how do they relate to students who are so unlike themselves?

Children who live in poverty may attend schools in areas of high unemployment, high-minority population, or low levels of school funding. Further, during the last decade, homelessness of school-age children has risen; in 2009, 41 percent of the homeless population was composed of families. The McKinney-Vento Act which ensures the right to attend public school regardless of where a child may reside, includes children who may live in a homeless shelter outside the school's primary attendance area. This is important enough to say here that children and youth are considered homeless if they are

- sharing the housing of other persons due to loss of housing, economic hardship, or a similar reason (sometimes referred to as *doubled-up*);

- living in motels, hotels, trailer parks, or camping grounds due to lack of alternative adequate accommodations;

- living in emergency or transitional shelters; abandoned in hospitals; or awaiting foster care placement; have a primary nighttime residence that is a public or private place not designed for, or ordinarily used as, a regular sleeping accommodation for human beings;

- living in cars, parks, public spaces, abandoned buildings, substandard housing, bus or train stations, or similar settings; and

- migratory children who qualify as homeless because they are living in circumstances described above (U.S. Department of Education, p. 2).

Poverty plus homelessness can have devastating results for children in public schools unless the teachers and school personnel are sensitive to, and supportive of, those children. Until we see a significant economic recovery from the current recession, we are likely to be confronted with the problems of poverty and homelessness. How educators respond to these children will have profound effects on the future of our nation.

The articles in this unit were selected so that the readers could begin that conversation about relating to the children born into, or living in, poverty. Further, the articles offer some new ideas about how to change the mindset of both teachers and the children of poverty. And lastly, the articles will offer examples of schools and teachers who are making a difference for children, not just by raising test scores, but also by changing lives.

Where are America's poor children? If you answered *in the inner city* you will be surprised to know that just over one-quarter (28 percent) of America's poor children live in urban settings. However, the majority live in small cities and rural areas (39 percent) and the second largest group are from the suburbs (33 percent). We should be careful that we do not fall into the trap of the "culture of poverty" often found in the work of Charles Murray and Ruby Payne. In this unit you will read about poverty in the middle land between inner city and rural countryside. These articles offer strategies for working with suburban families who live in poverty and homelessness.

As teachers we should be concerned that schools in areas of high poverty are making a difference in the education of children. If we look to the rest of the world as well as disadvantaged areas of the United States, we can note that better schools and more successful academic programs are essential for students who live in poverty. However, while there will remain some obstacles to raising the achievement gap, we can learn strategies and action to take from top-ranked countries.

As you read these articles, you will learn who the poor are and where they live. You will read about engaging students with important content learning in successful schools in high poverty areas that have principals and teachers who have a set of common characteristics and are highly qualified educators. Most importantly we are reminded that all teachers need to use a fundamental set of research-based teaching strategies regardless of who they teach because good teaching is essential to students so that they acquire basic skills and the knowledge they need. The primary focus of this unit is to help readers learn that the most effective teachers ensure that all students acquire, rehearse, and connect background knowledge while receiving sufficient instructional support. Finally, we are asked to remember that best practices teaching is grounded in cognitive science research and cognitive supports as well as observation of master teachers.

References

Jensen, E. 2009. *Teaching with Poverty in Mind: What Being Poor Does to Kid's Brains and What Schools Can Do About It*. Alexandria, VA: Association for Supervision and Curriculum Development.

National Coalition for the Homeless, 2012. Homeless Families with Children. Author. Retrieved on 22 June 2014 from www.nationalhomeless.org/factsheets/families.html

Rawlinson, R. M. 2007. *A Mind Shaped by Poverty: Ten Things Educators Should Know*. New York: Universe, Inc.

U. S. Department of Education (n.d.). Guidance for the Education for Homeless Children and Youth. Author. Retrieved on 22 June 2014 from www2.ed.gov/programs/homeless/guidance.pdf

Smiley, A. D., and R. J. Helfenbein. 2011. "Becoming Teachers: The Payne Effect." *Multicultural Perspectives, 13* (1): 5–15

Article   Prepared by: Rebecca B. Evers, *Winthrop University*

Growing Income Inequality Threatens American Education

Rising economic and social inequality has weakened neighborhoods and families in ways that make effective school reform more difficult.

GREG J. DUNCAN AND RICHARD J. MURNANE

Learning Outcomes

After reading this article, you will be able to:

- Describe the origins and nature of income inequality.
- Explain the educational consequences of income inequality.
- Summarize additional and long range outcomes of income inequality.
- Generate ideas and solutions for the educational consequences.

America has always taken pride in being the land of opportunity, a country in which hard work and sacrifice result in a better life for one's children. Economic growth has made that dream a reality for generations of Americans, including many people who started out poor. The quarter century following World War II was a golden era for the U.S. economy, as high- and low-income families shared the benefits of substantial economic growth. But storm clouds began to gather in the 1970s. In particular, computer-driven technological changes favoring highly educated workers, plus demographic shifts such as the rise of single-parent families, have produced sharply growing income gaps among families.

In the past, America's public schools have responded well to the challenges of a changing world. Indeed, America's world leadership in education has fueled much of its prosperity and made the twentieth century the "American Century" (Goldin & Katz, 2008). But technological changes, globalization, and rising income inequality have placed great strains on the decentralized American approach to public education. We are constantly reminded that the math, science, and language skills of our children and young adults lag far behind those of children in other countries. In international rankings, our college graduation rate has fallen from 1st to 12th.

In this article—the first of two appearing in consecutive months—we describe the origins and nature of growing income inequality and some of its consequences for American children. We document the increased family income inequality that's occurred over the past 40 years. An increase in income disparity has been more than matched by an expanding gap between the money that low- and high-income parents spend on enrichment activities for their children.

Most distressingly, increasing gaps in academic achievement and educational attainments have accompanied the growth in income inequality. Differences in the reading and math achievement levels of low- and high-income children are much larger than several decades ago, as are differences in college graduation rates.

What accounts for these widening gaps? Drawing from the first part of our recent book, *Restoring Opportunity: The Crisis of Inequality and the Challenge for American Education* (Harvard Education Press and the Russell Sage Foundation, 2014), we explain that the evidence supports pathways operating through both families and schools. In addition to growing differences in the resources spent by poor and rich families on their children, declining real incomes for low-income families have affected maternal stress, mental health, and parenting.

Rising residential segregation by income has led to increasing concentrations of low- and high-income children attending separate schools. Peer problems, geographic mobility, and challenges in attracting and retaining good teachers have made it difficult to provide consistently high-quality learning experiences in schools serving a large proportion of low-income students.

Widening Gaps

Based on U.S. Census Bureau data, the left-hand bar in each set of bars in Figure 1 shows the average income in a particular year (in 2012 dollars) for children at the 20th percentile of the nation's family income distribution. This means that, in a given year, 20% of children lived in families with incomes below that level, while 80% had incomes above it. In 1970, the dividing line was drawn at $37,664.

The middle bar in each set shows the average family income in a given year at the 80th percentile of the distribution, which was about $100,000 (in 2012 dollars) in 1970. The right-hand bar in each set shows the average income for very high-income families—those with incomes exceeding those of 95% of U.S. families (a little more than about $150,000 in 1970).

In contrast to the two decades before 1970, when the incomes of these three groups grew at virtually identical rates, economic growth over the next four decades failed to lift all boats. In 2010, family income at the 20th percentile was more than 25% lower than the inflation-adjusted corresponding family income in 1970. In contrast, the real incomes of families at the 80th percentile grew by 23% to $125,000 over these four decades, while the incomes of the richest 5% of families rose even more. Census Bureau data also show that the decline of

the incomes of families at the lower end of the spectrum is reflected in the nation's child poverty rate: Over 16 million U.S. children—more than 20%—were living in poor families in 2012, up sharply from the 15% child poverty rate in 1970.

During this same time period, the gap between the average reading and mathematics skills of students from low- and high-income families increased substantially. As illustrated in Figure 2, among children who were adolescents in the late 1960s, test scores of low-income children lagged behind those of their better-off peers by four-fifths of a standard deviation—which represents about 80 points on the scale used to measure SAT scores. Forty years later, this gap was 50% larger, amounting to nearly 125 SAT-type points (Reardon, 2011). We were surprised to discover how much the income-based gap grew during this period in view of the decline in the racial gap in test scores in the decades following the 1954 U.S. Supreme Court decision in *Brown vs. Board of Education.*

Given the importance of academic preparation in determining educational success, it should come as no surprise that growth in the income gap in children's reading and mathematics achievement has contributed to growth in the corresponding gap in the rate of college completion (Figure 3, which is based on Bailey & Dynarski, 2011). Among children growing up in relatively affluent families, the four-year college graduation rate of those who were teenagers in the mid-1990s was 18 percentage points higher than the rate for those who were teenagers in the late 1970s. In contrast, among children from low-income families, the graduation rate was only 4 percentage points higher for the later cohort than for the earlier one. Analysts differ in their assessments of the relative importance of college costs and academic preparation in explaining the increasing gulf between the college graduation rates of affluent

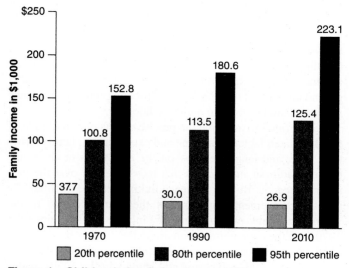

Figure 1   Children's family income over time

Note: Chart shows 20th, 80th, and 95th percentiles of the distribution of family incomes for all children ages 5–17. They are based on data from the U.S. Census Bureau and are adjusted for inflation. Amounts are in 2012 dollars. Reprinted with permission from *Whither Opportunity?* © 2011 Russell Sage Foundation.

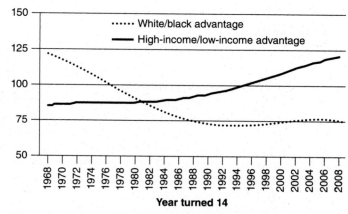

Figure 2   Race and income-based gaps in reading achievement in SAT-type units

Reardon, S.F. (2011). Reprinted with permission from *Whither Opportunity?* © 2011 Russell Sage Foundation.

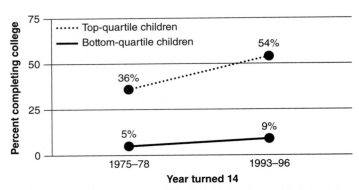

Figure 3   College graduation rates for high- and low-income children

Bailey, M.J. & Dynarski, S.M. (2011). Reprinted with permission from *Whither Opportunity?* © 2011 Russell Sage Foundation.

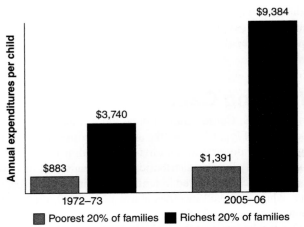

Figure 4   Family enrichment expenditures on children

Author's calculations are based on data from the Consumer Expenditure Surveys. Expenditure patterns vary across families and include child care. Books, fees for sports activities and equipment, and summer camp enrollment fees are examples of common "child enrichment" expenditures. Amounts are in 2012 dollars. Reprinted with permission from *Whither Opportunity?* © 2011 Russell Sage Foundation.

and low-income children in our country. However, both cost burdens and academic performance are rooted, at least in part, in the growth in family income inequality.

Inequality Affects Skills Attainment

American society relies on its families to nurture its children and its schools to level the playing field for children born into different circumstances. More than any other institution, schools are charged with making equality of opportunity a reality. During a period of rising inequality, can schools play this critical role effectively? Or has growing income inequality affected families, neighborhoods, and schools in a manner that undercuts the effectiveness of schools serving disadvantaged populations?

Families

Very young children tend to be completely dependent on their families to provide what they need for healthy development (Duncan & Magnuson, 2011). Children growing up in families with greater financial resources score higher on many dimensions of school readiness upon entering kindergarten. An obvious advantage of a higher family income is that it provides more resources to buy books, computers, high-quality childcare, summer camps, private schooling, and other enrichments. In the early 1970s, high-income families spent just under $3,000 more per year (in 2012 dollars) on child enrichment than low-income families (Figure 4; Duncan & Murnane, 2011). By 2006, this gap had nearly tripled, to $8,000. Spending differences are largest for enrichment activities such as music lessons, travel, and summer camps (Kaushal et al., 2011). Differential access to

such activities may explain the gaps in background knowledge between children from high-income families and those from low-income families that are so predictive of reading skills in the middle and high school years (Snow, 2002).

Parents also spend different amounts and quality of time interacting with their children. High-income parents spend more time than low-income parents in literacy activities with their children. Most disparate is time spent in "novel" places—other than at home, school, or in the care of another parent or a childcare provider. Between birth and age six, children from high-income families spend an average of 1,300 more hours in novel contexts than children from low-income families (Phillips, 2011). These experiences, financed by the higher incomes of more affluent families, also contribute to the background knowledge that is so critical for comprehending science and social studies texts in middle school.

It is difficult to untangle the precise effects of a multitude of family-related factors—income and expenditures, family structure, time, and language use—on the disparities in children's school readiness and success that have emerged over the past several decades. But the evidence linking income to children's school achievement suggests that the sharp increase in the income gap between high- and low-income families since the 1970s and the concomitant increase in the income-based gap in children's school success are hardly coincidental.

In particular, two experimental studies in the 1970s examined the overall effects on children of income supplements that boosted family income by as much as 50% (Maynard, 1977; Maynard & Murnane, 1979). At two of the three sites, researchers found that children in families randomly assigned to receive an income supplement did significantly better with respect to early academic achievement and school attendance than children in families that received no income supplement.

Still more evidence on policy-relevant effects of income increases comes from a study that takes advantage of the increasing generosity of the U.S. Earned Income Tax Credit (EITC) between 1993 and 1997 to compare children's test scores before and after the credit was expanded (Dahl & Lochner, 2012). The authors found increases in low-income children's achievement in middle childhood that coincided with the EITC expansion.

The strongest research evidence appears to indicate that money matters in a variety of ways for children's long-term success in school. While some children always have enjoyed greater benefits and advantages than others, the income gap has widened dramatically over the past four decades and, as these research studies suggest, this has been a significant factor in widening the gap in children's school success as well.

Schools

Researchers have long known that children attending schools with mostly low-income classmates have lower academic achievement and graduation rates than those attending schools with more affluent student populations. Less well understood are the ways in which student body composition shapes school functioning and children's developmental trajectories and long-run outcomes.

In recent decades, it has been largely through an increase in income-based segregation of neighborhoods and schools that growing inequality of family income has affected the educational attainments of the nation's children. Residential segregation by income has increased substantially in recent decades, as high-income families buy homes in neighborhoods where less-affluent families cannot afford to live, and poor families are increasingly surrounded by neighbors who are poor as well (Reardon & Bischoff, 2011). This reduces interactions between rich and poor in settings ranging from schools and child care centers to libraries and grocery stores. Without the financial and human resources and political clout of the wealthy, institutions in poorer neighborhoods, including schools, may decline in quality.

Perhaps most important, increasing residential segregation by income has led to increasing school segregation by income. From 1972 to 1988, schools became more economically segregated, and teenagers from affluent families were less and less likely to have classmates from low-income families (Altonji & Mansfield, 2011). As a result, a child from a poor family is two to four times as likely as a child from an affluent family to have classmates in either elementary or high school with behavioral problems and low skills. This sorting matters because the weak cognitive skills and behavioral issues of many low-income children have a negative effect on their classmates' learning.

Student mobility resulting from these residential changes poses another threat to achievement. Urban families living in poverty move frequently, and, as a result of school sorting by socioeconomic status, children from poor families are especially likely to attend schools with relatively high numbers of new students arriving during the school year. Recent research has shown that children attending elementary schools with considerable student mobility make less progress in mathematics than do children in schools with less student turnover. Moreover, these negative effects apply to students who themselves are residentially stable as well as to those who are not and are likely to stem from disruption of instruction caused by the entry of new students into a class (Raudenbush, Jean, & Art, 2011).

Poor teacher quality, too, contributes to the weak performance of students in high-poverty schools. A substantial body of research has shown that schools serving high concentrations of poor, nonwhite, and low-achieving students find it difficult to attract and retain skilled teachers. In addition to preferring schools with relatively low proportions of low-achieving students, teachers favor schools in neighborhoods with higher-income residents and less violent crime (Boyd et al., 2011). In high-poverty schools, teacher commitment, parental involvement, and student achievement all tend to be lower.

Yet another challenge facing many of the nation's schools concerns the school placements of new immigrants, many of whom speak little English. Today's immigrants are more likely than their predecessors in the early 1970s to come from high-poverty countries. Black and Hispanic immigrants to New York City are much more likely to be poor than are white immigrants from Eastern Europe, and they are more likely to attend elementary and middle schools with native-born black and Hispanic students who are poor (Schwartz & Stiefel, 2011). Thus, while immigrants are not segregated from the native-born in New York City schools, their residential patterns contribute to segregation of schools by socioeconomic status and race.

Helping Low-income Children

By widening the gap in educational opportunities between children from low- and higher-income families, increasing income inequality jeopardizes the upward socioeconomic mobility that has long held our pluralistic democracy together. Improving educational outcomes for children growing up in low-income families is therefore critical to the nation's future and requires a combination of policies that support low-income families and measures to improve the quality of schools that low-income children attend.

The United States has implemented a range of policies to raise the buying power of low-income families, including the Child Tax Credit, the Earned Income Tax Credit, cash assistance programs, and the Supplemental Nutrition Assistance Program (formerly Food Stamps). Recent studies show that the increases in family incomes produced by these programs result in improved educational outcomes for young children and health in adulthood (Hoynes, Schanzenbach, & Almond, 2013). Unfortunately, these programs are under attack as Congress seeks ways to reduce the federal budget deficit.

Improving the quality of schools attended by low-income children poses even more important and difficult challenges. As a nation, we have failed to appreciate the extent to which technological innovations have brought changes in the skills needed to succeed in today's economy. Moreover, the rising economic and social inequality produced by technology and globalization has weakened neighborhoods and families in ways that make effective school reform all the more difficult. For a variety of historical reasons, our nation has not learned how to provide the consistent supports that schools—especially those serving large numbers of low-income children—must have to succeed.

Discussions of school reforms often center on simplistic silver bullets: more money, more accountability, more choice, new organizational structures. None of these reforms has turned the tide because none focuses directly on improving what matters most in education: the quality and consistency of the instruction and experiences offered to students.

References

Altonji, J.G. & Mansfield, R. (2011). The role of family, school, and community characteristics in inequality in education and labor market outcomes. In G.J. Duncan & R.J. Murnane (Eds.), *Whither opportunity? Rising inequality, schools, and children's life chances* (pp. 339–358). New York, NY: Russell Sage Foundation & Spencer Foundation.

Bailey, M.J. & Dynarski, S.M. (2011). Inequality in postsecondary education. In G.J. Duncan & R.J. Murnane (Eds.), *Whither opportunity? Rising inequality, schools, and children's life chances* (pp. 117–132). New York, NY: Russell Sage Foundation & Spencer Foundation.

Boyd, D., Lankford, H., Loeb, S., Ronfeldt, M., & Wyckoff, J. (2011). The effect of school neighborhoods on teachers' career decisions. In G.J. Duncan & R.J. Murnane (Eds.), *Whither opportunity? Rising inequality, schools, and children's life chances* (pp. 377–396). New York, NY: Russell Sage Foundation & Spencer Foundation.

Dahl, G.B. & Lochner, L. (2012). The impact of family income on child achievement: Evidence from the earned income tax credit. *American Economic Review, 102* (5), 1927–1956.

Duncan, G.J. & Magnuson, K. (2011). The nature and impact of early achievement skills, attention skills, and behavior problems. In G.J. Duncan & R.J. Murnane (Eds.), *Whither opportunity? Rising inequality, schools, and children's life chances* (pp. 47–70). New York, NY: Russell Sage Foundation & Spencer Foundation.

Duncan G.J. & Murnane R.J. (2011). Introduction: The American dream, then and now. In G.J Duncan & R.J. Murnane (Eds.), *Whither opportunity? Rising inequality, schools, and children's life chances* (pp. 3–26). New York, NY: Russell Sage Foundation & Spencer Foundation.

Goldin, C.D. & Katz, L.F. (2008). *The race between education and technology.* Cambridge, MA.: Harvard University Press.

Hoynes, H.W., Schanzenbach, D.W., & Almond, D. (2012). *Long run impacts of childhood access to the safety net.* Unpublished NBER Working Paper No. 18535.

Kaushal, N., Magnuson, K., & Waldfogel, J. (2011). How is family income related to investments in children's learning? In G.J. Duncan & R.J. Murnane (Eds.), *Whither opportunity? Rising inequality, schools, and children's life chances* (pp. 187–206). New York, NY: Russell Sage Foundation & Spencer Foundation.

Maynard, R.A. (1977). The effects of the rural income maintenance experiment on the school performance of children. *American Economic Review, 67* (1), 370–375.

Maynard, R.A. & Murnane, R.J. (1979). The effects of a negative income tax on school performance: Results of an experiment. *Journal of Human Resources, 14* (4), 463–476.

Phillips, M. (2011). Parenting, time use, and disparities in academic outcomes. In G.J. Duncan & R.J. Murnane (Eds.), *Whither opportunity? Rising inequality, schools, and children's life chances* (pp. 207–228). New York, NY: Russell Sage Foundation & Spencer Foundation.

Raudenbush, S.W., Jean, M., & Art, E. (2011). Year-by-year and cumulative impacts of attending a high-mobility elementary school on children's mathematics achievement in Chicago, 1995–2005. In G.J. Duncan & R.J. Murnane (Eds.), *Whither opportunity? Rising inequality, schools, and children's life chances* (pp. 359–376). New York, NY: Russell Sage Foundation & Spencer Foundation.

Reardon, S.F. (2011). The widening academic achievement gap between the rich and the poor: New evidence and possible explanations. In G.J. Duncan & R.J. Murnane (Eds.), *Whither opportunity? Rising inequality, schools, and children's life chances* (pp. 91–116). New York, NY: Russell Sage Foundation & Spencer Foundation.

Reardon, S.F. & Bischoff, K. (2011). Income inequality and income segregation. *American Journal of Sociology, 116* (4), 1092–1153.

Schwartz, A.E. & Stiefel, L, (2011). Immigrants and inequality in public schools. In G.J. Duncan & R.J. Murnane (Eds.), *Whither opportunity? Rising inequality, schools, and children's life chances* (pp. 419–442). New York, NY: Russell Sage Foundation & Spencer Foundation.

Snow, C. (2002). *Reading for understanding: Toward a research and development program in reading comprehension.* Santa Monica, CA: Rand Corporation.

Critical Thinking

1. Look at school report cards and demographic/economic information for a school district in the community around your school or home. How do they compare to the family income information offered in Figure #1? How is the income information reflected in student achievement scores found in the school report cards?

2. Research school reforms or initiatives that have been tried in local schools during the last five to ten years. How have those reforms affected student achievement? If possible, find reasons for their success or failure. If not possible to find researched answers, infer two-three reasons.

3. Generate three-four ways that private citizens might help schools in low-income neighborhoods or towns improve the achievement levels of students living in poverty. Explain and support your choices.

Internet References

Child Tax Credit
   http://www.irs.gov/Individuals/Child-Tax-Credit

Earned Income Tax Credit
   http://www.irs.gov/Credits-&-Deductions/Individuals/Earned-Income-Tax-Credit

National Center for Children in Poverty
   http://www.nccp.org

U.S. Census Bureau: Poverty
   http://www.census.gov/hhes/www/poverty/

GREG J. DUNCAN, is distinguished professor in the School of Education at the University of California, Irvine. **RICHARD J. MURNANE** is Thompson Professor of Education and Society at the Harvard Graduate School of Education, Cambridge, Mass.

Article   Prepared by: Rebecca B. Evers, *Winthrop University*

How High-Poverty Schools Are Getting It Done

Principals in high-achieving schools with a high percentage of students in poverty share characteristics.

KARIN CHENOWETH AND CHRISTINA THEOKAS

Learning Outcomes

After reading this article, you will be able to:

- Describe the personal qualities of principals in high achieving, high poverty schools.
- Explain why leadership styles and philosophies are important to building a successful school.
- Infer what steps would be next for these principals and their schools.

To anyone who cares about ensuring that all children are educated to a high standard, it is depressing to look at one of those graphs that show schools by percentage of low-income students on the x axis and academic achievement on the y axis. The steep slope down and to the right seems to demonstrate an iron law of probability: High-income schools have high achievement; low-income schools have low achievement. Even more uncomfortable for a country that often prides itself on having eliminated institutional discrimination, the same results can be replicated when race rather than income is used.

But if you take your eye to the upper-right quadrant of that graph, you'll often see an outlier or two—that is, high-achieving schools with a high percentage of students of poverty or students of color.

What are those schools like? Are they there because of a one-time fluke? Are their poor kids the children of impecunious grad students? Are their students of color the children of doctors or lawyers?

After eight years of studying schools in the upper-right quadrant, we can say that their presence there is rarely a fluke. Their poor children are like poor children everywhere, burdened with hardships children should not have to face. Their students of color are not primarily the children of upper-income professionals. And many of these schools have teachers trained in the same local colleges that trained teachers who work in less successful schools nearby.

These schools do, however, have something that helps explain their success: They all have excellent school leaders.

This should hardly come as a shock. Research has demonstrated that school leadership is key to school improvement (Louis, Leithwood, Wahlstrom, & Anderson, 2010). In fact, one study concluded that as much as one-quarter of all "school effects" on achievement can be attributed to principals—second only to teachers and far ahead of factors like composition of student body (Leithwood, Louis, Anderson, & Wahlstrom, 2004). A more recent attempt to see how leadership translates into student achievement showed wide variation between the most effective principals and the least effective (Branch, Hanushek, & Rivkin, 2012).

But that raises more questions: What are these effective leaders like, and what do they do to be so effective? Are they simply the exception that proves the rule? We set out to answer those questions.

During the past eight years, the Education Trust has been visiting schools that are high-achieving or rapidly improving and that have significant populations of students of color or students of poverty or both. It was clear that leadership was a key factor in these schools' successes. To fully understand the role of these leaders, we went back to those schools and collected detailed data on the leaders' work.

We ended up with a sample of 33 principals (including three assistant principals) representing 24 elementary, middle, and high schools in rural, suburban, and urban locales in 19 states. (Some schools were represented by more than one leader because successive principals led and sustained the improvement.) On average, 75 percent of students in these schools qualified for free or reduced-price meals, and 73 percent were children of color. All the schools had student achievement comparable to that of middle-class schools in their state, and some were at the top of their state.

In examining the work of these principals, we discovered four qualities that they tend to share.

No. 1. Their beliefs about student potential drive their work

The leaders we studied had spent, on average, more than a decade teaching in classrooms where they developed the clear and unwavering belief that all students can learn to high levels and that it is up to the schools to help them do so. Long-time educator Molly Bensinger-Lacy said, "Through my teaching experiences, I learned that my students were capable of learning just about anything I was capable of teaching." Bensinger-Lacy became principal of Graham Road Elementary School in 2004 when it was one of the lowest performing schools in Fairfax County, Virginia. When she left in 2009, it was one of the highest performing schools in the state.

The principals' belief in the capacity of all students pushes them to set a rigorous performance standard and honestly discriminate between excellence and mediocrity. We need to be clear here: That kind of honesty is tough. It is all too easy to accept mediocre work, particularly when you know that mediocrity represents enormous progress.

Graham Road's students are mostly children of low-income families that have recently immigrated to the United States, and they do not speak English at home. Most of the students arrive in kindergarten not knowing any of their letters or numbers. Kindergarten teachers would often be thrilled if, by the middle of the year, their students knew half their letters and could count to 10. At grade-level data meetings, they would, understandably, brag about such progress. Bensinger-Lacy would cheer the progress, but she would also talk about what she called the "elephant in the room": If students didn't make faster progress, they would be at risk of not learning to read, never graduating from high school, and living in poverty for the rest of their lives. That was tough for the kindergarten teachers to hear, and tough for her to say, but Bensinger-Lacy considered it her job.

This same drive appears among the leadership at Elmont Memorial High School in Nassau County, New York. Elmont is a large comprehensive high school with just under 2,000 students, almost all of whom are students of color—mostly black. Elmont graduates almost all of its students, with just about half graduating with an advanced designation, and its results on most of the New York Regents exams compare well with the rest of the state. It is an exceptional school, and it has refined its practice in many ways, not the least of which involves being willing to discriminate between mediocrity and excellence. Take a look, for example, at this recommendation a school leader gave to a teacher following an observation:

> At one point in the lesson you took a sub-standard response that was not elaborated on. You admitted that, in the interest of time, you took the response and moved forward with the lesson. As we discussed, setting standards and having students meet those standards includes the proper responses. In the future, make it a point to ensure that students have a true grasp of the concept.

What teacher hasn't glided over an inadequate answer from a student? With dozens of students in the class and lots of material to get through, it sometimes seems unavoidable. But it also leads to students developing misunderstandings and doesn't help them learn at a high level. If students are going to meet high standards, those standards need to be present at all times in classrooms. As uncomfortable as it is to call out this seemingly minor episode, these occurrences are opportunities for school leaders to help staff understand the standard they are working toward.

No. 2. They put instruction at the center of their managerial duties

Over the years, the expectations of principals have changed. Where once the job was primarily defined as a managerial one, principals are now expected not just to run a smooth operation, but also to be change leaders and improve achievement. When we asked the leaders how they defined the job, 76 percent defined themselves as instructional leaders. The rest emphasized their responsibility to set a vision of high achievement. But no matter how anyone defines the role, the managerial part of the principalship has not disappeared.

So how do these school leaders find time to improve teaching and learning? The answer is that instead of adding instruction to their to-do lists, they tightly manage their time, as well as student and staff time, putting instruction at the center.

Here's an example of what we mean. Many students begin school behind and need every minute of instruction they can get, and their teachers often need more time to collaborate than their districts provide. Therefore, leaders must ensure that master schedules maximize both instructional time for students and collaboration time for teachers.

At the same time, these principals establish schoolwide routines—and work with their teachers to create classroom routines—to ensure that fumbling with materials and getting caught up in unnecessary discipline issues don't distract from instruction. One former principal, for example, said she always bought her teachers a lot of pencils: "I didn't want any teacher fussing with students over a dang pencil."

Bensinger-Lacy arranged the schedule at Graham Road so that teachers from each grade level met weekly for one hour at the beginning of the contractual day (15 minutes before school started and continuing for the first 45 minutes of the school day). Back in their classrooms, aides began the day—supervising breakfast, collecting homework, and starting the students on their work. This routine gave teachers a solid hour of professional collaboration, with the topic alternating between reading and math. One teacher would spend about 20 minutes presenting research related to a problem the teachers were experiencing, and the teachers—including the special educator, coach, and English language teachers assigned to that grade level—would spend the remainder of the time working on how to put those findings into practice—sometimes even producing actual materials during the meeting.

On one such day, the literacy instructional coach presented research on phonemic awareness and phonics to the 1st grade team. Even though the teachers were spending classroom time on the sounds of the English language and how they map onto the alphabet, their students were still not successful. After reviewing the research, the teachers discussed its implications and began developing activities that they could use with students during the little interstices of time that even the most organized teacher finds during the day, such as when buses are late or the media specialist runs long with an earlier class. These included "sound bingo" cards they could keep in their pockets and a list of other activities, such as playing "I'm packing my suitcase, and in it I put something that begins with . . ."

Key to the success of this process was that Bensinger-Lacy usually attended these meetings, thus demonstrating their importance.

No. 3. They focus on building the capacity of all the adults in the building

These leaders know that teachers hold the greatest power over a student's achievement. But they also know that many teachers are underprepared. Further, they know that no one teacher, no matter how brilliant and experienced, can possibly reach every child all the time.

And so they have systems in place to build the capacity and problem-solving ability of their teachers and create a professional culture where knowledge and expertise are shared. Teachers are no longer expected to all be experts who shut their doors and work in isolation.

When Barbara Adderley became principal of M. Hall Stanton Elementary School in north Philadelphia in 2001, it was one of the lowest-performing schools in the city, which made it one of the lowest in Pennsylvania. Before setting foot in the door, Adderley went to the district office to look at teacher attendance data. Two of the most reliable teachers were Kathleen Shallow and Chrissie Taylor. When Adderley visited their classrooms, she found competent, caring educators. She quickly made them the literacy and math coach, respectively, and sent them to every district training that seemed promising.

Adderley used data from state assessments, student work, classroom walkthroughs, and student attendance and discipline rates to identify the most pressing needs and plan professional development accordingly. She found that most teachers didn't know how to do such basics as lead guided reading lessons and use math games. She began by leading professional development sessions on those topics herself but soon asked Shallow and Taylor to take over, bringing back what they had learned from district training sessions. As the entire faculty became more comfortable in the role, other teachers led professional development sessions in their classrooms on specific topics that they excelled in—setting up activity stations, organizing materials for smooth transitions, and so forth.

No. 4. They monitor and evaluate what leads to success and what can be learned from failure

These leaders are unsentimental empiricists. They want to see evidence so they can, as one said, "do more of what works and less of what doesn't." They set measurable interim goals to track progress, assess the rigor of instruction through student work products, and engage their staff with data to discuss instruction. The principals rely on evidence to know whether something is working, and they help teachers do the same.

For example, when Terri Tomlinson became principal of George Hall Elementary School in Mobile, Alabama, in 2004, few students in the school could read or do math at a level approaching the state standards. Her students live in a fairly isolated neighborhood and rarely leave it. Her teachers, recognizing that their students brought little background knowledge to school, argued that they should go on field trips. As one teacher said, "They live 10 minutes from the bayou and have never seen a boat."

Tomlinson, knowing that field trips are often massive time wasters, was initially wary of the idea. She asked the teachers to demonstrate how field trips would work with the curriculum, how they would build vocabulary and background knowledge, and how students would apply what they had learned. Satisfied with the teachers' work, she approved a few test field trips and asked the teachers to demonstrate that they had had the desired effect. Formative assessments, summative assessments, student essays, and blog postings were all examined as evidence of success, and today most students at George Hall go on monthly field trips, which Tomlinson and faculty members believe have helped the school become one of the highest-achieving schools in the state.

If the evidence had not supported continuing the field trips, that would not have been cause for recrimination; after all, Tomlinson and other principals want their teachers to continually look for new ways of doing things. Instead, it would have been cause to rethink and go in a different direction. "We don't look to place blame in this building," Tomlinson said. "Instead, we look for solutions."

The Next Step

It took years of research demonstrating the power that effective teachers have in changing students' lives to shift the conversation from "schools can't do anything" to "we need to make sure kids have good teachers." That was a step forward, but to ensure that kids have good teachers, the next step is to understand the role school leaders play both in helping ordinary teachers become excellent and in creating schools where excellent teachers want to work.

The existence of such leaders—and their commonsense approaches to problem solving—stands as a powerful argument that schools can do better not only for their most vulnerable students but also for all students.

References

Branch, G. F., Hanushek, E. A., Rivkin, S. C (2012). Estimating the effect of leaders on public sector productivity: The case of school principals (CALDER Working Paper No. 66).

Washington, DC: National Center for Analysis of Longitudinal Data in Education Research.

Leithwood, K., Louis, K. S., Anderson, S., & Wahlstrom, K. (2004). How leadership influences student learning. New York: Wallace Foundation.

Louis, K. S., Leithwood, K., Wahlstrom, K. L., & Anderson, S. E., et al. (2010). Learning from leadership: Investigating the links to improved student learning. New York: Wallace Foundation.

Critical Thinking

1. Of the four qualities, which one do you believe is the most important? Support your answer with research-based educational theory.

2. Generate a list of personal qualities you would like to develop for yourself. How do these qualities fit into your educational philosophy?

3. Outline a step-by-step plan describing how you will achieve at least two of the qualities you want to exhibit as a teacher or principal.

Internet References

National Center for Educational Statistics: Children Living in Poverty
   https://nces.ed.gov/programs/coe/indicator_cce.asp
Southern Education Foundation
   http://www.southerneducation.org
The Education Trust
   http://edtrust.org

Authors' Note—We describe our research sample, methodology, and findings in more detail in Getting It Done: Leading Academic Success in Unexpected Schools (Harvard Education Press, 2011).

KARIN CHENOWETH is writer-in-residence and Christina Theokas is director of research at the Education Trust.

Article   Prepared by: Rebecca B. Evers, *Winthrop University*

Building a Pedagogy of Engagement for Students in Poverty

The only surefire way to eliminate the achievement gap is to eradicate poverty. Since that's not going to happen anytime soon, educators can still take many research-proven steps to foster equality of opportunity in education.

PAUL C. GORSKI

Learning Outcomes

After reading this article, you will be able to:

• Discuss your personal disposition toward people who live in poverty.

• Consider the suggested classroom strategies for teaching students who live in poverty.

• Evaluate strategies for becoming an activist in your community.

I started kindergarten in 1976, a decade before personal computers were in vogue for people who could afford them. The image of largesse I remember from elementary school was the 64-count box of crayons—the one with the built-in sharpener. I didn't have language for it then, but I knew that box denoted privilege.

I also remember when poster board was the hot commodity. I watched some students tremble when teachers assigned projects requiring it. Russell, a classmate, was shamed into outing himself as poor when the teacher asked the class, "Who needs help getting poster board?" The teachers I most admired were subtler, dumping everybody's crayons into community bins and keeping a few sheets of poster board tucked behind a filing cabinet, distributing it discreetly to students whose families couldn't afford it. My family fell in-between. We could afford poster board, but I settled for boxes of 16-count crayons.

During a recent visit to a high-poverty school, I asked 8th graders how many of them had a working computer and Internet access at home; only a few of the 40 students raised their hands. Then I asked how many of them had been assigned homework that required access to computers and the Internet since the last grading period ended; everybody raised their hands.

Even before the e-revolution, Russell and other students who had no say in their families' financial conditions were at a disadvantage. That's when poster board was the commodity. Now it's computers. And the Internet. And printers.

It can be difficult to remember that many poor families simply cannot afford these technologies. It can be even more difficult to remember that the same families have reduced access to a bunch of other resources that influence learning, such as health care, recreational opportunities, and even clean air. And given shifting demographics and the recent recession, their numbers are growing, especially in suburban schools where many of us are unaccustomed to teaching low-income students.

That's important because, as David Berliner (2009) reminds us, the only sure path to educational equity is eliminating poverty itself. As long as inequality abounds, so will those pesky achievement gaps. Unfortunately education practitioners can't eliminate poverty on their own. And we can't afford to wait, and poor families can't afford to wait, for poverty to be eliminated. Even as I work toward that bigger change, I have to commit to doing what I can to address the inequities that students are experiencing right now.

This is why I've spent much of the past five years reading every bit of research I can find on what works when it comes to mitigating the effects of economic inequality in schools. This is the question guiding my research: What can teachers and administrators do today, not to raise low-income students' test scores—as that obsession, itself, is a symptom of one of those bigger societal things that needs to change—but to improve educational opportunity?

Promising Practices and a Couple Caveats

Before considering my suggestions, remember that low-income people are infinitely diverse. No researcher knows your students better than you know them. So, no matter how tempting the easy solution may seem, there simply is no silver bullet, no nicely wrapped bundle of strategies that work for all low-income students everywhere. Aside from advocating for the social change necessary to eliminate poverty, the best thing we can do in the name of educational equity is honor the expertise of people in poor communities by teaming with them as partners in educational equity.

Second, more important than any strategy are the dispositions with which we relate to low-income families. Any strategy will be ineffective if I believe poverty is a marker of intellectual deficiency (Robinson, 2007). So I need to check my own biases even as I enact these strategies.

Classroom Strategies

Express high expectations through higher-order, engaging pedagogies. According to Lee and Burkam (2003), students labeled "at-risk" who attend schools that combine rigorous curricula with learner-centered teaching achieve at higher levels and are less likely to drop out than their peers who experience lower-order instruction. Like everyone else, low-income youth learn best at schools in which pedagogy is driven by high academic expectations for all students—where standards aren't lowered based on socioeconomic status (Ramalho, Garza, & Merchant, 2010), and in classrooms where they have access to dialogic, inquiry-driven, collaborative pedagogies (Georges, 2009; Wenglinsky, 2002). Critical pedagogies and the development of critical literacies can be particularly helpful when it comes to school engagement among low-income students. Provide them with opportunities to tell stories about themselves that challenge the deficit-laden portrayals they often hear.

Enhance family involvement. Make sure opportunities for family involvement are accessible to parents and guardians who are likely to work multiple jobs, including evening jobs, who may not have access to paid leave, who may struggle to afford child care, and who may rely on public transportation. Start by providing transportation and on-site child care (Amatea & West-Olatunji, 2007; Van Galen, 2007).

Incorporate arts into instruction. Among the most instructionally illogical responses to the test score obsession is the elimination of arts programs—most commonly in lower-income schools—to carve out additional time for reading, writing, and math. Exposure to art, theater, and music education bolsters learning, engagement, and retention for all students and especially for low-income youth, whose families generally can't afford music lessons or art camp (Catterall, Chapleau, & Iwanaga, 1999; Pogrow, 2006). Take advantage of local artists and musicians, who might consider working with your students or helping you think about the arts in discipline-specific ways.

Incorporate movement into instruction. Low-income students also are losing access to recess and physical education. The lack of recreational facilities and green space in poor communities, costs associated with recreational sports, and work and family obligations, often means that recess or P.E. is the only opportunity for low-income youth to exercise. Students who are physically fit fare better in school, and childhood physical fitness is an indicator of how healthy a person will be as an adult (Fahlman, Hall, & Lock, 2006). Anything you can do to incorporate movement into learning will help mitigate these disparities.

Focus intently on student and family strengths. Having high expectations is not pretention. When teachers adopt a deficit view of students, performance declines. The opposite happens when teachers focus on student strengths (Haberman, 1995; Johns, Schmader, & Martens, 2005). It will be better for you, too. Robinson (2007) found in a study of 400 teachers in low-income schools that those who rejected a deficit view were happier with their jobs.

Analyze materials for class bias. Poor families often are depicted in stereotypical ways in picture books and other learning materials (Jones, 2008). A variety of useful tools exist to help us uncover these sorts of biases, such as the checklist of the National Association for the Teaching of English Working Party on Social Class and English Teaching (1982). Engage students in an analysis of the biases you uncover. And please retire that obnoxious picture of the "hobo" from your vocabulary wall. It's 2013.

Promote literacy enjoyment. According to Mary Kellett, "If we . . . acknowledge that literacy proficiency can be a route out of poverty . . . the most powerful strategy is to . . . promote reading enjoyment. This is likely to make the biggest impact on literacy proficiency" (2009, p. 399). This means literacy instruction should not focus solely on mechanics and should avoid practices that give students negative associations with literacy, such as forcing them to perform literacy skills publicly.

Reach out to families early and often. Many low-income parents and guardians experienced school as a hostile environment when they were students (Gorski, 2012). Any hesitance we experience when we reach out is not necessarily ambivalence about school. It might reflect reasonable distrust for the system we represent. It might be about long work hours or a lack of access to a telephone. Be persistent. Build trust. Most importantly, demonstrate trust by nurturing positive relationships. We can do this by facilitating ongoing communication rather than reaching out only when something is wrong, creating an equitable classroom environment across all dimensions of diversity, and refusing to invalidate concerns about inequalities that are raised by low-income families (Hamovitch, 1996).

A Few Higher-level Strategies

As we grow our spheres of influence, we might consider taking on some bigger battles for class equity.

Advocate universal preschool. Investment in early childhood education might be the most critical educational advocacy we can do, as disparities in access to early educational interventions compound throughout children's lifetimes (Bhattacharya, 2010).

Nurture relationships with community agencies, including health clinics and farms (for fresh food). Susan Neuman (2009) found that of all types of educational interventions for poor families, those based on coordinated efforts among educational, social, and health services were most effective.

Reduce class sizes. Despite the illusion of a debate, research shows that class size matters (Rouse & Barrow, 2006).

Increase health services in schools. Start by broadening vision screenings to include farsightedness, which relates to up close (book) reading (Gould & Gould, 2003). Other services and screenings should focus on risks that are elevated in low-income communities, such as asthma (Davis, Gordon, & Burns, 2011). Fight to keep nurses in low-income schools, where they are needed desperately (Telljohann, Dake, & Price, 2004).

Conclusion

It bears repeating that teachers are not trained and schools are not equipped to make up for societal inequalities. This is why we should commit to doing all that we can in our spheres of influence toward class equity. And once we have done that, we can expand those spheres.

References

Amatea, E.S. & West-Olatunji, C.A. (2007). Joining the conversation about educating our poorest children: Emerging leadership roles for school counselors in high-poverty schools. *Professional School Counseling, 11* (2), 81–89.

Berliner, D. (2009). *Poverty and potential: Out-of-school factors and school success.* Tempe, AZ: Education and the Public Interest Center & Education Policy Research Unit.

Bhattacharya, A. (2010). Children and adolescents from poverty and reading development: A research review. *Reading & Writing Quarterly, 26,* 115–139.

Catterall, J., Chapleau, R., & Iwanaga, J. (1999). Involvement in the arts and human development: General involvement and intensive involvement in music and theater arts. In E.B. Fiske (Ed.), *Champions of change: The impact of the arts on learning* (pp. 1–18). Washington, DC: Arts Education Partnership, President's Committee on the Arts and the Humanities.

Davis, D.W., Gordon, M.K., & Burns, B.M. (2011). Educational interventions for childhood asthma: A review and integrative model for preschoolers from low-income families. *Pediatric Nursing, 37* (1), 31–38.

Fahlman, M.M., Hall, H.L., & Lock, R. (2006). Ethnic and socioeconomic comparisons of fitness, activity levels, and barriers to exercise in high school females. *Journal of School Health, 76* (1), 12–17.

Georges, A. (2009). Relation of instruction and poverty to mathematics achievement gains during kindergarten. *Teachers College Record, 111* (9), 2148–2178.

Gorski, P.C. (2012). Perceiving the problem of poverty and schooling: Deconstructing the class stereotypes that misshape education policy and practice. *Equity & Excellence in Education, 45* (2), 302–319.

Gould, M.C. & Gould, H. (2003). A clear vision for equity and opportunity. *Phi Delta Kappan, 85* (4), 324–328.

Haberman, M. (1995). *Star teachers of children in poverty.* Irvine, CA: Kappa Delta Pi.

Hamovitch, B. (1996). Socialization without voice: An ideology of hope for at-risk students. *Teachers College Record, 98* (2), 286–306.

Johns, M., Schmader, T., & Martens, A. (2005). Knowing is half the battle: Teaching stereotype threat as a means of improving women's math performance. *Psychological Science, 16,* 175–179.

Jones, S. (2008). Grass houses: Representations and reinventions of social class through children's literature. *Journal of Language and Literacy Education, 4* (2), 40–58.

Kellett, M. (2009). Children as researchers: What we can learn from them about the impact of poverty on literacy opportunities. *International Journal of Inclusive Education, 13* (4), 395–408.

Lee, V. & Burkam, D. (2003). Dropping out of high school: The role of school organization and structure. *American Educational Research Journal, 40,* 353–393.

National Association for the Teaching of English. (1982). Checklist for class bias and some recommended books. *English in Education, 16,* 34–37.

Neuman, S.B. (2009). Use the science of what works to change the odds for children at risk. *Phi Delta Kappan, 90* (8), 582–587.

Pogrow, S. (2006). Restructuring high-poverty elementary schools for success: A description of the Hi-Perform school design. *Phi Delta Kappan, 88* (3), 223–229.

Ramalho, E.M., Garza, E., & Merchant, B. (2010). Successful school leadership in socioeconomically challenging contexts: School principals creating and sustaining successful school improvement. *International Studies in Educational Administration, 38* (3), 35–56.

Robinson, J.G. (2007). Presence and persistence: Poverty ideology and inner-city teaching. *Urban Review, 39,* 541–565.

Rouse, C.E. & Barrow, L. (2006). U.S. elementary and secondary schools: Equalizing opportunity or replacing the status quo? *The Future of Children, 16* (2), 99–123.

Telljohann, S.K., Dake, J.A., & Price, J.H. (2004). Effect of full-time versus part-time school nurses on attendance of elementary students with asthma. *Journal of School Nursing, 20* (6), 331–334.

Van Galen, J. (2007). Late to class: Social class and schooling in the new economy. *Educational Horizons, 85,* 156–167.

Wenglinsky, H. (2002). *How teaching matters: Bringing the classroom back into discussions of teacher quality.* Princeton, NJ: Milken Family Foundation.

Critical Thinking

1. Gorski states that the most important strategy for teachers is our own dispositional bias. Make a list of your experiences with persons who live in poverty; (i.e., homeless street people, panhandlers, or working with children in schools/churches.) Note how these experiences have influenced your thinking. Did you come away with positive or negative responses?

2. Which one of Gorski's classroom strategies do you think will be the easiest for you to use? Which will be the most difficult? Explain your answers.

3. Select one of Gorski's higher-level strategies to research. Pick one that you know is available in your community. Research how this strategy is being implemented and its perceived or real effectiveness. Share the information with your peers as suggested by your professor.

Create Central

www.mhhe.com/createcentral

Internet References

Donors Choose
www.donorschoose.org

Edutopia
www.edutopia.org

McKinney-Vento Act
http://www2.ed.gov/programs/homeless/legislation.html

Southern Poverty Law Center Teaching Diverse Students
http://www.splcenter.org/what-we-do/children-at-risk

PAUL C. GORSKI is an associate professor of integrative studies (education and social justice concentrations) at George Mason University, Fairfax, Va. He is author *of Reaching and Teaching Students in Poverty: Erasing the Opportunity Gap* (Teachers College Press, 2013) and coeditor of *The Poverty and Education Reader: A Call for Equity in Many Voices* (Stylus Press, 2013).

Article   Prepared by: Rebecca B. Evers, *Winthrop University*

Overcoming the Challenges of Poverty

Here are 15 things educators can do to make our schools and classrooms places where students thrive.

JULIE LANDSMAN

Learning Outcomes

After reading this article, you will be able to:

- Summarize actions educators can take to help students thrive.
- Critique the practice of teaching in different ways to students of different economic circumstances.

Last year, when I was leading a staff development session with teachers at a high-poverty elementary school, a teacher described how one of her kindergarten students had drifted off to sleep at his seat—at 8:00 A.M. She had knelt down next to the child and began talking loudly in his ear, urging him to wake up. As if to ascertain that she'd done what was best for this boy, she turned to the rest of us and said, "We are a 'no excuses' school, right?"

A fellow teacher who also lived in the part of Minneapolis where this school was located and knew the students well, asked, "Did you know Samuel has been homeless for a while now? Last night, there was a party at the place where he stays. He couldn't go to bed until four in the morning."

I couldn't help but think that if the "no excuses" philosophy a school follows interferes with basic human compassion for high-needs kids, the staff needs to rethink how they are doing things. Maybe they could set up a couple of cots for homeless students in the office to give them an hour or two of sleep; this would yield more participation than shouting at children as they struggle to stay awake.

This isn't the first time I've heard of adults viewing low-income children as "the problem" rather than trying to understand their lives. In a radio interview I heard, a teenage girl in New Orleans after Hurricane Katrina told her interviewer that she thought many people viewed poor families like hers as criminals. Crying, she described how it felt when city officials blamed her family for the lack of food and shelter they experienced after the hurricane.

A Forgotten Duty?

Sometimes it seems that we do not believe it's our duty to provide basic needs and an education for all children in the United States, no matter where they grow up. For instance, in some schools I know of, when a student cannot pay for a reduced-price meal, the lunch is dumped into the trash in front of the entire school, humiliating that child.

The attitudes of policymakers also reflect a shift toward teaching students in differing ways depending on their economic status. Teachers often hear that poor kids come from violent, chaotic homes and that only regimented curriculums will allow them to succeed. Although wealthier children are taught through a variety of approaches that emphasize developing the whole child, the emphasis for low-income children is often on developing obedience.

At the same time, many rural, urban, and suburban schools serving low-income students challenge such prescriptive teaching. They quietly provide, intellectually and materially, for high-poverty students. For instance, they create programs that arrange transportation for students to theaters, concerts, and museums. Because Saturday and Sunday are two days of the week many poor children go hungry, some schools send kids home for the weekend with backpacks of food. They create a welcoming environment where even the poorest parents feel comfortable.

Teachers and administrators at these schools offer challenging instruction while simultaneously addressing basic needs. This is a tricky balancing act that requires dedication, self-reflection, and reexamining what works—or doesn't. Here, gathered from schools that succeed with students living in poverty, are suggestions for how to manage that balancing act.

What Teachers Can Do
Make Time for Extras

Can you create times for students to make up schoolwork, work on a project for history class, or just enjoy music and art? It doesn't have to be every day. Teachers in a building might coordinate to set times before and after classes during which a child with an unstable home life can use a computer or read in silence—and when teachers can give guidance and build trust.

In one middle school where I worked, we let students spend their lunch hours with us, providing chess and checkers. It's amazing how much information young men and women will share over a game board, from tasks they're having trouble accomplishing to worries about food over the weekend. What we learned from these times helped us create programs that met students' greatest needs.

Tell Students to Ask for Help

Spell out that you expect learners to come talk with you about a low test score, a comment on a paper, or their needs for resources. Some students simply don't know the expectations regarding behavior, work, and interaction with their teacher. One teacher in a suburban high school assumed her students had access to the Internet and assigned work on the basis of that assumption. When she found out that many students had no Internet at home, she organized time after classes for students to work on school computers—and transportation home—giving careful instructions about what she wanted from their time online.

Cut deals with students who don't have essential supplies by providing those supplies while, at the same time, pushing these kids to work hard on their assignments. A homeless girl may have lost a pencil in the trudge around the city finding a place for the night or left her homework in the office of a shelter. A boy may not be able to get his work done by the due date because he has no quiet place to concentrate. By keeping a supply of pencils, paper, and notebooks handy and adjusting due dates for individual students, you can make sure students know you're willing to modify conditions but you expect work to be done.

Use Visuals to Help Organize Assignments

Students whose lives are chaotic need to be reminded of exactly what work is due and when. Calendars and charts are visual cues that help kids organize time and tasks together, especially if you refer to them often. Write different tasks and events connected to each assignment—outline due date, media center day, or first draft due—on the calendar squares. A calendar both reminds students of the day of the week and creates a visual map to future tasks.

Imagine Their Obstacles— and See Their Strengths

If you grew up with economic security, remind yourself that you might not understand the things adults and children in families with barely enough for the basics have to do just to survive—and the obstacles they face. Some schools expect parents to get to parent conferences in the evening, which can involve a bus ride, babysitting expense, or taking time off from the late shift. To illuminate what such expectations involve, one school's social worker surveyed parents and teachers to see how many owned cars. Every teacher and teacher's aide owned a car, but only 40 parents—in a school with 500 students—did.

Find ways to accommodate such realities. For instance, I worked as a visiting poet in a school where one-third of the students were homeless. We made sure each kid had two copies of the poems they wrote, one to leave at school and one to take to their parents, to keep their writing from getting lost in transit.

When high-poverty schools hire people from the surrounding neighborhood who are acquainted with the poverty there, these people can be experts regarding students' situations. Connect with these staff members; ask their advice on how to affirm and provide for particular children. Jared, a young adult hall monitor at a school where I taught writing, brought into my class a poetry book by rapper Tupac Shakur. I read some of those poems with my students. Soon Jared was visiting my poetry sessions during breaks from his work, helping students with their writing and homework.

Understanding students' obstacles should help you give them credit for their amazing resilience and delight in learning. Low-income children are often described in terms of what they *don't* have or *cannot* do. Reframe your thinking to recognize the strength it takes for a child who had to find a couch to sleep on last night to simply make it in the school door.

Listen

In our rush to create silent classrooms and push test preparation, we lose sight of the complexity of children's lives, and we lose our delight in knowing how they feel, reason, joke, or concoct ideas. In just 10 minutes, you can encourage students to write from a prompt like "I am from _____" or "I used to_____, but now I _____." Read their pieces to a small group or to the entire class. Elementary teachers often have a daily circle time and even in secondary school, you can pull the chairs into a circle at the end of class and ask students about their plans for the rest of the day or a neighborhood event.

This listening is an important part of your job. Listening means slowing down or stopping, even for a minute as a student lingers by your desk. It means having music playing as you work in your classroom in the morning and nodding to a student who comes in early. If you let that student relax there most mornings, he might make it a habit to talk with you before each day begins.

Don't Tolerate Teasing

By establishing clear classroom guidelines, including no teasing about clothes or possessions and talking with students about what these guidelines mean, you'll establish a climate of safety. Effective guidelines state positive behaviors, such as, Be Physically Considerate, Be Verbally Considerate, or Try New Things. Talk about what concepts like *consideration* mean; for instance, showing verbal consideration includes not taunting or hurting anyone's feelings. When you spend time up front working on behaviors, you save time the rest of the year. Classes become communities, and discipline problems diminish.

Connect Curriculum to Students' Interests

When possible, connect the content you're teaching to things students are fascinated with, like a song or video they keep talking about or the pollution in their neighborhood. By tapping into learners' concerns, you can develop bridges to literature, science, or math. You might engage students in projects connected to community issues or problems, like cleaning up a playground or advocating for a bus for summer programs. Students can write letters to the editor, ask scientists to come in and talk about pollution, or find journalists who will talk to the class about issues in their city. Such actions give low-income students a sense of agency and possibility. You might also infuse their families' traditions and talents into classwork. Financially poor students often come from families rich in culture.

Speak Out

Advocate for impoverished children by speaking up about which students are tracked into general courses versus gifted programs or advanced classes. Insist on the giftedness of some of your poorer students. Some schools have programs that parallel advanced classes yet don't require applicants to demonstrate academic skills that they may not have going in—but could develop. These demanding courses both challenge and support low-income students.

Other schools have opened up advanced placement or International Baccalaureate classes to anyone who wants to try them. Suggest similar programs and push for changes like providing bilingual conferences for parents who don't speak English. You may get push back from those who want no deviation from the status quo. Be willing to be unpopular for your advocacy.

Find Allies

It's hard to do this work in isolation. Forge a supportive network that keeps you going as you strive to make a difference for students and push for academic equity—through a book group, inquiry team, or lunchtime discussion on issues related to education and poverty. You'll have someone to call when you're trying to anticipate how your suggestions will go over at the next faculty meeting—and someone to talk with about how it went. There are more teachers willing to advocate for kids than is often apparent.

What Administrators Can Do

Principals and superintendents can do much to support both struggling students and committed teachers. Think in terms of getting resources to the neediest schools and students.

Develop a Trusting Relationship with Teachers

Can teachers talk with you about an idea or solution they have for addressing the needs of poorer students? One of the most successful urban principals I ever worked with asked teachers to come to him often with a problem combined with a suggested solution.

Standing up for overworked teachers builds trust. When the district tries to mandate more requirements or protocols in March or to add a new test, voice your concern for the load this might put on teachers, many of whom may be already providing for students materially. When you have a devoted staff, make sure they know you'll challenge those who would add more burdens.

Spend Time in Classrooms

Observe not to evaluate, but to see how teachers do what they do successfully. Administrators, counselors, social workers, and even superintendents can be remarkable supporters for teachers by coming to classrooms—to work with students on a project, play piano for them, or just talk to them. When done in cooperation with teachers, such encounters add a great deal to a school's collaborative climate.

Give Teachers a Picture of Students' Realities

Through tapping the insights of social workers and district demographic services, and through family surveys, find out what household income and resources are like in your area and what resources students probably do or don't have at home. Share with your faculty facts like the income ranges of your families or the absence of grocery stores or libraries in their neighborhoods—details that clarify what it means to be poor.[1]

This information will help teachers avoid assumptions about what students have in their homes and appreciate the resilience of youth from high-poverty families who get to school each day filled with hope and energy.

Advocate for High-Quality Classes

Be aware of how tracking works in your school or district. Are poor students getting slotted into classes for low-skilled students early in their lives? Advocate for low-income kids to receive gifted education services.

Get more teachers into the neediest classrooms. A principal who states publicly that having five classes each containing 45 students is unacceptable—and that he or she will work to change these conditions—wins teachers' trust.

Offer After-school Programs and Services

Work with teachers to find groups like the YMCA to provide volunteers for your school, so students have supervision and stimulation—including physical activities, art, and academic activities—more hours in the day. Local groups, businesses, and cultural venues will often contribute if approached by the principal or superintendent (see "Sources of Grants for Projects and Materials"). Consider providing wraparound services for your low-income students, such as access to medical and mental health professionals.

Communicate Commitment

Make clear that as an administrator, you're in this for the long haul and will work on long-term solutions to inequity for children in your district. It is important that your entire staff knows you will persist in getting the services and programs your building needs.

Toward Vibrant Classrooms

These are just a few ways educators can ensure students aren't marginalized by poverty—without making students feel they are a "problem." Each school district will need to explore what might work in its unique situation. But my hope is that no school ever becomes a place where sleepy children are yelled at or where teachers lose our human compassion. Let's create vibrant classrooms that tap into the brilliance of each child.

Sources of Grants for Projects and Materials

RGK Foundation awards grants for projects in K–12 education (math, science, reading, and teacher development) and after-school enrichment programs. The foundation is interested in programs that attract female and minority students into STEM.

National Geographic Education Foundation provides professional development and education materials connected to geography education.

American Honda Foundation supports youth and scientific education projects, including those that offer unique approaches to teaching youth in minority and underserved communities.

Dollar General Literacy Foundation funds programs for youth and adult literacy, school library relief, and preparation for the GED. Dollar General Grant Programs support nonprofits in U.S. states in which company stores are located.

The ING Foundation awards grants to nonprofits working in education, particularly physical education and for programs addressing child obesity.

Teaching Tolerance makes grants of $500 to $2,500 for projects designed to reduce prejudice, improve intergroup relations in schools, and support professional development in these areas.

Note

1. Many documentaries and public television programs (such as *A Place at the Table, Viva la Causa,* and *Why Poverty*) show what life is like for families living in poverty—for example, the realities of doubling up with relatives or taking two bus rides to get groceries.

Critical Thinking

1. Ask a teacher in a high poverty school what works for them. Compare with the list in this article. Reflect on similarities and differences and infer the reasons for differences.

2. Select one of the suggestions and develop a plan or activity to implement the suggestion.

3. Select one of the sources for grants and submit a grant for your school or a school you know.

Internet References

National Center for Children in Poverty
http://www.nccp.org

Southern Education Foundation
http://www.southerneducation.org

The National Association for the Education of Homeless Children and Youth
http://www.naehcy.org

JULIE LANDSMAN is a consultant on equitable education. She is the author of many books on education, including *A White Teacher Talks About Race* (R & L Education, 2005), and is the coeditor with Paul Gorski of *The Poverty and Education Reader* (Stylus, 2014).

Article

Prepared by: Rebecca B. Evers, *Winthrop University*

Advocacy for Child Wellness in High-Poverty Environments

CAROL A. MULLEN

Learning Outcomes

After reading this article, you will be able to:

- Summarize adverse conditions of poverty on student performance.

- Explain the wellness challenges that may prevent academic success as well as students' ability to thrive.

- Develop a plan to become an advocate for student wellness in addition to students' achievement.

Crumbling buildings are but one sign of poverty that stretches beyond the school to a community of families struggling to get by. Slum neighborhoods, violent behavior, drug dealing, poor health care, broken plumbing, expensive housing, makeshift shelters, food-bank lines, outdated books, and weather-damaged property are compounding signs of poverty. Hunger, poor nutrition, and disease are more commonplace in America, as well as around the globe, than one might think. These types of problems that span urban, rural, and suburban areas interfere with student learning and child wellness. Yet, educators in high-poverty schools are expected to rise to the occasion by satisfying the same standards for learning and performance of schools that are highly resourced and that serve children living in favorable conditions.

Bureaucrats and legislators, not always attuned to the extraordinarily adverse conditions children in poverty face, have unrealistic expectations for student performance (Tienken, 2012) and school performance (Darling-Hammond & Lieberman, 2012). Schools built for life in the early twentieth century put educators and students at a serious disadvantage. Given the unsatisfactory conditions of high-poverty schools, it should

be no surprise that students who lack twenty-first century skills such as proficiency with digital technologies and high-stakes standardized tests also have lower college acceptance rates than students from advantaged backgrounds (Mullen & Kealy, 2012; Tienken, 2012). In addition, an array of wellness challenges defines the learning landscape, which becomes a space to navigate just to survive, let alone thrive. Placing shame on teachers and students in underperforming schools produces a "trauma of failure" (Darling-Hammond & Lieberman, 2012, p. 73) that can manifest as dread of learning, fear of failure, or other negative emotions. All of these forces "conspire" to hold students and educators in disadvantaged school communities accountable in the same ways as their counterparts in modernized, well-resourced schools. Where is the equity in that?

Holistic Wellness

The daily struggles to learn are copious for children in dual school systems (that is, advantaged versus disadvantaged or segregated) and public schools segregated by race and class, both in urban and rural settings. Not only are these children challenged by economic poverty, but they also may face poverty that is situational (such as a family crisis). Poverty magnifies the threshold of distress in communities where children live in shelters or are homeless, move often during a single school year, or experience school life that excludes their history and culture (English, Papa, Mullen, & Creighton, 2012; Mullen & Kealy, 2012).

Especially in these circumstances, wellness must be viewed holistically. Achievement, while a critically important bar of significance, is not the only standard of progress where the whole learner is concerned. In 2007, UNICEF conducted an empirical, international research study concerning the holistic well-being of all children, and impoverished children and youth in particular. As explained by UNICEF (2007), wellness simultaneously affects the child from multiple directions:

> The true measure of a nation's standing is how well it attends to its children—their health and safety, their material security, their education and socialization, and their sense of being loved, valued, and included in the families and societies into which they are born. (p. 1)

Indicators of wellness, as identified by UNICEF (2007), cover these six dimensions:

- material well-being (e.g., low family income; "lack of educational and cultural resources," p. 10);
- health and safety (e.g., inadequate "child immunization rates," p. 13);
- education (e.g., below average achievement in reading and math literacy, p. 18);
- peer and family relationships (e.g., "living in single-parent families" and "stepfamilies," p. 21);
- behaviors and risks (e.g., experiences of fighting or being bullied, p. 26); and
- young people's sense of well-being (e.g., personal view of health as fair or poor, not liking school, or not feeling satisfied with their own lives; pp. 34–35).

Poverty can affect wellness, and poverty that is complex in nature (i.e., both situational and generational) can have a rippling effect on a student's well-being, including his or her educational performance and attainment. Viewed from the opposite direction, a child or adolescent who is granted the opportunity to build capacity in one area of wellness, such as education, may be able to do so in one or more of the other areas.

The UNICEF indicators from the 2007 study reinforce the holistic nature of well-being. A child's nurturance must go beyond the dimension of material well-being—the most readily understood indicator of child well-being—across the six dimensions of well-being. While material well-being obviously includes material comfort, it extends to that more nebulous area involving selfhood. One's sense of self, a key dimension of well-being (UNICEF, 2007), the sixth indicator, includes deeply personal beliefs and allows individuals to develop into advocates for change. If an individual believes in his or her ability to succeed in particular situations, especially challenging ones that involve considerable planning and exertion of effort, then that person may make a commitment and be driven to action (Schunk & Mullen, 2013). Sense of self stemming from hope and confidence is especially important in high-poverty schools that are burdened by "naming and shaming" couched in widely circulated, debilitating messages about teachers

having low expectations of student success in minority schools (Darling-Hammond & Lieberman, 2012, p. 73).

Teacher Advocacy for Students' Well-Being

In a world where children and youth live in extreme global economic poverty (Ki-Moon, 2013), educators must advocate for their students' well-being in ways not traditionally associated with schooling practices and teacher preparation. Consider Elizabeth. As an undergraduate student, Elizabeth gained experience as a self-identified "civil rights activist" through her involvement with the university's Black student union (Lieberman & Friedrich, 2010, p. 21). Now an urban middle school teacher, Elizabeth views her modeling of and writing about activism, community alliances, and classroom as "a laboratory for equity and social justice" in which students are taught about contemporary issues in context and through which they learn to advocate for themselves (Lieberman & Friedrich, 2010, p. 21).

Like Elizabeth, teachers can stand up for students' well-being in many different ways. However, positioning themselves to support and sponsor their students and to model advocacy begins with a comprehensive, holistic understanding of well-being. Armed with that knowledge, teachers can make a difference in their classrooms and schools, as well as in the community. They can prepare students to advocate for themselves in the real world by using the classroom as a safe haven for practicing these skills. Outside of the classroom, teachers can "advocate for the profession" by joining professional associations, learning about pressing issues in education, communicating with decision makers, and participating in person where policy, curriculum, achievement, performance, quality, and other salient matters are under the microscope (Bond & Sterrett, 2011, p. 2).

Teachers who develop agency and activism as twenty-first century skills and key areas of personal development will be more equipped to model these abilities for their students and to help them develop agency as a core aspect of their sense of self (UNICEF, 2007). Any person—whether a preservice teacher, inservice teacher, child, or youth—can be a spokesperson for well-being on his or her own behalf and that of others. Specifically, a teacher can advocate for children by creating a climate of awareness that extends to such stakeholders as parents and policymakers, and specifically by generating strategies for thinking about well-being holistically as related to curriculum, policy, and human development. In professional development trainings and when using curricular approaches to student wellness, teachers might create their own rubrics for clarifying as well as monitoring wellness relative to each student.

Elizabeth, the Advocate

Elizabeth, mentioned earlier, teaches in a rundown, poorly equipped infrastructure, in stark contrast to a classroom facility in a functioning school building with learning resources (Lieberman & Friedrich, 2010). Based on the vignette she penned, she exerts activism in the roles of "community organizer" and "political activist" by taking personal initiative and empowering her students through concrete actions that enliven "the conditions needed to support quality teaching and learning" (Lieberman & Friedrich, 2010, p. 24).

Serving as a child-centered advocate, Elizabeth involves parents in her own personal letter-writing, as well as other teachers and stakeholders from outside the school. With her help, her students develop their own self-identity by connecting their lessons to their lives and community. For instance, she exposes them to articles about the school that put issues of social justice, revolution, and racial segregation in context.

High-quality teachers like Elizabeth are vital in the turnaround of their struggling schools in disadvantaged neighborhoods. Yet even the most capable of teachers cannot alone bring about change. Teachers must find allies among parents and guardians, partner schools, sponsors, and colleges of education (Kosiczky & Mullen, 2013; Papa & English, 2011) and take advantage of opportunities to interact with those stakeholders.

Not only does Elizabeth harness "parent, student, and community power" to discover "resources needed to address their current issues," but she also encourages stakeholders to seek "solutions to the current problems they [are] facing," such as racial segregation (Lieberman & Friedrich, 2010, pp. 21–22). She accepts many requests to speak about the conditions of her school and its history, and leads her students in the exercise of writing testimonials for audiences that have spanned the Congressional Black Caucus, the United States Senate, Court TV and C-Span, and community organizations (Lieberman & Friedrich, 2010). As her students develop a democratic understanding of social justice, Elizabeth continues to deepen her self-understanding and, together, they engage in reciprocal learning about the value of "resistance, revolution, and rising up" (Lieberman & Friedrich, 2010, p. 21).

Elizabeth energizes her students to test newfound knowledge in their communities. She identifies her students as the primary stakeholders in charge of learning to advocate for themselves and like populations. With the vision of bringing about safer school conditions for all students from disadvantaged neighborhoods, her students wrote letters about a school modernization bill. As Elizabeth shared, her middle school students

drafted a petition letter to the members on the City Council Education Committee and collected over 400 petition letters from parents. They delivered these

during the public hearing for the School Modernization bill. . . . The petition letter-writing campaign and supporting actions not only had a direct impact on school modernization, but also resulted in the building of powerful alliances with parents, community members, and organizations. (Lieberman & Friedrich, 2010, pp. 23–24)

These students felt a shift toward being able to take charge of bettering their own worlds, even though they came to realize that racial issues of the school's past were still evident in some cases. Elizabeth and her students drew awareness by the collective to this issue by sharing this revelation with their constituencies.

At one point, Elizabeth temporarily moved her students to a space outside the school building until a permanent building with safer conditions became available. In relating her story, Elizabeth noted that seeking and finding safe spaces to learn is a form of activism. In addition, dimensions of wellness such as health and safety have the potential to support and reinforce a child's well-being.

Giving students firsthand experiences in putting civil rights history into context and translating its promises and perils to everyday life offers valuable lifelong lessons. Students become empowered as they develop into change agents. Schulten (2012), who advocated teaching the civil rights movement, would likely applaud Elizabeth's sociocultural teaching commitments. By focusing on issues that have societal merit, students have opportunities to explore important topics such as discrimination by employers and policymakers, wage gaps for females and minorities, and unemployment rates for minorities.

Social Contracts and Advocacy

To care about the well-being of children and youth is to care about the "social contract"—that is, the agreed-upon principles or two-way promises teachers have with students, whether actual or figurative. Educators make a difference by insisting on having their own social contracts with students that account for well-being across different dimensions. Imagine schools taking action by producing advocacy-oriented social contracts with students that could extend to include stakeholders. Social contracts in many classrooms are basically written rules which children must follow that equate with behavioral conduct, such as respecting others, staying focused, listening to others, and exhibiting self-control. A former classroom teacher described hers as a "shared social contract, clear expectations, a sense of purpose, and a set of logical consequences" (Shindler, 2010, p. 10).

To make them even more meaningful, advocacy-oriented social contracts could focus on the development of students and concerned citizens as advocates, support the teacher's own development in this area, and impact the school culture. Such social contracts could help articulate aspirational goals oriented at making a difference in the world; establish shared goals for developing networks outside the school and at the local, national, and international levels; identify problems within the community that could be targeted for assessment and change; name strategies for fostering collective action around a vision; and promote personal and collective identity formation around change agency as world citizens.

Elizabeth's students assumed advocacy roles by critically evaluating policy governing school buildings and linking the problems to action, with the purpose of modernizing outdated school campuses. Thereby, they took steps toward leveling the playing field for disadvantaged student populations. By their example, these students addressed the dimensions of health and safety, education, and relationships.

Taking Stock of Our Situations

Reflecting on Elizabeth's efforts can help educators envision ways to engage in the struggle to build capacity for children's well-being as well as their own. She made advocacy and accountability part of her students' daily mantra by teaching them to advocate for themselves while being accountable through their words and actions to constituents, such as their own parents and communities. Beyond the UNICEF (2007) study's emphasis on what is important, Elizabeth's story has added value because it gives evidence of what is possible and "achievable in practice" (Lieberman & Friedrich, 2010, p. 3).

All educators can join in this cause, regardless of their respective positions within schools, colleges of education, and elsewhere by "provid[ing] both government and civil society with the information to argue for and work towards the fulfillment of children's rights and the improvement of their lives" (UNICEF, 2007, p. 3). As educators, we can and must take action to influence governments and impact our own communities. Examples of pathways educators can take include "build[ing] a constituency for economic and educational change in urban [and other] communities" and thereby "connect[ing] movement building in education to political–economic justice issues"; "teach[ing] a critical, thought-provoking curriculum"; and utiliz[ing] the classroom to discuss issues their students face" (Anyon, 2014, p. 171). In addition, educators can mobilize by joining proactive organizations such as the National Coalition of Educational Activists, Educators for Social Responsibility, and Kappa Delta Pi, as well as participating in conferences or caucuses that foster work on behalf of students and critical thinking about policy and society.

As an introduction to advocacy through mobilization, educators also can be encouraged to act by taking stock of their situations. For example, they can explore the stories of their students, other educators, and their schools. Focused on the story of schools, Parrett and Budge (2012) suggested that educators can assess their ability to take action by reflecting on their willingness to make changes in support of, for example, child well-being. The self-assessment tools (rubrics) they provided focus on educators' ability and willingness to work with disadvantaged students (Parrett & Budge, 2012). By identifying perceptions of colleagues' capacities in that area, educators can elicit beliefs about individual personal, political, and academic capital. Further, such assessments—taking stock, identifying gaps, and measuring growth—could be expanded to incorporate entire schools and communities of learners.

The "Elizabeth" of this essay believes that she has a good understanding of what it means to live in poverty and what it takes to change a school culture so that it becomes safe as well as educative for all children and youth. Additionally, she sees children in the fundamental role of actively educating citizens who live in poverty. Children are not passive recipients of the change process in this worldview; they are active shapers of the future who can benefit from role modeling provided by their teachers, mentors, sponsors, and peers (English et al., 2012; Lieberman & Friedrich, 2010).

In her own social movement building, Elizabeth enlists others, including children's parents. Seeing herself as part of a larger whole, she does not try to take on this challenge alone. Educators who change their environments knowingly function within a tapestry of complex collectives even though much is to be discovered and cannot be known in advance. They gain the support of others in the effort to improve a child's world and thereby increase their own chances of success at mobilizing for the greater good (Anyon, 2014). Effective "problem-solvers" and "puzzle-unpackers" (Papa & English, 2011, p. 4) like these teachers and principals "go to the mat for their kids" (community activist cited in Anyon, 2014, p. 171), working beyond their campus and enlisting many players in a common cause.

Advocacy on a Broader Scale

Systems thinkers and activists described by Parrett and Budge (2012) have suggested that educators who turn around low-performing or failing schools

- build leadership capacity within themselves and others, including children and youth;
- foster a learning environment that is safe, healthy, and supportive; and
- enable the learning of all stakeholder groups at the individual and systems level.

How do effective educators in turned-around schools enact UNICEF's indicators of well-being? What more can each school and teacher do? How can schools get started? Much of this work is complicated and unknown. The stories, such as Elizabeth's, are only partial, but do connect wellness with issues of health and safety, education, and some of the other indicators.

Digging deeper to find answers raises additional questions. Who are the expert educators working in high-achieving, high-poverty schools to improve the well-being of their students? What do they do to turn around their schools and increase the capacity for wellness of disadvantaged children and youth? How can educators find out more about the dynamics that go into turning around low-performing schools?

These concerns were raised by superintendents, school board members, professors, and other leaders at the inaugural Virginia Tech School of Education Leadership Advisory Council in February 2014. Using the UNICEF dimensions of wellness as a focal point for the transformative work of educators in distressed circumstances, the Advisory Council members considered the comprehensive but unique dilemmas that influence the work of teachers in urban and rural settings, as well as the importance of understanding child wellness on an entirely new level.

The Advisory Council embraced the concept of child well-being and advocacy for the rights of children within schooling contexts and across nations as a starting place for collective advocacy among superintendents and other leaders from school divisions and higher education programs. Meeting attendees established the groundwork for continued discussion about child advocacy with stakeholders ranging from division superintendents, to principals, to school board members, and to other groups such as teacher consultants and prospective donors.

Outcomes from the meeting underscored the importance of the Advisory Council being action-oriented in the areas of child advocacy and lobbying. Attendees committed to further study of (a) the unintended consequences of high-stakes testing, (b) professional development opportunities in Virginia for principals and teachers, and (c) leadership styles needed for Title 1 schools. All of these areas intersect with child poverty and well-being, and the role of educators as advocates.

Through partnerships such as those formed through the Advisory Council, as well as organizations that provide expert assistance such as the National Center for Children in Poverty and Kappa Delta Pi (2013), educators can find out more about advocacy development for teachers and on behalf of students. Well-being for children around the world necessitates awareness of and action against unsafe living conditions, abuse, stress, and myriad other problems. Children everywhere, no matter their circumstances, can be taught to advocate for themselves. Teachers assist this advocacy mind-set by developing into strong, mindful advocates themselves and modeling discoveries.

Closing Thoughts

Notably, Elizabeth proactively helped her students think and act as change agents and integrate that sensibility into their belief system. They were being positioned to shape a world in which they could speak up and act on their own behalf. They were also being guided to research solutions and possibilities for a better world, identify resources and key players, and seek to be educated in a safe, healthy environment. Developing an advocacy mind-set, children and youth will become adults who manage the old and broken systems left behind by their elders.

Good work is being done in some P—16 schools and communities to tackle pressing challenges faced by students. An awareness of child well-being from a holistic perspective can help ensure that human rights are observed in the daily learning of students and their development over time. A holistic approach to well-being is a practical gauge that educators can use for combating the status quo of poverty and for turning around low-performing schools in which capacity is being built for positive learning, critical thought, and informed action. Knowing the international indicators of well-being can be helpful to teachers for shaping and assessing lessons and for guiding advocacy and activism within receptive and unreceptive school contexts alike.

References

Anyon, J. (2014). *Radical possibilities: Public policy, urban education, and a new social movement* (2nd ed.). New York: Routledge.

Bond, N., & Sterrett, W. (2011). A beginning teacher's guide to advocacy. *New Teacher Advocate, 19*(1), 2–3. Retrieved from www.kdp.org/teachingresources/pdf/vz/A_Beginning_Teacher_Guide_to_Advocacy_Bond.pdf

Darling-Hammond, L., & Lieberman, A. (Eds.). (2012). *Teacher education around the world: Changing policies and practices.* New York: Routledge.

English, F. W., Papa, R., Mullen, C. A., & Creighton, T. (2012). *Educational leadership at 2050: Conjectures, challenges and promises.* Lanham, MD: Rowman & Littlefield Education.

Kappa Delta Pi. (2013). *Find resources: Disadvantage children.* Retrieved from www.kdp.org/resources/tr/disadvantaged.php

Ki-Moon, B. (2013). *The millennium development goals report, 2013.* New York: United Nations. Retrieved from www.un.org/millenniumgoals/pdf/report-2013/mdg-report-2013-english.pdf

Kosiczky, B., & Mullen, C. A. (2013). Humor in high school and the role of teacher leaders in school public relations. *Journal of School Public Relations, 34*(1), 6–39.

Lieberman, A., & Friedrich, L. D. (2010). *How teachers become leaders: Learning from practice and research.* New York: Teachers College Press.

Mullen, C. A., & Kealy, W. A. (2012). Poverty in school communities. *Kappa Delta Pi Record, 49*(2), 70–77.

Papa, R., & English, F. W. (2011). *Turnaround principals for underperforming schools.* Lanham, MD: Rowman & Littlefield Education.

Parrett, W. H., & Budge, K. M. (2012). *Turning high-poverty schools into high-performing schools.* Alexandria, VA: ASCD.

Schulten, K. (2012, January 27). *Reader ideas: Teaching the civil rights movement* [blog]. Retrieved from http://learning.blogs .nytimes.com/2012/01/27/reader-ideas-teaching-the-civil-rights-movement/?_php=true&_type=blogs&_r=0

Schunk, D. H., & Mullen, C. A. (2013). Toward a conceptual model of mentoring research: Integration with self-regulated learning. *Educational Psychology Review, 25*(3), 361–389.

Shindler, J. (2010). *Transformative classroom management.* San Francisco: Jossey-Bass.

Tienken, C. H. (2012). The influence of poverty on achievement. *Kappa Delta Pi Record, 48*(3), 105–107.

UNICEF. (2007). *Child poverty in perspective: An overview of child well-being in rich countries.* Florence, Italy: The United Nations Children's Fund. Retrieved from www.unicef.org/media/files/ChildPovertyReport.pdf

Critical Thinking

1. Are the six indicators of wellness present in every school in your local district? If not, which indicators are missing? What effect do the missing indicators have on student wellness and achievement? Think beyond standardized test scores to other ways of knowing.

2. Note what the advocate, Elizabeth, did in her community. Which of her actions might you select to use as an advocate? Explain your answer.

3. Sometimes teachers feel that they cannot solve such large social issues. Elizabeth did what she could quite effectively. Think about what you and your peers might do; just one thing to help children in your area. Develop a plan to begin that one thing.

Internet References

National Center for Children in Poverty
http://www.nccp.org

The National Association for the Education of Homeless Children and Youth
http://www.naehcy.org

UNICEF: Child Protection and Development
http://www.unicefusa.org/mission/protect/education

Mullen, Carol, "Advocacy for Child Wellness in High-Poverty Environments", *Kappa Delta Pi Record,* October-December 2014, pp. 157–163. Copyright © 2014 by Phi Delta Kappan. Used with permission.

Article

Prepared by: Rebecca B. Evers, *Winthrop University*

Struggling in Suburbia

Many suburban schools are facing what for them is a new problem—poverty.

DAVID McKAY WILSON

Learning Outcomes

After reading this article, you will be able to:

- Summarize the actions teachers and their schools can take to counteract their perceptions of students who are at-risk.

- Describe the socioeconomic context of schools.

In Denver's western suburbs, a social studies teacher thought up a novel approach to teaching her students the unsettling realities of urban homelessness. She assigned them the task of sleeping overnight in the backseat of the family car.

But the assignment held a surprise in store for the teacher—one that provides a glimpse into the reality of 21st-century poverty in America. The teacher did not realize that one of her students was homeless. The girl had already spent many nights in her parents' car.

"These days in suburbia, you never know who you will have in your class," says Sheree Conyers, homeless liaison for the Jeffco Public Schools of Jefferson County, Colorado. "These are hard times. So many of our families are in transition."

A decade ago, the Jeffco Schools had just 59 homeless students in a district that serves about 86,000 students. By 2012, there were close to 3,000, representing 3 percent of the district enrollments. At Parr Elementary School, 28 percent of the students were homeless, according to a 2012 report.

The increasing poverty in Jefferson County, where close to one in three students qualifies for free and reduced price lunch, reflects the explosion of poverty in suburbs nationwide. Throughout the 2000s, the suburbs were home to the largest and fastest-growing poor population in the nation, according to a 2011 analysis of U.S. Census data by the Brookings Institution. From 2000 to 2010, the report also says, poverty grew by 53 percent in the nation's suburbs.

This rapid change has left many educators behind. They are still teaching as if the suburbs have remained immune from the poverty that has long troubled urban areas, says M.J. Lechner, a University of Colorado-Denver professor who oversees seven student teachers at Parr. "Some teachers have been responsive [to the changes]," she says, "while others are still struggling to give up the notion that all kids are the same as they were 10 years ago."

A Poorly Defined Problem

The explosion in suburban poverty is part of a larger, more disturbing trend. Childhood poverty nationwide is at its highest point since 1993, with 16.5 million, or 22 percent of children ages 18 and under living in poor families, according to the 2010 U.S. Census. Race is still a factor. For African-American children, the poverty rate was 38 percent; for Latino children, it was 32 percent.

Being classified as "poor" means that a family of four earns no more than $22,314. However, the National Center for Children in Poverty at Columbia University estimates that families typically need twice that income to cover their basic needs. That looser definition puts 44 percent of American children in low-income families.

The growth in suburban poverty has had a major impact on suburban schools, like those near Denver. Without the safety net of social services that city governments provide for the urban poor, suburban schools have had to scramble to set up programs that address basic needs, such as adequate food and clothing, for their students from low-income families.

The Jeffco district has established school-based food banks and an emergency fund for health needs, such as eyeglasses or medication. It also has held clothing drives at schools with large homeless populations. Schools feed students free or low-cost meals during the week, but not on the weekends. So 13 Jeffco schools have partnered with community sponsors and local food banks to provide food for the weekends.

At Parr, school officials have even altered the curriculum to accommodate homeless students. But some teachers have not adjusted to the new reality. "If a student has neither the place nor the tools with which to complete tasks sent home, they are often reprimanded or punished by missing recess," Lechner says. "This makes our homeless population feel even more singled out and ostracized."

WHERE DO PEOPLE IN POVERTY LIVE?

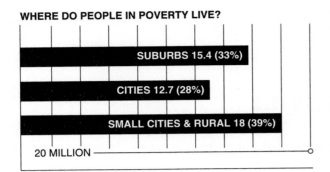

SUBURBS 15.4 (33%)

CITIES 12.7 (28%)

SMALL CITIES & RURAL 18 (39%)

20 MILLION

Who Are the New Suburban Poor?

According to Scott Allard, an associate professor at the University of Chicago, the new suburban poor are a mix of old and new poverty. In more mature cities, like Chicago and New York, poverty has grown up around the inner-ring suburbs, where urban families have migrated from rundown city neighborhoods and the recession has deepened financial need. Many such communities experienced a spike in poverty during the economic downturn of the late 1980s.

The new suburban poverty, says Allard, has developed in the outer-ring suburbs, which underwent tremendous growth in the 1990s and 2000s. New immigration patterns have brought immigrants directly to the suburbs as well, unlike previous waves of newcomers who first settled in urban areas. In addition, Allard says, these outer-ring suburbs were hit hard by the recession, and by the subprime mortgage bust, which has led to foreclosure on more than 6 million homes.

"It's not unusual for immigrants now to go straight to the suburbs and become part of the working poor," says Allard. "The changes in the suburbs have been significant."

This means that the face of suburban poverty can be diverse. Impoverished immigrants may lack both language skills and job prospects. In addition, some who were once members of the suburban middle class have lost their jobs and their homes. A traditional view of America's underclass is that poverty is a cultural phenomenon that gets passed down from generation to generation. But the new suburban poverty, at least in part, comprises families descended from the middle class who find themselves suddenly poor.

How Educators Can Help

Teachers can help low-income students simply by knowing all their students better. A teacher who's aware that a student is sleeping in a car—or just struggling to stay in her house—will be more sensitive about approaching topics like homelessness. Teachers can also help by confronting biased attitudes against low-income neighbors. Jokes about "rednecks," "white trash" or dressing "ghetto" should be addressed as they come up in classrooms and hallways.

Combating the "Culture of Poverty"

Educators grappling with the new poverty in the suburbs often turn to popular writers such as Charles Murray and Ruby Payne. They will find themselves misled.

According to *The New York Times*, "The libertarian writer Charles Murray has probably done more than any other contemporary thinker to keep alive the idea of a 'culture of poverty,' the theory that poor people are trapped by distorted norms and aspirations and not merely material deprivation."

Murray reinforced that idea in his 2012 book, *Coming Apart: The State of White America, 1960–2010.* One of his long-held beliefs is that social programs make the problems of poverty worse, not better. But Murray's libertarian beliefs leave him little room to do more than call for less government. "I don't do solutions very well," he says.

Payne, an educational consultant, has had a more direct impact on schools. Her work is rooted in a long-held view that much of American poverty is generational, with children growing up in families that have been mired in the underclass for two or more generations. Although her outlook is popular, critics argue that her characterizations are overly simplistic, even bigoted, and harm relations between teachers and students.

According to Payne, children whose families have been poor for generations tend to value relationships over achievement, believe in physical fighting to resolve conflicts, view the world through a strictly local lens and value food for its quantity rather than quality.

Low-income children run into problems, says Payne, because their schools are run on the hidden rules of the middle class. These rules hold that work and achievement are the driving forces for decision-making, that fights are conducted with words rather than fists, the world is defined in national terms, and food is valued for its quality rather than quantity.

Paul Gorski, an assistant professor of integrated studies at George Mason University, says that Payne's approach—considered a "deficit" model because it focuses on what low-income children lack—doesn't hold up. The increasing diversity of the poor in the suburbs, he says, makes such an approach even harder to justify. "The suburban poor are diverse, and becoming even more diverse, so the stereotypical version of the poor, urban person just doesn't work anymore."

Gorski says that educators need to move away from a focus on the "culture of poverty." Instead, they should look at more structural issues, such as the lack of resources in some schools that teach the poorest children. Today, that includes suburban schools struggling to address the needs of a new wave of impoverished children.

"We talk about education being the great equalizer, yet our poorest students are in the least equipped schools," he says. "We don't need to fix poor people. We need to fix the system."

SUBURBAN POVERTY INDEX

5 MILLION
number of suburban
families added to
poverty rolls since
2000

ONE THIRD
portion of the
nation's poor
who live in
suburbs

2.7 MILLION
the number by
which suburban
families outnumber
urban families
living in poverty

But much of the most important work needs to take place at the administrative level. Here are some tips for school administrators who might be seeing widespread poverty at school for the first time:

Watch for changes of address. Families facing sudden poverty may move a lot. In many cases, the parents are understandably afraid their children will be forced out of a desirable school or district. This puts great stress on the students—stress the school or district can ease in part by helping the parents understand their rights.

Work around the car culture. Gasoline and car maintenance can be huge expenses. Don't assume that parents can always shuttle their kids to and from school activities.

Become familiar with the McKinney-Vento Act. This federal law guarantees the rights of children and youth experiencing homelessness to a free and appropriate public education. It requires a local homeless education liaison in every school district. It also ensures enrollment, access to services, school stability and academic support.

Help with fees. Students who are suddenly impoverished usually avoid field trips and extracurricular activities that require fees. In some cases, they'll even misbehave right before a big event to be prohibited from going. Make sure teachers are on the lookout for this behavior, and make sure the school has a response. For example, see if the PTA can create a fund to keep these students from being marginalized.

Find out what's needed. Ask parents what's needed to help their children stay in school. Perhaps they need the library open late a few nights a week to have a place to go after school. Perhaps students need more computer access to complete assignments. Perhaps they need help with meals or transportation.

Provide services. After the problems have been identified, advocate for ways to address them.

Conyers, Jeffco's homeless liaison, says one of the simplest things educators and support staff can do is to simply remain alert. A student's sudden poverty is likely to show up in increased absences, exhaustion, mood changes, change in performance and an unkempt appearance.

Also, educators should understand that the families of these students now face the daunting task of navigating the labyrinthine social-service network—a disorienting and often embarrassing task. "These former middle-class families don't know how to apply for food stamps, they don't know where to begin," Conyers says. "There needs to be more hand-holding."

Critical Thinking

1. Why is it important to revisit the popular views of who is poor, why they are poor, and where they live?

2. How does this article change your perception about teaching in a suburban school district?

3. Look at the poverty levels in the largest city in the state where you are (or your home state) and compare that rate with the poverty levels found in at least two of the suburbs near that city. What do you find? Does it match the data in the article? If not, research or speculate what might be the reasons for the difference?

Create Central

www.mhhe.com/createcentral

Internet References

Brookings Institute
www.brookings.edu/research/books/2013/confrontingsuburbanpovertyinamerica

Unit 3

UNIT

Prepared by: Rebecca B. Evers, *Winthrop University*

Literacy Is the Cornerstone of Learning

In this unit of the *Annual Edition,* we focus on two core literacy skills that are taught in all public schools: reading, and writing. We have selected this topic because these skills are fundamental skills acquired from printed materials that are a primary source of information in most of our public schools. Additionally, being able to read and write are fundamental rights of all citizens in a democratic society. Many of us who read for both learning and pleasure cannot imagine a life without books or reading, and writing remains a primary source of communication, especially within the hallowed halls of public schools.

Reading is the single skill every person must have to be successful in school, at work, and in life activities. However, if we look at the assessment of adult reading skills in the United States, we find that 14% of the adult population score Below Basic literacy skills and another 29% score at the Basic level. This is 43% of the United States population or approximately 93 million adult citizens. Of the Below Basic demographic, 55% did not graduate from high school. Further, a total of 59% Below Basic readers were persons of color: 39% Hispanic and 20% African American (National Assessment of Adult Literacy, 2003).

Comparing the reading scores of 8th graders nation-wide, we find that trends in overall reading levels as well as reading levels across race/ethnicity are rising. However, we continue to have large numbers of children of color who are not performing at the Proficient level. In 2013, The Nation's Report Card indicated that African American eighth graders scored as follows: 39% Below Basic, 44% Basic, and 16% at Proficient levels. Hispanic students scored in similar patterns: 32% Below Basic, 46% Basic, and 20% at Proficient levels. American Indian*/Alaska Natives performed about the same: 38% Below Basic, 44% Basic, and 18% at Proficient levels (The Nation's Report Card, 2013).

Although we are making progress in raising reading scores for all students, we still have work to do. The data clearly indicates that by 8th grade at least one-third of students across three racial/ethnic groups are not reading at a level that would allow them to continue their education after high school, find the job or career they desire, or perhaps even complete four years of high school. In addition, limited access to books, effects of poverty, lack of access to caregivers or significant adults who read, and disabilities are just some of the factors that can have profound effects on learning to read. These factors alone can derail all that is done in classrooms. So what is a teacher to do? Some suggestions and classroom based strategies are offered here.

We know that children are more likely to be strong readers when they are surrounded by books and adults who read, both to the children and for their own pleasure. One suggested action for helping children learn, improve, and embrace reading skills is to raise the reading skills of the adults in their lives. Library adult literacy programs can collaborate with community businesses, authors and booksellers, teachers, and community agencies with adult literacy programs. These collaborations can engage entire communities in reading and other literacy activities. Teachers might do well to seek out these collaborating community groups to get and give support to students of the adults engaged in learning to read.

Perhaps a teacher can tap into the student's sense of right and wrong by using moral and ethical dilemmas taken from fairy tales, short stories, and young adult literature to engage students in real life decisions. Students read, make decisions about characters' actions, form discussion groups, share their opinions, and defend their decisions. This activity covers several Common Core standards of reading, problem solving, and critical dialogues.

A frequent bit of advice given to teachers who are teaching struggling readers is to use lower level books with levels of high interest for the student. However, caution is important here. Low level books can mean low vocabulary or abridged versions of required readings. These may not be in the best interest of the reader and may provide an unsatisfactory reading experience as important details may be excluded when books are abridged. But what if you could get the students to read unabridged books simply by putting an e-book reader in their hands or by providing access to digital copies for their iPhone or tablet. Students see reading differently when it comes in familiar and handy form; no losing, forgetting, or even accidentally destroying the book. In addition, students reported less bullying about reading when they were engaged with an e-reader.

Writing can be a creative activity which many adolescents like. Regardless of the fact that their world is filled with text messages, Instagram, and Twitter, youth continue to write for themselves in diaries, personal journals, blogs, and even on Twitter. However, in schools we often turn writing into a chore with those dreaded class journals with assigned topics or Word-of-the-Day lessons for end of course assessments and other standardized tests. Scholars have concerns that standardized test preparation has forced teachers to coach students on writing to very specific prompts that focus on the correctness of the response rather than on reflection, inquiry, or synthesis. When a group of students was given the opportunity to meet before school to write, critique, and discuss writing they found their voice. This, according to the researchers, is something missing in middle school now and reaffirms their conclusion that nurturing the heart of adolescent identity development is being lost in highly structured schedules of core content lesson plans with little flexibility. Writing for inquiry, pleasure, and reflection should not be lost in a true middle school experience that will lead to adults who can use written communication effectively in the world of Twitter and Facebook.

Notes

*Term American Indian used in the report of assessment results.

References

National Assessment of Adult Literacy, 2003. Key findings. Author. Retrieved 21 June 2014 from http://nces.ed.gov/naal/fct_performance.asp

The Nation's Report Card, 2013. What proportions of student groups are reaching Proficient? Author. Retrieved 21 June 2014 from http://nationsreportcard.gov/reading_math_2013/#/student-groups

Article

Prepared by: Rebecca B. Evers, *Winthrop University*

The Fight for Literacy in the South

Illiteracy remains a serious problem in the U.S., even though the issue has been overshadowed in recent years by the economy and the war on terror. Even data documenting changes in literacy in each state is hard to attain.

PAIGE CRUTCHER

Learning Outcomes

After reading this article, you will be able to:

- Outline the facts presented about adult literacy.
- Name the participants in the fight for literacy.
- Justify why schools and teachers must be concerned about adult literacy.

The most recent comprehensive report—"The National Assessment of Adult Literacy"—was released in 2003, yet many literacy efforts benchmark their progress based on those findings. Still, nonprofits in a number of Southern states are making progress in helping more people learn to read using ESL and GED programs, intensive tutoring, training, and workshops.

The Literacy Council of Buncombe County in Asheville, N.C., founded in 1987, has more than 200 volunteer tutors who give over 15,000 hours annually and provide literacy tutoring to more than 350 students. The council's focus is on programs for adult education, English for speakers of other languages, and the Augustine Project, which provides, free of charge, to low-income children who read below grade-level one-on-one time with highly trained tutors. Ashley Lasher, executive director of the Literacy Council of Buncombe County, notes that nearly 20% of adults in the county do not have a high school diploma or GED, and one in 10 cannot read at or above a basic level. Lasher explains that her organization is just one of many working to improve reading skills across North Carolina: "There is a North Carolina Literacy Association of organizations such as ours working all across the state. Some of our organizations are large in terms of budget, students served, and volunteers, others

are quite small. But we all strive to teach reading, writing, and English language skills to those most in need."

In Mississippi, the 2003 study by the National Assessment for Adult Literacy showed somewhere between 5% and 22% of adults in Lafayette County lacked "basic prose literacy skills." Meridith Wulff, director of the Lafayette County Literary Council, says, "I receive calls every week—and sometimes every day—from adults seeking help for themselves or someone they know. We know that improving a person's ability to read usually brings improvements in other aspects of a person's life: their ability to get a job, how their kids do in school, and so on. So it is essential to improving the individual's quality of life and the quality of life in our community." The Lafayette County Literacy Council's programs include a grade-level reading initiative that helps to ensure kids read at their grade level, and a partnership with the local United Way on the campaign. Other initiatives include a two-year pilot reading intervention program called Reading Rockets, targeted at second graders reading below grade level and repeating first graders, as well as a partnership with Dolly Parton's Imagination Library, with workshops this fall for families who receive Imagination Library books to help teach parents how to maximize reading in their home.

South Carolina has what Eileen Chepenik, executive director of Trident Literacy Association, calls, "a critical problem." Trident Literacy serves Charleston, Berkeley, and Dorchester counties, and in the tricounty area there are 60,000 adults without high school credentials, and as many as 20,000 of them have less than a ninth-grade education. "Low literacy skills are directly related to higher welfare costs, increased healthcare costs, and higher incidences of incarceration. Moreover, they perpetuate the generational cycle of illiteracy and poverty," says Chepenik. Trident Literacy works with adults to improve their educational functioning levels. "Many earn their GEDs and WorkKeys Career Readiness Certificates, and get jobs. Each person's improvement is a success story, and we have so many of them," says Chepenik. While Trident's successes don't keep up with the school dropout rate, its programs enable its students to make dramatic improvements to their literacy levels and enhance their future prospects. Trident Literacy's core programs are Basic Literacy, GED-prep, English as a Second Language, and Basic Computer Use.

Working with parents and children is key to getting literacy rates up. "Parents are the children's most important teachers. There's a greater likelihood a child will be unable to read and write if the parent is challenged as well," says Gregory Smith, executive director of the Florida Literacy Coalition Inc. The lack of visibility about illiteracy is often what prevents adults from seeking help. "Illiteracy is not a reflection of your intelligence. Literacy is a skill like any other skill," Smith says. He believes the best spokespeople for literacy "are the people who have been there—through the voices of those who have gone through programs and been successful." The Florida Coalition created its *Adult Learner Essays* book to provide these voices. "It is a catalyst, or motivator, for people to not just write an assignment for class but also to be included in a publication."

Giving kids the motivation to read comes in many forms for the literacy councils and coalitions. The Lafayette County Literacy Council sponsors a young adult author to speak at the Young Authors Fair as part of the Oxford Conference for the Book, held every March. "It is important to us that we reach the kids who are not already readers and, hopefully, help turn them into lifelong readers," Wulff says.

Literacy problems also reach into the wealthiest counties in the region. The Literacy Council of Williamson County, Tenn., was founded in 1986 when a man walked into the library and asked a librarian, "I can't read. Can you help me?" At a loss, the county librarians were referred to the Nashville Adult Literacy Council, which helped them form their organization. Twenty-seven years later they're still combatting illiteracy in one of the state's most affluent counties. Many of the adults in Williamson County have high school diplomas, but are incapable of competing in today's job markets because their level of literacy is so low, according to Rita Dozier, executive director of the Williamson County Literacy Council. Dozier estimates close to 9,000 people in Williamson have less than a ninth-grade education. "Most of our GED students are working toward being accepted into higher education or getting a better job," she says. "Our ESL students who are making Williamson County their home are anxious to be a part of our community."

Author and Bookseller Support

Author support of councils and coalitions makes a difference in the fight for literacy. "We are lucky enough to have an incredibly vibrant literary community here in Oxford," says Wulff,

"which makes reading a big part of our local culture. We're even luckier to have a number of authors who live here and feel passionately about the issue of literacy and get involved." The Lafayette County Literacy Council also receives support from the independent bookstore Square Books.

To raise funds, the Literacy Council of Buncombe County hosts an annual Authors for Literacy Dinner & Silent Auction, where a bestselling author donates his or her time to be the keynote speaker of the evening. This year's event, on August 23, will feature National Book Award—winning author Charles Frazier (*Cold Mountain, Thirteen Moons, and Nightwoods*). "In the past, our event has featured Elizabeth Kostova, Sara Gruen, John Hart, Ron Rash, and Jill Conner Browne," says Lasher. The Literacy Council of Williamson County just hosted its ninth Author! Author! event, where multiple authors keynote to raise funds for the council. "The funds from Author! Author! are crucial to the ongoing work of the Literacy Council," notes Dozier. Local authors, like bestselling Lisa Patton (*Whistlin' Dixie in a Nor'easter*), do more than keynote and emcee events; they also volunteer evenings to help teach classes for the council.

Booksellers are also hard at work in the fight against illiteracy and often partner with literacy councils and nonprofits. Many are committed to finding ways to give back and foster reading in their communities. Becky Quiroga Curtis, children's book buyer and children and young adult events coordinator for Books & Books in Miami, notes, "As a company, we are very committed to literacy." The store's efforts include Sunrise Little Free Libraries—a community service project in the city of Sunrise to put free books into the hands of underprivileged children—as well as donating book baskets to nonprofits and passing along extra ARCs to homeless shelters, prisons, and underprivileged schools.

Valerie Koehler, owner of Houston's Blue Willow Bookshop, is committed to both literacy and aliteracy. To that end, Blue Willow partnered with the charity Family Point Resources when the bookstore's neighborhood library moved too far away for patrons who walked there. "We have a large multifamily neighborhood adjacent to the shop and to my neighborhood. There is a huge disparity in income, lifestyle, and education. Family Point identified the need to build a library within [the charity's] building so we decided to kick-start the library. Our customers came through with donations of new books, used books, cash, and best of all—time. Time to build the library, build the collection, and spend time with the children. It makes me smile every time I walk into that space," Koehler says. Blue Willow has also partnered with the Literacy Council of Fort Bend County for Reading Between the Wines. This year they brought authors together with donors for an evening of talks, food, and book signings.

For other booksellers looking to create partnerships with organizations for literacy projects, Koehler advises that stores should just start the conversation. "I believe it is my responsibility as someone who is fortunate in both education, health, and wealth to help in whatever way I can," she says.

Critical Thinking

1. Outline the social and economic issues associated with low adult literacy rates.
2. How are community organizations and booksellers working to eradicate illiteracy?
3. Research the literacy rates in your community and answer the following questions:
   a. What is the rate?
   b. To what can you attribute this rate?
   c. What can schools and teachers do to make sure adolescents do not leave school unable to read?

Create Central

www.mhhe.com/createcentral

Internet References

Center on Rural Education
http://www.ed.gov/rural-education

International Association of Reading
www.reading.org/General/Default.aspx

Read, Write, Think
www.readwritethink.org

The Rural School and Community Trust
http://www.ruraledu.org/

Article

Prepared by: Rebecca B. Evers, *Winthrop University*

Putting the Heart Back into Writing: Nurturing Voice in Middle School Students

The authors share five areas of inquiry that emerged as the result of a voluntary weekly before-school writing program.

BARB RUBEN AND LEANNE MOLL

Learning Outcomes

After reading this article, you will be able to:

- Discuss why writing is not taught in many schools.

- Articulate the needs and reasons to provide more writing instruction.

- Explain how to incorporate more writing practice into your content area.

> **"If you pay me a million dollars for me to stop writing, it would never work."**
>
> —Carrie, 11-year-old middle school student

For many middle grades students, writing facilitates a search for meaning; writing can foster self-expression and self-discovery and can help students cope with economic and family issues that are out of their control. Susannah [pseudonym] captures the voice of a middle school student perfectly in her short story:

> Zodiac grabbed an apple. "There's not much to tell. Okay, you wanna hear? Fine. I am now best friends with a slut with a rock for a brain. My science teacher is a hippie. My history teacher is a hard-ass army freak. My math teacher is a rainbow Madonna. My social studies teacher is a freakin' Calvin Klein model. My Spanish teacher is a hopeless romantic. My wellness teacher is a douche bag with 7 sons AND a divorce. And my language arts teacher is an air-head rag city ghetto girl." Zodiac cried loudly, "I have a crush on my new friend's BOYFRIEND!" Zodiac got out five pages of homework Mrs. Brown had assigned her. Zodiac wiped away her tears. "Now leave me alone." Ryuzaki nodded.

In our experience working with a team of adolescents, we witnessed young authors using writing as a vehicle to explore their innermost thoughts, their struggles with identity, relationships, cancer, love, religion, and fears. Their voices rang true as they wrote by choice, within the loosely structured setting of a before-school writing team.

Many researchers have reported the adolescent years mark declining motivation for some students to write (Anderman & Maehr, 1994; Eccles, Wigfield, & Schiefele, 1998; Romano, 2007). Much of the research reveals that adolescents do write for their own authentic purposes, but this usually happens outside school (Yost & Vogel, 2012). Our experience as before-school writing team instructors contradicts these claims. At a high-poverty school with troubling test scores, students clamored for the opportunity and space to write. Our students responded enthusiastically to school writing time that nurtured their search for meaning. They wanted a quiet, safe venue to write, with support, about topics of their own choosing.

Faced with expectations of increasingly higher academic standards and accountability, along with extreme budget cuts, school districts have narrowed their focus to raise student scores on statewide literacy and math tests. Teachers nationwide are increasingly pressured to use class time for test preparation in core subjects linked to high-stakes tests. Writing is not always considered a core subject (Applebee & Langer, 2006; Dillon, 2006; The National Commission on Writing for America's Families, Schools and Colleges, 2006). A key stance in the philosophy of The National Commission on Writing (2006) is that effective writing instruction is time-consuming for students and teachers, and students are not spending enough time writing at school. If writing is addressed in the classroom, it is often in preparation for the statewide writing assessment, not for its benefits to the "whole child"—nurturing curiosity, exploration, integrative thinking, and problem-solving. Applebee and Langer (2006) noted how state and district writing assessments limit the scope of a broad writing curriculum in favor of coaching students on how to respond to narrow prompts or questions in limited genres. With a focus on high-stakes test performance come more restricted tasks, often centered around structural concerns and a "correctness" mindset, not focused on inquiry or synthesis of a student's classroom life with life beyond the classroom.

Even in classes where teachers make time for writing instruction, Applebee and Langer (2006) found, "Students seem not to be given assignments requiring writing of any significant length or complexity" (p. 11). According to Loveless (2012), the Common Core State Standards will not ameliorate this lack of writing time or instruction. In fact, the Common Core Standards focus narrowly on argumentative and research writing, leaving little room for journaling, poetry, fiction, memoir, and other popular student-choice genres (Common Core State Standards Initiative, 2011).

River Middle School [pseudonym] is no exception. Located in a blue-collar suburb of a large urban city in the Northwest, River has more than 1,000 students. Sixty-five percent of the students qualify for free and reduced-price lunch, and 24% are English language learners. River is ranked as *troubled* by the state for repeatedly missing benchmarks. Although its state ranking is satisfactory for achievement, outstanding for attendance, and outstanding for percent tested, only 70% of its students are at grade level in reading, compared to the state average of 80%. Most significant, is its seventh grade writing scores with 60% of the students testing below grade level on a state writing assessment. With new state high school graduation requirements demanding passing scores on state writing assessments, writing instruction has become a priority.

The 2011–2012 academic year was a rough year at River Middle School. Due to budget shortfall, the school was forced to lay off nine young staff members. Remaining teachers accepted 14 furlough days. With the addition of sixth grade, came an additional 340 students. Of the 48 teachers, 19 were new. Two-thirds of River's $1,000+ students were also new to the school. Class periods were reduced by five minutes to create a seventh period strictly devoted to intensive literacy instruction. Class sizes grew to more than 40 students.

Despite this disruptive environment, in stark contrast to best practices, school staff remained dedicated to ensuring their students were ready for high school. They viewed literacy as a civil right. Monthly professional development meetings were dedicated to instructional improvement. The expectation was that the principal, or coach, could walk into any classroom and see learning and language targets posted for each lesson, along with what students were expected to learn and how students would achieve those targets. All teachers were required to follow a lesson architecture that included active student engagement, formative assessment, and a literacy component for every lesson.

While this initiative was essential to achieving basic literacy for all students, it left little time for student creativity and choice. Furthermore, with more than 40 students in a language arts class, and shorter class periods, little time remained for students to participate in an authentic writer's workshop. Students no longer had the luxury of writing on a topic of their own choosing over an extended length of time without a specific product and a generic learning target in place. Staff felt a sense of urgency that students must be taught "the basics" they need for success in high school. However, something critical was lost in the shuffle. Students no longer had the freedom to write for the joy of writing about a topic of their choosing in a genre they personally wanted to explore.

By October of 2011, the principal started receiving notes from students complaining about their language arts classes. Several eighth grade students reported that they were no longer allotted adequate time for writing during class sessions. Students complained about the limits placed on their choice by writing assessment-like prompts and a focus on informative writing. In response to the students' concerns, the school established a before-school, once-a-week writing team—the River Writing Team. Subsequently, 26 students (or nearly 2.6% of the school's population) applied to participate. During the weekly late openings, we (a professor involved in a university-school partnership and a former River teacher teaching writing at a community college) volunteered to facilitate a one-hour writing team time for students who loved to write. No academic grade was attached, no learning target posted, and no specific genre, topic, or length of writing was required. Students wrote what they wanted to write. For the culminating event, students were invited to attend a state-wide, all-day writing festival at a local university.

As instructors for the River Writing team, we wanted to try to understand what was motivating these students to come to school early voluntarily and to engage willingly in the difficult task of choosing a genre and topic, drafting, revising, and polishing writing. We asked ourselves, what are the intrinsic motivators that drive these young students to write? What are the components of a nurturing writing environment? How can we understand student motivation so that we can nurture student interest in writing within the constraints of large classes and the current emphasis on Common Core standards? For students who are already intrinsically motivated to write, how can teachers nurture—and not lose—these intrinsic, self-regulated writing interests? In what ways can a before-school writing team nurture young adolescents' natural craving to use writing as a tool for augmenting adventure and discovery?

Background Literature

What motivates middle grades students to write? Little research exists on developing motivation to write (Bruning & Horn, 2000). Researchers agree that both motivation and practice are essential to becoming a more effective and efficient writer (Daniels, 2010; Dredger, Woods, Beach, & Sagstetter, 2010; Zumbrunn & Krause, 2012). Generally, students feel most motivated when they have a sense of autonomy or control (Ryan & Deci, 2003); they feel connected to their instructor, to their class, and to the school (Daniels, 2011; Ryan & Deci, 2003); and they have self-efficacy—they feel they possess the skills necessary to meet the challenges of writing, and their needs for instruction are being met (Lipstein & Renninger, 2007).

Students learn they have control over their choices, thoughts, and actions when teachers successfully create a motivating learning environment. (Daniels, 2011; Zumbrunn & Krause, 2012). They are more likely to learn the material or complete the tasks when they feel it is their choice (Anderman & Maehr, 1994). Daniels (2011) asserted that the autonomy of students to make their own choice increases motivation and participation in school. When students engage because they see value in the learning experience, their intrinsic motivation leads to increased engagement (Daniels, 2010). If young adolescents are more motivated to write when they sense a worthwhile, authentic purpose for their expression and when they feel competent and safe in their self-expression and written analysis, how can teachers harness these motivations in a way that can advance their fluency in writing? This is what we hoped to explore during our time working with the River Writing Team.

Parameters of this Study

Through this study we wanted to gain a deeper understanding of young adolescent motivation and developmental needs

as our nation plunges ahead with the national Common Core Standards and their implications for writing instruction. We pondered five questions as we studied our middle school writing team.

1. What intrinsic motivators drive these young students to write?
2. What components create a nurturing writing environment?
3. How can we understand student motivation so that we can nurture student interest in writing within the constraints of large classes and mandates to address Common Core Standards?
4. For students who are already intrinsically motivated to write, how can teachers nurture and even deepen—not lose—this student interest in written performance?
5. In what ways can a before-school writing team nurture young adolescents' natural craving to write?

All participants were students at River Middle School, a high-poverty school. Students' names have been changed to protect confidentiality. All students in grade level literacy classes were invited to apply to join a special school writing team. Of the 200 students who received the announcement, 26 students submitted short essay applications in December 2011. We decided to accept all applicants, anticipating attrition once students realized they were going to have to arrive an hour early to school once a week, without the school providing transportation. On the first day, 22 students arrived; they were evenly divided between sixth, seventh, and eighth graders. Only two boys joined the team. Some students had parents drop them off at school, but most took public transportation, which resulted in arriving a half-hour earlier than the original start time. Sixteen students continued to attend regularly throughout the remaining 15 weeks. The final distributions of students consisted of seven sixth graders, three seventh graders, and six eight graders. By the fourth week one of the boys stopped attending, leaving one eighth grade boy as the only remaining male in the group.

The students were native English speakers testing at or above grade level in reading. Four of the students were in the school orchestra. Two of the students were studying dance outside school. The one boy was in foster care with a history of running away. He admitted attending primarily to be away from home.

Findings

The participants' writings reflected a strong sense of self-efficacy. All 22 students were strong readers, comfortable with rich language, confident in their writing ability, willing to take risks in writing, and willing to take feedback to make their writing strong. Four of them mentioned their intention to work as professional writers when they grow up. They were writing by choice, on topics of their choosing. Students felt a sense of autonomy and control, which is consistent with research on motivation (Anderman & Maeher, 1994; Bruning & Horn, 2000; Daniels, 2010 and 2011). They asked for time, guidance, and the tools necessary to be successful writers. The primary audience for these writers seemed to be themselves.

Commitment to Writing

Participants demonstrated a serious commitment to writing. They talked about their love of writing, including writing outside school. Teresa wrote, "I love the feeling of having a story come to life on paper." Ann explained, "I love to write. . . . I have a great vocabulary, yet I still strive for better." They recognized writing as a powerful vehicle for exploring who they were as people. Blake, an eighth grade boy, captured this perception clearly when he wrote:

I truly enjoy it [*writing*], I see it as a way of saying something but not really saying it. It's a sense of security, a sence [*sic*] of honesty I can have with myself.

Carmen, an eighth grade girl, reflected a sense of urgency these students felt for a venue to write as a way to explore options beyond their difficult lives:

I can make a world, people, or anything to escape the horrible world we live in. . . . I am the kind of writer who could fill pages of description on a character so [that] the reader sees what I do.

Student Self-efficacy

We saw evidence of students' strong sense of self-efficacy in their applications to be part of the team. For instance, Jennifer wrote about her desire to write for a larger audience beyond her parents and teachers. Her rich language was reflective of the group:

I love writing, it is my passion. . . . I still wish more than just my mom, dad, and my language arts teacher . . . could see what just pours out of me like a waterfall.

Nancy, an eleven-year-old, demonstrated a notable ability to articulate her writing strengths:

I can write in a number of genres, I have a very developed vocabulary (required for an intense story), and I have a wild imagination, perfect for writing love or adventures stories (my best two genres).

Adult Influence

Two students mentioned past teachers' comments on their writing competence. For instance, Susannah wrote, "My fifth grade teacher said that I have a gift for writing and she couldn't teach the kids what I know and how I can write."

On a number of occasions, students mentioned wanting to emulate favorite authors, indicating a comprehension of the relationship/correlation between reading and writing. For example, Sarah explained:

I love the way Norton Juster, author of *The Phantom Tollbooth,* can describe his characters and create places, like the "Sea of Knowledge," "Point of View," and the "Valley of Sound." Norton Juster's writing is logical, clear, and witty.

When one of the instructors commented on Molly's rich language, she responded. "Well, I am trying to write like Suzanne Collins." She was motivated to revise and edit, explaining she was striving for what she perceived as strong, powerful writing.

Student Choice

The most dominant theme that emerged from the River Writing Team was the power of student choice in writing. Students were instructed to write on any topic they wanted. Most of the students had no trouble coming up with topics and sticking with them throughout the four months of the team sessions. Topics ranged across a broad spectrum, from a memoir of a participant's visit to the public library to get her first library card; a fantasy set in Munchkin Land; a multi-chapter, complex science fiction fantasy; to a violent horror story. No one chose nonfiction expository writing, and only one student chose personal narrative. Five students wrote poetry.

Student Voice

Students recognized the importance of voice. Nancy dropped a story after five weeks, insisting she could not continue because the protagonist was 17, and at 12 she felt inadequate to capture the appropriate voice because she "had not experienced being 17." Instead, she switched to writing very powerful poetry full of angst—more reflective of her current circumstances.

One student, very involved in dance outside school, worked on a fictional memoir of a former dancer, now in her eighties. Through flashback, she describes the protagonist's first audition for a major role and the trade-offs and sacrifices necessary to become professional. Molly, who has been fighting cancer for two years, wrote a 25-page imaginative story set in "Chemoland," the world she imagined while attending her daily (now monthly) chemotherapy sessions:

I stood up and looked Chemo straight in the eye and said, "I hate you! Taking me away from my family, making me lose my hair, my mind, making me feel sick and look super skinny!" I dashed to my room ripped off my hat and stared in the mirror. I didn't even see me anymore.

I saw a sick bald person. What happened to me, who had I become? I didn't want any more presents. I was fed up with being that tough 11 year old. I wanted to be with my family again. I wanted to go home.

At the end of the story, she included an epilogue describing her personal experience with cancer and dedicating the story to the other children she had grown close with during her experiences over the last two years.

Two students wrote disturbing poetry about suicide, cutting, and extreme angst. Nancy successfully captures the soul-searching angst of young adolescents in this poem.

Family told me it would be alright [sic], that I would make other friends,/but they don't get it, and they never have. . . . /I had given up on myself, already decided that I wasn't worth anything, that nobody wanted me to deal with, that nobody would or ever could love me./And I knew it, all along I was just lying to myself, drunk with hope and longing. I hoped for a better life, to be prettier, smarter, more successful. I longed for something I could never have./And so I stopped trying, stopped wanting, stopped everything./I gave up, and I never forgave myself.

Patty wrote about love and relationships in a poem entitled "Heart Breaker": "My best wasn't good enough/it never has been, no matter how hard i try, it's never enough." Her second poem, about her next boyfriend, starts out, "He is my savior, in everything i do,/he is the one who keeps me from the dark."

Blake, the one male participant, was at first resistant to sharing his work with anyone. Ultimately, he was comfortable using the Google Docs application to share his poetry with the researchers and specific students and to give feedback to other participants. An example of his writing on his vision of Utopia reveals the anger and powerlessness he feels as a 14-year-old in foster care:

Unlike most Utopian societies, mine doesn't have a set of rules. There is no religion, there are no false hopes, there are no lies, and there is no sunlight. There is only truth, only direct answers, no hidden faces or emotions, there is only everyone and their darkness within. A place for people who others think couldn't be any less conceded (sic). A place for the depressing, the indifferent, the so-called "freaks" of common society, a place where they can feel safe with their own kind, the avoidable or invisibles. A place for people to be themselves.

Not atypical of disenfranchised youth, Blake appeared to relish taking on the persona of the "other."

Perseverance

Students demonstrated perseverance that some might argue not developmentally possible for young adolescents. Many worked on a single piece of writing the entire 16 weeks, putting in many hours beyond the once-a-week meeting. Virtually no discipline issues occurred during the sessions. Students wanted to be there. They wanted quiet. They wanted to go deeper into the writing process than a 49-minute English class period allows. The wanted the time to think, write, revise, edit, and produce their personal best.

Providing an external authentic audience, or an authentic audience that went beyond the classroom, was less valued than we had expected. Students persevered, developing and reworking the same pieces of writing for weeks at a time. The original flier announcing the establishment of the writing team made clear that the culminating event was attendance at a statewide writing festival, where they would share their writing with students from around the state, attend writing workshops, and hear a presentation from a popular professional young adult author. However, of the 16 consistent participants, only 11 actually attended the festival. All 11 who attended the festival were positive about the experience. However, responses to the exit questionnaire indicated that the writing festival did not drive the students to attend the early-morning sessions. Apparently, an outside audience was not a necessary motivator for these students.

School attendance records indicated a slight increase in attendance on Wednesdays, the writing team days. A parent of an eighth grader informed us she used the writing team as an incentive to get her daughter to do homework. This parent reported that Wednesdays were the only day her daughter jumped out of bed eager for school.

Concluding Thoughts

The young adolescents who chose to be part of the school writing team saw themselves as writers. They sought out a place that would allow them a sense of autonomy, voice, and a venue to explore who they were as people and writers. Their dispositions toward writing were in alignment with the research literature. These students demonstrated an intrinsic motivation to write. They craved the autonomy implicit in this weekly unstructured time; they could choose what and how they would write, without a tight deadline and with easy access to adult guidance when they wanted it (Zumbrunn & Krause, 2012; Ryan & Deci, 2003). They clearly exhibited self-efficacy as they confidently shared their writing with each other, instructors, and complete strangers at the state writing festival (Klassen, 2002; Schunk & Zimmerman, 1997). The River Writing Team did not achieve the strong connections between students and teachers or as a class community that many researchers identified as necessary for young writers (Daniels, 2011; Ryan & Deci, 2003). The students' intrinsic drive to write was so strong, the classroom environment appeared to play a secondary role in their motivation. As long as the room was quiet and students could work uninterrupted, they remained content and focused (Lipstein & Renniger, 2007). The statewide writing festival, as an authentic audience, appeared to be less motivating than we had anticipated. Instead, the group of students appeared to provide an authentic audience for each other.

In this era of intense accountability, schools often focus on struggling students who are below grade level. The newly-adopted national Common Core Standards' emphasis on expository writing and informational text will move the focus further away from options for student choice than ever before (Applebee & Langer, 2006; Common Core, 2011).

Many young adults feel powerless and trapped in adolescence; contrary to the central foci of authentic middle schools, their natural developmental needs to search for identify and meaning are not being met within the current school system (Erikson, 1968; Yost & Vogel, 2012). They need more than the basic academic skills so centrally characteristic of a junior high. True to the middle school model, young adolescents need a venue to try on identities, to explore who they are as people, and to figure out their place in the world. Writing is an appropriate, safe venue for that exploration. Students have no say in the national obsession with standards, testing, and accountability. The emphasis on remedial work to ensure we are leaving "no child left behind" means those already at grade level are ignored. Students are forced to write to controlled writing prompts designed to match or even replicate a test, denying them personal relevance and the autonomy necessary for self-exploration.

Schools must find the time to continue to nurture young people's search for meaning through storytelling. If there is not time during the regular language arts class periods, then time needs to be provided through an elective, before school, after school, or even during lunch, for students who want a quiet, safe venue to write about topics of their own choosing with support.

To ensure all students meet all standards, we, as educators, adhere to a tightly-run schedule, with carefully construed lesson plans with explicitly targeted specific standards, for every period of every school day. Certainly, this approach is efficient. However, something vital is lost in this process—the heart of adolescent identity development. We need to hear and value the voices of young writers, especially if we seek to create true middle schools.

References

Anderman, E., & Maehr, M. (1994). Motivation and schooling in the middle grades. *Review of Educational Research, 64*, 287–309.

Applebee, A. N., & Langer, J. A. (2006). *The state of writing instruction in America's schools: What existing data tells us.* Albany, NY: Center on English Learning and Achievement. Retrieved from http://www.albany.edu/cela/reports.html

Bruning, R., & Horn, C. (2000). Developing motivation to write, *Educational Psychologist, 35*, 25–37.

Common Core State Standards Initiative. (2011). *Key points in English language arts.* Retrieved from: http://www.corestandards.org/about-the-standards/key-points-in-english-language-arts

Daniels, E. (2010). Creating motivating learning environments: What we can learn from researchers and students. *English Journal, 100* (1), 25–29.

Daniels, E. (2011). Creating motivating learning environments: Teachers matter. *Middle School Journal, 43* (2), 32–37.

Dillon, S. (2006, March 26). Schools cutting back subject to teach reading and math. *New York Times.* Retrieved from http://www.nytimes.com/2006/03/26/education/26child.html?pagewanted=all

Dredger, K., Woods, D., Beach, C., & Sagstetter, V. (2010). Engage me: Using new literacies to create third space classrooms that engage student writers. *Journal of Media Literacy, 2* (2), 85–101.

Eccles, J., Wigfield, A., & Schiefele, U. (1998). Motivation to succeed. In N. Eisenberg (Ed.), *Handbook of child psychology: Vol. 3, Social, Emotional, and Personality Development* (pp. 1017–1095). New York, NY: Wiley.

Erikson, E. H. (1968). *Identify: Youth and crisis.* New York, NY: Norton.

Klassen, R. (2002). Writing in early adolescence: A review of the role of self-efficacy beliefs. *Educational Psychology Review, 14*, 173–203.

Lipstein, R. L., & Renniger, K. A. (2007). Interest for writing: How teachers can make a difference. *The English Journal, 96* (4), 79–85.

Loveless, T. (2012). *How well are American students learning?* Washington, DC: Brown Center on Education Policy at Brookings. Retrieved from http://www.brookings.edu/research/reports/2012/02/16-brown-education

The National Commission on Writing for America's Families, Schools, and Colleges. (2006). *Writing and school reform including the neglected "r"—The need for a writing revolution.* New York, NY: The College Board. Retrieved from http://www.host-collegeboard.com/advocacy/writing/

Romano, T. (2007). Teaching writing from the inside. In K. Beers, R. Probst, & L. Rief (Eds.), *Adolescent literacy: Turning promise into practice* (167–178). Portsmouth, NH: Heinemann.

Ryan, R. M., & Deci, E. L. (2003). Intrinsic and extrinsic motivations: Classic definitions and new directions. *Contemporary Educational Psychology, 25*, 54–67.

Schunk, D. H., & Zimmerman, B. J. (1997). Developing self-efficacious readers and writers: The role of social and self-regulatory processes. In J. T. Guthrie & A. Wigfield (Eds.), *Reading engagement: Motivating readers through integrated instruction* (pp. 34–50). Newark, DE: International Reading Association.

Yost, D., & Vogel R. (2012). Writing matters to urban middle level students. *Middle School Journal, 43* (3), 40–47.

Zumbrunn, S., & Krause, K. (2012). Conversations with leaders: Principles of effective writing instruction. *The Reading Teacher, 65*, 346–353.

Critical Thinking

1. Present three reasons or arguments for a school-wide writing program in your school.

2. Consider your content area as you explain two ways you could incorporate writing into your daily or weekly routine.

3. Researchers asked five questions in this study. Now that you have read the results, construct two questions you want answered. Provide a brief rationale.

Create Central

www.mhhe.com/createcentral

Internet References

National Council of Teachers of Writing
http://www.ncte.org/

The National Writing Project
http://www.nwp.org/cs/public/print/resource/922

Virginia Department of Education
http://www.doe.virginia.gov/instruction/graduation/project_graduation/online_tutorials/english/materials/writing_middleschool.pdf

BARB RUBEN is an assistant professor of curriculum and instruction at Portland State University. LEANNE MOLL is a college writing coach and English teacher at Catlin Gabel School in Portland, OR.

Article

Prepared by: Rebecca B. Evers, *Winthrop University*

Character Analysis and Moral Development

Exploring moral dilemmas gives students greater insight into literary characters.

KIMBERLY KODE

Learning Outcomes

After reading this article, you will be able to:

- Discuss the use of Kohlberg's Theory of Moral Development in the study of literature.

- Debate the benefits and drawbacks of teaching using this method.

- Extend this method into other curricular areas.

How do we get students, often geniuses at getting *out* of work, to actually put more time and effort *into* their reading and the class conversations that follow? How do we get them to delve beyond the basic *who-what-where-when* of their short stories and novels?

Incorporating Lawrence Kohlberg's Theory of Moral Development into literature study develops readers who are not only more interested in what they are reading, but are more analytical about the actions and attitudes of the characters.

Introducing Kohlberg's Theory

Psychologist Lawrence Kohlberg sought to explain how individuals make decisions about moral issues and how that reasoning changes as they mature. Through his research, he identified three levels of moral development: Preconventional, Conventional, and Postconventional. Each level comprises two distinct stages (see box). He believed that each stage had its own unique characteristics, representing a sequence through which individuals must pass as they develop. These stages are hierarchical—an individual's moral development always moves forward without skipping any stages.

In conducting his research, Kohlberg created a "dilemma" story that serves as an excellent way to introduce how to apply his moral development theory to story characters:

Heinz and the Drug Dilemma

In Europe, a woman was near death from a special kind of cancer. There was one drug that the doctors thought might save her. It was a form of radium that a druggist in the same town had recently discovered. The drug was expensive to make, but the druggist was charging 10 times what the drug cost him to make. He paid $200 for the radium and charged $2,000 for a small dose of the drug.

The sick woman's husband, Heinz, went to everyone he knew to borrow the money, but he could only get together about $1,000 which was half of what it cost. He told the druggist that his wife was dying, asked him to sell it cheaper or let him pay later. But the druggist said, "No, I discovered the drug and I'm going to make money from it." So Heinz got desperate and broke into the man's store to steal the drug for his wife.

Should Heinz have done that? Was it wrong or right? Why?

After reading through the dilemma as a class, ask students to (1) write down their opinion about what Heinz did and (2) explain their rationale. Then group students randomly and ask them to discuss their answers among themselves.

After a short time, students move back to the large class setting to participate in a teacher-led discussion to determine at which stage of moral development Heinz might be, based on Kohlberg's stages.

For example, if the students' opinion is that Heinz should not have stolen the drug, then it could be concluded that Heinz's moral development is at the Law and Order stage in the Conventional Level because by not stealing the drug, he is following the rules and showing respect for the authority of the druggist.

Conversely, if the students think Heinz is justified in stealing the drug because his wife will die without it, it could be concluded that because he stole the drug not for his own good but for that of his wife, Heinz is at the highest stage of moral development, Universal Principles in the Postconventional Level; his decision to steal was based on his value of human life.

After drawing conclusions about Heinz's level of moral development, students can then consider the moral development of the druggist, who both invented the drug and set the exorbitant price.

More Practice Using Kohlberg's Theory

After examining Kohlberg's dilemma story together, students are ready to try their hand at a form of literature with which most are already familiar: classic fairy tales. Because of their limited length and well-defined good and evil characters, fairy tales can serve as an easy jumping off point as students develop their understanding of Kohlberg's theory. Additionally, most students have prior experience reading and considering fairy tale elements such as universal theme and story structure.

Following the instructional procedure previously used with the Heinz dilemma, the class begins their analysis by examining the popular fairy tale, *Sleeping Beauty.*

Although the characters in *Sleeping Beauty* may be considerably more one-dimensional and straightforward when compared to characters in full-length narratives, this fairy tale provides the opportunity for students to move their focus beyond that of the main character, allowing them to expand their consideration to include the moral development of both major and minor characters including Sleeping Beauty, the king and queen, the prince, the princes who died trying in their efforts to find the castle, the good fairies, and the fairy who cast the evil spell.

This can propel interesting class discussions as students consider the idea that Sleeping Beauty, the protagonist of the story, and the fairy who cast the evil spell, the antagonist of the story, both may be operating at the stage of The Marketplace in the Preconventional Level because both characters behave to serve their own desires: Sleeping Beauty when she ignores all that she has been taught and touches the spinning wheel, and the

wicked fairy when she punishes Sleeping Beauty by casting her to sleep when she unintentionally is not included at a party in the kingdom.

A Step Beyond

The next step is to move into short works of more appropriate grade-level fiction where perhaps the moral developmental stages are not quite so clear. A shorter piece of literature can help students gain the confidence needed for the later analysis of longer narratives.

A good example of literature of the appropriate length is Pearl S. Buck's *The Big Wave.* Short enough to read in class together over one or two sessions, it nonetheless provides a complex storyline with characters facing a variety of difficult moral choices.

Again, there are numerous characters within the book that students can consider, including the main characters Kino and Jiya, as well as the Old Gentleman, Kino's father, and Jiya's father.

When using this text, it may be helpful to stop one time in the middle of the book to discuss the students' perceptions of the characters' moral development because not all of Buck's characters are at the stage they appear to be.

Students often believe the moral development of the Old Gentleman, who takes in the children orphaned by the tidal wave, to be at either the Social Contract stage or the Universal Principles stage of the Postconventional Level because he does such a wonderful thing by taking in so many.

However, when Jiya later decides not to be his son, the Old Gentleman becomes angry and spiteful, leaving students to reconsider, wondering if instead he is at the Good Boy/Good Girl stage of the Conventional Level and is only doing these good works to impress the people in the village with his kindness.

After so much guided practice, students are ready to work independently and in small book discussion groups to apply Kohlberg's Theory of Moral Development to the characters in other narratives.

These texts may include Arthur Roth's *The Iceberg Hermit,* Gary Paulsen's *Canyons,* Robert Louis Stevenson's *Treasure Island,* Jeanne Wakatsuki Houston and James D. Houston's *Farewell to Manzanar,* Conrad Richter's *The Light in the Forest,* Carolyn Meyer's *Where the Broken Heart Still Beats,* Scott O'Dell's *Sing Down the Moon,* Bette Greene's *Summer of my German Soldier,* Esther Forbe's *Johnny Tremain,* Katherine Paterson's *Park's Quest,* Cynthia Voigt's *Solitary Blue,* Patricia Clapp's *The Tamarack Tree,* and James Lincoln Collier and Christopher Collier's *My Brother Sam Is Dead.*

Group discussions are elevated to new heights as students break into camps and defend their opinions, considering such

Kohlberg's Theory of Moral Development

I. **Preconventional Level**
   A. **Obedience and Punishment:** The individual obeys rules to avoid punishment and achieve gratification
   B. **The Marketplace:** The individual is motivated by their own needs and wants. A philosophy of "you scratch my back, I'll scratch yours" is common.

II. **Conventional Level**
   A. **Good Boy/Good Girl:** The individual behaves in order to impress others and avoid their disapproval. Good behavior is the behavior which pleases others.
   B. **Law and Order:** The individual does not question laws or social institutions but simply follows their rules. Right behavior consists of doing one's duty, showing respect for authority, and maintaining current systems.

III. **Postconventional Level**
   A. **Social Contract:** The individual develops a sense of responsibility to the group as a whole. Right behavior is the behavior that does not violate the rights of others. What is good for the group determines the right decisions.
   B. **Universal Principles:** Individual morality is based on decisions of conscience and based on chosen principles. These principles are abstract and center on the value and dignity of human life, equality, and justice.

Developing Understanding

Too often when teachers prompt literature discussions through the use of open-ended questions, middle school students react with a blank stare and are unable or unwilling to articulate their opinions. In this format, students want to discuss their opinions and are able to analyze the characters in a manner more insightful than what occurs during typical class discussions.

Incorporating Kohlberg's Theory of Moral Development into literature discussions provides an avenue for students to move past lower levels of understanding into a more mature examination of the literary characters.

Critical Thinking

1. How do you think parents and community leaders in your area might respond to this teaching method? Would you agree with them?

2. What are the benefits to students when teachers use this method to teach literature? What drawbacks might be encountered?

3. Other than in Language Arts classes, how could teachers incorporate the use of dilemmas into other content areas?

Create Central

www.mhhe.com/createcentral

Internet References

Common Core Standards
   http://www.corestandards.org/
International Association of Reading
   www.reading.org/General/Default.aspx
Kohlberg's Theory of Moral Development
   http://en.wikipedia.org/wiki/Lawrence_Kohlberg's_stages_of_moral_development
Read, Write, Think
   www.readwritethink.org
The National Council of Teachers of English (NCTE)
   http://www.readwritethink.org/professional-development/strategy-guides/supporting-comprehension-strategies-english-30106.html

KIMBERLY KODE is an assistant professor in the dual early elementary/special education program at York College of Pennsylvania.

questions as whether Woodrow, Jeanne's older brother in *Farewell to Manzanar,* who functions in the role of the father during the course of the book, is operating at the Law and Order stage in the Conventional Level or at the Social Contract stage in the Postconventional Level, which is a higher level of moral development.

As a cumulative project, students are tasked with creating one-page opinion papers discussing their perception of a character's level of moral development and their rationale for their decision.

Article   Prepared by: Rebecca B. Evers, *Winthrop University*

Rekindle the Love of Reading

Giving students Kindles reinvigorates young readers and improves their reading achievement.

MARK ISERO

Learning Outcomes

After reading this article, you will be able to:

- Retell the experience of one teacher's attempt to improve student reading habits and skills.

- Evaluate the viability of the teacher's actions and the results of those actions.

- Formulate a plan to replicate this teacher's reading program in your school.

If you ask a typical 9th grader about reading, you'll get a range of responses, but two trends will likely emerge: resignation and regret. If the student feels resigned, you'll hear, "No way, I don't read much," or "I haven't finished a book in years." Reading will be characterized as "boring," particularly in comparison to phones and video games, Instagram, and Snapchat. The student will sometimes tell stories of fake reading or of getting by in classroom discussions by mimicking peers.

If you keep listening, feelings of resignation will turn into regret. You'll hear, "I wish I read more," or "It's too hard for me." The student may smile when sharing her favorite book as a child but then quickly look away. After some silence, she may remember that she used to be a reader and wonder why that changed. Then, the "shoulds" will take over: "I know I should read more," and "I should find more time to read."

A few years ago, after more than a decade teaching English, I began asking students about their reading lives. After doing more than 100 informal interviews, I made a big decision. Instead of cajoling my 9th graders unsuccessfully to read great books like *Night* and *Things Fall Apart,* I launched an independent reading program as part of my curriculum. Influenced by reading gurus Nancie Atwell, Donalyn Miller, and Kelly Gallagher, and invigorated by an article in *The New York Times,* I built a fledgling classroom library of 500 titles and encouraged students to read books they liked, in addition to the books I required them to read.

For the most part, the experiment worked. My students read more than ever, improved their reading skills, and said they liked to read. But not all students felt that way. To some, reading was boring, no matter what. Reading wasn't worth their time. Many said they hadn't read a book since 4th grade. I needed to reach these students, too.

One November during reading workshop I noticed a boy with his head down and eyes closed. This was not the first time he had chosen sleeping over reading. He'd been consistently clear about his hatred for reading. His book, though, was still propped open—an advanced move by an advanced fake reader. By this time, I was exasperated by his reluctance to read, and I didn't know what to do next. Instead of my normal intervention—approach the student, rouse him with a hand on his shoulder, and ask him if anything is wrong—I decided to do something different. I let him borrow my Kindle.

The boy, after a quizzical look, immediately sat up and quickly switched books—from Khaled Hosseini's *The Kite Runner* (my choice) to Tupac Shakur's *The Rose that Grew from Concrete* (his choice). He played around with the buttons and made the font bigger. Then, for the first time in nearly four months, the 9th grader read without interruption. This was not fake reading. At the end of class, he smiled and said, "This is so much better!" I asked him whether he wanted to take the Kindle home for the weekend. "Really?" Sure. By the next Monday, he'd finished *The Rose,* his first book of the year.

Start a Kindle Project

The best part of the Kindle Classroom Project is that it is easily replicable. In fact, many teachers across the country—like Denise Fullerton in Berkeley and Meg Griswold in Nashville—have also experienced success using Kindles with students. With education budgets tight and less money to fund school libraries, many teachers fill the gap themselves in order to get good books in students' hands. With the same amount of effort it takes to build a rich, physical classroom library, teachers can begin a Kindle project of their own. Here are a few suggestions:

- **Start small.** Let a student borrow your Kindle for a few days and see what happens. Most likely she will read more, but, in addition, her friends and family will notice. Within days, students will approach you with jealous complaints and hopeful requests that you loan them the Kindle next.

- **Get the word out that you're looking for used Kindles.** With tablets and phones now the preferred way to read on a screen, many people in your community have old Kindles lying around their homes, ready to be read. I made my project public on my blog, but that's not necessary. Most teachers ask their family and friends or make announcements in the school or community newsletter. Others have found success using DonorsChoose or by creating an Amazon wish list. The donations may begin slowly, but once word-of-mouth gains momentum, the Kindles will flow in faster.

- **Create a separate Amazon account.** This is crucial. You don't want to share your personal Amazon account and its link to your credit card. Best to set up a new account without a credit card number for your Kindle classroom. Unfortunately, it's not easy to transfer books from your personal account to this professional one, so if your personal library contains a book your 9th graders would like to read, you may need to buy an additional copy. But this way you don't have to worry that students will go on an Amazon shopping spree.

- **Invest in excellent books.** Many people think the best library is the biggest one. On the Kindle, it's more important to have high-interest books that pop. Students dislike combing through swaths of mediocre titles searching for a book they like. If you already have an independent reading program, it's best to start with the popular books that are never out of circulation.

- **After buying e-versions of those titles, listen to students.** What are their favorite books? Which books have changed their lives? Depending on your budget and your fund-raising, make frugal decisions when building your e-library. Remember that each title can be shared on six Kindles simultaneously, so your $10 investment becomes $60, at least virtually.

- **Catalog your Kindles and load up your books.** Go to the Manage Your Devices page on your Amazon account and rename your Kindles so they're easy to track. I also put a sticker on the back of each Kindle for easy identification. Next, register the Kindle under the classroom library's email address. Once that is completed, check the Kindle web site to ensure that the device is listed and that everything got saved properly. The last step is to download books onto the devices, easily the most labor-intensive step. Despite Amazon's policy to allow sharing titles to up to six devices, you must send each book to each device, one by one. If your e-library contains many titles, you may want to round up some help and speed up this step using multiple computers simultaneously.

- **Charge up your Kindles and release them to students.** Depending on its model, a Kindle keeps its charge for as little as a week and as much as a month. Either way, once you charge the devices, you won't need to give out Amazon cables, especially if students keep Wi-Fi turned off. In the case of an around-the-lock avid reader, you can leave chargers in the classroom, but any Android phone charger will work.

- **Maybe the hardest step in starting a Kindle program is the last one: determining which students should get the e-readers first.** Because my intent is to serve the most reluctant readers first, struggling readers get priority. Also, some may be hesitant over worries they'll break or lose the Kindle, or concerns that by accepting the device they must don a reader identity. In my experience, this process takes no more than a few moments, and, once the Kindle is in their hands, students are off and reading.

Once that happens, once students are reading again—not fake reading—the power of the story takes over. With the help of a Kindle, students begin inhabiting a new world filled with fantasy and possibility. Meanwhile, there is also a return to childhood, when reading was bright and joyful. As students read on their Kindles, they build their futures as they revise their pasts. All of a sudden, they're readers again.

—*Mark Isero*

Last year, the Kindlers read more books on average than their physical book-reading peers, and their reading scores climbed much more than the non-Kindlers.

Since that day, I've collected Kindles and loaned them to reluctant readers to motivate them to read. My Kindle Classroom Project now serves 139 9th graders and has a library of 449 high-interest titles. Last year, the Kindlers read more books on average than their physical book-reading peers, and their reading scores climbed 1.9 grade levels, much more than the non-Kindlers' 0.9. To be sure, my experiment was by no means a scientific study. But one thing remained clear: The 9th graders who read on Kindles told me they liked to read. Their resignation and regret gone, these students had reclaimed their love of reading.

It's Time to Read

What made this reading resurgence happen? My gut says the Kindle helps students build a new relationship with reading. Many of my students wouldn't risk being caught reading a physical book—not in class, and certainly not on the bus home. It's much cooler, and maybe even safer, to break out an iPhone than a book. Though the Kindle is no longer a cutting-edge device, it still gives my students enough tech-cred to appease leery onlookers. The e-Ink version offers them the perfect mix of digital and analog: digital enough to maintain status among their friends, while analog enough to prevent a theft by their enemies.

Students say the Kindle's clunky interface keeps them focused on reading. One student told me, "There's no distractions. It's just me and the words." Her sentiment is absolutely true. Once a student chooses a font, nothing gets in the way of the reading experience. Even the touchscreen Kindles barely go on the Internet, and by no means are students trying to post Facebook or Twitter updates. When it's time to read, it's time to read. Several students said they leave their phones in another room when they're reading at home so that texts won't compete for their attention.

The Kindle Classroom Project has been successful because it directly meets the needs of struggling readers.

Over time, my students come to call the Kindle theirs. When I loan one out, the student hears, "Here's something valuable to show that I care about you and that I want you to read." As a result, much more than with physical books, students take care of their Kindles. One June, I was walking down the hallway and spotted a copy of Jay Asher's *Thirteen Reasons Why* (a great book!) in the garbage can, likely the victim of a year-end locker-clearing celebration. That doesn't happen with the Kindles. Students keep them in cases and don't cram them into backpacks. In fact, in the three years my students have used them, only three devices have stopped working, perhaps because of negligence, but more likely due to old age.

Not losing Kindles also means not losing the e-books they contain. Because the books are safe in the Amazon cloud, they're impossible for students to misplace or leave indefinitely at their cousin's house. Their covers also don't get tattered; there's never need for contact paper. Many teachers spend countless hours at the end of the year pleading with their students to return paperbacks. "If a book doesn't come back, at least I know someone's reading it," goes the common refrain. Yet the teacher still has to spot the $15 to replace the title. In contrast, with Kindles I'm freed up to listen to students, take book requests, and raise money for new titles to expand our e-library.

Another important benefit of this approach: Students can read the same title at the same time. Because most Amazon e-books can be shared among six devices simultaneously on the same account, there is no wait for popular books. When five girls all of a sudden wanted to read Simone Elkeles' *Perfect Chemistry* two years ago, I didn't have to rush to Barnes & Noble to order multiple copies of the book. The same thing happened with the boys and *My Bloody Life: The Making of a Latin King,* by Reymundo Sanchez. After several months, when the popularity of those titles waned, the books did not end up on remainder tables. Moreover, friends can form informal book clubs and talk about the books they're reading. Students tell me that reading is much more enjoyable when it's social. While they prefer to read silently and on their own, students like discussing the characters and major themes. A healthy "how-far-are-you-in-the-book competition" spurs students to keep up the reading pace outside of class. Stories, because they're shared with friends at a critical stage of adolescence, carry deep meaning and create lasting memories.

Struggling Readers

Above all, I believe the Kindle Classroom Project has been successful because it directly meets the needs of struggling readers. A Kindle cuts through the stigma that students have felt for many years and gives them another chance to identify as readers. Specifically, since all the Kindles look similar, kids need not disclose what they are reading. They can enjoy a book at the 3rd-grade level without fearing the taunts and condescension of peers and teachers. One of my students—a hulking, burly young man—got turned on to E.B. White's *Charlotte's Web* last year. No way would he have read that book, with Wilbur and Charlotte prominently displayed on its cover, in class or on the city bus.

In addition to being able to choose whatever titles they want, struggling readers invariably crank up the font size on the Kindle, sometimes to the largest setting. It's easier for them to focus on a screen with larger text and fewer words per page. Readability is crucial. No longer do students drown in an ocean of tiny text, and rarely do they repeat lines, a common occurrence when text is small. With fewer words per page, struggling readers can feel the joy of finishing pages and wondering what will happen next. And because the Kindle maintains its thickness, never giving away the heft of a big book, a long story does not overwhelm the student in the same way a physical book would.

In short, for too long 9th-grade students—particularly those who have struggled with reading—have been told that reading is not for them, that they can't read, that they're dumb, that they should fake read instead of trying honestly, or maybe that they should give up reading altogether. Collecting Kindles and loaning them out to students changed this script and offered them a chance to reclaim their love of reading.

Critical Thinking

1. What are the important points of this article for teachers to remember?

2. This is one teacher's story of his experience. If you were going to research the viability of his experience, what research questions would you ask? What data would you collect?

3. Your principal has read this article and has asked you to head a task force at your school to collect Kindles and give one to every student who is reading below grade level at Best Practice Elementary School. Before you chair the first meeting of the group, you outline the first five actions you would take to make this happen. What are those?

Create Central

www.mhhe.com/createcentral

Internet References

Bill & Melinda Gates Foundation
www.gatesfoundation.org/topics/Pages/high-schools.aspx
Center for Comprehensive School Reform and Improvement
www.centerforcsri.org
Donors Choose
http://www.donorschoose.org/

MARK ISERO taught English and social studies for 15 years before becoming a literacy coach for Envision Education, a charter school network based in Oakland, Calif. Now in its fourth year, his Kindle Classroom Project serves students in California communities in San Francisco, Oakland, and Hayward.

Unit 4

UNIT

Prepared by: Rebecca B. Evers, *Winthrop University*

Improve School Climate to Improve Student Performance

All of us are situated in social, political, and economic circumstances which inform and develop our values. Our values are usually derived from principles of conduct that we learn during interactions with others. This is to say that societal values develop in a cultural context. Teachers cannot hide all of their moral preferences, personal biases, or ethical principles. They can, however, learn to conduct just and open discussions of moral topics without succumbing to the temptation to indoctrinate students with their own views. In democratic societies, such as the United States, alternative sets of values and morals co-exist. What teachers perceive to be worthwhile and defensible behavior informs their reflections on what educators should teach. We may be conscious of some of the values that affect our behavior, but we may not be as aware of what informs our preferences. Values that we hold without being conscious of them are referred to as tacit values: these are values derived indirectly after reasoned reflection on our thoughts about teaching and learning. Much of our knowledge about teaching is tacit knowledge, which we need to bring into conscious cognition by analyzing the concepts that drive practice. We need to acknowledge how all of our values inform—and influence—our thoughts about teaching. In many cases teachers must grapple with the dilemma of their own values versus the values of their students. Teachers with dispositions for viewing each student with an open mind and heart will be able to treat each individual as unique and valuable. This is a first step in building a classroom climate that is accepting of and inviting to everyone.

As students grow older, they need to develop a sense of genuine caring both for themselves and others. Therefore, teachers must model and teach students how to be a caring community of learners by building positive relationships with the students, their parents, and the community outside the school. The quality of the school climate has become increasingly important in the last decade. The increased incidents of bullying, both face-to-face and cyber-bullying, as well as the frequent school shootings have made schools consider and add more rules and restrictions on student behavior and dress. These actions have an effect on how teachers, children, and youth think about their environment. Even teachers and school staff may be more stressed as they worry about what might take place and having to enforce the stricter rules. Teachers need to be able to straddle the line between creating an accepting environment and enforcing the rules and restrictions to keep students safe. The articles in this unit offer practices and suggestions to help teachers create caring communities of learners.

While most teachers are very aware that words have power and some words are taboo, it is the little words that can count the most. Comments made when Cheryl fails the math quiz, such as "Oh, well, most girls are not very good at math" or when an African American student scores the winning goal a someone says, "They are the best athletes" are little throw away comments that have a profound impact over time whether they come from parents, teachers, or peers. Children and youth hear those and form their prejudices and biases. These little comments can build on one another to become more extreme beliefs and prejudices. We are being asked to consider how the psychology of prejudice is formed and that through discrimination and the use of "isms" students can be marginalized. We are also asked to consider how these acts can build into more dangerous actions.

Age-appropriate social skills are an important component of caring communities of learners. Some schools have opted for gender-specific classrooms rather than coed. There are some interesting discussions occurring around this trend. One scholar suggests that separation by gender might be as harmful as racial segregation. Another concludes that in a classroom free of labels and gender expectations, a more integrated classroom can be developed where social skills and productive relationships are created. What effects might this sorting by gender have on the emotional and social development of students?

We have often heard that it is important to have a relationship with students built on mutual respect and trust. In practice that can be difficult, however some teachers are able to accomplish this and are rewarded by the students and acknowledged by their peers. The work of one of these teachers has been the topic of an award winning documentary film and he has been awarded grants to fund his work. Another discussant argues that teacher education programs that only educate teacher candidates to be highly qualified in their subject area are missing a vital piece of those candidates' professional preparation. Attention must be given to the importance of the candidates' drive to do what is necessary to engage students. That it is the enthusiasm for one's students that produces lifelong learners. Establishing positive relationships and making sure that we use the appropriate currency to motivate students does not mean we are "fluffy" or "soft" in our attention to the real work of schools. Further, we must consider how the policies we establish in

schools affect our children, especially in the areas of bullying and our zero tolerance of infractions of school rules.

Teachers worry and complain about how much or how little parents engage with the school community. We know that their participation is critical to the well-being of the school and to any real change or reform. Generally, we think that parents simply do not want to do their parental duty or do not care enough about their child's education. Not once in my long teaching career have I ever heard a teacher say "I wonder if it is the size of the school?", "Maybe they do not feel safe in this building." or "Maybe the parents don't actually see us as open to their presence or suggestions." Four hypotheses were tested for their effect on parent engagement and the results are both interesting and useful to school personnel.

Article   Prepared by: Rebecca B. Evers, *Winthrop University.*

Why Our Approach to Bullying Is Bad for Kids

Safe schools—for a safer world.

SUSAN PORTER

Learning Outcomes

After reading this article, you will be able to:

- Debate the positive and negative issues associated with how we define and label incidences of bullying.

It's hard to avoid the topic of bullying these days. From parents chatting about it on the soccer field sidelines, to op-ed pieces calling for police presence on school campuses, to the President and First Lady hosting webcasts on the subject—just about everyone with a soapbox, real or virtual, is talking about how to deal with the bullying scourge that is sweeping the nation's schools. And, boy, is it bad.

The next time you've got a spare moment, Google "statistics on bullying" and see for yourself. When I last looked, this is what popped up:

- One in five kids is bullied.
- Twenty-three percent of students say they have been bullied several times.
- One in four kids is bullied.
- Fifty percent of kids are bullied, and 10 percent are bullied on a regular basis.
- Seventy-four percent of 8- to 11-year-olds said teasing and bullying occurs at their schools.
- Seventy-seven percent of students say they've been bullied recently.
- It is estimated that more than half [emphasis added] of school bullying incidents are never reported.

Despite the fact that the statistics are wildly inconsistent, even the lowest percentages are scary, and they suggest that our kids aren't safe in schools because they're hurting one another at alarmingly high rates. At best, the data suggest that we've got a serious problem on our hands.

Or do we?

Parents often ask me what's behind the rise of bullying among children, and whether or not kids today are different from those of previous generations. As a school counselor, with almost 25 years of experience, I tell parents that kids haven't changed much over the years, but something significant has changed recently, and that's how our culture thinks about, talks about, and deals with aggressive childhood behavior. And the change is profound.

A Shift in Definition

A few years ago, a K-12 school asked me to consult on the subject of bullying. This was about the time many schools were implementing "Zero Tolerance Anti-Bullying" policies. In preparation for my presentation, I researched the topic by reviewing local and regional policies on bullying, and articles in the professional literature. I was stunned by what I learned.

First, I discovered that bullying was everywhere. The statistics were as disturbing and wide-ranging then as they are today. Admittedly, I was shocked. Here I was, a school counselor with years of experience as both a mental health clinician in schools and a consultant to schools, and somehow I had missed all of this. Of course, I had dealt with cases of bullying in my own work, but the sweeping nature of the phenomenon, as suggested by my research, had eluded me. The ground under my professional feet started to shake. As I digested the information I felt horrible. How could I have been so blind?

But then, as I researched further, I learned another important thing about bullying. According to the many definitions I read, the term had come to include not only the classic forms of harassment between children, behaviors such as shaking down a kid for lunch money, beating up a smaller kid in the schoolyard, or repeated hate speech. Now, it also included behaviors such as social exclusion, name-calling, teasing, sarcasm, and being unfriendly. I also noted a corresponding shift in the telltale signs expressed by the victims of bullying, which in addition to extreme symptoms, such as school phobia and depression, now included symptoms such as feeling upset and being sad.

As I considered all of this, I realized what I'd missed in my work was not a rise in incidents of classic bullying, but rather the creeping expansion of the definition of bullying, which according to the average anti-bullying policy was now a catchall term for the routine—albeit nasty—selfishness, meanness, and other social misfires that characterize childhood and adolescence. I call this the expanded definition of bullying.

As I completed my research, I sensed that this expanded definition of bullying was doing more than just attempting to protect kids. It was also making a lot of normal childhood behaviors seem pathological and dangerous. Many of the behaviors described in the bullying literature were almost inevitable, given brain development, but this didn't seem to matter. What mattered instead was setting unrealistic guidelines for children's behavior in the hopes of preventing them from feeling pain. Lost, it seemed, was the intention of helping kids learn from their mistakes and developing resilience in the face of adversity.

The Preadolescent and Adolescent Brains and Development

The preadolescent and adolescent brains can be characterized in many ways, the most important of which, when it comes to the expanded definition of bullying, is that they are not yet fully developed. And the most important part of the brain that has not yet developed is the prefrontal cortex, the part of the brain that deals with functions such as impulse control, judgment, and empathy. These functions are often referred to as executive functions, and researchers believe we continue to develop these functions well into our twenties.

This means children, even older teenagers, have brains that are not yet capable of being consistently in control of themselves, even when they try really, really hard. As children age, however, the executive functions start to kick in more predictably, and therefore older teenagers can be entrusted, for example, to drive a car or babysit a younger child or do their homework without a nightly battle. That said, the key is consistency, and even the best-behaved and seemingly mature teenager can have lapses in judgment and behave without the benefit of fully formed executive functions.

If you consider the expanded definition of bullying in light of brain development, and think about behaviors such as teasing, name-calling, and social exclusion, you can see why kids and teenagers might exhibit these behaviors, given the fact that their brains simply aren't fully formed yet. Being polite, keeping their hands to themselves, not saying everything that pops into their heads, staying on task, and being thoughtful—these are the things kids work on every day, and their brains won't master these tasks for years. The brain constantly makes mistakes as it develops these capacities, and often these mistakes come at the expense of another person's feelings.

Add to this various aspects of development, such as the marked self-consciousness that characterizes adolescence, and you have a recipe for insensitive behavior. When kids walk down school hallways, they aren't thinking about other people's feelings; they're thinking me, me, me. This is normal. But this leaves them vulnerable to making big mistakes when it comes to attending to the needs of others, and acting with these needs in mind.

So, regardless of what we'd like, we can't expect kids to sail through childhood and adolescence without blundering—especially given that the average adolescent brain, still under construction, is hardwired to behave in ways that are irritating and selfish at times. This explains, in part, the prevalence of bullying (the expanded version) these days.

There are other reasons why the milder bullying behaviors are rampant (and always have been), and why we can't eradicate them.

First, brains at this age are prone to misinterpreting facial cues, a fact that has huge implications when it comes to social interactions. For example, the teenage brain might interpret a classmate's frown to mean, "She really hates me! She doesn't want to be my friend," when, in fact, it probably means something completely different. A missed cue of this kind, coupled with the self-absorption of the age, can turn a non-situation into an emotional drama, as the teenager imagines her classmate's expression to be both (A) extremely negative, and (B) necessarily about her.

Second, brains at this stage tend to respond very emotionally to social situations. For example, Cathy looks at Susie the wrong way. Unlike an adult, Susie isn't unaffected by Cathy's expression, or simply annoyed by it. Susie takes it personally. She may feel overwrought. This is especially true if Susie believes Cathy's expression indicates that she (Cathy) wishes to exclude her (Susie). Research has shown that the threat of social exclusion is one of the scariest things for a pre-teen girl's brain to deal with, so Susie's response to Cathy's expression could conceivably cause Susie's brain to initiate a fight-or-flight response, sending Susie on an emotional roller-coaster ride that terrifies her.

An important point to understand about a situation like Susie's is that her reactions and feelings are real to her, but that doesn't mean they are an accurate gauge of the outside situation. Our current approach to bullying places so much emphasis on a child's inner experience that I often deal with children (supported by their parents) who believe that their feelings are facts. In today's social climate, Susie's very real, albeit internal and emotional response to Cathy's frown can be sufficient evidence to Susie that Cathy has done something really bad. And, if Susie claimed that Cathy had repeatedly acted this way, and if Susie had some very wounded feelings as evidence, then Cathy could be in big trouble. At the very least, she'd probably get a stern talking-to from a teacher or school administrator. And for what, making a face? But with our expanded definition of bullying, Susie's pain is the trump card.

Finally, bullying is widespread because kids at this age tend to see the world in black and white terms. Their brains are just developing the capacity for abstract thought, and while they may have glimpses of it here and there, for the most part, and especially when it comes to social situations, the world to them is pretty cut and dried. As such, there is little room for a nuanced interpretation of painful situations, so a perceived social attack is usually interpreted in dire terms.

Unfortunately, in our desire to protect perceived victims, we downplay or ignore these essential truths about development such that, over the past decade or so, we have succeeded in redefining many unpleasant childhood behaviors as bullying, and thus the epidemic. With this expanded definition of bullying in place, the average child, behaving in an average way, is statistically likely to be branded a bully at some point, and to become a victim of bullying—and this troubles me.

None of this means that we should ignore children's bad behavior or pain. But our current approach to bullying, which superimposes on the childhood brain an adult-like capacity for intent and self-control, gives little encouragement for growth and change. It also ignores children's capacity for resilience, and it does both through its use of labels.

Fixed Mindsets and the Problem with Labels

Labels are everywhere when it comes to bullying, and they are an important part of how anti-bullying rhetoric aims to educate kids about aggression. Go to any anti-bullying website, or review anti-bullying curricula, and you will see what I mean. The labels are ubiquitous: active bully, passive bully, lieutenant, henchman, bystander, ally, hero, and, of course, victim. They constitute the dramatis personae of the bully play. In learning about bullying, students are instructed to identify the players, imagine what roles they play, and clearly distinguish between the wrongdoer and the wronged. It's all fixed, perhaps in an effort to simplify what is usually an inherently complicated situation. And with these labels, the painful dynamics that occur among children become carved in stone.

By now, most educators are familiar with the work of Stanford University psychologist Carol Dweck. In *Mindset: The New Psychology of Success,* she describes the two lenses through which we make sense of the world: the fixed mindset and the growth mindset. The fixed mindset is characterized by a belief that personality and intelligence are static qualities, and that they can't be developed. A growth mindset, on the other hand, is characterized by a belief that these qualities can change and develop, and that effort leads to learning and therefore growth.

Our approach to bullying is problematic, if for no other reason, because it provides kids (and adults) with little conceptual room to maneuver. When a child misbehaves and is labeled a bully, the label declares something about his character, not just about his behavior. For adults, the bully label affixed to a child sticks in our minds, and encourages us to view the child's behavior—past, present, and future—through this lens. If we consider that children don't develop the capacity for abstract thought until early adolescence (if then), we see how problematic labels are. Children can't see beyond the concrete, so they

will take labels like bully or victim and run with them, usually to their own detriment. But adults should know better. Our goal is to facilitate growth and change.

I encourage readers to carefully examine their own schools' and states' anti-bullying policies and curricula to bring this point home. I have yet to come across a policy that approaches the issue of problematic childhood and adolescent behavior from a growth mindset. These policies, in their presumed effort to protect kids and shape behavior, do little more than make us view children and their behavior in a fixed framework. The formulaic ways in which aggression among kids is described, and a general indifference to context through the use of easy-to-apply labels, let us off the hook for approaching problematic situations between children with compassion for all parties involved.

The use of labels, and the accompanying fixed mindset they engender, does nothing to help us help kids. Children need us to understand their social lives and behavior in dynamic, not static, terms, and to separate their behavior from their characters. Children should be allowed to make mistakes, and these mistakes, even if egregious, should not result in the children receiving labels that limit our ability (and possibly our desire) to help them develop into responsible adults.

But labels aren't bad for just the bullies; they're bad for the victims, too. Remember, mindsets are about whether we see the world through fixed or growth lenses, and the victim label is as fixed and inflexible as the bully one. Both discourage self-exploration and faith in change. The bully has no incentive to change as long as the adults (and children) around him see him in wholly negative terms, while the victim has no incentive to develop resilience if he is continually identified with and reminded of his wounds. In my experience, victims are often the biggest losers when it comes to labeling because, as victims, they are encouraged to identify with their vulnerability, and as a result, their sense of agency often derives from their feelings of helplessness and pain.

The other labels used in the bully rhetoric—such as bystander, ally, and hero—are also problematic. For starters, they give children, and especially young children, the incorrect impression that they are responsible for preventing other people's pain. In addition, they lead children to believe that they must be vigilant at all times, and know when and how to intervene in complex social situations. Sure, kids should be encouraged to help out other kids, but it is neither their role nor their duty to assume this much responsibility for situations beyond their control, and yet this is the impression our use of labels gives them.

If nothing else, we should abandon labels and the fixed mindset around bullying because they alienate parents, and we need to work closely with parents if we want to help children change their behavior. I routinely tell parents to stop listening if someone (let's say a teacher or another parent) calls their child a bully. Why? Because when adults use the term bully, they have stopped seeing a child's potential, and they aren't focused on helping that child grow. Using the term bully is an easy way out, and it allows adults to avoid the very hard work of helping children change their behavior. This is not just an issue

Code of Conduct for XYZ Academy

Middle School (or High School) is a time of tremendous physical, psychological, and emotional growth and change, and the expectations for XYZ Academy students reflect the capabilities of adolescents (or children) at this developmental stage and the aspirations the community has for them.

All XYZ Academy students are expected to behave in ways that support the well-being, health, and safety of themselves and others. To this end, students should be respectful in their interactions and relationships and learn to recognize how their actions, including their speech, affect others. XYZ students should aim to be courteous, kind, and inclusive, and accept constructive feedback and criticism as being essential parts of learning and membership within the community.

As an educational community, XYZ recognizes that social-emotional development, as any other subject, takes time to master, and involves mistakes and missteps. As such, adults are charged to help students reflect upon their behavioral choices, especially when these choices hurt or deny the rights of others. In cases of severe or repeated negative behavior that falls short of expected conduct, disciplinary action may be taken.

of semantics, as any parent of an accused child can attest. It's about believing in growth or not.

An Alternative Approach

In order to do right by our students, we must first understand brain and psychological development and set reasonable expectations for student behavior. We must recognize that the brain doesn't fully develop for years, and that it makes plenty of mistakes along the way, whether in mathematics or history or relationships. We succeed as educators when we help students solve academic problems. Likewise, we succeed when we help students solve behavioral problems. And just as we avoid labels when it comes to students as academic learners, we should avoid labels when it comes to students as social-emotional learners.

We must also abandon the conceptual frameworks and rhetoric that encourage us to understand childhood aggression in simple and formulaic ways, and we should adopt policies that reflect a growth mindset. To this end, I have included a Code of Conduct statement that approaches behavior and expectations from a growth mindset. You will note that it does not specify certain behaviors or reactions to behaviors, as do most anti-bullying policies. It is aspirational, open-ended, and doesn't dictate how a school should respond to complex social situations among students.

As educators, it is our job to lead the way. When we stop seeing the potential for growth and change in children, it's time for us to retire.

Critical Thinking

1. Porter holds what may be considered a controversial view on bullying. Do you agree or disagree with her new definition and primary concerns about bullying? Justify your answer with at least three reasons.

2. Think back to your childhood, particularly during "tween" years. What bullying label would you give yourself? At what point in your life did that label no longer apply to you? Now, describe how and why your behavior changed. Does your experience support or deny Porter's assertions?

Create Central

www.mhhe.com/createcentral

Internet References

Wrightslaw on Bullying
www.wrightslaw.com/blog/?tag=bullying

Susan Porter is dean of students at The Branson School (California). Her book, *Bully Nation: Why America's Approach to Bullying Is Bad for Everyone,* is scheduled to be released by Paragon Press in the spring of 2013.

Porter, Susan. From *Independent School*, vol. 72, no. 2, Winter 2013, pp. 72–78. Copyright © 2013 by Nancy Porter. Reprinted by permission.via Rightslink.

Article   Prepared by: Rebecca B. Evers, *Winthrop University*

Deconstructing the Pyramid of Prejudice

On the surface, negative comments by students about race, gender, or sexual preference may seem to be part of the benign banter of youth, but they're exactly where teachers should start their battle—and lessons— to build a better child and world.

DAVID LIGHT SHIELDS

Learning Outcomes

After reading this article, you will be able to:

- Discuss the psychology of human prejudice while describing the three levels of the "Pyramid Principle" of prejudice.

- Examine the need to address prejudice in the classroom.

- Defend either the legal or educational solutions to acts of prejudice and hate.

Every teacher has heard them, often several times a day: comments that rub them the wrong way but seem too innocent to challenge. "Boys will be boys," Mr. Shubert says in response to a playground tussle. After Ernie gets 99% on the math quiz, Jamie blurts, "Figures; he's Chinese." "That's so gay," Tricia moans when her teacher assigns tough homework. Teachers who want to help students become competent, caring adults cannot just help Ernie learn math. They need to help Mr. Shubert, Jamie, and Tricia see the harm in their seemingly innocuous comments.

While subdued forms of everyday prejudice may seem harmless, appearances can be deceiving. Such commonplace prejudices form the foundation upon which more extreme acts of prejudice build. And they also leave us vulnerable to costly errors of judgment that can have tragic consequences. That is why addressing prejudice in the classroom is as crucial to our youth's education as learning to read.

Comprehending the pyramid principle of prejudice and its profound educational implications is the first step toward reducing the violence, discrimination, hatred, and bigotry that spread like wildfires in the dry climate created by everyday prejudice.

Before we explain the pyramid principle, though, let's take a quick scan of the psychology of prejudice and how it relates to discrimination and the "-isms."

The Psychology of Prejudice

We all know what prejudices are. They are prejudgments that rely on stereotypes (Allport, Clark, & Pettigrew, 1979). They are assumptions made about people based on their association with certain groups. Prejudices arise and persist because they serve important social and psychological functions.

In one sense, prejudices reflect an inevitable part of human cognition. The world is such a complex place that simplification is necessary for understanding. We would be overwhelmed if we tried to approach each new individual with no preconceived ideas. Before we even consciously think about it, we already have formed opinions about that boy who walked into class on the first day sporting a Mohawk and skull shirt. Stereotypes are cognitive maps that help us simplify our highly complex social world. To some extent, they are necessary for mental efficiency and ease (Dalrymple, 2007). Still, that efficiency comes at the cost of accuracy and fairness.

The psychological roots of prejudice also extend deep into our emotional selves (Whitley & Kite, 2010). One major source of prejudice is the pervasive human need for positive self-regard. We want to feel good about ourselves and the groups with which we identify. As a male, I want to feel good about being a man. As a member of this nation, I want to feel patriotic. A powerful way to buttress our sense of worthiness, competence, and belonging is to compare ourselves to others we perceive as inferior. We might muse: "I'm so glad I'm American; we're better than the French," even if we're sensitive enough not to say it aloud. This need for favorable social comparison provides fuel to the fires of prejudice. Prejudices, after all, guarantee in advance that "we" will compare favorably to "them."

Prejudices support numerous other psychological functions that need not concern us here. But one more deserves special mention. For those who are relatively privileged in society, prejudices can blind us to the injustices that protect our privileges. For example, not long ago a wealthy presidential candidate who spent his early years in security and abundance, who attended expensive private schools and benefitted from the models and social networks that his family, neighborhood, and schools afforded, still claimed that his wealth was all his own doing (Pareene, 2012). With that incredulous claim comes implicit blame: Those who are caught in poverty can be blamed for their plight. From this vantage point, the structural inequalities that perpetuate class divisions are hidden. Blaming the victim (Ryan, 1971) is a resilient form of subtle prejudice; it takes a hundred forms, and it benefits the privileged in a thousand ways.

Prejudice and Discrimination

We've hinted at the deep connection between prejudice and discrimination. While prejudice is largely attitudinal, discrimination is more behavioral. Discrimination refers to actions, policies, or social arrangements that disadvantage people based on the group to which they belong (Whitley & Kite, 2010). The Boy Scouts long-standing exclusion of gay boys was discriminatory. Fortunately, the Scouts recently reversed this policy (Eckholm, 2013), though discrimination persists in that openly gay troop leaders are banned.

Discrimination is often codified in the policies and practices of organizations. Continuing discriminatory policies does not depend on the individual prejudices of those who implement them. For example, imagine that a college requires a minimum score on a standardized test before granting admission. Imagine further (it should be easy) that the test is culturally biased. If admission officers simply apply the rules, they can further discrimination even though individually they may not be prejudiced against the disadvantaged applicants.

Prejudice and the "-isms"

Prejudice is often confused with the "-isms," such as racism or classism. However, there is an important difference. Prejudice refers to the attitudes and beliefs held by an individual or group that inform their decisions and actions. When we refer to a statement as racist, however, we mean something more than that the statement reflects a racial prejudice. A statement is racist when the prejudice it expresses reinforces the prevailing racial division of power and privilege (Tatum, 1997). The "-isms" represent the ways that certain prejudices and practices perpetuate and fortify unequal access to the goods of society (social, economic, political, etc.). Thus, sexism goes beyond individual prejudice; it occurs when gender prejudice buttresses unequal power hierarchies that privilege males at the expense of females. The "-isms" are fundamentally about prejudices combining with power, though the power may be exercised in subtle and indirect ways.

The "Pyramid Principle" of Prejudice

In society, when our sight is sharpened by honesty, we see that the blatant acts of hate or discrimination carried out by the troubled few are actually ugly and exaggerated reflections of imperfections in ourselves. The pyramid principle of prejudice states that the blatant prejudices of the few are magnifications of the latent prejudices of the many (Shields, 1986).

Have you ever been to a carnival fun house with mirrors that distort your image, creating exaggerated and ugly reflections of yourself? Such mirrors provide an analogy for the pyramid principle. Just as the twisted image in the fun house mirror could not exist without someone standing in front of it, neither would gross acts of violence be possible without the "minor" violence of widespread and largely inconspicuous prejudice that lines the base of the prejudice pyramid.

The bottom of the pyramid is where most people can be found. The prejudices and discriminatory acts of people metaphorically residing at the base often go unrecognized; they have a quiet, inconspicuous, everyday quality to them. If confronted, most people at the base would be puzzled; they don't consider themselves prejudiced. As you move higher up the pyramid, fewer and fewer people are represented, but the prejudicial attitudes and discriminatory actions become increasingly overt, obvious, and extreme. At the top of the pyramid are the truly horrendous acts carried out by tiny numbers.

The key point is that every vertical movement up the pyramid builds from and depends upon the attitudes and behaviors established by the levels below. Still, people at each level typically perceive "the problem" to be limited to those higher in the pyramid. "Yeah, I laughed at the [racist] joke, but I don't use the 'n' word," says Malcolm as he refuses to accept any sense of personal responsibility for the continuation of racial prejudice in society.

Life at the Base

Most people, in most situations, neither think of themselves as prejudiced, nor do they exhibit overtly prejudicial speech or

The Pyramid Principle of Prejudice

Interpreting the Pyramid

As you move up the pyramid, attitudes and actions become more extreme but fewer people express or accept them.

As you move down the pyramid, the actions and thoughts become less extreme, but are reflected in larger numbers of people.

Each higher elevation of the pyramid builds on and amplifies the thinking and behavior of the lower parts of the pyramid.

Legal action is appropriate for dealing with actions at the upper end of the pyramid.

Educational action is necessary to address the thoughts and behaviors at the lower end of the pyramid.

Everday, seemingly trivial, attitudes and behaviors that are widely overlooked as instances of prejudice or discrimination, including teasing and humor based on stereotypes.

Extreme expressions of prejudice and/or discrimination, including housing and job discrimination, violent hate crimes, and inequitable distribution of educational opportunities.

"Jump that Muslim."

"She was asking for it."

"Don't admit Janelle. She probably cheated to get those test scores."

"We can't do anything about the achievement gap because black culture doesn't value education."

"Rather than Chemistry, why don't you take cooking, Susan? Remember, the way to a man's heart is through his stomach."

"No, John, you can't bring Jason to the prom."

"Of course, you'll take your husband's name when yoy ger married."

"Why are you upset? You bipolar or something?"

"How many Hispanics does it take to screw in a lightbulb?"

"Don't cry; be a man." "He throws like a girl." "Oh, that's so lame."

---

behavior. But none of us are completely free of bias, most of which is unconscious. As psychologists over the past couple decades have demonstrated, most of our thinking occurs outside conscious awareness (Evans, 2009). In terminology popularized by Nobel Prize-winning researcher Daniel Kahneman (2011), our "fast thinking" is invisible to our conscious mind. And it is within our fast thinking that most biases and prejudices operate (Anderson, 2010).

Consider gender. In schools, stereotypes about "boys" and "girls" are as common as pencils. Typically, comments about "boys' toys" and "girls' toys" by a kindergarten teacher would raise no eyebrows. Complimenting girls for their looks and boys on their athleticism may occur with little notice. When Tom describes Kim as "feminine," he is likely unaware of how his "fast thinking" engaged in complex comparisons between observed attributes and cultural stereotypes. No doubt he would reject the idea that his comment about Kim is prejudicial. Still, all references to "masculinity" or "femininity" are premised on stereotypical depictions of gender that can't help but reinforce a bias against those who do not fit or conform to the dominant cultural patterns of gender expression.

Consider race. Everyday racism is widespread but largely hidden, especially to those who are not victimized by it. White dolls are more common in preschools than black dolls. An active African-American boy may be described as "aggressive," while a white boy exhibiting the same behaviors may be described as "spirited." Even without recognizing it, the teacher of a diverse classroom may be more alert to rule violations by black than white children. The examples could be multiplied a hundredfold. While the cumulative effects of such patterns of prejudice and discrimination are weighty, each individual instance seems inconsequential.

Most prejudices at the base of the pyramid have few immediate and obvious negative outcomes. Their cost comes from their cumulative effect and the launching pad they provide for expressions of prejudice at higher levels. Still, even unobserved biases can sometimes explode in tragedy. This may well have been the situation in the Trayvon Martin case. Though no one can get inside George Zimmerman's head as he followed, then shot the unarmed teenager, it is improbable that he was immune to stereotypes that link black male teenagers with crime. Even George Zimmerman may not be aware of his own "fast thinking" about race. The fact that we are becoming an increasingly armed society paves the way for subtle prejudices to be amplified by weapons into disastrous encounters.

Moving up the Pyramid

Stereotypes about blue and pink clothes are at the base of the pyramid. Higher up are stereotypes about intellectual competencies and capacities that channel boys toward math and science and girls toward art and literature. While girls may benefit from learning poetry, there is no poetic justice in this; everyone should have equal access to every field of study. Similarly, racial prejudices at the mid-range of the pyramid are more explicit than those at the base. Stereotypes that claim blacks are "natural" athletes hurt African-Americans in the classroom. In many urban schools, there is a continuous flow of students into the justice system; the school-to-prison pipeline is fueled by stereotypes about "what works" with disadvantaged youth.

I was at a workshop recently where a coach from a predominantly Native American high school recounted how his team often endures humiliating racially charged jeers and gestures by fans of opposing teams. Group dynamics can sometimes whip subtle prejudices into actions higher in the pyramid.

Prejudice against gays and lesbians, though lessening, is still common on middle and senior high school campuses where these youth face frequent social marginalization from their classmates. The tragic fate of 15-year-old Lawrence King illustrates multiple levels of the pyramid (Saillant, 2008). Throughout Lawrence's life students made seemingly innocuous remarks or jokes that expressed prejudice against gay people. Metaphorically standing on their backs, a few carried it further and Lawrence was bullied, the victim of name calling and wet paper towels thrown at his head. Then, one student climbed to the top of the prejudice pyramid. On Feb. 12, 2008, Brandon McInerney, 14, shot Lawrence twice in the head.

Of course, at the pyramid's peak are attitudes and behaviors that are so extreme that they are widely condemned. Rising to this level are the brutal but relatively rare acts of hate groups. Not far below are overt patterns of discrimination in such things as housing, wages, employment, and health care. These clearly remain significant societal problems. But whose responsibility is it to deal with prejudice and discrimination in its various forms?

The Remedy: Legal or Educational?

One last dimension of the pyramid is this: The higher you go in the pyramid, the more the legal system is the appropriate remedy; the lower you go, the more it is the educational system that needs to take responsibility. If housing discrimination is occurring, it should be challenged in court. If women don't receive equal pay for equal work, laws need to be enforced. In states where gay and lesbian couples cannot marry, constitutions need to change.

When you get closer to the base of the pyramid, the remedies are necessarily educational rather than legal. To collapse the whole pyramid, we need to attack it at its base. That is where schools and teachers need to shoulder responsibility.

Unfortunately, educators who desire to tackle the base of the prejudice pyramid may be silenced by the retort, "You're just being PC." Many individuals are so fearful of being accused of political correctness that so-called minor injustices are readily tolerated. "It's not that serious," we say to ourselves. "So what if we refer to 'Muslim terrorists' as if that communicates something valid? So what if we don't confront a student who says, 'that's so gay' in the hallway?" Yet these minor expressions of prejudice are important. Every act at the bottom of the pyramid is shouldering part of the responsibility for those acts residing above.

Concretely, what can educators do? The first step is self-awareness. Despite its many forms, all prejudices work through creating some form of "us/them" dichotomy. A white girl and a Latina girl get in a fight during recess, and the teacher on duty—who just so happens to be white—automatically singles out the Latina as the aggressor. While readers may feel justifiable anger at that teacher, we need to look in the mirror. We all behave similarly. What are the "us/them" divisions in our own thinking? We will never eliminate them completely, but we can make progress.

The second step is to speak up. I'm not suggesting that each expression of everyday prejudice needs to be met with a protracted debate. But silence should not be our default option. Silence endorses. Silence leaves harmful patterns uninterrupted. Speak with humility and grace, but speak up when everyday prejudices are expressed or exhibited.

Hopefully, speaking up can lead to schoolwide dialogue. Spotting prejudices in others is easier than seeing them in ourselves, and an open, honest discussion can be helpful. Dealing with the adult culture of the school is a prerequisite to dealing effectively with students and their peer culture.

Schools with character education programs (Shields, 2011) can integrate prejudice reduction efforts into them since a concern for diversity and social justice are cornerstones of character. Moreover, pedagogical strategies widely used in character education also work well to reduce prejudices. For example, cooperative learning can be effective for both developing character and addressing cultural difference (Johnson & Johnson, 2012). Done right, competition, too, can have its place (Shields & Bredemeier, 2009, 2010). The old "boys against the girls" strategy for creating teams, however, is out. If competition is used, people with diverse backgrounds must be on the same team where they can build bridges.

Finally, take advantage of opportunities to address the plethora of "-isms" when doing so fits within the curriculum. Virtually every subject can be a means to address problems of prejudice and associated patterns of discrimination. If you teach math, discuss the cultural stereotypes that interfere with some students progressing as well as others. If you teach biology, why not challenge the false dualism of male and female? If you teach health and physical education, why not reflect on why there are significant health disparities across racial and ethnic groups or why gay athletes have a hard time coming out? If you teach literature, social studies, or history, the possibilities are nearly endless. Whatever your grade level or subject area, a quick Internet search will reveal an abundance of resources for addressing prejudices and social injustice.

There is much that you can do, and it begins with comprehending the realities captured by the pyramid principle of prejudice.

References

Allport, G., Clark, K., & Pettigrew, T. (1979). *The nature of prejudice: 25th-anniversary edition.* New York, NY: Basic Books.

Anderson, K. (2010). *Benign bigotry: The psychology of subtle prejudice.* Cambridge, MA: Cambridge University Press.

Dalrymple, T. (2007). *In praise of prejudice: The necessity of preconceived ideas.* New York, NY: Encounter Books.

Eckholm, E. (2013, May 23). Boy Scouts end longtime ban on openly gay youths. *New York Times.* www.nytimes.com/2013/05/24/us/boy-scouts-to-admit-openly-gay-youthsas-members.html?_r=0

Evans, J.S. (2009). Dual-processing accounts of reasoning, judgment, and social cognition. *Annual Review of Psychology,* 59, 255–278.

Johnson, D.W. & Johnson, R.T. (2012). Restorative justice in the classroom: Necessary roles of cooperative context, constructive conflict, and civic values. *Negotiation and Conflict Management Research,* 5 (1) 4–28.

Kahneman, D. (2011). *Thinking, fast and slow.* New York, NY: Farrar, Straus, and Giroux.

Pareene, A. (2012, September 18). Mitt Romney, self-made man. *Salon.com.* www.salon.com/2012/09/18/mitt_romney_self_made_man/

Ryan, W. (1971). *Blaming the victim.* New York, NY: Pantheon Books.

Saillant, C. (2008, October 3). Teen accused of killing his gay classmate had white supremacist materials. *Los Angeles Times.* http://articles.latimes.com/2008/oct/03/local/mebriefs3.S4

Shields, D.L. (1986). *Growing beyond prejudices: Overcoming hierarchical dualism.* Mystic, CT: Twenty-third publications.

Shields, D.L. (2011). Character as the aim of education. *Phi Delta Kappan,* 92 (8), 48–53.

Shields, D. & Bredemeier, B. (2010). Competition: Was Kohn right? *Phi Delta Kappan,* 91 (5), 62–67.

Shields, D. & Bredemeier, B. (2009). *True competition: A guide to pursuing excellence in sport and society.* Champaign, IL: Human Kinetics.

Tatum, B.D. (1997). *"Why are all the black kids sitting together in the cafeteria?" And other conversations about race.* New York, NY: Basic Books.

Whitley, B.E. & Kite, M.E. (2010). *The psychology of prejudice and discrimination,* 2nd ed. Belmont, CA: Wadsworth Cengage.

Critical Thinking

1. Explain why prejudice is part of the human condition.

2. Examine the differences between prejudice, discrimination, and the "-isms." Provide at least one example of each that you have witnessed or experienced in public schools.

3. Reflect on what you have learned as you read and discussed this article. What do you think we can or should do to change the minds and hearts of educators, children, and youth who are prejudiced?

Create Central

www.mhhe.com/createcentral

Internet References

National Association for Multicultural Education (NAME)
www.nameorg.org

Safe Schools
http://www.safeschoolscoalition.org/

Teaching Tolerance
http://www.tolerance.org/

What Kids can do
http://whatkidscando.org/

DAVID LIGHT SHIELDS is teacher education program coordinator in the department of social and behavioral sciences, Saint Louis Community College-Meramec, St. Louis, Mo.

The Enduring Influence of School Size and School Climate on Parents' Engagement in the School Community by Lauri Goldkind, et al.

81

Article

Prepared by: Rebecca B. Evers, *Winthrop University*

The Enduring Influence of School Size and School Climate on Parents' Engagement in the School Community

LAURI GOLDKIND AND G. LAWRENCE FARMER

Learning Outcomes

After reading this article, you will be able to:

- Describe the negative effects of school size.
- Explain the factors that influence parental engagement in their child's school.
- Discuss why school size has the greater effect on parental participation.

Introduction

Parental involvement in schools continues to be a critical issue for the stakeholders of the nation's education system (i.e., teachers, parents, educational administrators, policymakers, etc.; Epstein & Jansorn, 2004; Fan & Chen, 2001; Fege, 2000; Lloyd-Smith & Baron, 2010; Teicher, 2007). Parents' involvement as educators in the home, participants on school committees, and advocates for school reform both outside and within the system has been found to have positive impacts both individually, resulting in increased academic performance of the recipient daughter or son, and on the school community as a whole (Fan & Chen, 2001; Green, Walker, Hoover-Dempsey, & Sandler, 2007; Walsh, 2010). For those seeking to promote parental involvement, Hoover-Dempsey and Sandler (1995, 1997) provide a framework which identifies associated factors. In this model, the school environment (school climate), teachers, and children contribute to parents' motivation to be involved (Hoover-Dempsey et al., 2005). The extent to which both the school and their children invite parents and provide opportunities for involvement shapes the nature and extent of involvement (Hoover-Dempsey et al., 2005). The school improvement/reform literature has focused on the school's structure and management practices as important aspects of the school which shape parents' perceptions of the invitations for involvement. School reform models, for example, "Success for All" (Slavin, Karweit, & Madden, 1989) and the Social Development Model (Comer & Haynes, 1991), seek to promote parental involvement by making changes in school governance which will increase the opportunities for parental involvement (Magolda & Ebben, 2007). School reform efforts targeting school size also seek to promote greater student and parental involvement (Hartmann et al., 2009; Semel & Sadovnik, 2008). In the face of these reform efforts, there continues to be a need to better understand how structural aspects of school, for example school size, are related to parents' perception of the extent to which the school welcomes parental involvement.

Literature Review

Hoover-Dempsey and Sandler (1995, 1997), using a psychological framework, view parental involvement as having its beginnings in a set of perceptions parents have about their role as a parent, their self-efficacy within the school domain, and opportunities and invitations for involvement they receive from their child and the school personnel. Perceived opportunities for involvement focus on parent perception of the extent to which the school and their child want them to be involved. While limited, the literature indicates that children's stage of social-cognitive development and approaches to learning are all factors that are associated with the types of invitation for involvement provided to parents (Hoover-Dempsey et al., 2005). The decline in parental involvement that is associated with the transition from middle to senior high school is often attributed to parents' natural response to their child's increasing developmental need for autonomy (Hoover-Dempsey et al., 2005). Aspects of the school environment such as staff attitudes towards parents and numbers of communication attempts to parents have been found to be associated with parental involvement and the nature of the invitations for involvement provided by the school (Lavenda, 2011).

School Size and Academic Progress

The structure and quality of the school environment is believed to play an important role in providing opportunities for student and parental involvement. Large, impersonal, bureaucratic comprehensive schools are believed to present many barriers to involvement (Meier, 1997). Case studies of effective alternative schools provide evidence of the importance of school size in promoting involvement (Wehlage, Rutter, Smith, Lesko, & Fernandez, 1989). Attending small general education secondary schools has been associated with improved student achievement (Cotton, 1996; Darling-Hammond, Ancess, & Ort, 2002; Haller, Monk, & Tien, 1993; Kahne, Sporte, de la Torre, & Easton, 2008). Research has also shown that small schools promote more equitable access to academically demanding courses (Bryk, Lee, & Holland, 1993), more equitable gains in achievement (Darling-Hammond et al., 2002; Lee & Smith, 1995), and lower dropout rates (Darling-Hammond et al., 2002; Kahne et al., 2008; Pittman & Haughwout, 1987).

Gardner, Ritblatt, and Beatty (2000) found that the dropout rate was significantly higher in the larger California public high schools than in small schools. Their finding is consistent with the previous investigations in examining dropout and schools size (Werblow & Duesbery, 2009). The general belief is that in small schools, adolescents develop a sense of belonging, and when young people are part of a small, connected environment, they are less likely to drop out of school (Gardner et al., 2000).

The bonds that young people make with their peers and adults are needed to facilitate the development of social capital which promotes successful school completion (Coleman, 1988). There is evidence that school climate improves when larger schools are converted into smaller ones (Hartmann et al., 2009; Huebner, Corbett, & Phillippo, 2007). In the late 1990s, we witnessed the reorganization of schools around the country focused on reducing the size of schools (Hartmann et al., 2009). By 2001, the Bill and Melinda Gates Foundation had made grant awards totaling approximately 1.7 billion dollars to school districts seeking to create smaller school settings for their students.

School Size and Parental Involvement

Mechanisms by which school structural variables are associated with the behavior of parents and their children have not received a great deal of attention in the literature (Datar & Mason, 2008). Additionally, much of the work examining the association between school size and parental involvement has focused on class size during the primary grades K-3 (Datar & Mason, 2008). Studies of class size provide evidence that, during the primary school years, parental involvement is associated with class size in a complementary and substitutable manner (Bonesrønning, 2004; Walsh, 2010). For example, in the study of Norwegian primary school children, decreases in class size were found to result in increases in parental involvement. In a study of United States middle and senior high school students, increases in school size were associated with decreases in parents' volunteer activities (Walsh, 2010). While the work of Bonesrønning (2003, 2004, 2010) and Walsh (2010) provide insight into the role school size might play on parents' perceptions and their potential involvement in education, more attention to other potential mediators is needed.

School Size and Safety and Respect

Hoover-Dempsey & Sandler's (1995, 1997) model of parental involvement, along with the existing school climate (Hoy & Miskel, 2005) and school violence (Espelage, Bosworth, & Simon, 2000) literature, highlight the role that perceptions of school climate play in shaping students', teachers', and parents' behavior. A comprehensive case study of 14 effective alternative high schools carried out in the latter part of the 1980s provided evidence of the importance of creating a school climate that is respectful of the student's and family's needs as a critical component in facilitating both student and parent involvement which led to improved academic achievement (Wehlage et al., 1989). Motivated in part by an understanding of the importance of creating a safe and respectful learning environment as a contributor to a school's effectiveness, several school reform initiatives that focused on reducing school size in order to create a school climate supportive of high achievement were developed in the early 1990s (Neiman, 2011). Several of the prominent reform efforts include the School District of Philadelphia's "Going Small" initiative (Benson & Borman, 2010) and similar initiatives in the New York City Public Schools and Chicago Public Schools, both funded out of a 1.7 billion dollar fund established by the Bill and Melinda Gates Foundation (Lachat, 2001). The New York City Public Schools have moved through three waves of small-schools-based reforms starting in the 1970s (DiMartino, 2009). A study of the 2006 graduates of

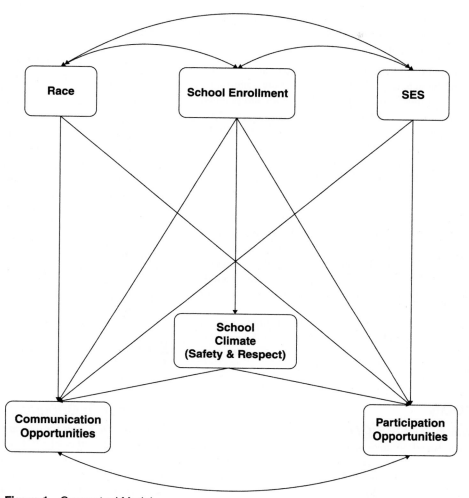

Figure 1 Conceptual Model

14 small schools established in 2002 provided evidence of the potential for these schools to promote safety and respect within the school setting, along with positive academic engagement and performance (Huebner et al., 2007).

Aims of the Present Study

Building on Hoover-Dempsey and Sandler's (1995, 1997) model of parental involvement, this study investigates the potential mediating role that a parent's perception of the extent to which their child's school provides a safe and respectful environment plays in the relationship between school size and perceptions of the invitations for involvement provided by the school. Green et al. (2007) describe invitations for parent participation as schools presenting explicit opportunities to participate via open school nights and parent-teacher conferences, as well as implicit environments that encourage participation, such as parent literature written in accessible language, welcoming greetings when parents are dropping students off at school, and otherwise creating a climate where parents can be comfortable helping students to assimilate into the school culture.

This study sought to determine if parents' perceptions of the school climate in the areas of safety and respect mediates the relationship between the enrollment size of a school and parents' perceptions of the degree to which the school provides opportunities for involvement (i.e., opportunities for communication and participation in school activities). An analysis of secondary data from the New York City Department of Education's Learning Environment Survey (LES), completed by parents in the Spring of 2008 was used to examine the study's mediation hypothesis. Figure 1 diagrams the hypothesized relationships among enrollment, school climate, and parental involvement that will be examined in this study. The following hypotheses will be tested:

H1: Enrollment size is directly related to parents' perceptions of the extent to which schools provide opportunities for communication between the school and parents.

H2: Enrollment size is directly related to parents' perceptions of the extent to which schools provide opportunities for parents to participate in school activities.

H3: Safety and Respect are directly related to parents' perceptions of the extent to which schools provide opportunities for communication between the school and parents.

H4: Safety and Respect are directly related to parents' perceptions of the extent to which schools provide opportunities for parents to participate in school activities.

H5: Safety and Respect mediate the relationship between enrollment size and parents' perceptions of the extent to which schools provide opportunities for communication between the school and parents.

H6: Safety and Respect mediate the relationship between enrollment size and parents' perceptions of the extent to which schools provide opportunities for parents to participate in school activities.

Methods
Sample and Design

This study is based on an analysis of secondary data from the 2008 parents' version of the annual New York City Department of Education's Learning Environment Survey (LES). First implemented in 2007, the LES is the largest survey of its kind in the U.S. and asks all 1.5 million public school parents, teachers, and 6th- through 12th-grade students about a variety of topics related to the quality of their school experience (Nathanson et al., 2013) The units of analysis in this study are schools, in particular, middle and senior high schools. Those schools providing services primarily to special education youth or other alternative educational programming, for example, schools designed to transition youth from the juvenile justice system back into the general education program, were excluded from this study. Schools of special emphases, for example, magnet and charter schools, were included in the analysis only if they serviced middle and senior high school students and were not primarily serving a special education population. For the purposes of this study, only general education middle and senior high schools with parent response rates of 30% or higher were included. This response rate cutoff was set in order to insure that each school had an adequate representation of their parents in the sample. Approximately 70% of the middle and senior high schools surveyed had parental response rates of 30% or higher.

Certainly, the use of a cutoff score like 30% raises the question of whether the "included" schools, that is, the schools with parental participation rates greater than or equal to 30%, differ from schools which have lower participation rates (i.e., the "excluded" schools). For two variables, the proportion of students receiving a free or reduced fee lunch and the proportion of students who were Black or Latino, both of which were available for the study sample and the population of schools from which the sample was drawn, negligible differences were found between the distributions of the included and excluded schools (details available upon request from the first author).

We have reason to believe that a response rate of approximately 30% is typical for a survey of this type. For example, The Fort Worth Independent School District's 2011–2012 Parent Survey report indicates a response rate of 28.3%, an actual decrease of three percentage points from the prior year's survey (Morrissey & Yuan, 2012). The Los Angeles Unified School District's average parent response rate in 2012 was only 18% (LAUSD, 2012).

Endogenous Variables

Two areas of invitations for involvement were assessed by the survey: Participation and Communication Opportunities.

Participation Opportunities

All composite scores for the various subscales used in this study were created by the school district. Individual parent responses were not made available to the researchers. All composite scores were based on an average of the parents' responses for each school. Eight items were used to assess parents' perceptions of the extent to which, over the recent academic year, the school encouraged caregiver participation either by inviting them to a school function or by designing school activities in a manner that would facilitate caregiver participation. Some of the items asked about attitudes; others asked about the frequency of specific behaviors. Example items included: "My child's school makes it easy for parents to attend meetings by holding them at different times of day, providing an interpreter, or in other ways." and "I feel welcome in my child's school." Parents responded to items like this one using a rating scale that ranged from 0 "Strongly Disagree" to 10 "Strongly Agree." Items asking about frequency of specific behaviors included the following example: "How often during this school year have you been invited to a workshop, program, performance, or other event at your child's school?" Parents responded to items like this one using a rating scale that ranged from 0 "Never" to 10 "More than once a month." The average rating for the eight items was used to create the composite score for the subscale.

The secondary data set available for analysis only contained the school-wide composite score of the measures. Higher composite scores indicated that parents at the school perceived that the school provided more opportunities for participation in school activities. Thus, the unit of analysis was the school, not individual parents.

Communication Opportunities

As was the case with the Participation Opportunity measure, individual items were not made available, and the unit of analysis was the school. The Communication Opportunities subscale on the survey measured a parent's perception of the extent to which the school provided opportunities for the parent to communicate with school personnel about their child's academic progress and behavior. This subscale consists of 10 items. Example items included: "The school keeps me informed about my child's academic progress." and "The school contacts me when my child breaks school rules." High scores indicated parents' agreement with the idea that the school provided information about its educational goals and offered appropriate feedback on each student's learning outcomes. Parents responded to items using a rating scale that ranged from 0 "Strongly Disagree" to 10 "Strongly Agree." The data set available for secondary analysis only contained the composite measures. Higher composite scores indicated that parents at the school perceived that the school provided more opportunities for communication with parents about their children's progress in school.

Exogenous Variables
Student Race/Ethnicity

For the purpose of this paper, student race/ethnicity has been operationalized as the proportion of each school which is Black and/or Latino.

Student Socioeconomic Status

School socioeconomic status (SES) is operationalized as the proportion of the students in each school receiving a free lunch.

Enrollment

Enrollment size (or enrollment) refers to the total number of students on a schools official roster. This variable is reported annually.

Mediator Variable: Safety and Respect

The subscale Safety and Respect assessed parents' perceptions of the extent to which the school worked to develop a school environment focused on keeping individuals free from physical or emotional harm. Ten items made up this subscale on the parents' survey. Parents responded to the items using a ten-point rating scale. Example items included: "My child

is safe at school," and "Discipline is fairly enforced." Parents responded to items like these using a rating scale that ranged from 0 "Strongly Disagree" to 10 "Strongly Agree." The school district recoded negatively worded items when appropriate (e.g., "School staff are disrespectful to students."). High scores indicated perceptions of a positive school climate. The data set available for secondary analysis only contained the composite of the measures; the average rating for the ten items was used to create the composite score for the subscale.

Analysis Strategy

Descriptive analysis will be reported below. Figure 1 provides the conceptual model that will be estimated to evaluate the study's hypotheses. The path analysis model will be estimated using full-information maximum likelihood in Mplus 7.0. The bootstrapped-t method (Dang et al., 2011) will be used to estimate the significance of the indirect effects. Estimation of the statistical significance of the indirect effect using the bootstrapped-t method has been shown to be more robust than other methods, for example, the Sobel test (Sasser & Bierman, 2011).

Results
School Characteristics

Table 1 contains the descriptive statistics for the schools that participated in the study. A total of 545 (73%) of the 727 possible schools were included in the sample. Of the schools included, 42.7% were middle schools (grades 6–8), 9.7% were middle-senior high schools (grades 6–12), and 47.6% were senior high schools (grades 9–12). Approximately 30% of the total population that met the selection criteria for this study was excluded from the analysis because their response rates dropped below 30%. The middle-only schools declined by 40%, the middle-senior high schools declined by approximately 29%, and the senior high schools-only schools by approximately 18%. The schools ranged in size from new charter schools with enrollments under 50 to large, traditional high schools with enrollments above 4,900. Lastly, all five boroughs of New York City were represented in the sample in a manner that was not markedly different from the representation in the population.

Table 2 contains the product moment correlation matrix along with the means and standard deviations for the study variables. There were approximately 2.5% of missing data. Following a set of procedures outlined by Mertler and Vannatta (2010), distributions of the variables were examined visually with boxplots and bivariate graphs, and a Kolmogorov-Smirnov test was carried out. With the exception of enrollment, there was no evidence of any serious violation of the normality or linearity assumptions. Following the recommendations of Mertler and Vannatta (2010), extreme outliers, variables with

Table 1 2008 Survey Data: Sample Characteristics

	Percentages	
	Sample (N = 545)	Total Population (N = 747)
School Type		
Middle	42.7	49.7
Middle/Senior High	9.7	9.6
Senior High	47.6	40.7
Enrollment Size (total student enrollment)		
42–200	14.6	13.4
201–400	30.0	29.0
401–600	29.3	27.0
601–800	6.5	7.2
801–1000	6.5	6.6
1001–1200	4.9	4.7
1201+	8.2	12.0
Borough		
Bronx	27.4	26.8
Brooklyn	29.5	31.6
Queens	14.8	15.3
Manhattan	24.4	23.4
Staten Island	3.9	2.9

z-score greater than +3 or less than −3, were recoded to the highest values. School enrollment ranged from 42 to 4,944 with a mean of approximately 590. The natural log of the enrollment was taken to reduce skew. There were significant associations among enrollment and the other study variables. In all cases, higher enrollment was negatively associated with parents' perceptions of safety and respect, invitations for engagement, and communication. Also, there were positive associations among safety and respect, invitations for engagement, and communication.

Study Hypotheses Results

H1: Enrollment size is directly related to parents' perception of the extent to which schools provide opportunities for communication between the school and parents.

H2: Enrollment size is directly related to parents' perceptions of the extent to which schools provide opportunities for parents to participate in school activities.

Hypotheses 1 (H1) and 2 (H2) state that enrollment size will be directly related to both the parents' perceptions of participation and communication opportunities. These hypotheses were tested in the context of a "direct (total) effects only" path model (Figure 2) which also included percent Black/Latino and percent receiving a free school lunch as confounders. The direct effect of school enrollment on communication ($\beta_{\text{enrollment size} \rightarrow \text{Communication}} = -.20$, $p < .05$) and on participation ($\beta_{\text{enrollment size} \rightarrow \text{Participation}} = -.15$, $p < .05$) are, as expected, inversely and significantly related to both outcomes. In substantive terms, parents in larger schools report fewer opportunities for both communication and participation with the adults responsible for educating their children. Given that both direct effects are statistically significant, we move on to consider the role of school climate as a potential mediator of these direct effects.

H3: Safety and Respect is directly related to parents' perceptions of the extent to which schools provide opportunities for communication between the school and parents.

H4: Safety and Respect is directly related to parents' perceptions of the extent to which schools provide opportunities for parents to participate in school activities.

Parents' perceptions of the extent to which the school environment is both physically and emotionally safe for their children

Table 2 Variables Intercorrelations, Means, and Standard Deviations

Variables	1	2	3	4	5	6
1. Communication	—					
2. Participation	.09	—				
3. School Climate	.80	.80	—			
4. Enrollment	−.27	−.19	−.27	—		
5. Student Race	.26	.16	.02	−.31	—	
6. Socioeconomic Status	.17	.08	.05	−.22	.67	—
Mean (Standard Deviation)	7.74 (.53)	7.65 (.48)	8.32 (.55)	67.53 (71.94)	78.91 (26.13)	76.28 (18.25)

Note: All correlations were significant at the $p < .01$ level.

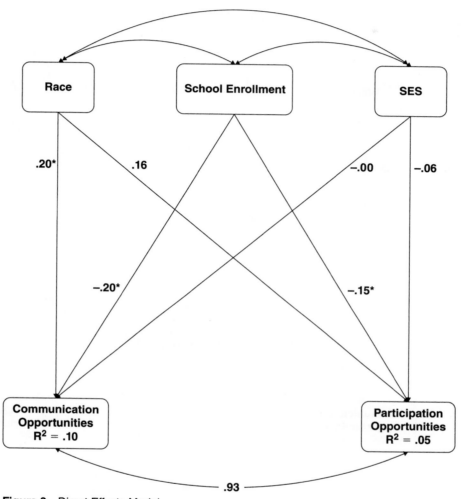

Figure 2 Direct Effects Model

are, as hypothesized, positively associated with parents' perceptions of the opportunities the school provides for both communication and participation in the school ($\beta_{\text{Safety \& Respect} \rightarrow \text{Communication}}$ = .80, $p < .05$; $\beta_{\text{Safety \& Respect} \rightarrow \text{Participation}}$ = .82, $p < .05$).

> H5: Safety and Respect mediates the relationship between enrollment size and parents' perceptions of the extent to which schools provide opportunities for communication between the school and parents.
>
> H6: Safety and Respect mediates the relationship between enrollment size and parents' perceptions of the extent to which schools provide opportunities for parents to participate in school activities.

Hypotheses 5 and 6 are necessarily considered in the context of an augmented path model in which the presumptive mediator,

Safety and Respect, is now included as an additional endogenous variable. As seen in Figure 3, and in marked contrast to their counterparts in Figure 2, the direct effect of school enrollment on communication($\beta_{\text{enrollment size} \rightarrow \text{Communication}}$ = .03, $p > .05$) and the direct effect of school enrollment on participation ($\beta_{\text{enrollment size} \rightarrow \text{Participation}}$ = .09, $p < .05$) are noticeably smaller than the direct effects of school enrollment on communication and participation in the direct effects model and as shown in Figure 2 (i.e., −.20, $p < .05$ and −.15, $p < .05$).

Summary

There is evidence that the negative relationships between enrollment size, communication, and participation opportunities are mediated through a parent's perception of the extent to which the school environment is both physically and emotionally safe for

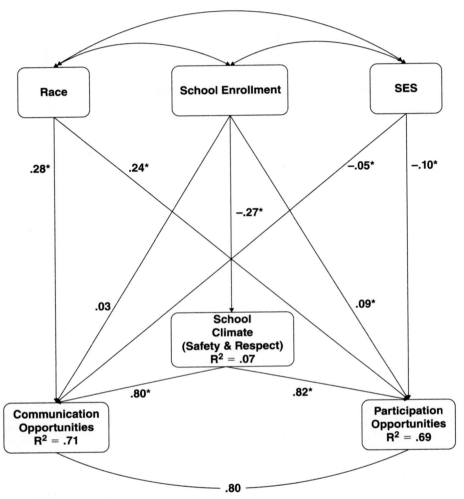

Figure 3 Path Model Direct and Indirect Effects

the child. However, the extent to which this is the case varies by outcome. Specifically, the association between school enrollment (i.e., school size) on communication opportunities is completely mediated by safety and respect, whereas most, but not all, of the association of school size on participation opportunities is so mediated. That is to say, the association of school size on participation is partially mediated by school size. For both outcome variables, the mediated effect was larger than the direct effect, especially the indirect effect of school size on communication opportunities. (IE = $-.21$, .95 CI $(-.30, -.13)$ is the product of the direct effect of school size on school climate ($\beta = -.267, p < .05$) and the direct effect of school climate on communication opportunities ($\beta = .80, p < .05$). With regard to participation opportunities, the indirect effect (IE = $-.22$, .95 CI $(-.31, -.13)$ is the product of the direct effect of school size on school climate ($\beta = -.267, p < .05$) and

the direct effect of school climate on participation opportunities ($\beta = .82, p < .05$).

Discussion

Maximizing parental participation in the school community is a critical objective of various school reform initiatives. This study represents an initial attempt to test the role of school climate as a mechanism which may facilitate parental perceptions of the opportunities provided by the school for parental participation. Smaller schools have been found to be more effective in providing opportunities for parental participation than larger schools (Walsh, 2010). For example, smaller schools, precisely because they are smaller, have been able to emphasize relationships among their stakeholders, for example, prioritizing school-parent relationships, which in turn promote parental participation and ultimately enhance academic achievement.

This investigation has identified the importance of two aspects of school climate, specifically, the safety which characterizes the school environment and the respect shown by the members of the school community to one another. We argue that school climate is an important "conduit" potentially influencing the effect of school size on both communication and participation opportunities for parents. We have tested this claim by developing a path analysis model which empirically evaluates whether and, if so, to what extent, data collected from the parents in the largest school system in the United States can be said to support this claim. Our findings indicate that schools of different sizes report corresponding differences in the safety and respect which can be said to characterize them. These safety and respect differences, in turn, seem to affect the levels of parental engagement in these schools. In more substantive terms, our findings indicate that larger schools are generally characterized by less safety and less respect, and this type of school climate suppresses the level of communication and opportunities for involvement as perceived by parents of students in these schools.

Needless to state, this is not a welcome state of affairs. It would be useful and important to identify factors in the school environment which might buffer or mitigate the negative impact of school size on school involvement transmitted via the climate of unease that often characterizes our larger schools. Identifying these potential moderators of this indirect effect of school size on parental involvement would seem to be the logical next step. In addition, there are almost certainly other mediators of the causal process by which school size affects school involvement.

Aside from the identification of additional factors which would enhance our ability to better explain parental involvement, we also recognize that we have estimated an aggregate model, that is, a model in which the unit of analysis is the school; therefore, our conclusions can only be said to characterize schools per se. This type of model, while appropriate for this purpose (i.e., characterizing schools), eliminates the individual variability among the parents in these schools.

It would be a useful complement to this study to be able to test our model using the individual parents as the units of analysis. Finally, it should be understood that explaining parental involvement is really an intermediate step toward developing a more comprehensive understanding of how school size affects academic achievement, the ultimate purpose for which schools exist.

Limitations

While the findings indicate evidence of school climate serving as a mediator of parents' communication and participation, several limitations exist within the study. These constraints include making use of secondary data sources, relying on a self-selected group of respondents, possible socially desirable responding, reliance on the subjective perceptions of the conditions in the schools rather than on objective measurements of them, and, perhaps most importantly, using correlational data to draw "causal" inferences. In addition, it should be understood that the units of analysis are schools, not the individual parents whose children attend these schools. That is to say, the analyses are analyses of the perceptions of these parents aggregated to the school level.

Mahoe (2004) describes some of the disadvantages of using secondary data. She cautions that one major disadvantage of using secondary data sets is a lack of access to the instruments used to originally collect data. Frequently, the researchers did not design these instruments, and their original intent may have been to achieve different goals (Cowton, 1998; Mahoe, 2004). In addition, DunIsmuir and Williams (1990) suggested that the biases and potential inaccuracies are impossible to check. A question of note in the literature arises around whether or not data can be separated from the mechanisms of data collection and the context in which the data were collected (Cowton, 1998; Dunsmuir & Williams, 1990).

The survey data that the authors utilized comprises the responses of over 1.5 million parents and students. It is likely that several groups of parents are either underrepresented or not reflected at all in the results. For example, a parent experiencing disenfranchisement with the school system or conflicts with their child's school will likely not have completed a survey on behalf of the Department of Education. Similarly, parents who are new to the country or for whom English is not their primary language may not have participated in the survey due to perceived cultural biases or inhibitors. Even among those schools whose parents did elect to participate in the survey, 30% were excluded from the study sample because their response rates were below 30%. However, it should be noted that the discrepancies between the study sample and the population of schools is fairly minimal, at least with regard to the variables available for inclusion in this comparison.

In addition, the possibility of socially desirable responding should be acknowledged to the extent that parents are "invested" in seeing their children's schools as more than adequate for the purpose of educating them. In a related vein, the study relies upon the parents' subjective perceptions of the availability of opportunities for communication and participation, whether or not they are affected by socially desirable responding. These should not be confused with or for objective measurements of these same opportunities. Still, it may well be the case that the parents' subjective perceptions of opportunities for communication and participation are no less relevant or "real," at least to them, than objective measurements of these same phenomena.

Finally, and perhaps most importantly, the correlational, cross-sectional design of the Department of Education's

Learning Environment Surveys limit the explanatory power of the findings reported herein. It should be clearly understood that observational studies do not and cannot provide a rigorous evaluation of causal claims. Only a true experimental design can provide the imprimatur for such claims.

Areas of Future Inquiry

One of the claims of the small schools movement is that small school environments lead to increased academic achievement outcomes, a more positive school climate, and decreased incidents of suspension and expulsion. Further testing of the models described in this paper will include the addition of academic achievement indicators such as attendance rates, standardized test performance including middle grade state exams and high school level Regents exams, as well as suspension rates. If the small school proponents are to be believed, then we would expect to see the positive indirect effect of school climate on academic achievement indicators.

Also bearing investigation are the individual demographic factors that may impact how parents, guardians, and students experience school climate, engagement, and communication. Many scholars have documented the achievement gap that exists between children of color and White youth. Latino and African American children are far more likely to experience school failure than are White children. Analysis of desegregated data of the National Assessment of Educational Performance (Campbell, Reese, O'Sullivan, & Dossey, 1996; Ladson-Billings, 2006; Lubienski, 2002) illustrate the large gap between the performance of White children and their Latino and African American counterparts (Campbell et al., 1996). There is a strong possibility that families with children of color may experience home-school communication, school climate, and opportunities for participation differently than White families.

Conclusion

School reform movements in major urban areas nationwide have invested millions of dollars to try and implement new policies, create new schools, and reconfigure existing schools in the service of increasing the academic achievement of young people. One essential element that has been found to enhance academic performance is parent involvement. This study's models suggest that school climate and the dimensions of perceived safety and respect are important conditions for parents to actualize their invitations to participate in the school community and to maximize communication opportunities. With a national wave of policymaking focusing on the creation of and benefits imparted by smaller schools, it is more important than ever to understand the impacts of enrollment on a school's climate and culture and how those create more engaging environments for

students and their families. While brick and mortar issues such as the sizes and shapes of existing structures may lend themselves to creative rearrangements, small schools, academies, and houses within larger schools and other configurations of learning environments have become a fixed part of the public education landscape. Policymakers and practitioners must partner with researchers to understand the impacts of these new learning environments on students' academic performance and on family engagement. This article is a beginning attempt to understand the role of school size, school climate, and parents perceptions of invitations to participate in their children's education.

References

Benson, J., & Borman, G. (2010). Family, neighborhood, and school settings across seasons: When do socioeconomic context and racial composition matter for the reading achievement growth of young children? *Teachers College Record, 112* (5), 1338–1390.

Bonesrønning, H. (2003). Class size effects on student achievement in Norway: Patterns and explanations. *Southern Economic Journal, 69* (4), 952–969.

Bonesrønning, H. (2004). The determinants of parental effort in education production: Do parents respond to changes in class size? *Economics of Education Review, 23* (1), 1–9. Retrieved from http://www.sciencedirect.com/science/journal/02727757/23/1

Bonesrønning, H. (2010). Are parental effort allocations biased by gender? *Education Economics, 18* (3), 253–268. doi:10.1080/09645290902843514

Bryk, A. S., Lee, V. E., & Holland, P. B. (1993). *Catholic schools and the common good.* Cambridge, MA: Harvard University Press.

Campbell, J. R., Reese, C. M., O'Sullivan, C., & Dossey, J. A. (1996). *NAEP 1994 trends in academic progress.* Retrieved from http://nces.ed.gov/nationsreportcard/pubs/main1994/97095.asp

Coleman, J. S. (1988). Social capital in the creation of human capital. *American Journal of Sociology, 94* (supplemental), 95–120.

Comer, J. P., & Haynes, N. M. (1991). Parent involvement in schools: An ecological approach. *Elementary School Journal, 91* (3), 271–277.

Cotton, K. (1996). Affective and social benefits of small-scale schooling. *ERIC Digest.* Charleston, WV: ERIC Clearinghouse on Rural Education and Small Schools.

Cowton, C. J. (1998). The use of secondary data in business ethics research. *Journal of Business Ethics, 17,* 423–434.

Dang, T. T., Farkas, G., Burchinal, M. R., Duncan, G. J., Vandell, D. L., Li, W., . . . Howes, C. (2011). *Preschool center quality and school readiness: Quality main effects and variation by demographic and child characteristics.* Evanston, IL: Society for Research on Educational Effectiveness.

Darling-Hammond, L., Ancess, J., & Ort, S. W. (2002). Reinventing high school: Outcomes of the coalition campus schools project. *American Educational Research Journal, 39* (2), 639–673.

The Enduring Influence of School Size and School Climate on Parents' Engagement in the School Community by Lauri Goldkind, et al.

91

Datar, A., & Mason, B. (2008). Do reductions in class size "crowd out" parental investment in education? *Economics of Education Review, 27* (6), 712–723.

DiMartino, C. (2009, April 13–17). *Redefining leadership: Public and private partnerships in the new small schools movement.* Paper presented at the Annual Meeting of the American Education Research Association, San Diego, CA.

Dunsmuir, A., & Williams, L. (1990). *How to do social research: Sociology in action.* Glasgow, UK: Collins Educational Publishing.

Epstein, J. L., & Jansorn, N. R. (2004). School, family, and community partnerships link the plan: A program of partnerships linked to school improvement plans. *Education Digest, 69* (6), 19–23.

Espelage, D. L., Bosworth, K., & Simon, T. R. (2000). Examining the social context of bullying behaviors in early adolescence. *Journal of Counseling & Development, 78* (3), 326–333.

Fan, X., & Chen, M. (2001). Parental involvement and students' academic achievement: A meta-analysis. *Educational Psychology Review, 13* (1), 1–22. doi:10.1023/a:1009048817385

Fege, A. F. (2000). From fundraising to hell raising: New roles for parents. *Educational Leadership, 57* (7), 39–43.

Gardner, P. W., Ritblatt, S. N., & Beatty, J. R. (2000). Academic achievement and parental school involvement as a function of high school size. *The High School Journal, 83* (2), 21–27.

Green, C. L., Walker, J. M. T., Hoover-Dempsey, K. V., & Sandler, H. M. (2007). Parents' motivations for involvement in children's education: An empirical test of a theoretical model of parent involvement. *Journal of Educational Psychology, 99* (3), 532–544.

Haller, E. J., Monk, D. H., & Tien, L. T. (1993). Small schools and higher-order thinking skills. *Journal of Research in Rural Education, 9* (2), 66–73.

Hartmann, T., Reumann-Moore, R., Evans, S. A., Haxton, C., Maluk, H., &Neild, R. C. (2009). *Going small: Progress and challenges of Philadelphia's small high schools.* Philadelphia, PA: Research for Action.

Hoover-Dempsey, K. V., & Sandler, H. M. (1995). Parental involvement in children's education: Why does it make a difference? *Teachers College Record, 97* (2), 310–331.

Hoover-Dempsey, K. V., & Sandler, H. M. (1997). Why do parents become involved in their children's education? *Review of Educational Research, 67* (1), 3–42.

Hoover-Dempsey, K. V., Walker, J. M. T., Sandler, H. M., Whetsel, D., Green, C. L., Wilkins, A. S., &Closson, K. (2005). Why do parents become involved? Research findings and implications. *The Elementary School Journal, 106* (2), 105–130.

Hoy, W. K., &Miskel, C. G. (2005). *Educational leadership and reform.* Greenwich, CT: Information Age.

Huebner, T., Corbett, G. C., &Phillippo, K. (2007). *Rethinking high school: Inaugural graduations at New York City's new high schools.* New York, NY: New York City Public Schools.

Kahne, J. E., Sporte, S. E., de la Torre, M., & Easton, J. Q. (2008). Small high schools on a larger scale: The impact of school conversions in Chicago. *Educational Evaluation and Policy Analysis, 30* (3), 281–315.

Lachat, M. A. (2001). *Data-driven high school reform.* Providence, RI: The Education Alliance.

Ladson-Billings, G. (2006). From the achievement gap to the education debt: Understanding achievement in U.S. schools. *Educational Researcher, 35* (7), 3–12.

Lavenda, O. (2011). Parental involvement in school: A test of Hoover-Dempsey and Sandler's model among Jewish and Arab parents in Israel. *Children and Youth Services Review, 33* (6), 927–935. doi:10.1016/j.childyouth.2010.12.016

Lee, V., & Smith, J. (1997). High school size: Which works best and for whom? *Educational Evaluation and Policy Analysis, 19,* 205–227.

Lloyd-Smith, L., & Baron, M. (2010). Beyond conferences: Attitudes of high school administrators. *School Community Journal, 20* (2), 23–71. Retrieved from http://www.schoolcommunitynetwork.org/SCJ.aspx

Los Angeles Unified School District (LAUSD). (2012). *Results of the 2012 School Experience Survey: LAUSD high schools.* Los Angeles, CA: Author. Retrieved from http://reportcardsurvey.lausd.net/surveys/getpdf?language=EN&grade_level=HIGHSCHOOL&school_name=&school_code=&location=LAUSD&school_year=2012&district=&prop=TCIBCfwDEq8ZVcVy%2B845cpt9NdNIwJRFLFVlTtUSwE08kvgrEG2z2xuN%2FAlpeQIdjPnhsq6V%2BXrF%0D%0Aq28UDVx4Gb9XSkg5tA7%2FebzJg39zN6ZUl4jbPiwaxkq5VPCtU5%2BiHWX7GMJPQvvRh9GSjjOkC9Nj%0D%0AbndzEFMoJ1HZWZcCm8RM0v3c8vqsRg%3D%3D

Lubienski, S. T. (2002). A closer look at Black-White mathematics gaps: Intersections of race and SES in NAEP achievement and instructional practices data. *The Journal of Negro Education, 71* (4), 269–287.

Magolda, P., &Ebben, K. (2007). From schools to community learning centers: A program evaluation of a school reform process. *Evaluation and Program Planning, 30* (4), 351–363.

Mahoe, R. (2004). The doctorate in education. *Educational Perspectives, 37* (2), 34–38.

Meier, D. W. (1997). Can the odds be changed? *Educational Policy, 11* (2), 194–208.

Mertler, C. A., &Vannatta, R. A. (2010). *Advanced and multivariate statistical methods: Practical application and interpretation* (4th ed.). Los Angeles, CA: Pyrczak Publishing.

Morrissey, G. E., & Yuan, W. H. (2012). *2011–2012 Parent Survey Report.* Fort Worth, TX: Fort Worth Independent School District. Retrieved from http://www.fwisd.org/adq/Documents/Final Report Parent Survey_2011–2012.pdf

Nathanson, L., Kemple, J., Gold, T., Brand, J., Baker-Smith, C., & McCormick, M. (2013, March). *Developing measures of effective learning environments from the New York City school surveys.* Society for Research on Educational Effectiveness Conference, Washington, ID. Retrieved from http://steinhardt.nyu.edu/research_alliance/research/projects/CriticalLearningEnvironmentFactorsForHighSchools

Neiman, S. (2011). *Crime, violence, discipline, and safety in U.S. public schools: Findings from the school survey on crime and safety: 2009-10* (NCES 2011–320). U.S. Department of Education, National Center for Education Statistics. Washington, DC: U.S. Government Printing Office.

Pittman, R. B., &Haughwout, P. (1987). Influence of high school size on dropout rate. *Educational Evaluation and Policy Analysis, 9* (4), 337–343.

Sasser, T., &Bierman, K. (2011). *Inattention and impulsivity: Differential impact on school readiness capacities.* Evanston, IL: Society for Research on Educational Effectiveness.

Semel, S. F., &Sadovnik, A. R. (2008). The contemporary small-school movement: Lessons from the history of progressive education. *Teachers College Record, 110* (9), 1744–1771.

Slavin, R. E., Karweit, N. L., & Madden, N. A. (Eds.). (1989). Effective programs for students at risk. Boston, MA: Allyn & Bacon.

Teicher, S. (2007, February 15). Schools strive for "no parent leftbehind." *Christian Science Monitor.* Retrieved from http://www.csmonitor.com/2007/0215/p13s02-legn.htm

Walsh, P. (2010). Is parental involvement lower at larger schools? *Economics of Education Review, 29* (6), 959–970.

Wehlage, G., Rutter, R. A., Smith, A. S., Lesko, N., & Fernandez, R. R. (1989). *Reducing the risk: Schools as communities of support.* New York, NY: The Falmer Press.

Werblow, J., &Duesbery, L. (2009). The impact of high school size on math achievement and dropout rate. *High School Journal, 92* (3), 14–23.

Critical Thinking

1. In a bulleted list, summarize the results of this study.

2. Based on this study what actions should school administrators, teachers, and parents take to increase parent engagement?

3. Write 1–3 research questions that remain unanswered or that address the limitations of this study.

Create Central

www.mhhe.com/createcentral

Internet References

Coalition of Essential Schools
www.essentialschools.org

Office of Safe and Drug-Free Schools
http://www2.ed.gov/about/offices/list/osdfs/index.html

What Kids Can Do
http://www.whatkidscando.org/

LAURI GOLDKIND is an assistant professor in the Graduate School of Social Service at Fordham University. She has a deep commitment to social justice and a keen interest in work that focuses on creating equity and equal opportunities for urban youth from underresourced communities. Prior to joining the faculty at Fordham, she held numerous positions in youth development and juvenile justice organizations in New York City. Dr. Goldkind's current research work centers on the intersection of the juvenile justice and public education system's impact on urban youth. **G. LAWRENCE FARMER** is an associate professor in the Graduate School of Social Service at Fordham University. Prior to joining Fordham in 2005, he held several positions in the Dade County, Florida public school system including serving as a school social worker and a district assessment coordinator. His scholarly work focuses on understanding those personal factors (i.e., educational expectations and future orientation interests), family factors (i.e., parental educational expectations and parental involvement), and institutional and environmental factors (i.e., school safety and access to social capital) that impact youth's ability to adopt and employ those values and behaviors that will allow them to succeed in primary and secondary educational settings. His current research interests include school social work practice, youth risk and resiliency, and quantitative research methods.

Lauri Goldkind and G. Lawrence Farmer, *The Enduring Influence of School Size and School Climate on Parents' Engagement in the School Community,* School Community Journal, 2013, pp. 223–243. Copyright © 2013 by the Academic Development Institute. All rights reserved. Used with permission.

Article

Prepared by: Rebecca B. Evers, *Winthrop University*

Creating a Climate *for* Achievement

To turn around achievement at this Title I school, teachers collaborated to enhance both academic and social-emotional learning.

DEBORAH D. BRENNAN

Learning Outcomes

After reading this article, you will be able to:

- Explain how the three tiered Response to Invention helped turn around a Title I school.

- Use practical suggestions for improving a school's climate.

Four years ago, I was the first principal of a new Title 1 school in Round Rock, Texas. My excitement at this opportunity was tempered when I studied the assessment results for the incoming students. Nearly 300 of the approximately 850 students entering Robert P. Hernandez Middle School had failed the state assessment in reading. Even more had failed in math.

Clearly, the reality for our student population didn't resemble that of the traditional Response to Intervention pyramid, in which 75–85 percent of a school's students flourish with Tier 1 instruction (the instruction and preventive strategies all students receive). We needed to immediately strengthen our Tier 1 instruction while providing Tier 2 help—academic intervention and supports—for a large group, a tall order in itself.

I realized, however, that it wasn't only academic support Hernandez students needed to thrive; they also needed social-emotional skills that would enable them to learn. Many students who'd been forced to transfer to Hernandez were upset at the loss of friends. Our first year, behavior problems threatened to derail plans for improved instruction. Fights in the girls' bathroom broke toilets and sinks, graffiti tagged the school, and groups wore certain colors to show allegiance with gangs. Student divisions often appeared to be based on race.

The first order of the day for tackling both academic and behavioral challenges was to collaborate to strengthen our instruction and relationships within the school.

Strengthening Our Academics

Staff development was a big part of innovating instruction in the first two years of the school. Our staff studied Robert Marzano's *Art and Science of Teaching* (ASCD, 2007) and John Hattie's *Visible Learning* (Routledge, 2008) and chose to try these high-yield strategies: clearly articulated learning goals aligned with our state's standards, formative assessment, tracking of student learning, and targeted interventions on the basis of student data. I broke down the research into three steps toward improving academics.

1. *Setting—and Sharing—Learning Goals*

   We needed to set learning goals together, to help our instruction match the thinking level the standards required. So our school schedule maximized planning time for course-alike teachers. Teachers met weekly as subject-matter departments (grades 6–8) and daily as content-alike teams during one of their planning periods.

   In these meetings, teachers discussed the kind of student work they'd accept as evidence of mastery. They planned units to ensure that instruction included all standards, was aligned across grades, and would lead to mastery of each standard at the right level of rigor. An instructional coach attended planning meetings and guided this work.

Teachers designed graphic organizers of unit standards to create a map of the intended learning. Each classroom teacher posted these organizers (plus daily learning targets) and referred to them during instruction. They discussed with students how classroom learning activities supported each goal, emphasizing the relevance and real-world connection of the learning.

2. *Creating Assessments and Tracking Learning*

As part of creating common summative assessments, teachers discussed how to assess each standard in a way that would yield reliable data about learning. They asked questions like, Is there sufficient evidence that a standard has been mastered? Does the test question match the rigor of the standard?[1] Schoolwide, we talked about formative assessment. I provided resources for such assessment, like clickers, and teachers began checking for understanding often to catch students before they failed a unit test.

After each teacher-created summative assessment and district-created benchmark test, we disaggregated assessment results by student sub-populations and by the standard assessed. Doing this after teacher-created tests was especially powerful. Teachers together analyzed results, reflected on their instruction, and improved it on the basis of what assessment data showed.

We also helped students track their own progress. As more departments adopted the graphic unit organizer, teachers had students use them to track their individual formative and summative assessment results. In science classes, students tracked their own progress in mastering standards by tracking scores on each assessment in their class notebook.

3. *Intervening Early*

Hernandez students weren't allowed to fail. We committed to filling students' learning gaps rather than moving through the curriculum and leaving students behind. Although teachers weren't required to reteach and retest content or standards that a group of learners had missed, doing so became the norm. Reteaching happened through before- and after-school tutorials, with all our dedicated teachers pitching in. Tutorials focused on particular standards. Students who hadn't demonstrated mastery on that standard were strongly urged to attend.

Our science teachers were more intentional. They set up a series of Saturday sessions focused on standards many students missed. Although these were open to all students, low-scoring students were specifically invited. As word spread about the effectiveness of this intervention, social studies and math teachers adopted the practice.

Results—and Looking for Reasons

By the end of our third year using these practices, Hernandez students showed small gains in their passing rates on state assessments in most subjects. They showed passing rates of 82 percent (with 12 percent scoring as advanced) in science and 68 percent (with 11 percent scoring as advanced) in social studies.

Because all staff had attended the same trainings and collaborated in these processes, we explored what accounted for the greater success in science and social studies. These teachers had set their students up for achievement by not only planning collaboratively, but also intentionally creating routines to implement research-based practices. For instance, science teachers dedicated one wall in their classrooms to a graphic organizer illustrating what students would study the entire semester, with each standard broken down into key concepts and vocabulary. As each new unit was introduced, teachers would unveil a portion of the graphic organizer.

The science and social studies departments also used their planning time in a highly productive way. Each teacher shared benchmark and other assessment data among the department's teachers at all grade levels. For example, 8th grade United States history teachers shared with all their social studies colleagues the fact that their students showed a lack of understanding on standards related to the U.S. Constitution and Bill of Rights. The 7th grade Texas history teachers promised to build a foundation of vocabulary and background information about major government documents during lessons on the Texas constitution.

Strengthening Social-Emotional Learning

At the end of year two, I came to a realization: The students who were failing classes and state assessments were the same ones who were visiting the office for discipline, were suspended, or were often absent.

Although as a staff we had talked about relationships, classroom management, and discipline matrices, we'd left the implementation up to each teacher rather than setting up a schoolwide system for forging relationships and positive discipline. I didn't understand at first how intentional we needed to be. Emotional connections with students had always been a part of my teaching experience, and I thought every teacher naturally made connections with students that transcended the classroom. I soon saw that we needed to become intentional in our approach to the social-emotional side of education, to work as hard on that aspect of learning as we worked on academics.

Creating a strong social-emotional school culture begins with the people who have the most direct contact with students: teachers. In year three, we focused on creating a sense of a team with a shared purpose among our faculty. We looked for small gains in our data and had the teachers behind those wins share their insights and practices. Each faculty meeting began with staff members thanking one another for small acts of kindness or sharing good news. Several teachers began to form a greeting line to shake hands with people as they entered faculty meetings. Our mission and vision statements were painted on the walls and discussed at meetings. We started to refer to ourselves as the "Bulldog Nation." Staff members developed pride in their school and one another.

During the summer before our third year, we used grant funds to train teachers in the Capturing Kids' Hearts[2] approach and brought expert Eric Jensen in to discuss the effects of poverty on children. We created teacher-led committees to build systems that would support a strong campus culture and empower teachers to solve problems collaboratively.

We revamped our interventions for students who were struggling with behavior and strengthened our classroom procedures, just as we had done on the academic side of the Response to Intervention pyramid.

Building Relationships

The first step was guiding teachers to be intentional in relationship building. Most teachers care about students; it's why they teach. Unfortunately, many students, especially struggling or diverse students, don't perceive that message from their teachers. Each teacher was required to be in the halls between periods and encouraged to interact positively with students—to comment on activities or just greet a student. Each class created a social contract about how they would treat one another. Besides starting each day with the pledge, "Today, tomorrow, and always, I will treat others with kindness and respect," many classes adopted the faculty's practice of sharing "good things."

Our training with Eric Jensen helped teachers understand students' need for social learning and active engagement. We trained teachers in how to teach students behaviors that support productive group interaction and encouraged teachers to arrange students' seating in groups.

We began celebrating students who showed positive behavior and attributes. The teacher committee charged with celebrations created not only staff events, but also reward rallies,

attendance celebrations, and other gatherings for students. We turned our student of the month recognition into a dog tag celebration, featuring dog tags in different colors for each behavior attribute (principled, caring, and so on). At a morning reception for parents and students, teachers presented each honored student with a dog tag in the color matching the attribute that student exemplified.

I instituted a Principal's Advisory Committee. Advisory teachers identified about 20 students in each grade level whom other students tended to follow—for good or bad. I met with these students, talked about school pride and the behaviors we expected from all students, and empowered them to together choose activities the school should offer as options for all students. These students led their advisory classes toward meeting high behavior expectations.

Grading for Hope

Hernandez teachers wanted to ensure that grades supported student learning. Our belief was that all students must learn— and that some might take more time than others. So one of our committees guided creation of a campuswide grading policy. This policy allowed students to retest and even turn in work late without penalty. For the most part, zeros weren't assigned. Homework was referred to as "home practice" and often wasn't given a grade that would go in the grade-book. When teachers called parents to alert them to their child's impending low grade, they told parents about extended opportunities for students to learn the material.

Using Proactive Discipline

Discipline was probably the most challenging area to change. Too many of our minority students, especially black boys, had discipline referrals. Our training with Eric Jensen gave teachers some insight, and Capturing Kids' Hearts gave us practices to try. I knew we had to get in front of the discipline issue, however, so we started tracking which students had problems in which classes.

We focused on 6th graders so we could change the history of discipline problems that came with many of them from elementary school. Each school counselor worked on positive peer interactions with a group of 6th graders about whom they had discipline concerns. In partnership with a community group, we began to hold leadership classes, and adults from this group mentored students who struggled behaviorally.

Our discipline committee created our Friday Academy. Teachers handled day-to-day classroom discipline, contacted parents, and supervised teacher detentions; if these measures didn't work, they recommended a student for Friday Academy. With parent permission, these students stayed after school for two hours on Friday and performed community service, supervised by volunteer teachers who built relationships with each student during the activities. Only a handful of students who experienced this intervention were repeat offenders.

Results—and Hope

The school's test scores remain high—higher than those of schools in our district that have lower percentages of students living in poverty. By implementing practices that address the behavioral side of the Response to Intervention pyramid as well as the academic one, we hope to break the correlation between high poverty and low student achievement at Robert Hernandez Middle School.

Notes

1. We trained teachers on "cut scores" so they could differentiate among a student response that was at mastery level, above mastery level, or not quite at the required level for mastery.

2. Capturing Kids' Hearts (www.flippengroup.com/education/ckh. html) is a program that helps educators build positive, trusting relationships among themselves and with students.

Critical Thinking

1. If you could only implement two of the six steps for creating a climate for achievement, which would they be? Defend your answers.

2. Using what you know about educational psychology and child development, explain why the six steps used in this school were successful.

3. Allowing students to retake failed assessments and hand in required assignments late has some critics. What do you think about these policies? Be sure to look at both the student and teacher side. Also, think about long term consequences.

Internet References

Capturing Kids' Hearts
http://www.flippengroup.com/education/ckh.html

National School Climate Center
http://www.schoolclimate.org/

What Kids Can Do
http://www.whatkidscando.org/

DEBORAH D. BRENNAN is the former principal of PFC Robert P. Hernandez Middle School in Round Rock, Texas.

Article   Prepared by: Rebecca B. Evers, *Winthrop University*

The Failure of Zero Tolerence

From the Editors: Ironically, zero tolerance policies once promoted as a solution to youth violence have created a school to prison pipeline. Widespread discipline practices of suspension, expulsion, and arrest for school behavior problems are turning kids in conflict into criminal offenders. The preeminent researcher on zero tolerance reviews the evidence about these practices and proposes a preventive model to insure school safety without discarding our most marginalized youth.

RUSSELL J. SKIBA

Learning Outcomes

After reading this article, you will be able to:

- Outline the reasons that Zero Tolerance became a popular school policy.

- Describe major effects of Zero Tolerance on school policies and students.

- Evaluate the effectiveness of Zero Tolerance as a policy to make schools safer.

- Analyze the lessons learned through use of Zero Tolerance policies.

Introduction

There is no doubt that the safety of our children in our schools and in our communities is paramount. Incidents of school violence in the United States have motivated researchers and practitioners to explore and employ effective methodologies and strategies to promote safety in classrooms and schools. Still, issues of disruptive behavior top the list of concerns about education among teachers and parents.

The controversies about promoting safety and discipline in our schools are not about whether to address those issues, but rather how best to address them. For the last 20 years, fear for the welfare of our children has led us down a "no-nonsense" path of increased punishment and school exclusion in responding to school and community disruption through an approach

that has come to be known as *zero tolerance*. These policies have dramatically increased the number of students put out of school for disciplinary purposes, and may be accelerating student contact with law enforcement. In today's climate it seems school leaders are being asked to make a tough choice between keeping their school safe and ensuring that all students have the continued opportunity to remain in the school learning environment. The message of zero tolerance is intuitively appealing. When disruption and disorder threaten our schools and communities, it becomes increasingly easy to accept the notion that greater authority and force are necessary in order to keep schools secure. Faced with the undeniable need to preserve the safety of our children, which of us would not engage in strong actions for their sake when left with no alternative? The presumption that increased force was necessary in our schools motivated the vast social experiment called zero tolerance and has maintained it in one form or another for over 20 years.

As that policy has been implemented in our schools and communities, however, its outcomes have led many to the realization that increasing punishment creates unintended consequences for children, families, and communities. Moreover, the data that has emerged from this 20-year social experiment has overwhelmingly failed to demonstrate that school exclusion and increasing levels of punishment keep our schools and streets safer. Instead, the data suggest that suspension, expulsion, and the increased use of law enforcement in school settings are themselves risk factors for a range of negative academic and life outcomes.

Are the goals of keeping our schools safe and keeping our students in school necessarily mutually exclusive? This article suggests that exclusionary, zero tolerance approaches to school discipline are not the best way to create a safe climate for learning. Increasingly, there are sound alternatives available to schools that can promote a safe school climate conducive to learning without removing large numbers of students from the opportunity to learn or creating a more negative school climate through increased punishment. Where did the philosophy of zero tolerance come from? What do we know about its effects?

The Rise of Zero Tolerance Philosophy

In the United States in the 1980s and 90s, fears concerning violence in schools and classrooms led to a dramatic increase in the implementation of so-called zero tolerance school discipline policies. The first recorded use of the term appears to be the reassignment of 40 sailors for drug usage on a submarine in the Norfolk, Virginia, shipyard. Although the policy was controversial from the start, it also found influential supporters. Not long after this first incident, First Lady Nancy Reagan appeared with the Secretary of the Navy to highlight the new "no-nonsense" approach to drug enforcement. Indeed, one can imagine that it was the First Lady's influence that moved the philosophy forward. By 1986, the Reagan Administration had proposed the first zero tolerance legislation for our nation's schools, although the bill was defeated in Congress.

Yet in an era in which it was widely believed that schools were being overwhelmed by violence, the term zero tolerance resonated. Although data has since refuted this presumption—school violence has stayed relatively stable for 30 years—school districts in the late 1980s and early 90s began reframing their disciplinary policies to increase both the number and the length of suspensions and expulsions for an ever-widening range of infractions, including fighting (or witnessing fights), wearing hats, even failure to complete homework. The Clinton Administration and Congress soon jumped on the bandwagon, passing the Gun Free Schools Act in 1994, mandating a one calendar year expulsion for possession of firearms on school grounds.

At the core of zero tolerance philosophy and policy is the presumption that strong enforcement can act as a deterrent to other potentially disruptive students. Relying primarily upon school exclusion—out-of-school suspension and expulsion and increases in security and police presence—the philosophy of zero tolerance is based on the "broken-window" theory. The theory is that communities must react to even minor disruptions in the social order with relatively strong force in order to "send a message" that certain behaviors will not be tolerated. Conversely, zero tolerance advocates believe that the failure to

intervene in this way allows the cycle of disruption and violence to gain a solid toehold in our schools and community.

The Effects of Zero Tolerance

Since the philosophy of zero tolerance is to treat all incidents as worthy of severe intervention, it is not surprising that there have been literally thousands of incidents in the United States in which the punishment seems out of scale to the offense. News reports have documented a seemingly endless stream of cases in which students in U.S. schools have been suspended or expelled for bringing a knife in a lunchbox to cut chicken, pointing a gun drawn on paper at classmates, bringing a plastic axe to school as part of a Halloween costume, or calling one's mother stationed in Iraq on a cell phone. Some of these cases have led to community outrage, even lawsuits. Zero tolerance policies in Fairfax County, Virginia, recently became the center of intense controversy when a successful student-athlete committed suicide after his removal from school for possession of a legal but controlled substance (St. George, 2010).

Similar unfortunate incidents have followed the rise of increased police presence in schools. In Toledo, Ohio, a 14-year-old girl was arrested for a dress code violation when she came to school wearing a midriff shirt. In Palm Beach, Florida, a 14-year-old student with disabilities was arrested after he was caught stealing $2 from a classmate; although it was his first arrest, he was held for six weeks in an adult jail. The prosecutor filed adult felony charges but dropped them after a crew from *60 Minutes* arrived at the boy's hearing. In Chicago, Illinois, in 2009, two dozen 11- to 15-year-old students in a charter school were arrested and detained overnight for a food fight.

These incidents, noteworthy enough to be highlighted in the media, may well be only the tip of the iceberg in terms of how exclusionary policies have changed school outcomes. The use of out-of-school suspension has approximately doubled since 1973, and almost tripled for Black students (Kim, Losen, & Hewett, 2010). In some school districts, these increases have been dramatic. In Chicago, Illinois, after the implementation of zero tolerance in 1995, the number of expulsions rose from 81 to 1,000 three years later. Evidence suggests that the number of referrals to juvenile justice from schools is also increasing. In Pennsylvania, a 2010 report found that the number of referrals to juvenile justice has tripled over a period of seven years. In Florida, there were over 21,000 arrests and referrals of students to the state's Department of Juvenile Justice in 2007–2008. A large proportion of these school arrests or referrals are for misdemeanor offenses or disorderly conduct. This has resulted in complaints by judges who worry about clogging up the juvenile justice system and courts with behaviors that could have been managed in the classroom or at school.

Has Zero Tolerance Made our Schools Safer?

Clearly, the rise of a punishment- and exclusion-based philosophy of school discipline has created very real consequences for students. Yet given the responsibility of educators to keep students safe, more extreme approaches to school discipline might well be viewed as justified if those approaches could be shown to lead reliably to safer or more orderly school climates. Ultimately then, the most important question in examining zero tolerance is its effectiveness. Does the data show that zero tolerance has led to improvements in student behavior or school safety? Does it do so fairly and equitably for all students? The question might be framed as one of costs and benefits. Does the removal of troublesome students from school reduce disruption and improve school climate enough to offset the inherent risks to educational opportunity and school bonding that come from removing students from the school setting? Three criteria that we might use in judging the effectiveness of school removal are consistency of implementation, outcomes, and fairness of application across groups. In all of these areas, the data are surprising, often disconfirming what we commonly expect.

Inconsistency of Implementation

A basic rule of intervention effectiveness is that, for an intervention or procedure to be effective, it must be implemented in the way it was intended. Procedures such as conflict resolution, for example, demand a high level of training of both staff and students—if that training does not occur, it is almost certain the procedure will be less effective. This criterion—often referred to as *treatment fidelity* or *treatment integrity*—means that, unless an intervention can be implemented with some degree of consistency, it is impossible to know whether it could be effective.

One of the common findings of studies about the application of school suspension and expulsion is its high rate of inconsistency. Rates of suspension and expulsion vary dramatically across schools and school districts. Although one would presume that, as a more serious punishment, the use of school suspension would be reserved for more serious offenses, national data suggest that out-of-school suspension is used in response to a wide range of behavior from fighting to insubordination, and that only a small percentage of suspensions actually occur in response to behavior that threatens the safety or security of schools (Heaviside, Rowand, Williams, & Farris, 1998).

Further, although it is often presumed that suspension and expulsion are a direct response to student disruption, which student actually gets suspended or expelled is determined as much or more by the unique characteristics of that particular school.

School climate and school governance, school demographics, and principal and teacher attitudes all play significant roles in determining the rate of school discipline. It is not surprising, for instance, that there are significantly higher rates of out-of-school suspension and expulsion at schools with principals who favor a zero tolerance approach (Skiba & Rausch, 2006).

In short, there appears to be a high rate of inconsistency in the use of school suspension and expulsion, and its application is based as much on school attributes as on student behavior. It must be assumed that this failure to demonstrate treatment integrity limits the effectiveness of application of zero tolerance suspensions and expulsions.

Poor Outcomes

No data exist to show that out-of-school suspensions and expulsions reduce disruption or improve school climate. If anything, disciplinary removal appears to have negative effects on student outcomes and the learning climate. A number of researchers have found that students suspended in late elementary school are more likely to receive office referrals or suspensions in middle school than students who had not been suspended, prompting some researchers to conclude that suspension may act more as a reward than as a punishment for many students (Tobin, Sugai, & Colvin, 1996). School rates of out-of-school suspension are moderately associated with lower graduation or higher dropout rates and greater contact with the juvenile justice system (Council of State Governments Justice Center, 2011). Indeed, it has been documented that suspension or expulsion are used by some administrators as a tool for "pushout" in an attempt to rid the school of perceived troublemakers or those whose long-term chances of success at school are seen as low. Somewhat surprisingly, however, purging the school of such students does not improve school climate. Schools with higher rates of school suspension have been found to have lower parent and teacher ratings of school climate and school governance (American Psychological Association, 2008). Most importantly, schools with higher suspension and expulsion rates have been found to have lower outcomes on statewide test scores, regardless of student demographics (Davis & Jordan, 1994). It is difficult to argue that zero tolerance approaches are necessary in order to safeguard an orderly and effective learning climate when schools that use school exclusion more have poorer academic outcomes.

Unfair Application

One of the more consistent findings when looking at school discipline has been a high degree of racial disparity in school suspension and expulsion. In the United States, Black students are consistently suspended at rates two to three times higher than those for other students, and are similarly overrepresented in office referrals, expulsions, and corporal punishment. Those disparities have increased over the last 30 years. Although it is widely believed that racial disproportionality in discipline is an issue of poverty, not race, the data say otherwise: Statistical analyses show that racial gaps in discipline are as likely or more likely to occur in rich, suburban districts as they are in poor, urban districts (Wallace, Goodkind, Wallace, & Bachman, 2008).

Nor do the data support the widely-held perception that Black students earn a higher rate of school exclusion by acting out more. If anything, studies have shown that Black students are punished more severely for less serious and more subjective infractions. One study, "The Color of Discipline," explored the differences in infractions leading to office referrals between Black and White students. Where there were differences, White students were referred more than Black students for more objective offenses, such as smoking and vandalism, while Black students were referred more than White students for more subjective offenses, such as disrespect or loitering (Skiba, Michael, Nardo, & Peterson, 2002). Researchers since then have consistently found that disciplinary disparities between Black and White students occur most often in subjective categories, like defiance and disrespect. Some evidence suggests that these disparities are caused at least in part by cultural mismatch or insufficient training in culturally responsive classroom management (Vavrus & Cole, 2002).

What Have We Learned?

Clearly, there was a hope in the United States in the 1990s that the increased surveillance and punishment associated with zero tolerance would send a strong message that could deter violence, crime, and disruption in schools. Yet data that have accumulated since those policies were first implemented have been highly consistent in showing that such an approach simply has not worked in promoting improved student behavior or school safety. The American Psychological Association, in response to concerns about zero tolerance, commissioned a Zero Tolerance Task Force to study the approach and make recommendations. After a year of reviewing extensive research and documentation, that Task Force concluded that:

An examination of the evidence shows that zero tolerance policies as implemented have failed to achieve the goals of an effective system of school discipline. . . . Zero tolerance has not been shown to improve school climate or school safety. Its application in suspension and expulsion has not proven an effective means of improving student behavior. It has not resolved, and indeed

may have exacerbated, minority over-representation in school punishments. Zero tolerance policies as applied appear to run counter to our best knowledge of child development. By changing the relationship of education and juvenile justice, zero tolerance may shift the locus of discipline from relatively inexpensive actions in the school setting to the highly costly processes of arrest and incarceration. In so doing, zero tolerance policies have created unintended consequences for students, families, and communities. (American Psychological Association, 2008, p. 860)

Fortunately, during the last decade, there has also been considerable growth in knowledge of alternative strategies that appear to hold far more potential for reducing school disruption and ensuring the safety of students in school. What have we learned?

Over five decades of study, behavioral psychologists have amassed data that should lead us to be highly skeptical of the effectiveness of punishment for changing the behavior of children. While setting limits is often an important part of many programs, the effects of punishment are always unpredictable. Rather than changing their behavior, children and youth are just as likely to respond to punishment with anger and aggression or running away. As many school districts relying on suspension and expulsion have found, students eventually become immune to a certain level of punishment, requiring ever longer and more severe penalties. In schools and systems that rely solely on punishment to contain student behavior, more and more staff effort and resources are progressively devoted to a system that over time seems less and less effective. This is not an abstract problem: Every year, our reliance on school exclusion for discipline means that the educational career and life course of students across the nation are disrupted, moving them away from educational success and toward increased contact with the justice system. Fortunately, there are alternatives.

Preventive Discipline

In the last 10 to 15 years, a comprehensive model of preventive discipline and behavior support has begun to emerge as the model most likely to successfully address issues of safety, disruption, and discipline in schools. The approach is grounded in a primary prevention approach to mental health and behavior planning, targeting three levels of intervention simultaneously. First, school-wide prevention efforts, such as conflict resolution, improved classroom behavior management, and parental involvement, can help establish a climate less conducive to violence. At the second level, schools assess the seriousness of threats of violence and provide support to students who may be at-risk for violence and disruption through such interventions as mentoring, anger management screening, and teaching pro-social skills. Finally, schools that are prepared to prevent violence have plans and procedures in place to effectively respond to disruptive or violent behaviors that do occur, including school-wide discipline plans, procedures for individual behavior plans, and cross-system collaboration, especially between education and juvenile justice.

A preventive model of school discipline assumes that there is no one simple solution that can address all problems of school disruption. Rather, developing safe and orderly schools conducive to learning requires comprehensive, long-term planning, an array of effective strategies, and a partnership of education and juvenile justice, families, the community, and students themselves. The following have been demonstrated to be effective components of a comprehensive program to ensure school safety:

- *School-wide Behavioral Planning and Improved Classroom Management.* School-wide discipline plans and behavior support teams, through programs such as Positive Behavior Interventions and Supports, build the consistency and communication that is critical in effective responses to school disruption. Appropriate strategies for handling misbehavior and teaching appropriate behavior can help prevent minor misbehavior from accelerating into a classroom or school crisis.
- *Social Emotional Learning.* Social instructional approaches can help establish a non-violent school climate, by teaching students alternatives to violence for resolving interpersonal problems.
- *Parent and Community Involvement.* Rather than blaming parents as the cause of discipline problems, schools, courts, and communities are beginning to find that it is more useful and effective to include parents as active partners in the process of behavior planning.
- *Early Screening for Mental Health Issues.* Early identification of students who may be at-risk for antisocial behavior or emotional disorders increases the chances of providing behavioral support to those students, so that unmet social and behavioral needs do not escalate into violence.
- *School and District-wide Data Systems.* Improved data collection on discipline, office referrals, and law enforcement contact, and in particular the disaggregation of such data by race and ethnicity, can be used to evaluate school and district progress in handling both major and minor disciplinary incidents. Disaggregation of those data for those groups who have been disproportionately affected by school discipline is key in bringing equity to our school discipline systems.

- *Effective and Ongoing Collaboration.* Reducing referrals to juvenile justice and school-based arrests will require collaboration between education, juvenile justice, and law enforcement in order to develop effective alternative strategies, such as restorative justice, that can contribute to school safety while reducing the risk of student involvement in the juvenile justice system.

Conclusion

In the nineteenth century, the dunce cap served as a potent symbol of the prevailing belief that failure to learn was a character flaw that could not be remediated. In the intervening years, we have come to understand that mistakes are simply the first step in the learning process and that, with perseverance and improved teaching, all students can learn. We are due for a similar realization with respect to student misbehavior. We can no longer afford simply to throw away those who transgress in our schools, especially when such exclusions continue to disproportionately impact those who have been marginalized throughout our history. The cost to society of an ever-expanding prison population, and to our communities of an increasing crime rate as more children spend more time out of school, is simply too great. Schools and communities across America are discovering that safety and academic opportunity are in no way mutually exclusive and that, by employing strategies to teach students what they need to know to get along in school and society, we strengthen our children, our systems, and our communities.

References

American Psychological Association Zero Tolerance Task Force. (2008). Are zero tolerance policies effective in the schools? An evidentiary review and recommendations. *American Psychologist, 63* (9), 852–862.

Council of State Governments Justice Center. (2011). *Breaking schools' rules: A statewide study of how school discipline relates to student's success and juvenile justice involvement.* Texas A&M University, Public Policy Research Institute. New York, NY: Council of State Governments Justice Center.

Davis, J. E., & Jordan, W. J. (1994). The effects of school context, structure, and experiences on African American males in middle and high schools. *Journal of Negro Education, 63,* 570–587.

Heaviside, S., Rowand, C., Williams, C., & Farris, E. (1998). *Violence and discipline problems in U.S. Public Schools: 1996–97.* (NCES 98-030). Washington, D.C.: U.S. Department of Education, National Center for Education Statistics.

Kim, C. Y, Losen, D. J., & Hewitt, D. T. (2010). *The school-to-prison pipeline: Structuring legal reform.* New York, NY: New York University Press.

St. George, D. (2011, February 20). Suicide turns attention to Fairfax discipline procedures. *Washington Post*. Retrieved from http://www.washingtonpost.com/local/education/suicide-turns-attention-to-fairfax-discipline-procedures/2011/02/14/AB9UtxH_story.html

Skiba, R. (2012). Reaching a critical juncture for our kids: The need to reassess school-justice practices. In New York State (Ed.), *Keeping kids in school and out of court: A collection of reports to inform the national leadership summit on school-justice partnerships* (pp. i–x). Albany, NY: New York State Permanent Judicial Commission on Justice for Children.

Skiba, R. J., Michael, R. S., Nardo, A. C., & Peterson, R. (2002). The color of discipline: Sources of racial and gender disproportionality in school punishment. *Urban Review, 34*, 317–342.

Skiba, R. J., & Rausch, M. K. (2006). Zero tolerance, suspension, and expulsion: Questions of equity and effectiveness. In C. M. Evertson, & C. S. Weinstein (Eds.), *Handbook for Classroom Management: Research, Practice, and Contemporary Issues* (pp. 1063–1089). Mahwah, NJ: Lawrence Erlbaum Associates.

Tobin, T., Sugai, G., & Colvin, G. (1996). Patterns in middle school discipline records. *Journal of Emotional and Behavioral Disorders, 4*, 82–94.

Vavrus, F. & Cole, K. (2002). "I didn't do nothin": The discursive construction of school suspension. *The Urban Review, 34*, 87–111.

Wallace, J. M., Jr., Goodkind, S. G., Wallace, C. M., & Bachman, J. (2008). Racial/ethnic and gender differences in school discipline among American high school students: 1991–2005. *Negro Educational Review, 59*, 47–62.

Critical Thinking

1. Clearly the author of this article believes Zero Tolerance is not a good policy. Do you think he has made his case? Support your answer with evidence from this article or other research you have found.

2. Look at school policy in your area; is it a Zero Tolerance? If you were a school leader who has read this article would you continue a Zero Tolerance policy? Justify your answer.

3. Skiba has suggested preventive discipline as an alternative to Zero Tolerance. What do you think must happen so that schools will be able to let go of Zero Tolerance, suspensions, and other punitive discipline methods?

Internet References

National Association of School Psychologist-Resources
http://www.nasponline.org/resources/factsheets/zt_fs.aspx

National Education Association-Alternatives to Zero Tolerance
https://www.nea.org/home/alt-zero-tolerance-policies.html

Teaching Tolerance
http://www.tolerance.org/

RUSSELL J. SKIBA, PHD, is a Professor in the School Psychology program at Indiana University. He is currently Director of the Equity Project, a consortium of research projects offering evidence-based information to educators and policymakers on equity in special education and school discipline.

Unit 5

UNIT

Prepared by: Rebecca B. Evers, *Winthrop University*

Teaching English Language Learners

The concepts of culture and diversity encompass all the customs, traditions, and institutions that people develop as they create and experience their history and identity as a community. In the United States, very different cultures coexist within the civic framework of a shared constitutional tradition that guarantees equality before the law. So, many people are united as one nation by our constitutional heritage. Some of us are proud to say that we are a nation of immigrants. Our country is becoming more multicultural with every passing decade. As educators, we have a unique opportunity to encourage and educate our diverse learners. The articles in this unit reflect upon all the concerns mentioned above. You can establish a classroom that is a place of caring and nurturing for your students, multicultural-friendly, equitable, and free from bigotry, where diverse students are not just tolerated but are wanted, welcomed, and accepted. Respect for all children and their capacity is the baseline for good teaching. Students must feel significant and cared for by all members of the classroom. Our diverse children should be exposed to an academically challenging curriculum that expects much from them and equips them for the real world.

The number of children (ages 5–17) who speak a language other than English at home has grown from 4.7 million in 1980 to 11,994,000 in 2012 (Annie E. Casey Foundation). Among these children, the percentage who speak English with difficulty is now around 2.5 million or around 5 percent. If we compare these students by age, the youngest had the most difficulty speaking English; while 7 percent of children ages 5–9 and only 4 percent of adolescents ages 14–17 spoke English with difficulty (U.S. Department of Education, National Center for Education Statistics, 2012).

On average, Hispanic students never perform as well as other students, not even in kindergarten. In some states, the Hispanic school-age population has nearly doubled since 1987 and is approaching one-half of all students. Unfortunately, these students are more likely to attend a hyper-segregated school, where the population is 90–100 percent minority and they are less likely to read or do math at grade level or earn a college degree. In fact, they drop out of high school at higher rates than all other categories of the student population (Coleman and Goldenberg, 2010).

These data appear to indicate that teachers and schools are making an impact on second language acquisition of students who do not speak English at home. The articles in this unit focus on the concept that caring, culturally responsive instruction from teachers with positive attitudes who look for student's assets can and will help English language learners (ELLs) be successful learners in school.

A shift in our thinking can make a powerful difference in how we approach and teach students who are ELLs. To begin with we might consider new ways to think and talk about students from other countries and cultural backgrounds. For example, we might consider that students who are ELLs have experiences that make them culturally different but not culturally deficient. The Network School in New York City has a graduation rate that is more than double the other schools in the city. There are lessons to be learned from those teachers who view their students who are ELL as assets.

A request from a general education middle school teacher to an ELL teacher caused them to consider how they might meet the needs of more ELL students and their teachers. As school populations of students who speak other languages has increased schools have not been able to find nor can they afford to hire as many ELL teachers as administrators need or want. Therefore, teachers are beginning to form groups to support each other as they work to teach and nurture ELL students.

Early Childhood classrooms are particularly interesting when young ELL or ESL students arrive. They are most likely dual language learners. While they are learning the language which they will use in school, they are continuing to learn their first language at home. These students may present a challenge to classroom teachers unless their teachers understand how to use each language to complement the learning of the other language.

Schools in rural areas have seen a rise in drop-out rates and corresponding drop in graduation rates for students who are ELL. Research data tells us that there is a positive correlation between ELL parent engagement, especially engagement with teachers, and the academic achievement of their children who are ELL. Some of the barriers to parent participation are identified as language, cultural differences, job schedules, and lack of transportation. With the rise in non-English speaking citizens in rural communities and the unsatisfactory drop-out and graduation outcomes, researchers were interested in discovering what factors influenced ELL parent-teacher relationships and interactions from the viewpoint of the parents. The results of this study offer valuable suggestions for teachers everywhere to consider.

References

Annie E. Casey Foundation, (N.D.). Data Center: Children who speak a language other than English at home. Author. Retrieved on 20 June 2014 from http://datacenter. kidscount.org/data/tables/81-children-who-speak-a-language-other-than-english-at-home?loc=1&loct=1#detailed/1/any/false/868,867,133,38,35/any/396,397

Coleman, R. & Goldenberg, (2010). *What Does Research Say about Effective Practices for English Learners?, Kappa Delta Pi Record,* Winter 2010.

U.S. Department of Education, National Center for Education Statistics. (2012). *The Condition of Education 2011* (NCES 2011-045), Indicator 6.

Article _____ Prepared by: Rebecca B. Evers, *Winthrop University*

ESL and Classroom Teachers Team Up to Teach Common Core

Lesli A. Maxwell

Learning Outcomes

After reading this article, you will be able to:

- State the purpose for ESL and classroom teachers to team up or collaborate.
- Critique three teaching methods proposed in this article.
- Compare the status of ESL teachers to general education teachers.

It started with an after-school conversation last spring between two teachers.

Barbara Page, a veteran English-as-a-second-language teacher, and Meredith Vanden Berg, an 8th-grade science teacher, were discussing a student from Somalia who had just arrived from a refugee camp in Yemen and landed at their ethnically diverse middle school in Beaverton, OR.

Vanden Berg wanted to know what more she could do to help the girl—who was just beginning to learn a few words of English—understand what was going on in her science classroom.

"I don't like when I see students staring off into space when I'm teaching and I know it's because of the language," said Vanden Berg. What could I be doing to convey the core concepts without completely losing her?"

That discussion was the spark for what has evolved into a much closer collaboration between ESL and content teachers at Meadow Park Middle School as they fully embrace the Common Core State Standards in English/language arts and mathematics this academic year.

Along with their math teacher colleague, Allison Shultz, Vanden Berg and Page have begun picking apart the standards, stripping them down to the essential concepts, simplifying the language, and developing strategies that all of them can use to support English-learners in both content and ESL classes.

It's a kind of collaboration and discussion that educators say needs to happen at schools across the country as teachers now stand on the front lines of helping an increasingly diverse student population meet the demands of the new standards.

Every student, whether a native English-speaker or a second-language learner, is expected to engage in conversation and discourse in the classroom, read and understand complex texts, and make effective oral and written arguments, among other high-level language practices in the new standards.

Both Shultz and Vanden Berg credit Page with helping them better understand how their own language of instruction can pose a major barrier to students whose English proficiency is still low.

"I see now how much we as content teachers take for granted," said Vanden Berg. "It takes a lot of words to explain the periodic table or an atom."

Shifting Relationships?

The nation's roughly 45,000 ESL teachers—many of whom split their time among schools with little chance to co-teach or plan with content teachers—have expertise and strategies that experts say all teachers will need to ensure that English learners are not shut out of the rigorous, grade-level content that the common core envisions will prepare all students for college and careers. Special education teachers, too, say schools need to foster closer collaboration between them and content teachers to support students with special needs.

But what role will ESL teachers play in this groundbreaking shift to the common core? Will there be a broader move to co-teaching or tighter collaboration between ESL teachers and their academic-content colleagues? What, if any, common-core professional development are ESL teachers receiving, and how is their expertise being tapped?

Earlier this year, the TESOL International Association, the professional organization for teachers who specialize in working with English learners, raised those issues during a convening of ESL professionals who work in school systems in and around Washington. There was strong consensus among the group that ESL teachers, in addition to working directly with students, need to be deployed as consultants to content teachers who will need guidance on how best to support English learners.

"If held to the same high and rigorous standards as their peers, the learning curve for English-learners is going to be longer and higher than most of their peers and therefore, the teachers who teach them need to be much better equipped," said Rosa Aronson, executive director of the Alexandria, VA-based TESOL group.

"What ESL teachers bring to the table is deep understanding of how language is acquired, the importance of teaching academic language, and the cultural issues for students who are English-learners. They are often closer to their students and families than content teachers and can be strong advocates for these students."

ESL Teacher Status

In many schools, ESL educators have not traditionally been seen as being as central to the enterprise of teaching students as their subject-matter peers, said AídaWalqui, the director of teacher professional development for WestEd, a San Francisco-based research group.

Often itinerant among schools, ESL teachers may serve multiple grade levels and are viewed by their content-area colleagues as being solely responsible for developing students' language skills. They are likely to spend their instructional time with English learners in stand-alone classrooms in the so-called "pullout" approach, though some districts, such as St. Paul, Minn., partner ESL and content teachers to keep English-learners in mainstream classrooms for all or most of the day.

ESL teachers are also less likely to become principals and take on other leadership roles in their schools than their content-area colleagues, All of that, said Walqui, makes elevating and recasting the role of the ESL teacher even more challenging.

"This is a major dilemma," she said. "What should the role of the ESL teacher be in this dramatically shifting environment of the common core?

Walqui argues that ESL teachers themselves, as well as their content-area peers, need to reconceptualize what language is and evolve from their concentrated focus on vocabulary and grammar or on how to make a request or express a hypothesis.

"Students are too often engaged in the production of sentences with vocabulary they have learned," Walqui said. "But a sentence is an isolated unit of language that would never really count as deep engagement with academic work, which is what the common core is all about."

Content All Day

Deep engagement with content is how a network of 16 high schools that specialize in serving recently arrived immigrants in California, New York, and Virginia, approaches instruction for English learners.

"Every single teacher is a teacher of language and content," said Claire Sylvan, the executive director and president of the Internationals Network for Public Schools, based in New York City. "If you want these students to learn rigorous academic content and gain dexterity in the new language, you better be doing more than 15 minutes a day of English-language instruction and better be doing rigorous content all day long."

In the Internationals network schools, students with varying levels of English proficiency, as well as those in different grade levels, are purposely mixed in classrooms. That way, more-experienced students help "acculturate" the newer arrivals, and a team of teachers sticks with the same group for two full years. That team—consisting of math, science, English/language arts, and social studies teachers, at least one of whom is also an ESL expert—share responsibility for the same cohort of students over time.

Each school is autonomous, but the network provides hundreds of digital lesson plans and other resources that integrate language instruction with content. Any teacher among the 16 schools can tap those.

"All the units our teachers have developed are designed to have students using their language in group projects, talking with each other, and actively engaged in discourse, no matter how imperfect it may be," Sylvan said.

While most of the teachers working in the Internationals schools are not necessarily trained in second-language acquisition or how to work with English-learners when they are hired, principals screen aggressively for prospective faculty members who are willing to learn.

"Push-In" Model

At another New York City school, John J. Pershing Middle School, where 40% of students are English-learners, Marcus Artigliere and his team of six fellow ESL teachers are working together, and with their core-content peers, to craft common-core lessons in English/language arts and math that outline explicit supports and "scaffolds" for ELLs, based on their proficiency levels.

They are doing that at the same time the school is shifting from pulling its ELL students out of mainstream classes for explicit language instruction to a "push-in" model in which the ESL teachers are always in the classrooms with content teachers.

"We think this is the only way that the shift to the common core is going to work for our English-learners," said "The goal is that you have the ESL professional right in the room to model for content teachers how you scaffold the content for English learners."

In Broward County, Fla, where state law requires all academic content teachers to have some training in the theories and practice of teaching second-language learners, the district's curriculum and instruction team has created an open-source digital professional-development resources around the common core, in addition to face-to-face training.

The district has produced a series of webinars to address particular instructional shifts in the new standards. Each webinar also has a companion webinar specifically targeting teachers who work with ELLs. Teachers in school-based professional learning communities watch the webinars together then discuss strategies and supports they can use for all students.

"All of our teachers, whether they are mainstream content teachers or ESL teachers, are getting this professional development and are doing it together," said Vicky B. Saldala, the director of the district's English-as-a-second-language department.

Saldala's team wrote a "best practices" document for English-learners meant for all teachers in need of understanding what types of classroom activities and supports work best for ELLs at different proficiency levels and in different subject areas. It also breaks down which supports are most effective across the four language domains of speaking, listening, reading, and writing.

Principal's Role

Key to meaningful collaboration and inclusion of ESL professionals in the rollout of the common core, said Aronson, are principals and district administrators willing to give faculty members the time and space to work together.

"The principal plays a huge role for encouraging and facilitating an inclusive school culture that promotes ESL teachers and content teachers working together, but unfortunately, they are the ones who often erect the biggest barriers to this," she said.

At Beaverton's Meadow Park Middle School, Principal Toshiko Maurizio is backing the work of the three teachers who have taken the lead in devising common core support strategies for the school's English learners. She has carved out staff-development time for them to collaborate and share their work.

Their work is particularly challenging because ESL teachers like Page do not work alongside content teachers in the classroom. English learners are pulled out for language instruction as part of their school day, and they are grouped based on proficiency levels, not grade level.

To help cross those barriers, Page created a Google document that all teachers in her school can access to write what key concepts they want their ELL students to understand in an upcoming lesson or unit. She plans her language instruction around those core-content requests, though she says it's an imperfect process.

"I'm really working on my juggling skills," Page said. "Folding in the core content at grade level into language instruction is really tough, especially when you are working with students at different grade levels. We don't have it all figured out, but we are trying. We are committed."

Critical Thinking

1. Interview an ESL teacher to discuss his/her reaction to this article. Ask what they would like to change about their interaction with general education teachers. Be prepared to discuss your interview.

2. How important is the school administration in this process? What should principals do to facilitate more collaboration among teachers?

3. Based on the age of the students you wish to teach or the content area you will teach, which of the three methods mentioned in the article would you like to use? Justify your answer.

Create Central

www.mhhe.com/createcentral

Internet References

Everything ESL
    www.everythingesl.net
Multicultural Education Internet Resource Guide
    http://www2.nau.edu/~jar/Multi.html
National Association for Multicultural Education (NAME)
    www.nameorg.org

LESLI A. MAXVOELL is a staff writer for Education Week.

Article

Prepared by: Rebecca B. Evers, *Winthrop University*

Involving the Parents of English Language Learners in a Rural Area: Focus on the Dynamics of Teacher-Parent Interactions

Jenna M. Shim

Learning Outcomes

After reading this article, you will be able to:

- Explain why Shim uses a postcolonial theory as a conceptual framework for his study.

- Argue the positive and negative effects of parental involvement.

- Apply the implications of this study to your teaching practice.

English language learners (ELLs) is the fastest growing population among the school-age group in the nation (Kanno & Cromley, 2013). Over the past 15 years, the number of English language learners has nearly doubled to about 5.5 million, and by 2025, it is predicted nearly one in every four public school students will be an ELL (National Clearinghouse for English Language Acquisition, NCELA, 2007; Winke, 2011). This growing wave of linguistic diversity is not limited to large metropolitan areas. In fact, growth has been much more rapid in less populated rural states. In this regard, O'Neal, Ringler, and Rodriguez (2008) reported that "ELL students and their families tend to settle in geographical locations that are rural" (p. 6). Similarly, Reed (2010) stated that rural areas are experiencing a rapid increase in racial and ethnic diversity in their student populations; therefore, schools

in rural states are facing unique educational challenges in meeting the needs of diverse student populations, including ELLs, a group with which teachers feel inadequately prepared to work productively. With respect to ELL students' academic achievement levels, many states reported that dropout rates for ELLs are significantly higher than dropout rates for non-ELL students (National Center for Education Statistics [NCES], 2011). In some rural states, dropout rates have increased and graduation decreased within the last five years mainly because of the educational and social challenges that ELLs face in their lives (Walker, 2012).

Research in the field of education is constantly striving to improve student learning, and the importance of parental involvement in student success at school now seems obvious. Indeed, parental involvement as an effective factor in improving student learning is no longer a subject of debate (Wei & Zhou, 2012), and a positive correlation between the ELL parental involvement and ELL student learning has been firmly established (Panferov, 2010). Meanwhile, just as is the case for non-ELL students, in particular those from low income families, difficulties associated with involving the parents of ELLs in their children's schools continue to be reported (e.g., Henderson, Jacob, Kernan-Schloss, & Raimondo, 2004; Hiatt-Michale, 2001; Panferov, 2010). Barriers that may prevent involvement of parents of ELLs have been identified as "language, cultural differences, work schedules, and lack of transportation" (Padgett, 2006, p. 44). With respect to parental involvement in general, Cox (2005), in her meta-analysis of 18 empirical studies, not only confirmed the correlations between parental involvement and students' academic achievements, but she also concluded that the most effective aspect of parental involvement efforts lies in the interactions between parents and teachers. Indeed, Padgett (2006) stated that parental involvement in school activities alone will not increase student achievement; rather, it is the quality of interactions and communication between teachers and parents that has a significant impact on student achievement.

Parental involvement in their children's education can take many different forms (Heymann & Earle, 2000), such as volunteering at school, assisting their children with homework, and becoming involved in school governance issues. However, since prior research has established that high quality interactions between parents and teachers are the most effective aspect of parental involvement effort, and, because exploration of ELL parental involvement is limited, the focus of this study is to investigate the dynamics of ELL parent-teacher interactions from the perspectives of the ELL parents. The research question that guided this study was: What are the factors that influence ELL parent-teacher relationship and interactions from ELL parents' perspective?

The importance of this study lies in several areas: rapid growth in linguistically diverse students in rural areas is now a mainstream issue and yet many rural teachers feel unprepared to work productively with ELL students and their families; the investigation of ELL parent-teacher relationships and the tensions within them remain an understudied area in the literature; and the perspectives of ELL parents do matter if we are serious about recognizing the contributions that ELL parents can make to the children's success in school. Lastly, this study, which takes place in a small town in a Western state, is important because the National Center for Educational Statistics showed that the ELL population in the Western states has more than doubled in the decade between 1995–2005 (NCES, 2006). The conceptual framework that follows briefly discusses Edward Said's (2003/1979) postcolonial theory and how it is employed as a guiding lens for this study.

Conceptual Framework

Despite the great influence and potentially positive impact of parental involvement and parent-teacher collaboration, parent-teacher relationships in general remain an area of tension (e.g., Lawrence-Lightfoot, 2003), including ELL parent-teacher relationships (e.g., Henderson et., al, 2004; Hiatt-Michael, 2001; Panferov, 2010). Indeed, Lawrence-Lightfoot (2003) stated that the borderlands between families and schools are a "most complex and tender geography" (p. xi). In investigating the dynamics of ELL parent-teacher interactions as intercultural relations,

Edward Said's (2003/1979) postcolonial theory is instructive because he explored how different cultures are represented especially by people who occupy a more dominant position. Put differently, Said was particularly committed to equal human rights, and given that the broader goal of this study is to increase more equitable educational opportunities for ELLs by exploring the dynamics of ELL parent-teacher interactions in which parents and teachers occupy different cultural and power positions, Said's postcolonial theory provides a robust conceptual framework upon which to ground this study.

In his most famous work, *Orientalism,* Said (2003/1979) foregrounds the social fact that neither individuals, nor social groups, nor cultures ever develop or exist on *a level playing field* (an equal power level) because individuals, social groups, and cultures are always constituted in and through discursive and material practices that are invisibly constituted by complex sets of asymmetrical power relations. Along these lines, Jandt and Tanno (2001) argue that the framework for postcolonialism can be used to expose not only colonial imperialism but also discursive and material practices that are invisibly constituted by *perceptual imperialism* in the present age. By perceptual imperialism, Jandt and Tanno mean "the process of observing and interpreting information about cultural Others through an underlying set of ideas based not so much on reality as on myth" (p. 120). Thus, the unequal power relations that constitute representational and differentiating practices in intercultural relations can be understood via the framework of postcolonial theory. In relevance to this study, ELL parent-teacher relationships are considered as intercultural relations because linguistic difference overlaps with cultural difference. Furthermore, ELL parent-teacher relationships are grounded in unequal power relations not only because of the different power positions that teachers and parents (like doctors and patients) occupy historically but also because of the different power positions that teachers, the majority of whom are European Americans and parents as racially and linguistically marginalized groups occupy historically (Luke, 2004).

From a postcolonial theoretical viewpoint, no discourse of knowledge, self, other or cultural relations and interactions is ever neutral (Said, 1994) and how problems of difference are understood depends on the political locations in which individuals stand. What this means for ELL parent-teacher interactions is that how teachers understand the cultural practices of ELL families, for instance, is never objective; rather, teachers' perceptions are influenced by their cultural, social, and political backgrounds. In this regard, intercultural relations are invisibly linked to discourses of unequal power relations between the members of the dominant and subordinated groups because the members of subordinated groups are represented by the members of the dominant group in ways that often serve the dominant group's interests—i.e., most often an unintentional act on the part of the members of the dominant group. Hence, when viewed through the lens of postcolonial theory, ELL parent-teacher interactions are not just individual-to-individual relationships and relationships in which knowledge and opinion matters in their interactions, they are linked to the power relations that are historically constituted and thus not always visible. In other words, ELL parent-teacher interactions can be constituted by the usually unconscious enactment of power of the teacher. In this regard, this study, which explores the dynamics in ELL parent-teacher interactions in a rural area from ELL parents' perspectives, postcolonial theory helps us understand the subject position of the ELL parents and why ELL parents feel the way they feel.

To further ground the study, the literature review explores the benefits of parental involvement and the factors inhibiting ELL parental involvement. Although this study investigates the dynamics of ELL parent-teacher interactions in a rural area, because current research on ELL parental involvement has been limited, parental involvement in children's schooling in general is reviewed.

Benefits of Parental Involvement

Parental involvement in its broad term has been defined as "the willingness of parents to participate in the education of their children" (Jeynes, 2003, p. 204), and it has become "one of the centerpieces of educational dialogue among educators, parents, and political leaders" (Jeynes, 2003, p. 203) for quite some time already. In this regard, numerous studies have shown that parental involvement has a significant influence on children's success at school (Heymann & Earle, 2000; Panferov, 2010; Walker, 2012; Wei & Zhou, 2012). With respect to rural areas, King (2012) reported that parental involvement serves as one of the factors that most impacts rural students' decisions to attend college. This finding is not surprising given that students become motivated when they observe their parents take an active interest in school because parent involvement communicates to students how important they are to their parents (Gonzales-DeHass, Willems, & Holbein, 2005). Other researchers have shown that the parents who emphasize their children's achievement as important and who are actively involved in their learning significantly impact student motivation (Marchant, Paulson, & Rothlisberg, 2001). Some studies have shown that parental involvement is also positively related to students' attitudes toward school and to reduced high school dropout rates (Rumberger et al., 1990; Jeynes, 2003). Others have even reported that parental involvement impacts time students spend on home work (e.g., Trusty, 1996; Gonzales-DeHass, Willems, & Holbein, 2005).

These studies have looked at parental involvement as parent-teacher collaborative tasks and relationships, which make a perfect sense given that parents and teachers, have

the mutual goal of children's success in school. With respect to ELL students, researchers have similarly shown that parental involvement has a positive effect on their second language learning, student motivations, and academic achievement (e.g., Kanno & Cromley, 2013; Walker, 2012; Wei & Zhou, 2012).

Many researchers have also argued that encouraging ELL parental involvement can be difficult (Kozol, 1991; Mace-Matluck, Alexander-Kasparik, & Qeen, 1998; Arias & Morillo-Campbell, 2008). Some studies have identified factors limiting ELL parents' school involvement as a mismatch between the parents' own experiences with, and expectations for school, as well as their English proficiency (Bosher, 1998; Hyslop, 2000; Jeynes, 2003; Muchinsky & Tangren, 1999). Others have identified obstacles as the lack of effective communication venues between parents and the teachers (Padgett, 2006; Scribner, Young & Pedroza, 1999); the low level of support and training provided by the school to encourage greater parent engagement (Gibson, 2002); and the lack of time and resources to take time off from work (Heymann & Earle, 2000). Also, Smith, Stern, and Shatrova (2008) have identified the factors inhibiting Hispanic parental involvement in their children's school as "the failure of the school to send correspondence, school calendar, lunch menus or newsletters written in Spanish; and the inability of the parents to speak and advocate for the right of their children" (p. 18).

Through a brief literature review on the different aspects and effects of parental involvement, what is notable is that many studies assume that parent-teacher collaboration occurs on an equal power level. So for instance, if English proficiency issues were solved, if schools provided more training and opportunities to support parental engagement, and if the time constraint from parents' work was taken into account more seriously, then productive and active parental involvement and successful teacher-parent relationships are attainable. In other words, the current parental involvement model often does not attend to the structural aspects and power asymmetry of parent-teacher relationships that can hinder productive collaboration. That said, the dynamics of ELL parent-teacher interactions in rural areas merit further research because (a) parent-teacher interactions hold great potential to improve student achievement (Cox, 2005), (b) the ELLs overall in the nations are underperforming academically when compared to their counterparts (Winke, 2011), (c) ELL parent involvement continues to be difficult (Kozol, 1991; Mace-Matluck, Alexander-Kasparik, & Qeen, 1998; Panferov, 2010), and (d) the rapid growth of ELLs in rural areas brings unique challenges to the schools in meeting their academic needs.

Methods

The study uses a general qualitative methodology to explore the dynamics of ELL parent-teacher interactions.

Setting

The context of this study is a town located in the south-central portion of a Western state in the U.S. The state is made up of primarily rural ranching communities, and the town has a population of 9300. Due to many employment opportunities linked to the state penitentiary and coal mines in the town, in the last two decades the town's mainly white population has become increasingly diverse, with the greatest increase in the Latino population, but also including individuals from China, Thailand, and Philippines. Consequently, the influx of ELLs has been noticeable in the town, and the public school ELL population in the town has more than doubled since the 1990s.

The town houses two elementary schools, one middle school, and one high school. Currently, 26.6% of the total student population is Hispanic, and Asians and Native Americans account for 4.1%. With regard to English as Second Language (ESL) services, 11.8% of the total student population qualifies and over 15% of the total student population lives in a home where one or both parents speak a language other than English.

Participants

Participants were recruited from middle school parents. The total student population of the middle school is 385, and according to an administrator of the school district, about 20% of the middle school population is ELL students. Initially, a district ESL program coordinator assisted the researcher in identifying and contacting the participants in person and by telephone calls. Six ELL parents whose children were enrolled in the middle school responded to the coordinator's invitation and volunteered to participate in this research project. Of the six parents, four parents spoke Spanish as their first language and two parents spoke Chinese as their first language. The number of years that the participating parents and their families lived in the town is between 3 to 10 years. Three of the Spanish speaking parents did not feel comfortable interacting in English with the researcher; for these three, a high school ESL teacher in the same school district who speaks Spanish as a second language fluently served as a translator. The other three parents spoke English to communicate with the researcher. One Spanish-speaking parent and one Chinese-speaking parent were fathers of their children, and the other parents were mothers of their children.

Procedures

The researcher and the six volunteer ELL parents met initially at an ELL parent night at the middle school. The middle school holds a parent night for ELL parents twice during a school year, and according to the district ESL coordinator, the attendance rate remains low. During the ELL parent night, the researcher and the ELL parents talked casually in a group but also on a one-to-one basis. Each individual conversation lasted about 15 minutes, and they all agreed to participate in future individual interviews. Following the ELL parent night, the researcher contacted each ELL parent and met with them individually for about an hour. All the interviews were tape-recorded, and as mentioned above, the translations for the three ELL parent interviews were provided by a high school ESL teacher. The main question that guided the interviews was: How do you feel about interacting with your child's teachers?

Data Analysis

Open coding strategy of grounded theory (Strauss & Corbin, 1998) was used to identify and analyze the patterns and themes within the participants.

Findings and Discussion

While the details of each ELL parent's interactions with their children's teachers were not identical, there were many similar dynamics that were found to be important. The discussions in this study pertain to the experiences of the participants in this study; thus, they cannot be generalized. In addition, this study does not deny the importance of the perspectives of teachers and their expertise. However, the present study focuses on the perspectives of ELL parents, and the findings from this study illuminate the general, yet important to acknowledge, asymmetrical power relations that shape the nature of ELL parent-teacher interactions. Following are the discussions of the findings, which are organized into different themes. Each theme is discussed with one or more examples from the statements made by the participating ELL parents.

Theme One: Teachers' Judgments

One of the most common misconceptions about linguistically diverse populations is that English language proficiency is linked to intelligence (Cummins, 2000). From such a myth, teachers can easily assume that students or parents who do not speak English fluently lack in their capacity to think at the same levels that people who speak English as their first language. In this regard, one Chinese ELL mother expressed her frustration about teachers' judgments toward her and her child.

> *They think our limited English and accents mean our IQs are low, and we cannot think for ourselves. One time a teacher generalized our values of education based on a single encounter with one other Chinese parent. Just because how we educate our children did not meet the teacher's expectation does not mean that we don't care about our children. Is there any parent who really doesn't care about her children and their education?*

The parent perceived the teacher prejudged the entire Chinese population based on a single previous encounter with another Chinese parent. She also expressed her surprise at a teacher assuming that Chinese parents do not care about their children's education, which she alluded to as being unfair. A Chinese father commented:

One time, my wife and I had a parent-teacher conference with our children's teachers. When we were talking about the teaching of math, my wife just wondered how math was taught since my wife felt that the teaching of math is rather slow here in the US. The teacher did not even explain how teachers taught math here and pointed out that research had shown that this was the best way to do it and that other ways to teach math are not as effective. The teacher also told us that we needed to catch up with how math is being taught here. Even though my wife and I wanted to say more, we felt intimidated by this teacher because we don't speak English very well. In our hearts, however, we know that it does not mean that we are not intelligent people.

This parent further expressed his frustration regarding teachers' unwillingness to be open about different ways of teaching math. This parent also commented that the teacher's insistence on focusing only on how math is taught in the US as opposed to other places in the world is not only unfair but not dehumanizing.

From a postcolonial perspective (e.g., Said, 1994, 2003/1979), the members of the subordinated groups are defined as inferior based on the members of the dominant group's perspectives. In this case, the parent perceives the teacher's judgment to be underpinned by prejudice, which is not based on objective facts but rather on myths that inhabit the unconscious mind of the teacher. From this perspective, the teacher is unconsciously and unknowingly operating within a colonial trajectory in which what is different from the dominant culture to which the teacher belongs, i.e., the different level of English proficiency and the different ways to educate children, are considered inferior. The teacher's perspectives, when viewed through the lens of postcolonial theory, are influenced by the complex history of which the teacher is probably not aware, and yet the teacher's judgment, which obviously influenced the ELL parent-teacher interaction, reflects the social fact that the presence of the past must not be denied or ignored.

Theme Two: Inability to Influence a Teacher's Decision Making

Another prominent postcolonial scholar, Gayatri Spivak (1988) in her influential work, *Can the Subaltern Speak,* discusses the importance of *speaking voice.* More specifically, Spivak argues that white men in colonial time represented brown women as if their representation was objective and neutral. Therefore, brown women did not have speaking voice. Here, what Spivak refers to as a speaking voice in her work is not limited to the actual act of talking but includes the power and influence that the speaking voice has or does not have. One Hispanic ELL parent in this regard stated that, "They tell us that our opinions are welcome and that we are free to voice our opinions but then they do whatever they want to do anyway."

Another Hispanic ELL parent echoed this statement and stated:

I always feel like I am being talked at but not talked with. They say that they are only interested in students' learning. My feeling is that teachers report how my children do in school, but they never ask me how my children do at home. They have all the answers ready for me but no question.

Similarly, another Hispanic ELL parent commented:

I feel like I am wasting my time when I talk to my child's teachers. They already made their decisions about many things, but they are trying to making it seem like it is also my decision. In reality, I know I am not at all a part of any decision making process. I feel pretty degraded when I am treated as if I have no ability whatsoever to see through how they are not really including me.

All three parents also expressed feelings of intimidation even when the teachers do not directly intimidate them. In his critical essay about a prescriptive model of dialogue, Nicholas Burbules (2000) asserts that a conception of dialogue is based on a neutral communicative process. However, Burbules contends that "a dialogue is not an engagement of two (or more) abstract persons" (p. 262), rather it is a "discursive relation situated against the background of previous relations" (p. 262) that is imbued with complex asymmetrical power relations. From such a perspective, the imbalance of power that accompanies ELL parent-teacher interactions impacts the dynamics of the interactions. Furthermore, such asymmetry cannot simply be discarded by teachers: the attributes of status, power, and authority have been socially and historically assigned to the teacher's position and as such may be at least a partial reason why these parents felt intimidated and talked at. While one parent felt that his opinions, even when given the floor, did not really count, the other parent felt that she was not given the floor at all to contribute to her children's school lives. From a postcolonial theoretical perspective, which attends to power asymmetry in intercultural relations, both are symptoms of unequal power differences that even assertive ELL parents and well-intended teachers cannot entirely escape.

Theme Three: Fear of Negative Repercussion against Speaking Up

Many ELL parents felt that teachers are not genuinely willing to respond to their questions. Said (1994, 2003/1979) contends that how the members of subordinated groups are represented and spoken for is largely affected by those who belong to the dominant group. So, for example, in the field of education, the more powerful (teachers who are from dominant groups), knowingly or unknowingly, and often in the name of equality, impose their values on subordinate groups (e.g., ELL students and their parents) without risking any disruption to their own positions. Thus, in the end, it is the ELL parents who are forced through normalizing grids constructed by the teachers. Furthermore, if the members of the subordinated group resist the values of the dominant, the consequences are often negative (Said, 1994). One Hispanic ELL parent stated:

> *I just feel that the only way to make them happy is if you remain quiet and you just agree with* everything they say. I feel *like they want to have all the control and when you question them about materials or extra support, they give you that face,* **how dare you?**

Another Hispanic ELL parent similarly claimed:

> *I recognize their expertise, and sometimes I just want to know more about how they are helping my child. But the minute I ask them a question, they become defensive and I realize I'd better not saying anything. Really, their professional knowledge is lost in their demeanor.*

In regards to remaining silent because of the fear of possible negative consequences, one Chinese ELL parent also stated:

> *There are many times I want to say something or ask something, but I end up not saying anything because I am afraid that my child will be penalized by a teacher because I made the teacher angry by asking her questions.*

The idea of possible repercussions that might result from ELL parents' communication with teachers played a big role in these parents' decisions to remain quiet. Essentially, these parents seem to calculate the risk before asking questions that might make teachers defensive. In other words, these ELL parents may have been asking if the potential benefits from asking questions is worth the risk of possibly angering their children's teacher, especially when teachers have an inordinate ability to affect their children's social, emotional and academic well-being. When viewed through the lens of postcolonial theory, the fear of these ELL parents about the repercussions makes sense, given that the members of the subordinate group suffer the consequences in one form or another for not remaining complicit and assimilating into the dominant values, whereas there are virtually no consequences flowing in the opposite direction for the dominant group.

Implications

Among the many factors that limit productive ELL parental involvement in a child's school, this study explored the dynamics of ELL parent-teacher interactions by looking at ELL parent-teacher interactions as intercultural relations in which ELL parents (who are from historically marginalized groups) and teachers (who are European Americans) occupy different power positions historically. The teacher population in the middle school described in this study is predominantly European American. At a broader level and similarly, the teacher population in public schools in the nation continues to remain predominantly European American (e.g., Berg, Denessen, Hornstra, Voeten, & Holland, 2010), and this is especially true in rural areas (e.g, O'Neal, Ringler, & Rodriquez, 2008). Moreover, this study focused on the perspectives of ELL parents not because the perspectives of teachers are unimportant or invalid, but to expose the voices of ELL parents in a rural area, which are often overlooked in the literature.

In this study, the three broad themes that emerged as obstacles that inhibit productive ELL parent-teacher interactions in a rural area are teachers' judgments toward ELL students and their parents; ELL parents' frustration about their inability to influence a teacher's decision making; and ELL parents' fear of repercussions for speaking up. These three themes were analyzed from a standpoint of postcolonial theory which showed that what impacts the ELL parent-teacher interactions includes the histories that are beyond immediate context and yet that constitute positions of ELL parents and teachers that are not on equal power levels. While these socially constructed subject positions are not reversible merely through good intentions, being aware of the unequal power dynamics and the tensions they cause has important implications for teachers working with ELL students and their parents. More specifically, even though unequal power dynamics do and will continue to exist in ELL parent-teacher interactions and even though such inequalities are the effects of systemic social conditions, if improvement is going to occur, it will be largely a function of how we as teachers act (or don't act) in relation to ELL parents. From such a commitment, following are a few implications drawn from this study for all teachers working with ELL students and their parents.

Making an effort to learn from differences, how parents know and view their children for instance, as not something that needs to be overcome, not something that need to be merely tolerated, but as something that serves as a generative ground in which teachers can move beyond their taken-for-granted ways of knowing and seeing children. While the campaign to respect differences in the field of education is not new, in practice, however, we do find it very hard to live together amidst difference (Boler, 1999). People are not all the same and the articulating of differences and truly listening to differences offers teachers fertile soil for thinking outside familiar frames of reference. Interacting with ELL parents who possess different values can be uncomfortable and at times even unsettling for teachers. However, if we are not willing to listen and learn from the parents of ELL students, we do stand to lose by not challenging ourselves and engaging constructively with ELL parents, who may not always share our point of view. This requires teachers to consider what it means to really respect and understand the ELL students and parents so that differences are not merely tolerated but rather may provide the foundations for creativity through which teachers can further assist their ELL students to succeed in school.

As shown in this study, some ELL parents feel intimidated, excluded, and even demeaned by a subtle message that teachers unknowingly communicate that the parents do not care about their children's education and have not adequately prepared their children to succeed in school. In conclusion, it may be helpful for teachers to make a conscious effort to be more self-reflexive in several ways. First, it is important to respond to the questions that ELL parents may ask in genuinely respectful ways to ensure that the parents are encouraged to ask more questions and to learn what parents do not understand. Second, it is also important to make an effort to not only report how an ELL student is doing in school but to be curious about and interested in learning about how the child is doing at home. In this regard, teachers need to learn to value the knowledge of parents and recognize the contributions that they can make to the children's success in school. In fact, it would serve teachers well to see the ELL parents as essential partners in ELL students' optimal learning. This means that teachers have to learn to listen—"patiently, intently, and respectfully—to parental perspectives on their children" (Lawrence-Lightfoot, 2003, p. 230), so that teachers learn about the child's life outside of school and convey to parents that they do care about their children.

Moreover, it is critical for teachers in rural areas, who are mostly whites and have little exposure to diversity, to remind themselves that a child's and parent's proficiency level in English and their accents cannot be equated with their intelligence level. While teachers may very well understand this concept theoretically, in practice, such judgments occur more often than not (e.g., Cummins, 2000), and it requires a conscious effort for teachers not to demean the ELL students and parents by making false assumptions. Lastly, this study is not suggesting at all that such reflexive work for teachers working in rural areas is easy. In fact, creating new spaces for ELL parent-teacher interactions in which teachers genuinely welcome parents' questions and their ways of seeing and knowing their child, and seeing them as invaluable resources for working successfully with their children may require a continual effort, struggle, and hard work. Such an effort is one of the critical requirements in facilitating ELL parent-teacher communication that are open and collaborative which in turn will benefit ELL students' educational, social, and emotional growth in rural areas. In this respect, teacher training programs need to focus more on teaching pre-service teachers about working with parents in general and with ELL parents more specifically.

References

Arias, M. B., & Morillo-Campbell, M. (2008). Promising ELL parental involvement: Challenges in contested times. Retrieved June 24, 2013, from http://greatlakescenter.org/docs/Policy_Briefs/Arias_ELL.pdf

Berg, L., Denessen, E., Hornstra, L., Voeten, M., & Holland, R. W. (2010). The implicit prejudiced attitudes of teachers: Relations to teacher expectations and the ethnic achievement gap, *American Educational Research Journal, 47* (2), 497–527.

Boler, M. (1999). *Feeling power: Emotions and education.* New York: Routledge.

Bosher, S. (1998). The composing processes of three southeast Asian writers at the post-secondary level: An exploratory study. *Journal of Second Language Writing, 7* (2), 205–233.

Burbules, N. C. (2000). The limits of dialogue as a critical pedagogy. In P. P. Trifonas (Ed.), *Revolutionary pedagogies: Cultural politics, instituting education, and the discourse of theory.* (pp. 251–273). New York: Routledgefalmer.

Cox, D. D. (2005). Evidence-based interventions using home-school collaboration. *School Psychology Quarterly 20* (4), 473–497.

Cummins, J. (2000) *Language, power and pedagogy: Bilingual children in the crossfire.* Clevedon, UK: Multilingual Matters.

Gonzales De-Hass, A, R., Willems, P. P., & Holbein, M. F. B. (2005). Examining the relationship between parental involvement and student motivation. *Educational Psychology Review, 17* (2), 99–123.

Gibson, M. A. (2002). *The new Latino diaspora and educational policy: Education in the new Latino diaspora: Policy and the politics of identity.* Westport, CT: Ablex.

Gonzales-DeHass, A. R., Willems, P. P., & Holbein, M. F. D. (2005). Examining the relationship between parental involvement and student motivation. *Educational Psychology Review, 17* (2), 99–123.

Henderson, A. B., Jacob, A., Kernan-Schloss, C., & Raimondo, B. (2004). *The case for parent leadership.* Lexington, KY: Prichard Committee for Academic Excellence.

Heymann, S. J., & Earle, A. (2000). Low-income parents: How do working conditions affect their opportunity to help school-age children at risk? *American Educational Research Journal, 37* (4), 833, 848.

Hiatt-Michael, D. (2001). *Preparing teachers to work with parents* (Report EDO-SP-2001-2). Washington, DC: ERIC Clearinghouse on Teaching and Teacher Education.

Hyslop, N. (2000). *Hispanic parental involvement in home literacy.* ERIC Clearinghouse on Reading, English, and Communication. (ERIC Document Reproduction Service No. 446340).

Jandt, F. E., & Tanno, D. V. (2001). Decoding domination, encoding self-determination: Intercultural communication research processes. *The Howard Journal of Communications, 12,* 119–135.

Jeynes, W. H. (2003). A meta-analysis: The effects of parental involvement on minority children, *Education and Urban Society, 35* (2), 202–218.

Kanno, Y., & Cromley, J. G. (2013). English language learners' access to and attainment in postsecondary education. *Tesol Quarterly, 47* (1), 89–121.

King, S. B. (2012). Increasing college-going rate, parent involvement, and community participation in rural communities. *The Rural Educator, 33* (2), 20–26.

Kozol, J. (1991). *Savage inequalities: Children in America's schools.* New York: Crown.

Lawrence-Lightfoot, S. (2003). *The essential conversation: What parents and teachers can learn from each other.* New York: Ballantine Books.

Luke, A. (2004). Two takes on the critical. In B. Norton, & K. Toohey (Eds), *Critical pedagogies and language learning* (pp. 21–29). New York: Cambridge University Press.

Mace-Matluck, B., Alexander-Kasparik, R., & Qeen, R. (1998). *Through the golden door: Educational approaches for immigrant adolescents with limited schooling.* McHenry, IL: Delta Systems and Center for Applied Linguistics.

Marchant, G. J., Paulson, S. E., & Rothlisberg, B. A. (2001). Relations of middle school students' perceptions of family and school contexts with academic achievement. *Psychology in the Schools, 38* (6), 505–519.

Muchinsky, D., & Tangren, N. (1999). Immigrant student performance in an academic intensive English program. In L. Harklau, K. Losey, & M. Siegal (Eds), *Generation 1.5 meets college composition: Issues in the teaching of writing to U.S.-educated learners of ESL* (pp. 211–234). Mahwah, NJ: Lawrence Erlbaum Associates.

National Center for Education Statistics. (2011). Retrieved June 24, 2013, from http://nces.ed.gov/nationsreportcard/pdf/studies/2011462.pdf

The National Center for Educational Statistics. (2006). Retrieved September 3, 2010 from http://www.ets.org/Media/Conferences_and_Eve nts/pdf/ELLsympsium/ELL_factsheet.pdf

The National Clearinghouse for English Language Acquisition and Language Instruction Educational Programs (2007). Retrieved September 3, 2012 from www.ncela.gwu.edu/expert/fastfaq/4.html

O'Neal, D. D., Ringler, M., & Rodriguez, D. (2008). Teachers' perceptions of their preparation for teaching linguistically and culturally diverse learners in rural eastern North Carolina. *The Rural Educator, 30* (1), 5–13.

Padgett, R. (2006). *Best ways to involve parents.* Retrieved April 15, 2013 from http://www.eddlgest.com.

Panferov, S. (2010). Increasing ELL parental involvement in our schools. *Theory into Practice, 49,* 106–112.

Reed, K. (2010). Multicultural education for rural schools: Creating relevancy in rural America. *The Rural Educator, 31* (2), 15–20.

Rhedding-Jones, J. (2002) English elsewhere: Glocalization, assessment and ethics. *Journal of Curriculum Studies, 34* (4), 383–404.

Rumberger, R. W., Ghatak, R., Poulos, G., Ritter, P. L., & Dornbusch, S. M. (1990). Family influences on dropout behavior in one California high school. *Sociology and Education, 63* (4), 283–299.

Said, E. W. (1994). *Culture and imperialism.* New York: Vintage.

Said, E. W. (2003/1979). *Orientalism* (25th anniversary ed.). New York: Pantheon.

Scribner, J. D., Young, M. D., & Pedroza, A. (1999). Building collaborative relationship with parents. In P. Reyes, J. D. Scribner, & A. Paredes Scribner (Eds.), *Lessons from high-performing Hispanic schools: Creating learning communities* (pp. 36–60). New York: Teachers College Press.

Smith, J., Stern, K., & Shatrova, Z. (2008). Factors inhibiting Hispanic parents' school involvement. *The Rural Educator, 29* (3), 18–29,

Spivak, G.. (1988). Can the subaltern speak? In C. Nelson & L. Grossberg (Eds.), *Marxism and the interpretation of culture* (pp. 271–313). Chicago: University of Illinois Press.

Strauss, A., & Corbin, J. (1998). *Basics of qualitative research: Techniques and procedures for developing grounded theory.* Thousand Oaks, CA: Sage.

Trusty, J. (1996). Counseling for dropout prevention: Applications from multicultural counseling. *Journal of Multicultural Counseling and Development, 24* (2), 105–117.

Walker, A. (2012). Collaborating with the community: A lesson from a rural school district. *Tesol Journal, 3* (3), 469–487.

Wei, M., & Zhou, Y. (2012). Effects of language-minority family's activities in early second language writing development. *Tesol Journal, 3* (2), 181–209.

Winke, P. (2011). Evaluating the validity of a high-stakes ESL test: Why teachers' perceptions matter. *Tesol Quarterly, 45* (4), 628–660.

Critical Thinking

1. Summarize the data on parent involvement found in this study. Then, list the benefits.

2. What conclusions can you draw from the information in this article?

3. Construct a matrix that includes the three major findings and the implications that correspond to each finding. Then describe what you would do in your classroom practice to change those findings.

Create Central

www.mhhe.com/createcentral

Internet References

Centers for Disease Control and Prevention
http://www.cdc.gov/healthyyouth/protective/parent_engagement.htm

National Educational Association
http://www.nea.org/tools/56945.htm

U.S. Department of Education
http://www2.ed.gov/admins/comm/parents/parentinvolve/index.html?exp=2

Article   Prepared by: Rebecca B. Evers, *Winthrop University*

Dual Language Learners

Effective Instruction in Early Childhood

CLAUDE GOLDENBERG, JUDY HICKS, AND IRA LIT

Learning Outcomes

After reading this article, you will be able to:

- Explain the need for early childhood education in preschool settings for students who are DLL.

- Examine the concept of learning two languages simultaneously.

- Evaluate the research analysis presented in this article.

A s the number of English learners in K–12 public schools has increased, so too has the population of preschool dual language learners, or DLLs. For preschoolers, the term dual language learners is preferred since young children are still in the midst of acquiring their first language. More than 4 million DLLs are enrolled in early childhood programs nationally. Thirty percent of the children in Head Start and Early Head Start are DLL.[1]

Although a large majority of preschool-age children in the United States attend some type of early education setting, Latino children and children of immigrants attend at a lower rate than do children of nonimmigrant parents.[2] This is unfortunate, since children who attend preschool during the year before kindergarten have an advantage in reading and math over their peers who are not enrolled in center-based care.[3] Many children who are learning English as a second language while they are gaining early proficiency in their home language are therefore disproportionately missing academic benefits that attending preschool provides.[4]

For those DLLs who do attend an early childhood care or education setting, early educators must be informed by what research has to say about creating optimal learning environments. Concern over the achievement of this population of students has led to a large number of recent research reviews and professional publications aimed at improving preschool DLLs' educational opportunities.[5] In this article, we survey this growing body of research to help inform educators responsible for creating settings for our young DLLs.

We organize our review of the research by addressing four key topics:

1. Employing children's home language in the early childhood curriculum;
2. Comparing effective practices for DLLs and English speakers in English-only programs;
3. Promoting language development in English and the home language; and
4. Involving families in supporting children's language learning.

1. Employing Children's Home Language in the Early Childhood Curriculum

The debate over bilingual education has been the most controversial aspect of the education of English learners for more than a half century and continues to be politically charged.[6] Bilingual education's basic premise is that students should be taught academic skills in their home language as they learn and acquire skills in English. According to this view, instruction in the home language strengthens the home language and creates a more

---

* For discussions of terms, see the CECER-DLL's website at http://cecerdll.fpg.unc.edu and the NCELA's glossary of terms at www.ncela.gwu.edu/files/rcd/BE021775/Glossary_of_Terms.pdf.

solid foundation for cognitive and academic growth in English; moreover, promoting bilingual competence is valuable in its own right. Opponents of bilingual education argue that instruction in students' home language both delays English learners' entrance into the academic and social mainstream and depresses English achievement; bilingualism might be fine, but the school should focus on rapid and effective English learning. Others have also raised concerns about the resources required to fund bilingual programs and whether the benefits justify the costs.[7]

Preschool studies tend to find that at best, instruction in the home language contributes to growth in both English and home language skills; at worst, there is no difference in English achievement but an advantage in home language achievement.[8] In addition to promoting bilingual language and literacy skills, utilization of the home language can also have psychological and social benefits that immersion in a second language cannot offer. One study[9] found that Spanish-speaking children who experienced Spanish interactions with their teachers were more likely to engage in more complex linguistic interactions than children who experienced only English interactions with their teachers. Teachers in classrooms where Spanish was used also tended to rate their students more positively in terms of the students' frustration tolerance, assertiveness, and peer social skills.

Teachers can also use the students' home language in various ways that support children's learning, even when instruction is essentially in English. For example, teachers could supplement a book they are reading aloud with explanations or brief clarifications in the home language or by pointing out a cognate (e.g., "Do you know what a market is? It sounds like *mercado,* right?"), which can make texts in English more accessible to DLLs and possibly make them aware of linkages across languages.

2. Comparing Effective Practices for DLLs and English Speakers in English-Only Programs

Studies of effective early childhood curricula have shown cognitive and social benefits for DLLs that may be comparable to or greater than those for native English speakers. Researchers in Nebraska, for example, found that a professional development literacy workshop series (HeadsUp! Reading) for early childhood educators was equally effective in promoting early literacy skills for children from English-speaking and Spanish-speaking homes.[10] In Oklahoma, one of the pioneers of universal high-quality pre-K education, preschools produce developmental gains across various demographic groups, including Latinos, approximately 70 percent of whom come from predominantly Spanish-speaking homes. Gains for these students (in English)

were stronger than for students from English-speaking homes;[11] this might be explained by the fact that the Spanish-speaking students began with far lower English levels than the English-speaking students.

Studies also illustrate the value for young DLLs of well-known elements of effective teaching, such as explaining vocabulary words encountered during reading and using them in different contexts.[12] In other words, successful teaching and curricula seem to be successful for most children, suggesting that there is probably considerable overlap between what is effective practice for DLLs and for students already proficient in English.[13]

Regardless of their level of English development, young DLLs who are working to master the rudiments of English probably need additional supports to help them participate fully in classroom learning activities if the activities are in English. Although preschool DLLs benefit from explanations about the meaning of words (just as English speakers do), one study found that children who began with lower English scores learned fewer words than children with higher English scores.[14] Pictures help DLL preschoolers with low levels of oral English learn story vocabulary (e.g., dentist, mouse, cap), suggesting that *visual representations,* not just *explanations,* provide these children with additional support for learning.[15] Video resources also have proven useful.[16]

Attempts to incorporate additional supports such as these into comprehensive programs and curricula have had mixed success. For example, a professional development program that succeeded in having early childhood educators add scaffolding strategies for DLLs into their core practices found that the improvements in child outcomes were limited to some phonological awareness measures.[17]

The key message is that what we know about effective instruction in general is the foundation of effective instruction for English learners of all ages. "Generic" effective instruction, however, is probably not sufficient to promote accelerated learning among ELs, although it is almost certainly a necessary base. While we have some intriguing clues about what else is needed to make programs effective for English learners, there is little certainty about how to incorporate these supports into programs that optimize developmental outcomes for DLLs.

3. Promoting Language Development in English and the Home Language

Language development is, of course, a high priority in early childhood programs. English language development is critically important, but so is promoting development of the home language. Developing the home language is important in its own right *and* as a means of promoting other important cognitive and social outcomes.[18]

In her volume, *One Child, Two Languages,* dual language researcher Patton Tabors describes the sequence that most young children follow as they begin learning a second language in preschool.[19] First, young children often attempt to use their home language. Then, when they realize their home language is not working in this context, they tend to become silent. DLLs listen and observe, gaining an understanding of the classroom language. Next, they begin to "go public," testing out some new words and phrases. Finally, they begin to produce the new language, using phrases and then sentences.

Children may approach English learning differently, so this developmental sequence is not universal and invariant. But when teachers are aware of the general sequence, they have the opportunity to support DLLs most effectively. For example, it is important to be able to recognize and respond to children's nonverbal requests and protests—a silent child has needs that must be met, and the teacher can couple meeting those needs with introducing new phrases. Additionally, children who are not yet communicating verbally can be encouraged to build relationships through shared interests (e.g., working with a partner on a puzzle or dressing dolls) and through humor. Children can also be provided with the space and time both to act as *spectators* and to *rehearse* what they hear and want to repeat. Furthermore, models of pragmatically appropriate phrases— that is, appropriate to the particular situation in which the word or phrase is used—can be very useful for children who are just starting to "go public" with their new language.

Explicit English language development instruction is also important. We know surprisingly little, however, about the relative effects, benefits, and disadvantages of different approaches to promoting English language development for DLLs in early childhood settings (or K–12 schools).

In early elementary settings, researchers[20] have found that a separate block of English language development instruction during the school day was somewhat more effective than only integrating English language development into other instruction throughout the day, although there certainly should be English language learning opportunities throughout the day as well. There is also evidence in the preschool context for a separate block of language development in the home language: for Spanish-speaking children in an English-immersion preschool, researchers found that a 30-minute block of Spanish-language development led to significant gains in children's oral proficiency in Spanish.[21] Second-language instruction should provide an appropriate balance of opportunities for meaningful, authentic communication and for more organized instruction and specific feedback on the proper use of conventional forms.[22]

4. Involving Families in Supporting Children's Language Learning

Families play an important role in helping to make children's preschool experiences successful. DLLs' parents consistently show interest in their children's education and are highly motivated to provide their support.[23] Unfortunately, teachers often underestimate language-minority parents' ability to help their children succeed in school.[24] Most parents are responsive to focused and sensitive efforts to help them play an active role in supporting their children's earliest school success. However, researchers have found variability on the impact of home intervention programs on children's academic learning, perhaps due to the range of design and implementation features of various programs.

An important issue that parents and teachers ask about is whether parents of DLLs should use the home language with children exclusively or try to encourage more English use. Research and experience have established that children can learn more than one language, either simultaneously or sequentially, with no adverse effects.[25] In fact, in addition to the social and cultural benefits, there are potential cognitive advantages to growing up bilingual.[26] Yet many parents—and teachers— assume it is common sense that speaking more English at home will promote higher levels of English proficiency for children. Correlational studies do tend to corroborate these intuitions; use of any language at home is positively associated with children's learning outcomes in that language and negatively associated with outcomes in the other language. But findings are mixed: one study[27] found that increased use of English by Spanish-speaking mothers did not accelerate English growth by children—but it did decelerate Spanish vocabulary growth.

Bilingual language development need not be a zero-sum game, and parents should be reassured that use of the home language will not undermine children's English language development. Continuing to speak the native language can also be important for other reasons in addition to the cognitive and linguistic benefits, such as maintaining cultural and family values and communication. In sum, although more research is needed in this area, current research suggests that preschool educators should use children's native language where possible, apply specific strategies for building English language skills, and build bridges with families to support children's learning.

Notes

1. Nikki Aikens, Sally Atkins-Burnett, and Eileen Bandel, *Approaches to Assessing the Language and Literacy Skills of Young Dual Language Learners: A Review of the*

Research, Research Brief #10 (Chapel Hill: University of North Carolina, FPG Child Development Institute, Center for Early Care and Education Research—Dual Language Learners, 2012).

2. Kristin Turney and Grace Kao, "Pre-Kindergarten Child Care and Behavioral Outcomes among Children of Immigrants," *Early Childhood Research Quarterly* 24, no. 4 (2009): 432–444.

3. Katherine Magnuson, Claudia Lahaie, and Jane Waldfogel, "Preschool and School Readiness of Children of Immigrants," *Social Science Quarterly* 87, no. 5 (2006): 1241–1262; and Russell W. Rumberger and Loan Tran, *Preschool Participation and the Cognitive and Social Development of Language-Minority Students* (Los Angeles: National Center for Research on Evaluation, Standards, and Student Testing, UCLA, 2006).

4. Lynn A. Karoly and Gabriella C. Gonzalez, "Early Care and Education for Children in Immigrant Families," *Future of Children* 21, no. 1 (2011): 71–101.

5. See, for example, Center for Early Care and Education Research—Dual Language Learners, research briefs #1–#8 (2011), available at http://cecerdll.fpg.unc.edu/document-library; and Linda M. Espinosa, *Getting It Right for Young Children from Diverse Backgrounds: Applying Research to Improve Practice* (Upper Saddle River, NJ: Pearson, 2010).

6. See, for example, Patricia Gándara and Megan Hopkins, eds., *Forbidden Language: English Learners and Restrictive Language Policies* (New York: Teachers College Press, 2010).

7. Oscar Jimenez-Castellanos and Amelia M. Topper, "The Cost of Providing an Adequate Education to English Language Learners: A Review of the Literature," *Review of Educational Research* 82, no. 2 (2012): 179–232; and Thomas B. Parrish, "A Cost Analysis of Alternative Instructional Models for Limited English Proficient Students in California," *Journal of Education Finance* 19, no. 3 (1994): 256–278.

8. W. Steven Barnett, Donald J. Yarosz, Jessica Thomas, Kwanghee Jung, and Dulce Blanco, *Two-Way and Monolingual English Immersion in Preschool Education: An Experimental Comparison* (New Brunswick, NJ: National Institute for Early Education Research, 2007); Judith K. Bernhard, Jim Cummins, F. Isabel Campoy, Alma Flor Ada, Adam Winsler, and Charles Bleiker, "Identity Texts and Literacy Development among Preschool English Language Learners: Enhancing Learning Opportunities for Children at Risk for Learning Disabilities," *Teachers College Record* 108, no. 11 (2006): 2380–2405; S. Jim Campos, "The Carpinteria Preschool Program: A Long-Term Effects Study," in *Meeting the Challenge of Linguistic and Cultural Diversity in Early Childhood Education,* ed. Eugene E. Garcia and Barry McLaughlin (New York: Teachers College Press, 1995), 34–48; Lillian K. Durán, Cary J. Roseth, and Patricia Hoffman, "An Experimental Study Comparing English-Only and Transitional Bilingual Education on Spanish-Speaking

Preschoolers' Early Literacy Development," *Early Childhood Research Quarterly* 25, no. 2 (2010): 207–217; Jo Ann M. Farver, Christopher J. Lonigan, and Stefanie Eppe, "Effective Early Literacy Skill Development for Young Spanish-Speaking English Language Learners: An Experimental Study of Two Methods," *Child Development* 80, no. 3 (2009): 703–719; and Adam Winsler, Rafael M. Díaz, Linda Espinosa, and James L. Rodríguez, "When Learning a Second Language Does Not Mean Losing the First: Bilingual Language Development in Low-Income, Spanish-Speaking Children Attending Bilingual Preschool," *Child Development* 70, no. 2 (1999): 349–362.

9. Florence Chang, Gisele Crawford, Diane Early, Donna Bryant, CarolleeHowes, Margaret Burchinal, Oscar Barbarin, Richard Clifford, and Robert Pianta, "Spanish-Speaking Children's Social and Language Development in Pre-Kindergarten Classrooms," *Early Education and Development* 18, no. 2 (2007): 243–269.

10. Barbara Jackson, Robert Larzelere, Lisa St. Clair, Marcia Corr, Carol Fichter, and Harriet Egertson, "The Impact of 'HeadsUp! Reading' on Early Childhood Educators' Literacy Practices and Preschool Children's Literacy Skills," *Early Childhood Research Quarterly* 21, no. 2 (2006): 213–226.

11. William T. Gormley Jr., "The Effects of Oklahoma's Universal Pre-Kindergarten Program on Hispanic Children" (policy brief, Center for Research on Children in the United States, 2008); and William T. Gormley Jr. and Deborah Phillips, "The Effects of Universal Pre-K in Oklahoma: Research Highlights and Policy Implications," *Policy Studies Journal* 33, no. 1 (2005): 65–82.

12. Molly Fuller Collins, "ESL Preschoolers' English Vocabulary Acquisition from Storybook Reading," *Reading Research Quarterly* 40, no. 4 (2005): 406–408.

13. Diane August and Timothy Shanahan, eds., *Developing Reading and Writing in Second-Language Learners: Lessons from the Report of the National Literacy Panel on Language-Minority Children and Youth* (New York: Routledge, 2008); and Claude Goldenberg and Rhoda Coleman, *Promoting Academic Achievement among English Learners: A Guide to the Research* (Thousand Oaks, CA: Corwin, 2010).

14. Collins, "ESL Preschoolers' English Vocabulary Acquisition."

15. Theresa Roberts and Harriet Neal, "Relationships among Preschool English Language Learners' Oral Proficiency in English, Instructional Experience and Literacy Development," *Contemporary Educational Psychology* 29, no. 3 (2004): 283–311.

16. Rebecca Silverman and Sara Hines, "The Effects of Multimedia-Enhanced Instruction on the Vocabulary of English-Language Learners and Non-English-Language Learners in Pre-Kindergarten through Second Grade," *Journal of Educational Psychology* 101, no. 2 (2009): 305–314.

17. Virginia Buysse, Dina C. Castro, and Ellen Peisner-Feinberg, "Effects of a Professional Development Program on Classroom

Practices and Outcomes for Latino Dual Language Learners," *Early Childhood Research Quarterly* 25, no. 2 (2010): 194–206.

18. Fred Genesee, Johanne Paradis, and Martha B. Crago, *Dual Language Development and Disorders: A Handbook on Bilingualism and Second Language Learning* (Baltimore: Brookes, 2004).

19. Patton O. Tabors, *One Child, Two Languages: A Guide for Early Childhood Educators of Children Learning English as a Second Language* (Baltimore: Brookes, 2008).

20. William M. Saunders, Barbara R. Foorman, and Coleen D. Carlson, "Is a Separate Block of Time for Oral English Language Development in Programs for English Learners Needed?," *The Elementary School Journal* 107, no. 2 (2006): 181–197.

21. M. Adelaida Restrepo, Anny P. Castilla, Paula J. Schwanenflugel, Stacey Neuharth-Pritchett, Claire E. Hamilton, and Alejandra Arboleda, "Effects of Supplemental Spanish Oral Language Program on Sentence Length, Complexity, and Grammaticality in Spanish-Speaking Children Attending English-Only Preschools," *Language, Speech, and Hearing Services in Schools* 41, no. 1 (2010): 3–13.

22. William M. Saunders and Claude Goldenberg, "Research to Guide English Language Development Instruction," in *Improving Education for English Learners: Research-Based Approaches,* ed. David Dolson and Lauri Burnham-Massey (Sacramento: CDE Press, 2010), 21–81; and Patsy M. Lightbown and Nina Spada, *How Languages Are Learned,* 3rd ed. (Oxford: Oxford University Press, 2006).

23. Claude Goldenberg and Ronald Gallimore, "Immigrant Latino Parents' Values and Beliefs about Their Children's Education: Continuities and Discontinuities across Cultures and Generations," in *Advances in Motivation and Achievement: Culture, Ethnicity, and Motivation,* vol. 9, ed. Paul R. Pintrich and Martin L. Maehr(Greenwich, CT: JAI Press, 1995), 183–228; Nancy J. Perry, Sascha Mitchell Kay, and Ashley Brown, "Continuity and Change in Home Literacy Practices of Hispanic Families with Preschool Children," *Early Child Development and Care* 178, no. 1 (2008): 99–113; and Ana Schaller, Lisa Oglesby Rocha, and David Barshinger, "Maternal Attitudes and Parent Education: How Immigrant Mothers Support Their Child's Education Despite Their Own Low Levels of Education," *Early Childhood Education Journal* 34, no. 5 (2007): 351–356.

24. Liz Brooker, "'Five on the First of December!': What Can We Learn from Case Studies of Early Childhood Literacy?," *Journal of Early Childhood Literacy* 2, no. 3 (2002): 291–313; and Claude Goldenberg, "Low-Income Hispanic Parents' Contributions to Their First-Grade Children's Word-Recognition Skills," *Anthropology and Education Quarterly* 18, no. 3 (1987): 149–179.

25. Genesee, Paradis, and Crago, *Dual Language Development and Disorders.*

26. Ellen Bialystok, *Bilingualism in Development: Language, Literacy, and Cognition* (Cambridge: Cambridge University Press, 2001); and Patricia K. Kuhl, "Early Language Acquisition: Cracking the Speech Code," *Nature Reviews Neuroscience* 5, no. 11 (2004): 831–843.

27. Carol Scheffner Hammer, Megan Dunn Davison, Frank R. Lawrence, and Adele W. Miccio, "The Effect of Maternal Language on Bilingual Children's Vocabulary and Emergent Literacy Development during Head Start and Kindergarten," *Scientific Studies of Reading* 13, no. 2 (2009): 99–121.

Critical Thinking

1. Why is early childhood education important for students who are dual language learners?

2. Summarize the main points under each key topic and rank the key topics in your preference for order of importance.

3. If you were given the funds to develop and implement a program for students who are DLL in your community, which of the key topics do you believe would be best or easiest to use as your start-up? Which would you leave until last? Justify your selections.

Create Central

www.mhhe.com/createcentral

Internet References

Center for Comprehensive School Reform and Improvement Center's Home page

http://www.centerforcsri.org

Center's link for resources on English Language Learners and Diverse Students

http://www.centerforcsri.org/index.php?option=com_content&task=view&id=678&Itemid=126

Larry Ferlazzo's Educational Blog

http://larryferlazzo.edublogs.org/

New Horizons for Learning

www.newhorizons.org

CLAUDE GOLDENBERG is a professor of education at Stanford University. Judy Hicks is a doctoral student in curriculum and teacher education at Stanford and a former elementary school teacher. Ira Lit is an associate professor of teaching at Stanford and the director of the Stanford Elementary Teacher Education Program. Previously, he was an elementary school teacher and the executive director for the Teachers for a New Era initiative at Bank Street College of Education. This article is adapted with permission from Claude Goldenberg, Judy Hicks, and Ira Lit, "Teaching Young English Learners," in Handbook of Research-Based Practice in Early Education, edited by D. Ray Reutzel (Guilford Press, 2013).

Claude Goldenberg, Judy Hicks, and Ira Lit, *Dual Language Learners: Effective Instruction in Early Childhood,* American Educator, Summer 2013, pp. 26–29. Copyright © 2013 by the American Federation of Teachers, AFL-CIO. All rights reserved. Used with permission.

Bilingual Education and the Role of Minority-Serving Institutions by Alice Ginsberg et al.

123

Article

Prepared by: Rebecca B. Evers, *Winthrop University*

Bilingual Education and the Role of Minority-serving Institutions

ALICE GINSBERG ET AL.

Learning Outcomes

After reading this article, you will be able to:

- Discern the critical issues facing education of students who are bilingual.

- Investigate programs and interventions established to serve this population.

English language learners (ELLs) and immigrants are the fastest growing student population in the United States. Currently, there are over 5 million ELLs in public schools, and this number will only increase as Loes and Saavedra (2010) project that they will comprise one in four students nationally in 2020. Arizona, California, Florida, New York and Texas presently educate about 70% of the total ELL student population. Interestingly, North Carolina, South Carolina, Tennessee, Arkansas, and Georgia are witnessing a rapid increase of over 200% in both ELL and immigrant student enrollment (Loes & Saavedra 2010).

Teacher education and certification programs are at the core of improving bilingual education.

Despite historic and far-reaching legal victories that proclaimed "language minority students may not be denied access to educational opportunities based on language or national origin," language of instruction continues to be a significant educational roadblock for ELL and immigrant students (Loes & Saavedra 2010, 4–5). In order to address this disjuncture, educational programs that emphasize language of instruction must be established upon a solid foundation of educational theory, research, and practice, and implemented with adequate support, resources, and personnel if ELL and immigrant students are to meaningfully take advantage of their recognized yet not fully tangible legal gains. Furthermore, ELL and immigrant students are arguably one of the most disenfranchised student populations in US schools. According to García (2010), ELLs who enter Kindergarten with limited English proficiency are in the lowest performing quartile in 5th grade reading and math. The achievement gap continues to grow as ELL students have the highest secondary school dropout rates and alarmingly low college placement rates.

While there have been increased efforts to improve bilingual education, especially in elementary education where interventions are the most critical and can be the most effective, the task before us is still a difficult one. As renowned ELL scholar Eugene García notes:

> Unfortunately, educational policy and practice discussions regarding the education of bilingual students are often overly simplistic and focus solely on linguistic deficiencies. . . . They tend to neglect the complex interweaving of students' cultural, linguistic and cognitive development (García 2010, p. 6).

García further elaborates that teacher education and certification programs are at the core of improving bilingual education. We cannot develop a more comprehensive and effective approach to serving ELL students *without* teachers who understand the cultural nuances of immigrant populations. Teachers must also be willing to engage in new, innovative, and ultimately more effective practices that build on students' strengths. According to García, "A vast body of research has documented a direct link between ELL students achievement and the expertise and experience of the classroom teacher," and that "To be effective, teachers must provide a classroom environment with ample opportunity for students to practice academic language thoughtfully and meaningfully" (García 2010, p. 8).

Kelly Salas, a former elementary teacher in the Milwaukee Public Schools who now works for the Milwaukee Teachers Education Association, warns that schools with high numbers of Limited English Proficient (LEP) students are more likely to encounter difficulties in filling teacher vacancies and mostly rely on under-qualified and substitute teachers. According to Salas, teachers in these schools are also "more likely to have provisional, emergency, or temporary certification than are those in other schools" (Salas 2014, 188).

The shortage of teachers who are qualified and prepared to teach ELL and LEP students led Garcia to ask critical questions: "Do teachers have at least three years of experience teaching ELLs? Do they use instructional strategies that are specifically responsive to students acquiring English in academic contexts? Do they receive the continuous professional development and classroom related support they need to determine the effect their instruction has on student outcomes. Are they given the support they need to use regular authentic assessments of student achievement to assess their impact?" (García, 2010, pp. 8–9).

To answer these important questions, it is significant that over 70% of all bachelor degrees awarded in bicultural/multilingual/cultural education hail from Minority-Serving Institutions (MSIs). This is but one example of how MSIs are paving the way for others to learn from and participate in more multifaceted and asset-oriented approaches to teaching ELL students.

An example can [be] found in the teacher education program at The University of Texas at El Paso (UTEP), which graduates over 50% of bicultural, multilingual, and cultural education teachers at MSIs. According to its College of Education's mission statement:

> Located in the bicultural, bilingual, and bi-national context of the border, the Department of Teacher Education seeks to prepare teachers and researchers who critically analyze educational practices in light of our diverse community and who can understand global issues in education. Highlights of our programs are the University's unique location on the U.S.-Mexico border and faculty with expertise in preparing teachers and researchers to work with Latino/as and English Language Learners.

UTEP is notable in that it engages in strong partnerships and ongoing service to community organizations and schools, including:

- Pro bono consulting to AVANCE of El Paso, to assist with the implementation of their family literacy program;
- Faculty facilitated establishment of a bilingual distance education program;

- Faculty-assisted curriculum development, parent power nights, and weekly literacy workshops at local schools;
- Library donations and reading tutorials with students from homeless shelters; and
- A yearly summer camp, TExPREP that involves about 300 middle school students from local schools.

These kinds of programs empower faculty to conduct cutting-edge research on language learning, bilugualism, international curricular issues, and immigrant education, which includes a recently awarded $1.8 million grant from the U.S. Department of Education for Project LEAD (Leadership in English Acquisition, Academic Achievement and Development). Project LEAD is a five-year collaboration between UTEP and the Socorro Independent School District (SISD) to improve and expand the knowledge of teachers who work with English language learners. Faculty at UTEP offer professional development, tutoring and mentors to SISD high schools and their feeder schools, as well as funding for participants to get ESL certificates, and for graduate students and teachers to earn advanced degrees in bilingual/biliteracy and second language acquisition.

Another MSI that is actively engaged in bilingual education is California State University, Fresno, which has developed a Mini Corps program that recruits university students familiar with migrant populations and prepares them to help classroom teachers in providing services to migrant children. Students interested in becoming teachers in migrant communities receive training, mentoring, advising, and financial support. In the 2013–2014 school year, 48 undergraduate students provided tutoring and mentoring to 680 K-12 migrant students, and worked collaboratively with 113 classroom teachers across 39 schools in Fresno County. Fresno State also offers a Reading Laboratory with literacy tutoring services for struggling school-age children from the community, summer writing programs and camps for local children, a family literacy program for parents and students, and a collaboration with a local Hispanic radio channel that disseminates information about their programs to potential teachers.

These are just a few examples of what MSIs are accomplishing in the field of bicultural, multilingual, and cultural education. As Salas reminds us: "All children need to learn how to communicate with people whose language and culture are different from their own. These abilities are highly valued, and many teenagers and adults spend years trying to develop them. Children who are raised from birth speaking a language other than English have a unique opportunity to cultivate these abilities from a young age. Our schools must help them seize that opportunity" (Salas, 2014, p. 189).

References

Loes, K. & Saavedra, L. (2010). *A new vision to increase the academic achievement for English language learners and immigrant students.* Washington, DC: The Urban Institute.

García, E. (2010). *Education and achievement: A focus on Latino "immigrant" children.* Washington, DC: The Urban Institute.

Salas, K. (2014). Defending bilingual education. In W. Au (Ed.), *Rethinking Multicultural Education: Teaching for Racial and Cultural Justice* (pp. 183–189). Milwaukee, WI: Rethinking Schools.

Critical Thinking

1. What data provided in this report was surprising to you? Explain why.

2. What actions would you take if the President appointed you as U.S. Secretary of Education?

Internet References

National Clearinghouse for English Language Acquisitions
http://ncela.ed.gov

Quality Education for Minorities
http://www.qem.org/

US Department of Education–Office of English Language Acquisitions
http://www2.ed.gov/about/offices/list/oela/index.html

Unit 6

UNIT

Prepared by: Rebecca B. Evers, *Winthrop University*

Technology Supports Learning

Technology has been a change agent in education. After experiencing early motion pictures in 1913, Thomas Edison declared that books would become obsolete in schools because we would be able to learn everything from movies. Most recently we have heard similar claims about digital books from advocates of Kindle, Nook, iPad, and other e-readers and sellers of audio books. What is really happening in our schools? Are textbooks disappearing? Is everyone connected? Are our students sitting all day laboring over a keyboard and staring at a screen? In this unit we will explore both the potential of the digital technology and the challenges of using this technology for teaching and learning.

There are significant trends noted by Bitter and Pierson (2002) that continue to be important to this discussion even now, thirteen years later. The first is the shift in demographics within our student population. We are seeing an increased numbers of students who do not live in traditional family structures, who have special needs at both the high and low ends of achievement, who are English Language Learners, or who live in poverty. For many of these students, the ability to access sophisticated technology may not exist in their homes or neighborhoods. Hence, schools are the only place where they can be exposed to and learn about the usage of technology. These students, many of whom will need technology to access the curriculum, will pose a considerable challenge to public schools. An additional challenge, according to Bitter and Pierson, will be the acceleration of technological change that correspondingly increases the pace of change in our knowledge base. Keeping up in one's field of expertise or areas of interest has become a full-time job of its own.

In most schools, regardless of where the school is regionally or economically, most teachers who use computers do so because computers make their jobs easier and help complete tasks more efficiently. The computer can do things the teacher cannot, or is unwilling to, do. We use them to keep digital grade books that will correctly calculate final grades in a flash; search for information to use in lectures; create photos and clip art to illustrate our PowerPoints; obtain lesson plans to meet state standards; and communicate with peers down the hall,

the principal, and even with parents. But too often the teacher's computer may be the only computer in a classroom. There may be a computer lab down the hall or a few computers in the media center, but very few schools have laptops or handhelds for all students. So almost 100 years ago, Thomas Edison may have been a bit hasty to declare books a thing of the past. In the *Education* 98/99, we published an article, *"The Silicon Classroom"* by Kaplan and Rogers (1996) in which they declared that schools were rushing to spend billions on computers without a clue on what to do with them. In present day classrooms, we continue to see the challenges that schools face in implementing computer usage in the classroom. These issues are economic, social, and philosophic. Why haven't we seen greater strides made to bring every school into the digital age? We hope the articles presented in this unit will challenge you to consider how you should and will use technology to remove barriers to the curriculum within your content area.

How do we respond when confronted with the accusation that too many teachers and schools are using 19th century methods to teach 21st century students? Some see a rebellion happening in schools as students are unable to relate to the teaching methods and materials presented in most classrooms. This is a non-violent rebellion, but it is nonetheless disturbing to see students who are not fully engaged in active learning experiences and frustrated in their desires for more.

If we are in the middle of a rebellion or revolution, even a non-violent one, we will need weapons to take into battle. The article on collaborative technology provides an interesting array of weapons, or rather technology tools, that are easily accessible to teachers and their students. Most of us know about Google Docs, but how does that software and other Web 2.0 applications support students' ability to meet Common Core Standards?

In an effort to make the most of face-to-face classroom time, many teachers are flipping their classes. Rather than looking for reasons and rationales for why students were failing, teachers should look for solutions. One teacher found her solution by *flipping*. This article is a good place to start if you are not sure what flipping a classroom means. Others are looking at collaborative online tools to support learning in and out of the classroom. Thinking in new ways has helped teachers in the specials such as physical education, art, and music integrate technology into teaching, learning, and assessing.

With the increasing diversity of students in our classroom, we need to provide more and more assistive technology to meet their needs. If we look around we can find technologies that will work for *all* students. Calculators may be available in math and even in science classes, but what about their use in social studies and language arts classes where students may want to average grades or percentages in class elections. Digital cameras can be used to document notes on the board from class discussions, posters they need to remember, or even a slide from a multimedia presentation. Dictionaries allow students with disabilities, who are ELL, or even gifted, to look up a definition of a new word (Melville, 2005).

Hopefully the articles in this unit will stimulate your imagination to consider using more technology in your classroom or using what you have more creatively.

References

Bitter, G. & M. Pierson. 2002. *Using Technology in the Classroom.* Boston, MA: Allyn and Bacon.

Melville, E. (2005). Cell Phones: Nuisance or Necessity. *Teaching Today.* Retrieved on 15 May 2012 from http://privateschool.about.com/gi/o.htm?zi=1/XJ&zTi=1&sdn=privateschool&cdn=education&tm=26&gps=234_220_1066_560&f=20&tt=13&bt=1&bts=1&zu=http%3A//www.glencoe.com/sec/teachingtoday/educationupclose.phtml/52

Article   Prepared by: Rebecca B. Evers, *Winthrop University*

Teachers Connect *with* Technology

Online tools build new pathways to collaboration

VICKI L. PHILLIPS AND LYNN OLSON

Learning Outcomes

After reading this article, you will be able to:

- Recognize the ways technology can support collaboration with educators within your school district and across the state or country.
- Explore online tools for learning and collaboration.

The Common Core State Standards promise to raise expectations for all students by establishing consistent college- and career-ready learning goals across the country. The standards build on the best of the current state standards informed by the experiences of top-performing countries. Most importantly, they focus on what is most essential at each grade level, bringing coherence and focus, rather than asking students and teachers to learn less and less about more and more.

Implementation of the Common Core provides an opportunity for states and districts not only to raise expectations, but also to rethink how they support teachers with instructional materials and professional learning. The Common Core will require teachers to shift their instructional practice in significant ways. To build long-term understanding and ownership, training and support should take advantage of teachers' own expertise and the power of teacher-to-teacher networks.

Professional Learning Needs

Teachers have expressed a strong desire for Common Core-aligned resources and support. In a 2012 Scholastic survey of teachers, supported by the Bill & Melinda Gates Foundation, teachers indicated they need more professional support and development to implement these standards. About six in 10 teachers requested professional learning focused on the standards and how to teach them, along with new English and math curricula and learning tools (Scholastic & Bill & Melinda Gates Foundation, 2012).

Yet traditional approaches for supporting educators following the introduction of new content standards will likely prove inadequate. As Learning Forward noted in *Meet the Promise of Content Standards: Investing in Professional Learning,* "Resorting to comfortable and familiar approaches to professional learning such as short-term awareness-building information sessions on what the new standards are and how they compare to previous ones will fall short of the intense, practical, content-focused professional learning needed to realize the promise of all students college- and career-ready at the end of high school" (Killion & Hirsh, 2012). Effective professional learning encourages collaboration among teachers over a sustained period to tackle the challenge of Common Core implementation.

A New Approach

At the Bill & Melinda Gates Foundation, we believe teachers need to be involved as critical partners in developing tools and resources to support Common Core implementation. When working together, teachers draw on their shared trust, expertise, and experiences to improve instruction. And when this collaboration focuses on student work, it builds educators' capacity to address students' academic needs immediately.

The foundation supports two examples of this kind of collaboration: the Literacy Design Collaborative (www.literacydesign collaborative.org) and the Mathematics Design Collaborative (www.mygroup genius.org/mathematics), through which groups of teachers, curriculum experts, and other educators work together to create high-quality, useful lessons and research-based instructional tools incorporating the Common Core State Standards. More than developing a free, online library of new lessons and units, these efforts are pioneering new pathways for how educators can work together to shift teacher practice.

For example, the Common Core State Standards recognize that, to succeed in college, students need to understand and write about nonfiction texts. But most high school science and social studies teachers, and even some English teachers, have little training in teaching reading and writing. In New York City, instructional experts from New Visions for Public Schools, a New York City-based nonprofit organization, are using the framework and tools developed by the Literacy Design Collaborative to help teachers across content areas embed standards-based literacy skills into their classrooms.

These skills include locating textual evidence, evaluating arguments, interpreting meaning, and synthesizing information from different sources. Teachers use templates aligned to the standards to develop their own curriculum modules that scaffold the writing process and enable teachers to assess student progress. These teachers are producing classroom-tested, Common Core-aligned modules that other teachers can adopt or adapt. And because all of the lessons are built off of a common set of templates, teachers are talking the same language, which makes sharing their work easier.

In mathematics, the standards ask teachers to weave together content knowledge and application. The Mathematics Design Collaborative addresses this by supporting teachers in enacting high-quality formative assessment through the use of lessons called classroom challenges. These two-day lessons help teachers understand where students are in their mastery of a topic, create learning experiences for students to develop rich understanding of a given topic, and give students opportunities to apply their learning in meaningful ways.

New Visions supports teachers in the math collaborative by facilitating grade-level team meetings to identify students' misunderstandings based on a preassessment. Teachers jointly design probing questions that will help address those misconceptions as students work collaboratively on challenging math tasks. Then teachers collectively review students' understandings once the task is completed to see if their instruction has been effective.

There is a buzz of enthusiasm in these schools as teachers embrace the work. Some say working with the collaboratives has been the best professional learning of their careers. Teachers report that they are covering fewer topics more deeply, that their expectations for student writing have increased, and that their students are more engaged and producing higher-quality work. Teachers also say that some of the extra time initially spent on these new instructional approaches is recouped later in the year because students can apply the skills learned to future lessons. Some teachers already are adapting these methods and performance tasks to the rest of their curriculum.

The collaboratives demonstrate that teachers are eager for meaningful opportunities to work together to create tools and resources that will improve student learning. And when teachers are engaged in developing instructional resources, they share them with each other, helping best practices spread faster than the common cold.

What Education Leaders Can Do

The collaboratives are just one model for engaging educators in Common Core implementation. State and district leaders can bring educators together to develop and adapt instructional materials aligned to the Common Core in a variety of settings—and the good news is they don't have to start from scratch. Teachers can find tools from the literacy and math design collaboratives at ASCD's EduCore (http://educore.ascd.org). In addition, organizations across the country are putting together collections of free, high-quality curriculum and instructional resources that can be adapted by local educators as part of a sustained program of professional learning.

For example, LearnZillion (http://learnzillion.com) offers short video lessons developed by teachers that illustrate key concepts in mathematics and English language arts for students in grades 3–12. In 2012, LearnZillion convened more than 100 teachers in Atlanta to create more than 2,000 lessons—with accompanying videos—aligned to the Common Core State Standards. Students can search the videos by content area, grade level, or topic to review material out of class, and teachers can access additional resources to plan lessons, engage parents, and monitor student progress.

Similarly, Better Lesson (http://betterlesson.com) provides free access to lesson plans, materials, and instructional resources created by successful teachers. Better Lesson was founded by a group of teachers from Boston and Atlanta who wanted to spread best practices to new and developing teachers. The organization is now working with high-performing mathematics and English language arts teachers to create Common Core-aligned courses and share strategies for effective instruction.

Technology allows teachers to access professional development resources when and how they want to, expanding the reach of summer workshops and professional learning days. Increasingly, innovative groups are tapping into the ability to provide tools and resources online. Student Achievement Partners (www.achievethecore.org) provides resources and professional development modules to help teachers understand the instructional shifts Common Core requires. The organization is working with the two national teachers unions to develop Common Core-aligned tools by teachers for teachers.

Teacher leaders who are part of the fellowship program at America Achieves (http://commoncore.americaachieves.org) have created lessons grounded in the Common Core, which other teachers can use or adapt, as well as videos of themselves teaching the lessons. The Teaching Channel (www.teaching channel.org) also allows educators to search for lesson ideas that are linked to the Common Core and then watch videos of teachers giving those lessons in real classrooms. Instead of inventing new techniques out of whole cloth, the Teaching Channel helps connect teachers with tactics, strategies, and methods that have been shown to work.

Reaching Teachers

These resources can only be effective if teachers know about them. Too often, we hear from teachers that they are in great need of resources but don't know what is available. Some states are addressing this by creating dedicated websites with information and links to materials. For example, the Tennessee Department of Education launched TNCore (http://tncore.org), which includes background on the standards and the instructional shifts they require, state-developed online training modules, and links to external resources.

District intranets and learning management systems also offer ways to connect teachers to high-quality online resources and to each other. Districts in Colorado, Illinois, and New York are now piloting new cloud-based services that connect content from a wide variety of publishers to information about student learning needs, giving teachers greater access to curriculum and assessment resources and the ability to personalize learning so that students get what they need, when they need it, in a format that works best for them.

The Power of Collaboration

From online lessons to streaming video of master teachers in the classroom, technology can be a powerful tool to help teachers explore and share best practices to implement the Common Core. Yet technology is best positioned to support, not drive, effective Common Core implementation.

The most important ingredient is the opportunity for teachers to collaborate and reflect together. To get Common Core implementation right, school and district leaders must take the time to ensure teachers have adequate resources and support to collaborate on the enormous shifts in instruction they are being asked to make on behalf of students.

Standards alone won't teach students how to closely read great literature or choose the appropriate mathematical strategy to solve a problem. For that, there is no substitute for great teaching. With the right supports, teachers are poised to take ownership of how to best implement the Common Core in their classrooms and to explore the teaching and learning possibilities opened up by the new standards.

References

Killion, J. & Hirsh, S. (2012). *Meet the promise of content standards: Investing in professional learning.* Oxford, OH: Learning Forward.

Scholastic & Bill & Melinda Gates Foundation. (2012). *Primary sources: 2012: America's teachers on the teaching profession.* New York, NY: Scholastic.

Critical Thinking

1. Develop a list of pros and cons for the use of the tools and websites discussed in this article. Explain which side you are on and why.

2. Reflect on your personal and professional use of technology, including social media, to connect with others. Now, create your philosophy of technology use that will enhance and guide your professional development as a teacher.

3. Using the websites in the article and referenced here, find two or three tools, websites, or online collaboratives that will fit into your content area and personal philosophy.

Internet References

Achieve the Core
   http://achievethecore.org/
EduCore
   http://educore.ascd.org/
Literacy Design Collaborative
   http://ldc.org/
Math Design Collaborative
   http://collegeready.gatesfoundation.org/Learning/MathDesign Collaborative

---

VICKI L. PHILLIPS is director of education, college ready, and Lynn Olson is advisor to the director of education at the Bill & Melinda Gates Foundation.

Phillips, Vicki L.; Olson, Lynn, "Teachers Connect with Technology: Online Tools Build New Pathways to Collaboration," *Journal of Staff Development: Learning Forward,* August 2013, pp. 34–37. Copyright © 2013 by Learning Forward: The Professional Learning Association. All rights reserved. Used with permission.

Article   Prepared by: Rebecca B. Evers, *Winthrop University*

Utilizing Technology in Physical Education: Addressing the Obstacles of Integration

The use of technology to enhance the educational experience has become a standard within all content areas. Physical education is not exempt from this standard, although implementation of technology use has been difficult because of the unique nature of the physical education classroom environment. The authors discuss the obstacles that teachers and administrators face while integrating technology into the physical education environment, as well as approaches that can be taken to overcome those obstacles.

BETH PYLE AND KERI ESSLINGER

Learning Outcomes

After reading this article, you will be able to:

• Justify reasons to overcome the roadblocks to integrating technology into physical education.

• Develop a lesson plan with two appropriate implementations of technology.

Technology and physical education (PE) are often considered at opposite ends of the educational spectrum— one sedentary and the other requiring movement. Tony Hall, in his keynote lecture given at the *International Association of Physical Education in Higher Education 2011 Conference,* addressed this very dilemma, suggesting that interactive technology needs be a solution to, rather than a reason for, "the serious contemporary educational and societal problems of inactivity, hypokinetic, and sedentary living" (Hall, 2012, p. 106). However, establishing or crossing the bridge with technology on one side and PE on the other can be difficult because of two major roadblocks—those from the perceptions of administrators and those self-imposed by physical educators. These roadblocks are not insurmountable, but they do require

a plan, resting on the important idea that technology should enhance teaching, not replace it (Juniu, 2011).

Administrative Roadblocks

Administrators and faculty technology committees often overlook the technology needs of PE. This oversight is not necessarily intentional but more often occurs because they are unaware of the technology possibilities within PE or because of financial restraints. Administrators may not consider the gymnasium a classroom. For instance, an interactive whiteboard is often out of the question in a gymnasium because of Internet capabilities, wiring, and safety concerns and because the gym is a multipurpose facility—often used for lunch, assemblies, interscholastic competitions, band and choral concerts, and so forth. Although having a separate classroom for PE would be ideal, it is rarely the reality, and many do not see retrofitting an older gymnasium with technology as being cost effective.

Self-Imposed Roadblocks

Even as administrators often overlook how technology and PE can be partnered, physical educators may also overlook obvious links that could create this needed relationship.

Most physical educators recognize the positives of technology in education but may not know how to implement them into the curriculum without taking away from activity time. Utilizing technology without adequate prep time for teachers to master its use may result in technology taking away from student learning and activity time (Sinclair, 2002). The key to maximizing the positive effects of technology in PE is to enlarge the physical educator's knowledge base. By starting small and enlisting the help of colleagues—with more than one person making an effort—the PE teacher can share and lessen frustration during the learning curve. For instance, creating a web page for PE on the school's website is a viable first step. Successfully implementing one piece of technology within PE will affirm its importance. It is also imperative that physical educators make administrators and technology committee members aware of the technology needs within PE.

Teacher Preparation

In teacher education, technology is frequently an area in which all student teachers must demonstrate competence. Teacher-preparation universities need to address how they are preparing future teachers in PE (Liang, Walls, Hicks, Clayton, & Yang, 2006) and emphasize the need for teacher candidates to meet technology standards (Southern Regional Education Board, n.d.). For instance, in Kentucky, technology is one of ten standards on which teacher candidates are evaluated. The candidate must display his or her ability to implement technology to (a) support instruction; (b) access and manipulate data; (c) enhance professional growth and productivity; (d) communicate and collaborate with colleagues, parents, and the community; and (e) conduct research (Kentucky Teacher Standards, 2008). The National Council for Accreditation of Teacher Education (NCATE) also emphasizes the importance of technology for teachers and for student learning.

Technology in PE

Technology can be implemented in a number of areas within the teaching of PE: unit and lesson plan preparation; classroom management; communication with parents and students; instruction and feedback; and assessment. However, too often physical educators implement technology only to meet the standards without discovering the how, why, and when to best use the technologies available ("Does Technology," 2012). Technology should be used to enhance student learning, to save time, and to motivate the student and the teacher. Technology should not be used just to meet state or district requirements. The challenge is how to find best uses of technology for PE.

Class preparation. The most common and accessible way for PE teachers to use technology is in their preparation for the school year. Numerous websites to which teachers can refer are available in this area: www.pecentral.com; www.aahperd.org/naspe; www.braingym.com; www.pe4life.org; www.letsmove.gov; and www.spark.org. At these sites, physical educators can find inspiration for units, outlines, lesson plans, and national and state standards as well as new ideas to augment their knowledge and experiences. In addition, physical educators from around the United States and the world can collaborate, share ideas, and problem solve, thereby further expanding their knowledge bases. Sharing via the Internet is also a valuable tool for new teachers as they prepare for their classes.

Classroom management. Keeping students meaningfully active is the primary goal of physical educators, but this is sometimes a difficult task. Music is a great addition to physical activities, useful for getting the students moving faster, keeping them motivated and moving, or calming them down. Software such as *GarageBand* (www.apple.com/ilife/garageband)—a tool that can create, write, or edit music as well as record songs—is advantageous to use in PE (Miller, n.d.). It allows a PE teacher to create musical loops with sound effects that the teacher then plays to signal students to move from station to station. For example, one piece of music can designate time for working at a station; a sound effect can signal equipment return at that station; another piece of music can then cue transition from one station to another; and a sound effect can signal students to begin the next station. This musical loop can be repeated until the students have moved through all the stations. Because the music is set up on a continuous loop, the PE teacher no longer needs to turn the music off and on manually or remotely to signal student rotation but can move freely about the gym, providing instruction and immediate feedback as well as monitoring off-task behavior.

Communication. A PE web page is a great technology tool with which to keep students, parents, colleagues, administrators, school board members, and the community informed. Daily PE routines, special events, review worksheets, exams, PE policies, and so forth can all be communicated to stakeholders via the Internet. Also, having an area on the web page for parents and other viewers to submit questions and concerns provides an additional opportunity for communication. PE advocacy is yet another reason for such a web page. Links to community recreation opportunities and tips on health and wellness can promote lifetime physical activity for the entire family.

However, a PE web page is only valuable if its contents are up-to-date; reading information that is 2 years old will not give others, including administrators, the impression that technology is important. PE teachers must have a systematic strategy in place to keep information current. For example, the organizational concept of *only handle it once* can be utilized to ensure timely information. PE teachers can write their units and assignments right into their web page while they plan, rather than having to plan, transfer, and update.

Instruction and feedback. Physical educators are often their own worst enemies when it comes to technology because they sense that technology operates against the very soul of their mission: to help students be physically active! *Technology and PE* appears to be an oxymoron, but the terms can complement each other. Video game consoles such as Wii (Nintendo, 2013), pedometers, heart rate monitors, iPads, active apps, interactive whiteboards, digital video recorders, and so forth can all be used to help students understand the relationships among the key components of physical education: motor skills, fitness, and physical activity. For example, a PE teacher may use a camcorder to record, share, and critique a student's performance. In their research, Banville and Polifki (2009) found a student's ability to learn and perform motor skills increased with the use of digital video recorders. Furthermore, digital videos are teacher friendly because they can be recorded and played back without any interruption to instructional time (Banville & Polifko, 2009).

Another application of technology to enhance instruction and feedback is to make available videos of appropriate skill performance and game play. Such videos can be used during the teaching, review, and assessment portions of a PE unit. Every day brings a new app for nutritional tracking, video feedback, PE rules, workout routines, and so forth. The number of apps and the rate at which they are hitting the market is astounding. Many schools are now providing iPads for each student or portable learning labs, so the possibilities of using apps for direct instruction and feedback are limitless.

Assessment. Although much of the physical skill assessment done in PE is time consuming by nature, technology can be a time saver if used properly (Graham, Holt-Hale, & Parker, 2013). For instance, to save precious in-class time for physical activity, teachers can assess cognitive knowledge with exams given online outside of class time; feedback on these exams can be immediate. Another advantage is that record keeping for student attendance and grades can be linked directly to the teacher's grade-reporting system for easy access and distribution from various mobile devices such as tablets, iPads, or smart phones. Students can also utilize these devices to self-assess motor performance by analyzing their skills immediately through videos. In addition, using software such as MovieMaker (Microsoft, 2013), students can showcase the

application of their PE knowledge and skill through the creation of instructional and performance movies. Technology makes this type of authentic assessment more meaningful for the student and the teacher (Kovar, Combs, Campbell, Napper-Owen, & Worrell, 2012).

Conclusion

Despite the roadblocks, a partnership of technology and PE is workable and beneficial for all involved. Frustrated by early failures with technology, many physical educators may give up or under-utilize technology just to say they are using it. The ability to understand technology may appear to some a natural-born trait; however, just like the acquisition of any skill-related endeavor in PE, time on task makes the difference. Once they invest the time and effort to learn technology, teachers who use it for unit and lesson plan preparation, classroom management, communication with parents and students, instruction and feedback, and assessment can save enormous amounts of time and energy. Truly, developing and improving the partnership between technology and PE is vital for student learning and needs to be a priority for all stakeholders—physical educators, administrators, classroom teachers, parents, and students.

References

Apple, Inc. (2013). GarageBand [Computer software]. Cupertino, CA: Author. Available from http://www.apple.com/ilife/garageband/

Banville, D., & Polifko, M. F. (2009). Using digital video recorders in physical education. *Journal of Physical Education, Recreation & Dance, 80*(1), 17–21. doi:10.1080/07303084.2009.10598262

Does technology in physical education enhance or increase the time available to engage in physical activity? (2012), *Journal of Physical Education, Recreations & Dance, 83*(7), 53–56.

Graham, G., Holt-Hale, S. H., & Parker, M. (2013). *Children moving: A reflective approach to teaching physical education.* New York, NY: McGraw-Hill.

Hall, T. (2012). Emplotment, embodiment, engagement: Narrative technology in support of physical education, sport and physical activity. *Quest, 64*(2), 105–115. doi:10.1080/00336297.2012.669324

Juniu, S. (2011). Pedagogical uses of technology in physical education. *Journal of Physical Education, Recreation & Dance, 82*(9), 41–49. doi:10.1080/07303084.2011.10598692

Kentucky Education Professional Standards Board. (2008). *Kentucky teacher standards*. Retrieved from http://www.kyepsb.net/teacherprep/standards.asp

Kovar, S. K., Combs, C. A., Campbell, K., Napper-Owen, G., & Worrell, V.J. (2012). *Elementary classroom teachers as movement educators*. New York, NY: McGraw-Hill.

Liang, G., Walls, R. T., Hicks, V. L., Clayton, L. B., & Yang, L. (2006). Will tomorrow's physical educators be prepared to teach in the digital age? *Contemporary Issues in Technology and Teacher Education, 6*(1), 143–156.

Microsoft, Inc. (2013). MovieMaker [computer software]. Redmond, WA. Retrieved from http://windows.microsoft.com/en-us/windows-live/movie-maker#tl=overview

Miller, A. (n.d.). Podcasting tool: GarageBand [web page]. Retrieved from https://sites.google.com/site/adammillerphysedandhealth/podcast

Nintendo of America, Inc. (2013). Wii [Video game system]. Redmond, WA: Author. Retrieved from http://www.nintendo .com/wii

Sinclair, C. (2002). A technology project in physical education. *Journal of Physical Education, Recreation & Dance, 73*(6), 23–27. doi:10.1080/07303084.2002.10607823

Southern Regional Education Board. (n.d.). *Technology standards for teachers*. Retrieved from http:/www.sreb.org/page/1380/

Critical Thinking

1. Review the roadblocks mentioned in the article. Then develop an argument for using technology to overcome two of the administrative and two of the self-imposed roadblocks.

2. Use the websites in the article and mentioned here to find at least three technologies (software or devices) to support your teaching. Write a letter to your principal or school board explaining how these tools would enhance students' skills and help them develop a healthy lifestyle.

3. To help your principal/school board understand the practical use of technology in physical education and support your request for technology, develop one or two lesson plans using the technology you have requested.

Internet References

iPhys-Ed.com
http://www.iphys-ed.com/technology-in-pe

PE Central
http://www.pecentral.org/

The PE Geek
https://thepegeek.com/

Pyle, Beth; Esslinger, Keri. From *Delta Kappa Gamma Bulletin*, Winter 2014. Copyright © 2014 by Delta Kappa Gamma Society. Used with permission.

Article

Prepared by: Rebecca B. Evers, *Winthrop University*

Implications of Shifting Technology in Education

Janet Holland and John Holland

Learning Outcomes

After reading this article, you will be able to:

- Assess the changing trends in technology.
- Reflect on your gaps in technological knowledge and skills.
- Implement research-based technology practices.

Instructional Gaps

While talking to an engineer volunteering to work with middle and high school students on a robotics competition, he expressed his surprise at how the students did not have a basic understanding of simple everyday concepts like clockwise and counterclockwise. A school nurse complained how sick students came into her office and when handed a phone to call their parents, they did not know how. At a recent workshop presentation for middle and high school students they were told to e-mail the information to the group leader then to their own account. It was surprising how many did not know how to do it. How can this be happening in this day and age? Were the students not taught the knowledge and skills through authentic experiences, did they not have access to the technology, are they using different terms or formats for communications? These events cause one to wonder what the root causes might be and to think about whether they need to be addressed. If so, how, especially when considering ourselves to be in this technologically advanced era?

Shifting Technologies

From simple observations, reading magazines, newspapers, and Internet articles, to watching the TV news we are seeing many new technologies arrive and old ones go away, so it is important to reflect on what we are gaining and losing in the shuffle. Think about the recent losses of or declines in the markets for stopwatches, calculators, compasses, print cameras, network TV, portable radios, tapes, CDs, DVDs, GPS units, big box games, rolodex organizers, maps, books, magazines, newspapers, travel agents, and greeting cards; just to name a few. Locally the large bookstores and news stands have disappeared, video stores closed, office supply store stocks dwindle, no local printing presses anymore, even the local newspaper is making deep cuts in hardcopy, while working to develop an online presence.

Radios and TVs are being challenged at every turn to keep people interested in their nearly real time media. We have a younger generation often more interested in what the Internet has to offer than the traditional entertainment options. The newer media offers a more personalized, interactive method of learning, socializing, and entertainment on a reduced or no cost basis.

The major greeting card companies are slowly reducing employees. This is happening as digital card use continues to grow with the added features of audio, video, and animation provided at a reduced or no cost basis. The selling of card stock paper for self-printed cards, again demonstrates the digital shift towards increasing user control. We are seeing traditional magazines and books going to digital formats. According to various popular press articles, more books are being sold as e-texts than as hard copy or paperback combined. Learners now have small, compact, increased access using mobile devices. The subsequent increase in self-publication software and apps provides a way for anyone to publish then share globally within a richer media platform while bypassing editor restrictions.

It seems like the current level of expectation to produce more at a faster pace has resulted in writing being shorthanded in most of our everyday communications. Elementary classroom teachers have been discussing whether students still need to know how to physically write with everything going digital today. Though typing electronically is quick, voice command typing is even faster. In addition, digital writing offers the support of immediate spelling and grammar checking. It is not fool proof and still requires a good foundation in writing basics. With the decline of writing checks for bill payments and an increase in electronic banking transactions, it is also reducing the need for handwriting. So, when reflecting on how handwriting has been so centrally necessary to building and preserving our culture, it takes a shift in mindset to see it should still be preserved even if performed electronically. I believe we can all agree, no matter what medium is used, students still need to have the knowledge and command of effective two-way communication skills including recording their thoughts, knowledge, opinions, discoveries, and inventions in a clear and concise way.

No sooner do we have to decide whether to save writing skills, and then smartphones arrive with their heavy and direct affect on new technology shifts. Most students are now packing an impressive set of apps used for learning, sharing, and even entertainment, all in their pocket with access at an all time high. One smartphone app called TuneIn (2012) currently advertises access to over 70,000 radio stations and two million podcasts with listeners from 230 countries. Talk about seductive and personalized, just shake your phone and it will locate similar stations, how sweet is that? It is only logical to see where this could be headed with continued growth. How long until our cars are standard equipped with this expanded access? Imagine the possibilities of students having this type of access to timely International news and the ability to hear reports in different languages, as we become a more global society.

Many of the older technology declines are directly attributable to technology shifts with quick direct open access through the Internet, for personal e-mail, chat, social media, new and improved software, tools, mobile devices, and apps. As a result, digital alternatives are quickly taking the place of our more traditional tools with the lure of small, mobile, quick, easy to use devices, improved quality, with increased user control and choice. It is not a bad thing, but there are implications, whether it is simply a new medium, or whether we might be missing some of the underlying bits of important knowledge needed to carry us forward in a digital era.

Technology Growth Areas

Where are consumers spending their money in the tech sector? According to CNN Money (2012), the "7 Fastest-Growing tech companies" include Cirrus Logic, making circuit components for tablets, Biadu China's search engine with a custom personalized homepage based on the users' search patterns, Apple's voice recognition phone, IGI Phototonics fiber lasers, 3D Systems creating three dimensional parts found in smartphones and other devices produced, Priceline online international travel booking, and Acme Packet security gateways reflecting the incredible growth and profits within the industry. The same consumer desires mentioned earlier are also reflected here with fast-personalized searches, shifts toward voice-activated communications, use of mobile devices, and increasing globalization.

Growth of technologies in the workplace are expanding to improve innovations and to expand the bottom line. The Deloitte Technology Trends annual report called "Elevate IT for digital business" (2012) examines actionable practices used to achieve improvements within five major technology forces over the past several years: analytics, mobility, social, cloud, and cyber security. Areas targeted for growth include; social business, gamification, mobility, user empowerment, cloud services, big data, geospatial visualization, digital identities, measured innovation, and outside-in architecture. Author's Cearley and Claunch (2012) (*The Top 10 Technology Trends for 2012*) point to Gartner's annual list reflecting the tremendous growth in mobile computing in the workplace. The top 10 strategies include, "media tablets and beyond, mobile-centric applications and interfaces, contextual and social user experiences, Internet of things, app stores and marketplaces, next-generation analytics, big data, in-memory computing, extreme low-energy servers, and cloud computing" (Cearley & Claunch, 2012, p. 1). It looks like one can find different items when looking at the various listings but it is easy to see major overlapping trends in mobile and social technologies. The current workplace knowledge-based economies are requiring more high-level creative thinking skills with workers adept in problem solving within expanded global markets.

Oftentimes, areas of growth in the workplace extend into the educational arena at some point in time. The "NMC Horizon Report > 2012 K-12 Edition", research from the Consortium of School Networking (CoSN), and the International Society for Technology in Education (ISTE) provides a list of the top emerging technologies, trends, and challenges impacting teaching, learning, and creative inquiry over the next five years. Within one year it is anticipated adoption will increase for, cloud computing, collaborative environments, mobiles, apps, and tablet computing. In two to three years adoption of digital identity, game-based learning, learning analytics, and personal learning environments is anticipated. From four to five years, augmented reality, natural user interfaces, semantic applications, and tools for assessing twenty-first century learning skills. Key trends are reflecting the shift towards more access, mobility, online, hybrid, and authentic active challenge-based collaborative learning models to develop leadership and creativity (NMC Horizon Report, 2013, p. 1).

According to authors Trucano, Hawkins, and Iglesias in EduTech (2012) blog article called "Ten trends in technology use in education in developing countries that you may not have heard about" provides a list of instructional technology trends in developing countries including, "tablets, social learning networks, translations, the great firewall of . . . everywhere, earlier and earlier, special needs, e-waste, open data, big brother data, getting school leadership on board, going global locally" (Trucano, Hawkins, & Iglesias, 2012, p. 1). The list reflects the trend towards increasing mobility and social learning within globalized learning environments.

With the release of mobile broadband wireless multiport Internet access, gaining Internet access on the go is ever more accessible, not only at home and from hotels, but literally traveling in the passenger seat riding the highways of America. It is arguably a step forward when exercising the potential for Internet access while becoming an effective use of what would normally be down time, now used productively. This is not to advocate working 24/7 but to create flexibility for hectic schedules. In the next section, we will examine some of the current best research-based instructional practices to see how they can be aligned with the use of new technologies.

Literature-Based Current Best Educational Practices

New technologies offer a great way to invigorate instruction, whether in traditional classrooms, online, or in blended learning environments. We are finding many new digital tools allow learners to actively research, collaborate, innovate, and share their ideas. Collaborative tools can be used to increase knowledge acquisition quickly and efficiently while making global connections for broader perspectives. Providing meaningful integration of new technologies through the careful selection of quality tools aligning to best instructional practices can alter how learners and instructors engage with concepts and each other to achieve powerful learning. The following sections provide some background knowledge on the current best instructional practices found in the research literature used as the bases for aligning instructional needs directed towards technology enhanced teaching and learning.

Mobility

One of the biggest trends in education is the ability to be mobile. *Time* magazine. April 1 (2013) states the percentage of U.S. phones that are smartphones has reached 57%. According to Apple's released reports, more than 40 billion apps were downloaded for the iPhone, iPad and the iPod Touch, in 2012. It is hard to deny the success realized with approximately 83 million iPads sold by the third fiscal quarter of 2012 (Nations, 2013). To put their impact into perspective, iPads have now surpassed Mac OS sales with the new mobile iOS (Caulfield, 2011). These sales reflect the strong consumer demand for this new media. There are many iPad contenders such as Amazon, Archos, Disgo, Acer, Asus, HTC, Google, Android, Motorola, Toshiba, BlackBerry, Sony, Samsung, Microsoft, Dell, Vizio, HP, and the e-book readers including the Kindle, Kobo, and Nook. Users are drawn to the sleek design, small portable size, long battery life, in store support, inexpensive, intuitive natural interface, with a vast number of quality content apps to run on the mobile devices, as well. Learning can then be extended beyond the classroom to working from home, on the go, and in the field. "We really have reached the point where we do have magic, and thus we have the opportunity to ask what we should do with it" (Quinn, 2012, p. 3). In the corporate environment educational applications range from training, performance support, increased access, and collaboration to learning. In the educational setting, learners are gaining new content, communicating, capturing information, analyzing data, presenting, sharing, and even using location based activities. "To have mobile learning work well, power has to shift from instructors and managers to the learners themselves" (Woodill, 2011, p. 165). It is a self-directed or do-it-yourself (DIY) approach to learning.

Problem-Based Learning

Problem-Based Learning is an instructional method in which learners, usually working in teams, are given complex authentic problems or challenges and are asked to solve them. This approach is often used to increase learner interactions by working together collaboratively. Teams determine the needs, and work through the steps to solve the problem. Barrows (1986) describes problem-based learning as a way to motivate students' solutions through self-directed explorations while gaining additional practice. Problem-solving models of instruction are based on contributions from Dewey (1916, 1938). Dewey defined a problem as anything giving doubt or uncertainty. His active learning experiences included providing an appropriate learning topic, which was important and relevant.

Inquiry Learning

The researchers Bigge and Shermis (2004), Holcomb (2004), Joyce and Calhoun (1998), Van Zee 2001), and others define inquiry learning as capitalizing on students' interests in discovering something new or finding alternatives to unsolved questions or problems. Learners often work together to conduct research, experiment, synthesize, classify, infer, communicate, analyze, draw conclusions, evaluate, revise, and justify findings. In inquiry learning, students are responsible for problem solving, discovery, and critical thinking in order to construct new knowledge through active experiences. "Inquiry teaching requires a high degree of interaction among the learner, the teacher, the materials, the content, and the environment. Perhaps the most crucial aspect of the inquiry method is that it allows both students and teachers to become persistent askers, seekers, interrogators, questioners, and ponderers" (Orlich, Harder, Callahan, Trevisan, & Brown, 2007, p. 296).

Motivating Learning

Keller's (1983) ARC (attention, relevance, confidence, satisfaction) model of motivation provides insight into providing motivating instructional learning environments. In general, gaining attention involves capturing learner interest, stimulating inquiry, and maintaining it. Relevance includes identifying learner needs, aligning them to appropriate choices and responsibilities, and building on prior experiences. Confidence includes building positive expectations, support, competence, and success. Satisfaction includes providing meaningful opportunities to apply new knowledge and skills, reinforcement, and positive accomplishments. In Gagne (1985) "Conditions of learning" he indicated it is necessary to gain students' attention before they will be able to learn. Ongoing studies in the field of educational motivation continued to expand with additional research by Wlodkowsky (1999), Brophy (1983, 1998), and others. They determined that additional traits of motivated learners include the desire to learn, work, meet a need, personal value, reach a goal, complete tasks, engaging, curiosity, successful effort or ability, achievement, and personal responsibility. In a constructivist framework, motivation includes both individual and group generated knowledge and concepts.

Communications and Collaborations for Learning

In the learning environment building professional relationships through collaborating, coaching, and mentoring are all social interactions directed towards learning to share ideas, give and receive feedback, and offer support (Carr, Herman, Harris, 2005). The concepts of social learning can be traced to Bruner (1961) and Vygotsky (1978) and others. Quality instructional design directed towards technology-enhanced learning requires a great deal of student interaction. Promoting learner-to-learner interactions can increase engagement through negotiations, reflections, and shared understandings. The interactions allow students to expand viewpoints and build social connections to

each other. Dialogue directed towards learning can provide students a way to expand ideas, extend concepts, and apply theory in authentic ways to solve challenges. "The focus of this work is ongoing engagement in a process of purposeful inquiry designed to improve student learning" (Carr, Herman, Harris, 2005, p. 1–2). "Collaboration forms the foundation of a learning community online-it brings students together to support the learning of each member of the group while promoting creativity and critical thinking" (Palloff, Pratt, 2005, p. xi). Some of the constructivists contributing to social learning included Piaget (1969), Jonassen (1995), and Brookfield (1995). Social presence creates the "feeling of community and connection among learners, has contributed positively to learning outcomes and learner satisfaction with online courses" (Palloff, Pratt, 2005, p. 7). Researchers finding a strong connection between social presence and improved learning, interaction, and satisfaction include Picciano (2002), Gunawardena and Zittle (1997), Kazmer (2000), and Murphy, Drabier, and Epps (1998). With the wide range of collaborative tools available for communications and collaboration, it forms the perfect foundation for social interactions and collaboration directed towards learning.

Multimedia Rich Learning

Multimedia refers to the use of text, graphics, sound, video, animation, simulation, or a combination of media. By appropriately aligning rich media to the content message, it can provide additional clarity and increase student focus rather than detract from it. Using a variety of media can increase interest and motivation while allowing unique opportunities to reach diverse learners. Mayer conducted many studies from comparing lessons presenting content with words, to lessons presenting content with words and relevant visuals (R. C. Clark & Mayer, 2003; Mayer 2001). The results have consistently demonstrated the positive impact of appropriate instructional visual selections. "Rich media can improve learning if they are used in ways that promote effective cognitive processes in learners" (Reiser & Dempsey, 2007, p. 315). Whether an educator prescribes to the learning principles of Skinner in the 30's by changing behavior, the 70's cognitive psychology focus on memory and motivation, the 80's constructivist focus on real world application, or a mixture of approaches, multimedia, used effectively, can help students to learn. Some media considerations include: gaining and keeping attention, memorability using an appropriate speed, level of difficulty, comprehension, placement, easy access, media matching the purpose, image content value, discovery, and level of interaction to improve effectiveness. "Ultimately good learning environments begin with the principles of learning and instruction, but require evaluation, revisions, and fine tuning to balance these competing values and ensure that the benefits are accrued for all intended learners" (Alessi & Trollip, 2001, p. 41). Multimodal learning can include a wide range of multimedia and interactive tools used to engage learners, thereby providing multiple modes of interfacing within the system.

Diverse Learners

Students learn in different ways and have unique abilities and preferences on how they best acquire new information. The exceptionalities in intellectual ability, communications, sensory, behavioral, physical, and combinations sometimes require special learning accommodations. One benefit digital tools can provide is the unique interface differing from traditional computing with gesture controlled navigation, the offering of computer-assisted programs, ability to increasing the size and contrast for text, images, audio, audio readers, audio text recording, audio commands, video media, interactive and collaborative tools to target specific learning needs. In addition, there is an increase in multi-language support. This can include assistance for both special needs, low and high, as well as the ever-increasing diversity of learners from all over the world joining our classes and workplaces.

Globalization

With the tremendous increase in travel, immigration, and communication technologies the world is becoming more diverse, connected, and interdependent. Globalization has accelerated the exchange of ideas and perspectives thereby increasing the overall knowledge base. Current digital tools provide increased opportunities for extending content and perspectives to transform knowledge into innovative. Using integrated curriculums, team teaching, and media rich instructional technologies, and forming partnerships, and fostering innovation, we can create knowledge and skills to prepare learners to work in future markets. Success in global markets, as we are now experiencing, demands successful interactions with a diverse, wide range of individuals and cultures. It begins with intercultural knowledge, skills, and respect for our combined contributions and strengths. As educators, we need to become international stewards sharing insights and preparing learners for the future. The dramatic increase in mobility and digital communications now "connects people and facilitates transnational understanding" in ways not previously possible (Bryan & Vavrus, 2005, p. 184). As a result, the international information infrastructure allows learners to interact and share multimedia resources easily with anyone across the globe. Current technology tools easily allow for original creations and global sharing.

It seems like it would be beneficial to offer classes on global language basics including key functional survival skill words through the use of immersive practice with multiple-languages. Subsequently, providing the potential to foster international relationships, travel, and commerce needed for an increasingly global society.

Active Hands-On Learning

Hands-on refers to the learning activity involving practice on actual equipment, or in this case digital tools. The learning activity is designed with the goal of promoting the transfer of knowledge through application. In an active learning environment students are active, working in teams, and socialization is directed toward learning productively. "Students must be actively involved in the learning process if their classroom experience is to lead to deeper understandings and the building of new knowledge. Students (and adults, as I have discovered) need to hear it, touch it, see it, talk it over, grapple with it, confront it, question it, laugh about it, experience it, and reflect on it in a structured format if learning is to have any meaning and permanence" (Nash, 2009, p. xi). The dialogue provides time for learners to digest new information, exchange ideas, and engage with others in authentic, active hands-on ways for expanded perspectives, and memorable learning experiences.

Creative Learning

Open-ended digital tools allowing for original solutions to problems or challenges provide the perfect environment for creative thinking. Students can demonstrate understanding through a wide variety of digital resources to present and share their unique solutions. It is critical to develop learners who can think beyond the box and lead us to new innovations. Simply reading and testing over material will not develop the creative, original thinking needed to move our society forward. Instructors often use Bloom's Taxonomy (1956) to ensure inclusion of high-level knowledge and skills as can be found in original creative work.

Learning New Content with Practice

The main consideration when selecting content resources is the relevance to the desired topic, and how clear the main ideas are communicated to learners. Providing learners with a graphic organizer is a nice way to show what will be studied by providing a brief overview of the content. By isolating facts, concepts, and generalizations, it makes it easier to understand new content. The higher level of knowledge integration teaches learners how items are related, similar, different, and how to compare so they can understand more complex relationships. Interactions with the content and others can provide additional practice to better retain new information. Some instructional activities are designed to provide learners with opportunities for review of previously learned information through repetition. Some digital tools provide the needed practice activities by using repetition to ensure retention into long-term memory. It is important to identify the objectives and align them with the learning activity.

Feedback, Support, and Assessment

By providing learners with timely information about their actions they will know how they compare to the desired level of criteria. "We should ensure that they receive feedback about their success and failure, are appropriately resourced with support to ultimately succeed, and ideally can share tasks and learning with one another" (Quinn, 2012, p. 24). Learner feedback can take many different forms such as traditional instructor exams with rating scales or comments for students. Another alternative is to use student self-evaluations using checklists or rubrics for individual or group work to learn to monitor their own success. Sometimes instructors will also use checklists or rubrics for evaluation and providing student feedback. Instructors can use a pretest to assess learners' current level of knowledge, diagnostic test to assess areas of strengths and weakness, formative assessments to measure ongoing progress, and summative letter grade assessments to make judgments on the quality and completion of projects. The data gathered by the instructor can be used to monitor learning and make adjustments as needed as the course progresses or for changes to be made before teaching the lesson, unit, or module again. It is important to identify the desired learning of "behaviors, activities, and knowledge you will be evaluating" (Orlich, Harder, Callahan, Trevisan, & Brown, 2007, p. 332). Instruction can include the teaching of knowledge, performance skills, and attitudes such as found in collaborative group work. Another consideration is whether the learning goal aligns to standards and provides feedback in this regard to students, parents, instructors, and administrators, as needed.

Objectives for Learning

Mager's (1975) model for objectives, indicates quality objectives including the following three elements: 1) statement of the conditions or context of performance, 2) statement of the task, and 3) measurable way to evaluate the performance. Meaningful objectives are the backbone for instructors to create learning activities designed for knowledge to be retained, transferred,

and applied to similar situations. It is accomplished by providing a specific statement of what learners will be able to do when they complete the lesson. A measureable performance objective statement describes the behavior students will demonstrate at the end of the lesson, the conditions under which they will be demonstrated, and the criteria for acceptable performance. Identifying the objectives becomes the guiding force for the selection of appropriate digital tools to get to the desired learner outcomes.

Flipped Classroom

Flipped classrooms are a more recent trend used to transform the way instructors are providing information by inverting traditional classroom lectures into online video and screencast presentations, so learners can view them prior to attending class. At home, learners can watch step-by-step explanations of concepts with visual examples to better understand complex concepts. The digital presentations allow each student to learn at their own pace with the ability to pause and replay as much as needed, on their own personal schedule when they are the most receptive to learning, to acquire the needed foundation knowledge. Class time is then flipped, so students complete homework and practice activities applying the new concepts in class. When attending class, students are engaged in student-to-student interactions, collaborations, and critical thinking with the instructor serving as a facilitator to support learners, as needed. The classroom is transformed into an active, authentic, learning environment where students can deal with complex issues related to the content topic. The Flipped classroom can be an alternative to traditional lecture-based models or can be used as a blended learning environment to engage student learning. Screencast technology is often used to leverage learning outside of class, so a teacher can spend more time facilitating project-based learning during class. This is most commonly being done using teacher-created videos that students view outside of class time. Then, the learners spend class time on problem solving, thereby increasing interactions between students and instructors. With the tremendous growth and availability of mobile devices, learners have ever improving abilities to view the videos on their own time. As noted, this just keeps increasing the chances the class time can be spent on problem-based collaborative learning.

Emerging Technologies

On a *CBS This Morning* show segment called "Gadgets and Gizmos Galore" with Brian Cooley, he reported on the 2013 Las Vegas, NV, International Consumer Electronics Show. He talked about how we are starting to move into a post-mobile era.

It does not mean getting rid of mobile devices but rather seeing a merger of devices such as computers, phones, TV, and tablets so we will not be thinking about what device we are using. One example of this trend is the movement towards hybrids such as the Phablet, where the phone and tablet are combined. Cooley also talked about exciting developments through body gesturing such as Vuzix's®™ eye motion control, Leap Motion's®™ sensor on the device screen controlled by hand movements, and InteraXon's®™ Muse headband reading brainwaves for device control. Within ten years we may no longer be using the mouse and touchscreen technology. It seems like the new devices will have the potential to increase usability access for diverse learners while being a more tactile and engaging way to interact with technology resources.

Conclusions and Future Implications

When searching the literature for recommendations practitioners could consider, when dealing with shifting technologies and the pursuit of quality learning environments within the K-12 setting, a Freakonomics podcast provides some insight. Stephen Dunbar's (2011) podcast tells about how the New York City Department of Education pilot program called "School of One" personalized educational plans so each individual student has a chance to excel. Dunbar interviewed the program founders Joel Rose, Chris Rush, and chancellor Joel Klein. They implemented a technology algorithm, similar in concept to what is used to personalize Pandora radio, to analyze how each individual student learns the best. Based on the analysis results, learning was customized the next day to maximize learning efficiency. The learning modality was also aligned to how each individual student learned best; whether alone, in small or large groups, synchronously or asynchronously to practice learning concepts. One shared success story pertained to a student who initially took ten to twelve exposures to learn, but after targeting how this individual student learned best, the number of exposures was reduced to two to three. Rather than guessing what students have learned, it is statistically analyzed at the individual level to ensure it is happening through personalization. Along the same line, the U.S. Department of Education report (2012) states

> The realization of productivity improvements in education will most likely require a transformation of conventional processes to leverage new capabilities supported by information and communications technologies. In sum, rigorous evidence is needed to support effective practices to foster the adoption of efficient, effective paths to learning.

We have three sets of insightful recommendations for higher education. They include "growth, even with the accompanying pains, is generally welcome because it provides energy, new ideas, and attention to innovations. Often, however, a snazzy new technology becomes the sole focus, not the ideas or innovative uses that lead to improved learning" (Wilson, 2005, p. 1). It is important to consider instructional needs alongside new and emerging technologies aligned to desired outcomes. If we do not, we may find ourselves marching towards obsolescence as we fail to adapt to changing educational goals, objectives, and new technologies. "Most universities are using the same methods to teach all of the same stuff. This is very dangerous as the world is changing so quickly that entire fields and bodies of knowledge risk being outdated/outmoded very quickly" (Moravec, 2013, p. 1). Moravec goes on to state we "need to stop behaving as consumers of education, but become creators, producers, and prosumers. At the same time, learning needs to become more immersive and personally-meaningful (subjective experiences) to each learner" (Moravec, 2013, p. 2). In a video interview with Douglas Rushkoff, he makes a good comment about how students need to ask themselves the following questions. "Am I learning? Am I becoming a smarter more innovative human being? That's what's going to serve you in the real job market of tomorrow. By the time the corporation has told the city college what skills it wants from its future workers you are going to graduate and those skills will have changed anyway" (Rushkoff, 2013, p. 3). The factory and banking models are no longer relevant and students are now demanding interactive, relevant learning experiences, as they well should.

Recommendations for business training include actionable improvements to add measurable value to the company. With the influx of digital natives into the workplace, social technology use is increasing. "Leading enterprises today are applying social technologies like collaboration, communication and content management to social networks—the connected web of people and assets that impact on a given business goal or outcome—amplified by social media from blogs to social networking sites to content communities. Yet it's more than tools and technology. Businesses are being fundamentally changed as leaders rethink their core processes and capabilities with a social mindset to find new ways to create more value, faster" (Ramsingh, 2012, p. 1). According to author Ron Zamir, keeping "learners engaged and motivated in training through rich media, bite-sized content and gamification are essential for creating training that is both palatable to the learner and creates real workplace change" (Zamir, 2013, p. 1). Zamir's goal is to design innovative solutions to create better training using new technologies "not just simply rehashing old, unchanged content" (Zamir, 2013, p. 1). Other current trends found from the Training Zone (2013) website include the integration of rich media, mobile learning, online learning, conferencing, and the shift to globalization. It is critical to first know the learners and organizational goals to better meet their needs. The best training is personalized, accessible, and engaging in both the training and support materials offered. The technology itself is not the magic bullet, it is what you do with it to reach the business goals. The training is a means to an end, with the end resulting in a positive impact.

Integrating quality research-based instructional practices as new technologies are released is one way to fight against knowledge gaps at all levels. When one analyzes the learning needs, goals, and objectives, then selects and aligns the best tools to accomplish the tasks, one increases opportunities for exceptional learning.

Looking at where we need to be going with technology infused education, *eSchool News* has an article called eSN Special Report: Keeping students on a path to graduation. The author states "educators are determined to find that relevance by giving students more of the skills they'll need to succeed in a globally competitive economy—the so-called "twenty-first-century skills" such as problem solving, critical thinking, communication, and collaboration" (Nastu, 2012, p. 1). By integrating technology through meaningful applications, learners are more likely to stay the course needed for college and future careers. Students tend to learn best through the application of concepts to functions via meaningful work tasks, integrating those concepts through authentic relevant connections.

With so many tremendous technological shifts happening, we need to be mindful of the missing bits of information which still need to be taught. Ask people from all walks of life what is missing, what are we no longer teaching that needs to be included no matter what medium is used? Keeping in mind, the knowledge and skills valued by our society are also in a state of flux.

The concepts of collaboration and social interactions directed towards learning can continue to play a great role in the digital transitions. Could we be at a point where we think those brains, properly educated and trained to collect data, to think about problems through deeper root cause evaluation processes might be ready to start coming up with solutions to issues, concerns, and problems? Could we be ready to embrace a little change? Might we be ready to start exploring ways to maximize the potential of each individual? This article points to the need to conduct various needs analyses, identify relevant learning goals and align them to current best research-based instructional practices, no matter what technologies are selected, while staying flexible and adaptable to the changes that are sure to come.

A story by Sugata Mitra from NPR's Ted Radio called Unstoppable Learning is a wonderful example of the resilience of learners. He found by putting computers in villages in rural India, that the residents who had never seen computers before, with absolutely no resources to teach them taught themselves how to use them. My favorite quote was "you gave us a machine that only works in English, so we taught ourselves English to use it" (Mitra, 2013). By providing challenges then standing back to watch we will be amazed at what the human spirit of inquiry is capable of learning.

In looking at the New Horizons Report (2013) for K-12, Higher Education, and online resources for new and emerging technologies in industry, there are some very exciting new developments happening from augmented reality, wearable technologies, 3D printing, and much more. It will be fun to see how these technologies can be used effectively to have a positive impact on learning.

Closing suggestions for future researchers include: continue to examine effective ways to personalize instruction, examine goals and learners, tailor instruction or training specifically to the learner. Then, we may find the keys to additional innovations in teaching, training, and learning.

References

Alessi, S., Trollip, S. (2001). *Multimedia for learning: Methods and development,* 3rd Edition. Allyn & Bacon, A Pearson Education Company, Needham Heights: MA.

Bryan, A., & Vavrus, F. (2005). The promise and peril of education: The teaching of in/tolerance in an era of globalization. *Globalization, Societies and Education,* 3(2), 183–202. Doi:10.1080/14767720500167033

Carr, J., Herman, N., & Harris, D. (2005). *Creating dynamic schools through mentoring, coaching, and collaboration.* Association for Supervision and Curriculum Development, Alexandria: VA.

Caulfield, B. (2011). Apple now selling more iPads than Macs; iOS eclipses Dell and HP's PC Businesses. Retrieved March 17, 2013 from http://www.forbes.com/sites/briancaulfield/2011/07/19/apple-didnt-just-sell-more-ipads-than-macs-ios-has-now-eclipsed-dell-and-hps-pc-business-too/

Cearley, D., Claunch, C. (2012). The top 10 technology trends for 2012. Retrieved Jan. 12, 2013 from: http://www.junctionsolutions.com/gartner-insights-the-top-10-technology-trends-for-2012/

CNN Money, 7 Fastest-Growing tech companies, Retrieved Nov. 2, 2012 from http://money.cnn.com/gallery/technology/2012/09/06/fastest-growing-tech-companies.fortune/index.html

Cooley, B. (2013). CBS This Morning, Gadgets and gizmos galore. Retrieved Jan. 8 from: http://www.cbsnews.com/video/watch/?id=50138517n

Deloitte, (2012). Tech trends 2012: Elevate IT for digital business. Retrieved Jan. 12, 2013 from: http://www.deloitte.com/view/en_US/us/Services/consulting/technology-consulting/technology-2012/index.htm?id=us_google_techtrends_02212&gclid=CIuI7Nqb47QCFYp_QgoduSsAcw

Dunbar, S. (2011). How is a bad radio station like our public-school system? A Freakonomics Radio Podcast Encore. Retrieved May 21, 2013 from: http://www.freakonomics.com/2011/12/21/how-is-a-bad-radio-station-like-our-public-school-system-a-freakonomics-radio-podcast-encore/

Hawkins, R. (2010). 10 global trends in ICT and education. Retrieved Jan. 12, 2013 EduTech: A World Bank Blog on ICT use in Education from: http://blogs.worldbank.org/edutech/10-global-trends-in-ict-and-education

Mitra, S. (2013). Unstoppable learning. NPR, Ted Radio Hour. Retrived May 23, 2013 from: http://www.npr.org/2013/04/25/179010396/unstoppable-learning

Moravec, J. (2013). The university of the future: Marching toward obsolescence? Education Futures. Retrieved May 21, 2013 from: http://www.educationfutures.com/2013/04/08/uni-future/

Nash, R. (2009). The active classroom: Practical strategies for involving students in the learning process. Corwin Press, Thousand Oaks: CA.

Nastu, J. (2012). eSN Special Report: Keeping student on a path to graduation, *eSchool News,* Retrieved Nov. 2, 2012 from: http://www.eschoolnews.com/2011/02/22/esn-special-report-keeping-students-on-a-path-to-graduation/?ast=95&astc=8784

Nations, D. (2013). How many iPads have been sold? Retrieved March 17, 2013 from: http://ipad.about.com/od/iPad-FAQ/a/How-Many-iPads-Have-Been-Sold.htm

New Media Consortium (2013). NMC Horizon Report. K-12 Education Edition and Higher Education Edition. Retrieved May 21, 2013 from: http://www.nmc.org/publications

Orlich, D., Harder, R., Callahan, R., Trevisan, M., & Brown, A. (2007). Teaching strategies: A guide to effective Instruction, 8th Edition. Houghton Mitllin Company, Boston: MA.

Palloff, R., Pratt, K. (2005). *Collaborating online: Learning together in the community.* Jossey-Bass, A John Wiley & Sons Inc. Imprint, San Francisco: CA.

Quinn, C. (2012). *The mobile academy mlearning for higher education.* Jossey-Bass a John Wiley & Sons, Inc. Imprint, San Francisco: CA.

Ramsingh, K. (2012). Reimagining business with a social mindset. Deloitte Tech Trends. Retrieved May 21, 2013 from: http://deloitteblog.co.za.www102.cpt1.host-h.net/2012/03/28/reimagining-business-with-a-social-mindset-%E2%80%93-deloitte-tech-trends-2012/

Reiser, R. & Dempsey, J. (2007). *Trends and issues in instructional design and technology,* Second Edition. Pearson, Merrill Prentice Hall, Upper Saddle River: NJ.

Rushkoff, D. (2013). Education in present shock: An interview with Douglas Rushkoff. Education Futures. Retrieved May 21, 2013 from: http://www.educationfutures.com/2013/05/03/education-in-present-shock-an-interview-with-douglas-rushkoff/

Training Zone (2013). Learning Technologies 2013. Retrieved May 25, 2013 from: http://www.trainingzone.co.uk/features/Technology

Trucano, M., Hawkins, R., & Iglesias C. (2012). Ten trends in technology use in education in developing countries that you may not have heard about, EduTech: A World Bank Blog on ICT use in Education Retrieved Jan. 12, 2013 from: http://blogs.worldbank.org/edutech/some-more-trends

Tuneln Radio, Retrieved Nov. 2, 2012 from http://tunein.com/press/

U.S. Department of Education (2012). Understanding the implications of online learning for educational productivity. Office of Educational Technology. Retrieved May 21, 2013 from: http://www.ed.gov/edblogs/technology/research/

Wilson, B. G. (2005). Choosing our future. Retrieved May 21, 2013 from: http://carbon.ucdenver.edu/~bwilson/ChoosingOurFuture.html

Woodill, G. (2011). *The mobile learning edge: Tools and technologies for developing your teams.* The McGraw-Hill Companies, New York: NY.

Zamir, R. (2013). Corporate training trends in 2013. Retrieved May 25, 2013 from: http://www.allencomm.com/2013/02/corporate-training-trends-in-2013/

Critical Thinking

1. The sections on shifting technologies and technology growth discuss an array of changes and new devices/software coming to market. Which of these new technologies will have the most impact on your personal life? Explain why and how it will impact your personal life.

2. Some sections of the article provide an overview of the current best educational practices. Which of these practices will have the most impact on your teaching practices? Do not consider finances, but think about your content area or grade level and technology expertise. Explain why and how it will impact your teaching. Now consider if and how your answers to these two questions are similar.

3. In their conclusion the authors ask, ". . . what is missing, what are we no longer teaching that needs to be included no matter what medium is used?" Ask two to three teachers with different years of teaching experience this question and include your own answer. Reflect on the implications of your findings.

Internet References

Center for Implementing Technology in Education
http://www.cited.org/

International Society for Technology in Education
http://www.iste.org/

US Department of Education- Use of Technology in Teaching and Learning
http://www.ed.gov/oii-news/use-technology-teaching-and-learning

Article   Prepared by: Rebecca B. Evers, *Winthrop University*

Assistive Tech for Everyone?

MICHELLE R. DAVIS

Learning Outcomes

After reading this article, you will be able to:

- State reasons why all technology should be available to all students all the time.

- Explain safeguards that should be put in place to ensure all students have equal access to, and appropriate devices for, high stakes testing.

- Identify the barriers to accessing technology that still remain in our schools and workplaces.

As students with disabilities in Virginia's Fauquier County district take online assessments, they have access to a toolbox of technologies that can make it easier to show what they know. An optic mouse can help magnify text; a text-to-speech tool provides a spoken version of exam questions; and various switches and joysticks, for those unable to use a mouse and keyboard, can be merged with the assessment.

But even students who don't have individualized education programs, or IEPs, have digital learning enhancements at their disposal in Virginia's online testing world, said Mary Wills, the 11,000-student district's director of testing. They have access to an electronic yellow highlighter that never runs out of ink, an electronic pencil for note-taking or math calculations, and an eliminator tool that narrows down the answers for multiple-choice questions.

"These tools are for all kids, not just for those with special needs," Ms. Wills said.

Assistive technologies and accommodations, once seen as primarily for students with disabilities, are now merging into the broader testing world, especially as more states and districts embrace online testing. Computer-based exams provide an opportunity to allow all students to tap into accommodations that could aid comprehension and focus.

"There are all types of interventions that came out to address the needs of students with disabilities, but anyone can benefit from them and should have the opportunity to use those accommodations if they want them," said Kimberly Hymes, the senior director of policy and advocacy for the Council for Exceptional Children, an Arlington, Va.-based advocacy group for students with disabilities. "Technology allows us to have those types of interventions readily available."

That philosophy is based on the concept of "universal design for learning," or UDL, she said. UDL calls for students to be presented with information and content in different ways and for providing multiple options to show understanding. The approach is intended to help all students, not just those with disabilities, Ms. Hymes said.

The Common-Core Effect

Some states, such as Virginia, have been doing online testing for years and have more experience with using assistive technologies and accommodations on assessments for students with disabilities, and for all students. But as the requirements for Common Core State Standards go into place, more districts in many states are going to be confronted with the issue. The two major coalitions developing online tests—the Smarter Balanced Assessment Consortium and the Partnership for Assessment of Readiness for College and Careers, or PARCC—are working to allow assistive devices for students with disabilities who need them and to provide other learning-enhancement tools to all students, said Brandt Redd, the chief technology officer for Smarter Balanced.

For specialized devices intended to help students with disabilities, for example, the coalition has developed a list of certified technologies that can work seamlessly with the online tests, such as certain input devices for students with motor-skills impairments or some text-to-speech readers, he said. Smarter Balanced's assistive technology certification process requires companies to pay $5,000 to have the coalition certify their devices work with the tests. Companies can also try out their devices with the assessment using Smarter Balanced's training tests online for free, but that does not provide certification.

Assistive "devices are allowed as long as the student uses it in regular instruction," Mr. Redd said. "We want to make sure no one is bringing in a device to artificially inflate" achievement.

It's also important that a student isn't using a device he or she had no experience with before test day, Mr. Redd said. The goal of the test is to measure academic abilities, not how adept the student is with technology.

Zoom Function

Smarter Balanced is approaching assistive technologies and supports from a three-tiered perspective. Some of those technologies—such as highlighters and zoom functions—will be available to all students. Others will be available to students who have had their uses approved by educators and other designated adults, such as translation tools for English-language learners or an English pop-up glossary. Still others, such as tools for translation into Braille, will be for students with IEPS that require those accommodations.

PARCC is approaching accommodations for its assessment in a similar way, said Jeffrey Nellhaus, the coalition's director of policy, research, and design. Supports embedded into the tests for all students include a magnifier and the option to change font size or background colors. Text-to-speech tools will be available to all students on tests in selected areas, Mr. Nellhaus said, but will be available for students with visual impairments on all parts of the test.

For math, that will be particularly helpful. "We want to make sure we're just measuring their ability to do the math, not their ability to read," he said.

PARCC doesn't require certification for assistive devices, but will produce a list of devices that work with their test as well as a list of technical guidelines for devices.

However, several advocacy groups have criticized PARCC for its failure to have all accommodations ready for its field testing this spring. In January, the National Federation of the Blind filed a lawsuit against PARCC, saying its upcoming field testing doesn't provide access for blind students who use Braille, representing a violation of the Americans with Disabilities Act. PARCC and the group have since settled the suit, with PARCC pledging to have Braille accommodations available for the practice test in spring 2014.

Patti Ralabate, the director of implementation for the Center for Applied Special Technology, or CAST, said her group, based in Wakefield, Mass., and others are watching to make sure supports for all students are provided and are not limited to small groups.

She's also eager to see whether devices not on certified lists are ultimately permitted.

"There are all kinds of issues around integrating assistive-technology devices with whatever technology is used to give the test," she said. Ms. Ralabate said it's important all accessability measures are working for the field test so that "all populations are taken into account."

The National Center and State Collaborative, one of two coalitions developing alternative assessments for students with severe cognitive disabilities, is pilot and field testing assessments with a high focus on assistive technologies, said Rachel Quenemoen, the project director. To ensure assistive devices work with assessments, the collaborative borrowed the most commonly-used devices to run compatibility checks and will work to resolve any barriers to the use of assistive devices before operational testing in the spring of 2015, she said.

Even aside from the common core, assistive technologies are blurring the lines between what students with disabilities get versus the rest of the student population.

In the 10,400-student Janesville, Wis., school district, for instance, many of the assistive technologies used are available for all students based on the concepts of universal design for learning, said Kathy White, an assistive-technology specialist for the district.

Word-prediction software, for example, which suggests words visually and aloud as students write, is one of the most commonly used assistive technologies in the district, according to Ms. White. It can help students with disabilities struggling to spell or conceptualize an idea, but it can also help an on-grade-level student writing about a historical period who needs unfamiliar vocabulary, or a kindergartner who wants to use a big word but doesn't know how to spell it.

Having such technologies available to all students takes away the stigma that can arise when it's just students with disabilities who use them, Ms. White said.

"I've seen a dramatic shift in the way these students look at technology," she said, referring to students with disabilities. "They used to say they didn't want to use it because they'd be different. Now we know everyone learns in a different manner."

Uneven Access

Districts also have to consider expenses. Some costs for assistive devices are down, because the technologies are now built into the assessments—like a text reader for example—or because the technology is getting cheaper. But that's not the case for everything, said Ms. Hymes.

Of course, the reality is that even as districts embrace assistive technologies and accommodations for more students, that approach doesn't necessarily carry over to students' experiences with state tests.

In the 210,000-student Houston school district, officials have taken up the UDL philosophy. Houston opted for laptops instead of tablets for its 1-to-1 computing initiative in part because that choice allows all students, including those with disabilities, to use the same technology, with some add-ons, said Sowmya Kumar, the assistant superintendent for special education. All students can also use Kurzweil software, a text-to-speech tool with built-in study aids, including a dictionary, a thesaurus, and an idea-organizing tool.

But on state tests, the majority of students who don't have IEPS won't have access to assistive technologies or accommodations. It's a practice that Ms. Kumar hopes to see shift in the near future.

Critical Thinking

1. What is the conceptual framework and research behind allowing the use of technology by all students?

2. Name the leaders who make a priority of providing access to technology and discuss what they have accomplished.

3. What do you think remain the primary barriers to access for all students?

Create Central

www.mhhe.com/createcentral

Internet References

Center for Applied Special Technology
http://cast.org/

Edutopia
http://www.edutopia.org/

Go2web20
www.go2web20.net

No Limits 2 Learning: Celebrating Human Potential through Assistive Technology
www.nolimitstolearning.blogspot.com

Article   Prepared by: Rebecca B. Evers, *Winthrop University*

From the Three *R*s to the Four *C*s
Radically Redesigning K-12 Education

The battle against nonliteracy has focused on teaching everyone to read and write text. But new technologies that facilitate more holistic learning styles, engaging all of the learner's senses, may open the locked stores of global knowledge for all. Instead of reading, 'riting, and 'rithmetic, we'll move to critical thinking, creative thinking, "compspeak," and calculators.

WILLIAM CROSSMAN

Learning Outcomes

After reading this article, you will be able to:

• Explain how technology supports the four *C*s in your content area or grade level.

From the moment that Jessica Everyperson was born, her brain, central nervous system, and all of her senses shifted into high gear to access and to try to understand the incredible new informational environment that surrounded her. She had to make sense of new sights, sounds, tastes, smells, tactile experiences, and even new body positions.

Jessica approached her new world with all of her senses operating together at peak performance as she tried to make sense of it all. Her new reality was dynamic, constantly changing from millisecond to millisecond, and she immediately and instinctively began to interact with the new information that poured through her senses.

Jessica's cognitive ability to access new information interactively, and to use all of her senses at once to optimize her perception of that ever-changing information, is all about her hardwiring. Jessica, like all "everypersons" everywhere, was innately, biogenetically hardwired to access information in this way.

For Jessica's first four or five years, her all-sensory, interactive cognitive skills blossomed with amazing rapidity. Every moment provided her with new integrated-sensory learning experiences that helped to consolidate her "unity of consciousness," as the ancient Greek philosophers called it. Because each learning experience was all-sensory, Jessica's perception of reality was truly holistic. This meant that the ways she processed, interpreted, and understood her perceptions were also holistic. Jessica was therefore developing the ability to both perceive and understand the many sides of a situation—the cognitive skills that form the basis of critical thinking and lead to a broad and compassionate worldview.

During those preschool years, she also became proficient in using the variety of information technologies (ITs) that continued to be introduced into her environment: radio, TV, movies, computers, video games, cell phones, iPods, etc. Early on, she stopped watching TV, which engaged only her eyes and ears, and switched to video games, which engaged her eyes, ears, and touch/tactility. Before she could even read a word, Jessica had become a multimodal multitasker, talking on her cell phone while listening to her iPod and playing a video game.

At this point in her young life, Jessica was feeling very good about her ability to swim in the vast sea of information using the assortment of emerging ITs. Not surprisingly, she was also feeling very good about herself.

Then, Jessica started school!

The Brightness Dims: Hello K-12, Hello Three *R*s (Reading, 'Riting, 'Rithmetic)

On Jessica's first day in kindergarten, her teacher was really nice, but the message that the school system communicated to Jessica and her schoolmates was harsh. Although none of the teachers or administrators ever stated it in such blatant terms, the message, as expressed via Jessica's school's mandated course curriculum and defined student learning outcomes (SLOs), was this: Reading/writing is the only acceptable way to access information. This is the way we do it in "modern" society. Text literacy is the foundation of all coherent and logical thinking, of all real learning and knowledge, and even of morality and personal responsibility. It is, in fact, the cornerstone of civilization itself.

And the message continued: Since you don't know how to read or write yet, Jessica, you really don't know anything of value, you have no useful cognitive skills, and you have no real ways to process the experiences and/or the data that enter your brain through your senses. So, Jessica, from now on, through all of your years of schooling—through your entire K-12 education—you and we, your teachers, must focus all of our attention on your acquiring those reading and writing skills.

The United States Department of Education holds every school system in the United States accountable for instilling reading skills, as well as math skills, in every one of its students, and it requires students to take a battery of standardized tests every year to see if both their reading scores and math scores are going up.

If the test scores trend upward, the schools are rewarded. If they stay level or decline, the schools are punished with funding cuts and threatened with forced closure. Schools literally pin their long-term survival on just two variables: First, do the tests show that students can read and write, and second, do the tests show that students can do math?

From that moment on, Jessica's learning experience took a radical downward turn. Instead of accessing a dynamic, ever-changing reality, she was going to have to focus almost entirely on a static reality that just sat there on the page or computer screen: text. Instead of accessing information using all of her integrated senses simultaneously, she was going to have to use only her eyes. And instead of experiencing information interactively—as a two-way street that she could change by using her interactive technologies—she was going to have to experience information as a one-way street: by absorbing the text in front of her without being able to change it.

Welcome, Jessica, to the three *R*s, the essence of K-12 education. Of course, Jessica and her schoolmates, particularly in middle and high school, will take other courses: history, chemistry, political science, and so on. However, these other courses count for almost nothing when students go on to college, where they have to take these subjects all over again (history 101, chemistry 101, political science 101), or when they enter the vocational, business, and professional world, where they have to receive specialized training for their new jobs. College admissions directors and workplace employers really expect only one narrow set of SLOs from students who graduate with a high school diploma: that the students should have acquired a basic level of text literacy.

Jessica, like almost all of her kindergarten schoolmates, struggled to adjust to this major cognitive shift. Actually, for the first year or so, Jessica was excited and motivated to learn to read and write by the special allure of written language itself. The alphabet, and putting the letters together to make words, was like a secret code that grown-ups used to store and retrieve information. The prospect of learning to read and write made Jessica feel that she was taking a step into the grown-up world.

However, this initial novelty and excitement of decoding text soon wore off, and most of the children in Jessica's first, second, and third-grade classes, including Jessica herself, had a hard time keeping up. By the fourth grade, numbers of students were falling further and further behind the stated text-literacy SLOs for their grade level. Their self-confidence was getting severely damaged, and they were feeling more and more alienated from school and education itself. Not surprisingly, Jessica was no longer feeling very good about herself.

Young People's Rebellion against The Three *R*s and Text Literacy

What's going on here with Jessica and young people in general? Our children are actually very intelligent. From the earliest age, their brains are like sponges soaking up and interpreting experiences and information that floods their senses. Almost all young children love to learn about everything, including about the learning process itself. They're continually asking "why?" in an effort to understand the world around them. It's a survival mechanism that we humans have evolved over millennia, much like the newborn deer kids that can stand and run minutes after they're born.

Young people's failure to excel, or to even reach proficiency, in reading and writing in K-12 is reflected in the school literacy rates that continue to fall or, at best, remain stagnant decade after decade. Look no further than the National Assessment of Educational Progress, an annual test that most experts consider a fairly accurate gauge of reading scores throughout the United States. The scores for 12th-graders declined from 292 in 1992 to 188 in 2009, while the scores of students in other grades only negligibly improved during that same time period—this despite gargantuan amounts of time, resources, and hundreds of billions of dollars that school systems burned through in an attempt to bring them up.

Yet another reflection of young people's dissatisfaction with reading is the tragic rising dropout rates of middle-school and high-school students, particularly African American and Latino students. The question that parents and educators need to ask themselves is: Do children become less intelligent as they pass through the K-12 years?

The answer is No! Studies consistently show that, although young people's text-literacy rates are falling, their IQs (intelligence quotients) are rising at an average of three points every 10 years. Researchers have been noting this trend for decades and call it the "Flynn Effect," after James Flynn, a New Zealand political science professor who first documented it.

What's going on here is that young people today are rebelling against reading, writing, and written language itself. They are actively rejecting text as their IT of choice for accessing information. They feel that it's no longer necessary to become text literate—that it is no longer relevant to or for their lives.

Instead, young people are choosing to access information using the full range of emerging ITs available to them, the ITs that utilize the fullness of their all-sensory, interactive cognitive powers. Because their K-12 education is all about learning to gather information via text, young people are rejecting the three *R*s-based educational system, as well. Why, Jessica is asking, do I need to spend years learning to read Shakespeare's *Hamlet* when I can download it and listen to it, or listen to it via audio book CD, or watch a movie or DVD of it, or interact with it via an educational video game of the play?

We may be tempted to point out to Jessica and her fellow text rejecters that, when they're text messaging, they are in fact writing and reading. But it's not really the writing and reading of any actual written language—and Jessica knows it. Texting uses a system of symbols that more closely resembles a pictographic or hieroglyphic written language than an alphabetic one. "♥2u" may be understandable as three symbols combined into a pictogram, but it's not written English.

In my opinion, "♥2u" exemplifies not a flourishing commitment to text literacy among young people, but rather the rejection of actual text literacy and a further step in the devolution of text/written language as a useful IT in electronically developed societies.

Replacing Text in Schools—and Everywhere Else

What is text/written language, anyway? It's an ancient technology for storing and retrieving information. We store information by writing it, and we retrieve it by reading it. Between 6,000 and 10,000 years ago, many of our ancestors' hunter-gatherer societies settled on the land and began what's known as the "agricultural revolution." That new land settlement led to private property and increased production and trade of goods, which generated a huge new influx of information. Unable to keep all this information in their memories, our ancestors created systems of written records that evolved over millennia into today's written languages.

But this ancient IT is already becoming obsolete. Text has run its historic course and is now rapidly getting replaced in every area of our lives by the ever-increasing array of emerging ITs driven by voice, video, and body movement/gesture/touch rather than the written word. In my view, this is a positive step forward in the evolution of human technology, and it carries great potential for a total positive redesign of K-12 education. Four "engines" are driving this shift away from text:

First, evolutionarily and genetically, we humans are innately hardwired to access information and communicate by speaking, listening, and using all of our other senses. At age one, Jessica just started speaking, while other one-year-olds who were unable to speak and/or hear just began signing. It came naturally to them, unlike reading and writing, which no one just starts doing naturally and which require schooling.

Second, technologically, we humans are driven to develop technologies that allow us to access information and communicate using all of our cognitive hardwiring and all of our senses. Also, we tend to replace older technologies with newer technologies that do the same job more quickly, efficiently, and universally. Taken together, this "engine" helps to explain why, since the late 1800s, we have been on an urgent mission to develop nontext-driven ITs—from Thomas Edison's wax-cylinder phonograph to Nintendo's Wii—whose purpose is to replace text-driven ITs.

Third, as noted above, young people in the electronically developed countries are, by the millions, rejecting old text-driven ITs in favor of all-sensory, nontext ITs. This helps to explain why Jessica and her friends can't wait until school is over so they can close their school books, hurry home, fire up their videogame consoles, talk on their cell phones, and text each other using their creative symbols and abbreviations.

Fourth, based on my study and research, I've concluded that the great majority of the world's people, from the youth to the elderly and everyone in between, are either nonliterate—unable to read or write at all—or functionally nonliterate. By "functionally nonliterate," I mean that a person can perhaps recognize the letters of their alphabet, can perhaps write and read their name and a few other words, but cannot really use the written word to store, retrieve, and communicate information in their daily lives.

Since the world's storehouse of information is almost entirely in the form of written language, these billions of people have been left out of the information loop and the so-called "computer revolution." If we gave a laptop computer to everyone in the world and said, "Here, fly into the world of information, access the Internet and the Worldwide Web," they would reply, "I'm sorry, but I can't use this thing because I can't read text off the screen and I can't write words on the keyboard."

Because access to the information of our society and our world is necessary for survival, it is therefore a human right. So the billions of people who are being denied access to information because they can't read or write are being denied their human rights. They are now demanding to be included in the "global conversation" without having to learn to read and write.

Three great potential opportunities for K-12 education in the coming decades arise out of this shift away from text.

- Using nontext-driven ITs will finally enable the billions of nonliterate and functionally nonliterate people around the world to claim and exercise their right to enter, access, add to, and learn from the world's storehouse of information via the Internet and World Wide Web.
- Voice-recognition technology's instantaneous language-translation function will allow everyone to speak to everyone else using their own native languages, and so language barriers will melt away. Consider the rate of improvement in voice-recognition technology over the last decade. As David Pogue points out in a 2010 *Scientific American* article, "In the beginning, you had to train these programs by reading a 45-minute script into your microphone so that the program could learn your voice. As the technology improved over the years, that training session fell to 20 minutes, to 10, to five—and now you don't have to train the software at all. You just start dictating, and you get (by my testing) 99.9% accuracy. That's still one word wrong every couple of pages, but it's impressive."
- People whose disabilities prevent them from reading, writing, and/or signing will be able to select specific functions of their all-sensory ITs that enable them to access all information.

The Brightness Returns: Goodbye, Three *R*s; Hello, Four IT *C*s

Every minute that Jessica and her friends spend getting information and communicating using video games, iPods, cell phones, and other nontext ITs, they're developing new cognitive skills.

Their new listening, speaking, visual, tactile, memory, interactive, multitasking, multimodal skills allow them to access information and communicate faster and more efficiently than ever before. I believe that Jessica and her friends are developing the very skills that will be required for successful K-12 learning as we move into the coming age of postliterate K-12 education.

Something good is also happening to Jessica's brain and consciousness as she uses her all-sensory, interactive ITs. Jessica is retraining her brain, central nervous system, and senses. She is reconfiguring her consciousness so that it more closely resembles its original, unified, integrated, pre-three Rs state. Jessica's worldview is broadening because she's perceiving and understanding the world more holistically. And she's feeling good about herself again.

Jessica's story—and there are millions of Jessicas struggling to succeed in our three Rs-based classrooms today—points the way to a new strategy for K-12 education in the twenty-first century. Basing K-12 education on the three Rs is a strategy for failure. We have the emerging ITs on which we can build a new K-12 strategy, one that has the potential to eliminate young people's academic nonsuccess and sense of failure and replace it with academic success and self-confidence.

Instead of the three Rs, we need to move on to the Four Cs: critical thinking, creative thinking, comp-speak (the skills needed to access information using all-sensory talking computers), and calculators (for basic applied math).

As text/written language falls more and more out of use as society's IT of choice for accessing information, so will the text-based three Rs. It's a trend that's already starting to happen. Videos as teaching-learning tools are surpassing textbooks in innumerable K-12 classrooms. Instructional interactive videos (we won't be calling them video "games" anymore) are already entering our classrooms as the next big IIT—instructional information technology—because students want to be interactive with information.

As the three Rs exit the K-12 scene, they'll leave a huge gap to be filled. What better way to fill that gap than by helping young people to become better critical and creative thinkers—the most crucial cognitive skills they'll need to help them build a more sustainable, peaceful, equitable, and just world? In order to store and retrieve the information they'll need to develop and practice these thinking skills, they'll also need to systematically acquire the all-sensory, interactive skills to access that information: the comp-speak skills.

These compspeak skills are the very same skills that Jessica and her classmates have been developing unsystematically by using their all-sensory ITs, but systematic training in listening, speaking, visuality, memory, and the other compspeak skills should be a central component of their post-three Rs education. It's ironic, and definitely shortsighted, that, in a difficult economic and budget-cutting climate, classes that support these compspeak skills are the first to be cut: music (listening, visual, body movement, memory), art (visual, body movement), physical education and dance (body movement, memory), speech (speaking, listening, memory), and theater arts (all of the above).

Over the next decades, we will continue to replace text-driven ITs with all-sensory-driven ITs and, by 2050, we will have recreated an oral culture in our electronically developed countries and K-12 classrooms. Our great-great-grandchildren won't know how to read or write—and it won't matter. They'll be as competent accessing information using their nontext ITs as we highly text-literates are today using the written word.

Critical Thinking

1. Reflect on the concerns Crossman outlines in this article. Do you agree that how we teach may be causing the very problems we are trying to remediate? Explain your answer.

2. Why do you think that teachers are not using more 21st-century teaching methods and materials, such as technology?

3. There are teachers who are using project-based learning (PBL) as a way to meet the needs of Jessica and her peers. Go to Edutopia's page on PBL www.edutopia.org/project-based-learning to find a video or page that you might use in your content area or grade level teaching. Be prepared to share in class discussion to explain your reason for the project you selected.

Create Central

www.mhhe.com/createcentral

Internet References

The Teaching Channel
    www.teachingchannel.org/
Open Thinking Wiki
    couros.wikispaces.com/TechAndMediaLiteracyVids

WILLIAM CROSSMAN is a philosopher, futurist, professor, human-rights activist, speaker, consultant, and composer/pianist. He is founder/director of the CompSpeak 2050 Institute for the Study of Talking Computers and Oral Cultures (www.compspeak2050.org). E-mail: willcross@aol.com.

Some of the ideas discussed in this article are discussed in greater depth in the author's book *VIVO [Voice-In/Voice-Out]: The Coming Age of Talking Computers* (Regent Press, 2004). This article is adapted from an earlier version in *Creating the School You Want: Learning@ Tomorrow's Edge* (Rowman & Littlefield, 2010), edited by Arthur Shostak and used with his permission.

Article   Prepared by: Rebecca B. Evers, *Winthrop University*

Common Core Standards: Transforming Teaching with Collaborative Technology

CATLIN TUCKER

Learning Outcomes

After reading this article, you will be able to:

- Describe how core standards can be adapted to all students with disabilities.

- Discuss what you consider necessary to improve teaching of students with disabilities.

The concept of group work—collaborative efforts by students—intrigued me from the earliest days of my teaching career.

I understood the myriad benefits of grouping students together to tackle challenges, explore topics, and work jointly to create a finished product. Unfortunately, the reality, in most cases, was very different from what I had hoped to achieve. There was no equity in student contributions during group tasks. One student usually dominated the work while the others chatted about random, unrelated topics. There was never enough time, and the finished product was almost always disappointing. It was not until I was able to embrace a blended learning model that combined online engagement with work in the classroom that I was successful in having students complete collaborative tasks.

Collaboration is an essential skill to success beyond high school. The Common Core Standards require students to "use technology, including the Internet, to produce and publish writing and to interact and collaborate with others." In addition to collaborating online, students must "prepare for and participate effectively in a range of [real-time] conversations and collaborations with diverse partners, building on others' ideas and expressing their own clearly and persuasively."

The process of working with others to produce or create something requires strong communication skills, a willingness to be open minded, and the understanding that the group's potential far exceeds any one individual's contributions. So how do we support students in cultivating the skills that are necessary for successful collaboration?

Luckily, educators today have access to a wide array of free technology geared toward fostering collaboration online. The relative ease of using these tools to group students, encourage communication, and drive creative problem solving make it possible to blend instructional mediums to engage students both inside and outside the classroom. Teachers are no longer limited to in-class group work to help students develop these competencies.

Collaboration requires that students be actively involved in the learning process. This is a new role for many students, who are used to sitting quietly in class passively consuming information. As a result, students need to learn how to actively engage with their peers to tackle academic challenges and become confident producers of information if they are going to be competitive beyond secondary school.

As schools deal with massive budget cuts across the nation, many teachers do not have the necessary professional development to support them in transitioning to the Common Core Standards. Increasingly, librarians and media specialists are becoming leaders on school campuses to support teachers in exploring technology and effectively integrating it into their curriculum.

I want to highlight some of the tools available to educators that can help them support their students in developing their communication and collaboration skills. Many of these tools offer educators the opportunity to share their best practices and lessons with each other. It is becoming easier for educators who may live and work on opposite sides of the globe to collaborate and learn from one another. With the guidance of a librarian and media specialists, teachers can explore how technology can be used to replace and improve what they already do instead of adding to their workload. They can also learn how to access a growing wealth of teacher-generated resources available on the Internet.

Collaborize Classroom: Online Discussions

I use Collaborize Classroom, a free online discussion platform, to teach communication skills and facilitate group discussions, debates, writing assignments, and group work. Most learning management systems have threaded discussions or a discussion board; however, I selected Collaborize Classroom because it focuses entirely on dynamic discussions. There is a variety of question types to structure discussions, teachers can embed media, and there is a results page where the outcomes of a conversation can be published in a colorful chart.

Teachers in upper elementary through postsecondary are using this discussion site to create online learning communities to complement their in-class work. The Common Core Standards state that students as early as kindergarten, "with guidance and support from adults, explore a variety of digital tools to produce and publish writing, including in collaboration with peers." This writing standard, which stresses the use of online tools to publish and collaborate, make it necessary for teachers to explore safe spaces where they can begin to cultivate these skills.

Results Page

Taking discussions online makes it possible for teachers to overcome many of the barriers that impede in-class conversations. Instead of a few students dominating the discussion, there is equity in the contributions. Students have the time and space to consider a question, articulate a response, and read the responses posted by their peers. This asynchronous flexibility makes it possible for every student to have a voice, which is necessary if they are "to understand other perspectives and cultures." This realization that other students in a class have different points of view or are influenced by their cultural backgrounds and past experiences is a necessary component of being college and career ready.

Online discussions are also an effective tool to teach students how to communicate in a respectful, supportive, and substantive way. These communication skills must be taught with intention. Too often teachers assume that students, as "digital natives," know how to navigate this space. They spend hours updating Facebook pages and firing off text messages, but they rarely see the impact their words have on others. They do not see the expression on the faces of the people receiving their messages. It is critical that they learn how to communicate orally and in writing, in person and online, to be successful in our rapidly evolving global economy.

I realized quickly that I needed to create a safe space online in the same way that I created a safe space in my classroom. I began by giving students a "Dos and Don'ts List for Online Communication" to ensure that students knew exactly what was appropriate in their online interactions. I engaged them in fun icebreaker activities to foster relationship building. Then we slowly built on that foundation, and I provided strategies for "Saying Something Substantial." I wanted to make sure students knew how to contribute to the conversation in a substantive way to ensure that the quality of conversations remained high.

This early work supporting students paid off as they quickly learned how to engage in academic conversations in a respectful and substantive manner. They also learned how to drive dynamic discussions without my involvement. These skills were the groundwork for the successful collaboration that blossomed out of their ability to clearly express themselves, engage respectfully with their classmates, and understand that the other thirty students in our class were incredibly valuable resources.

More than anything I did with my students, online discussions were essential in cultivating communication skills and raising awareness about our collective intelligence, which is so critical to successful collaboration.

I was surprised when the communication skills they developed online translated so seamlessly to the classroom. Students entered my class talking about discussions from the previous night. They began using each other's names in class and referring to specific ideas shared in the online space. As a result, our in-class discussions and group work were transformed. Students were more confident in their abilities and more eager to participate.

Teacher librarians can model the use of online discussions by inviting teachers to participate in an online book club using a technology like Collaborize Classroom. Engaging with other staff members using a specific technology provides teachers with an opportunity to explore the technology in a comfortable and enjoyable context.

Introducing a technology and allowing teachers to "play" with it helps them overcome many of the fears that can create a barrier to use. If teachers see the value of their online conversations, they are more likely to use the technology with their own students. It is also helpful to provide teachers with resources to support their efforts integrating technology. For teacher librarians interested in exploring this idea, there are resources available to them and the teachers on their campus regardless of the online discussion platform they use. There is a Collaborize Classroom Book Club sheet that provides an overview and a Book Club Facilitator's Guide with best practices, tips, and examples.

The Collaborize Classroom Topic Library makes it possible for teachers using the discussion site to archive and share their discussion topics with a global audience of educators. Currently, the Topic Library—a free extension of Collaborize Classroom—has over three thousand teacher-designed topics for a variety of subject areas and grade levels.

Google Docs

Google offers an array of free tools aimed at making collaboration simple. Google Docs is a suite of applications that include documents, forms, spreadsheets, drawings, and presentations. These can be shared with a single student, a group of students, or an entire class to allow easy synchronous or asynchronous work on a shared document.

Google Docs offers a vehicle to teach students how to communicate and collaborate while simultaneously helping them develop strong content knowledge. For example, English teachers who want to teach students how to read actively to comprehend complex texts can use a Google document to engage students in group annotations and discussions.

Teachers can copy and paste texts into the left column of a document and allow students to annotate and discuss the text in the right column. This makes it possible for students to use tools like "Define" or "Research" within the document to "determine or clarify the meaning of unknown and multiple-meaning words and phrases by using context clues, analyzing meaningful word parts, and consulting general and specialized reference materials."

In addition to identifying vocabulary that is unfamiliar, students are encouraged to "read closely to determine what the text says explicitly and to make logical inferences from it." This can be a challenging task, so it is helpful if students are encouraged to discuss the text and ask questions using the "Comments" feature or the real-time chat feature within a document. This creates a support network of peers who can offer insights and answer questions. Instead of traditional pen and paper homework, which leaves many students floundering when they encounter a question they do not understand, this is more engaging and fosters relationship building. As students lean on one another for support, ask questions, share ideas, and learn from each other, they begin to recognize peers as valuable resources in the class.

History and social science teachers who want to empower students can use Google Docs to group students and allow them to research a topic, become experts, and present that information to the class. This approach to flipping a lecture by allowing students to research and present the content addresses multiple Common Core Standards in a single activity.

First, students must research their topic using a shared Google Doc and utilize the "Research" tool. In doing so, students address writing anchor standards by conducting "short as well as more sustained research projects" and "gather relevant information from multiple print and digital sources."

Using the research tool inside of the Google document makes it possible for students to explore digital resources as a group to evaluate those online resources, identify key pieces of information, and discuss the importance of the facts they've found in relation to their topic. This teaches students to look at information with a critical eye, then consider how to present that information in a way that will interest other students.

Google Docs also makes it possible for students to create dynamic multimedia presentations to share their ideas with the class. It is important that students become media literate and learn how to communicate using images and video in addition to text.

Students today are inundated with media, but many do not think critically about the impact or purpose of media. Providing students with opportunities to create presentations requires that they "integrate and evaluate information presented in diverse media and formats, including visually, quantitatively, and orally." They have to think about details like citation or how an image might add to or detract from the content in their presentation. There are times when a picture can say more than words, but there are moments when a picture will distract or confuse an audience. These nuances of working with media are important to discuss with students to ensure that they are able to "present information, findings, and supporting evidence such that listeners can follow the line of reasoning and the organization, development, and style are appropriate to task, purpose, and audience."

The Common Core Standards for math emphasize several points that I think are important to discuss in this conversation about collaboration. When I was in high school, my math class consisted of reviewing a chapter in the math book then solving a collection of problems. Needless to say, the whole experience was not inspiring. I did not see the relevance of the formulas I was learning to life beyond the classroom

As I read through the Common Core math standards, I was excited to see a focus on real-world problem solving, higher-order thinking, and writing. Mathematically proficient students "construct viable arguments and critique the reasoning of others." They must be able to "Justify their conclusions, communicate them to others, and respond to the arguments of others." This requires that students be able to articulate their process and think critically about the way their peers have approached a mathematical problem A Google document can be used to present students with real-world scenarios that require problem solving and creative thinking. For example, [take] two different types of hair gel. . . . These two products essentially do the same thing, but this challenges students to look closely at the information about each gel. How many ounces does the bottle contain? How much is recommended for use? What types of ingredients are used? How much do they cost? Then they have to articulate a position about which hair gel they think is the "best deal" and support that position with evidence and a clear explanation.

I selected hair gel because it is a product many of my high school students are clearly using a lot of, so I knew it was relevant. It's a simple assignment that deals with a real-life scenario—bargain shopping—but also involves several variables and does not have a clear "right" answer. The task engages students in conversation and debate requiring that they clearly state their reasoning and evaluate the reasoning of their peers.

I could have used any number of items to create this document. Teachers who want to engage their students in designing problems for their peers to solve can empower students to create the product comparisons then share them with the class.

Teachers can also use technology to transform traditional exercises . . . . Adding online engagement makes the process more collaborative and interesting. Any teacher presenting students with a challenge can engage them in groups using Google Docs to brainstorm what they know about the problem, what they want to know, what they learned, and how they can apply their knowledge. The beauty is that their interactions and ideas are captured online and remain there for future reference and reflection.

Teacher librarians who want to share Google Docs with teachers on their campus should encourage teachers to begin by signing up for Gmail, which automatically provides them access to the full suite of Google apps. The template gallery available through Google Docs is a great resource for teachers using Google to create templates to collaborate and share their best practices.

Librarians model the use of Google tools by sharing documents with teachers who have a Gmail address so they can explore the potential for collaboration available via Google Docs. Modeling at every age level is effective for teaching. The more teachers have experience using a tool, the more likely they are to incorporate that into their teaching practice.

Most teachers are so overworked and overwhelmed by the current state of education that it is daunting to imagine shifting to a new set of national standards. Add to that the task of learning to integrate technology into their curriculum, and it becomes a staggering undertaking. If teachers understood that they could effectively teach a wide range of standards simultaneously with a single online assignment, this shift might not feel so overwhelming. The trick is to show teachers how to leverage the online space and their students' connectivity to actively engage students in collaborative tasks both inside and outside the classroom to prepare them for success beyond high school.

Critical Thinking

1. Tucker quotes a Common Core Standard that states students as young as kindergarten should use digital tools during writing activities in collaboration with peers. What is your opinion of beginning collaborative technology use at this age? Justify your answer.

2. Based on the information in the article, your own knowledge of collaborative technology and social media, and your chosen content area, develop two classroom activities that will involve students in collaborative technology for learning.

Create Central

www.mhhe.com/createcentral

Internet References

Quest Garden
www.questgarden.com

Go2web20
www.go2web20.net

CATLIN TUCKER is a Google Certified Teacher and CUE Lead Learner who has taught English language arts in Sonoma County since 2001. She authored Blended Learning for Grades 4–12: Leveraging the Power of Technology to Create Student-Centered Classrooms. She writes an education technology blog at www.catlintucker.com and is active on Twitter@CTuckerEnglish.

Unit 7

UNIT

Prepared by: Rebecca B. Evers, *Winthrop University*

Collaboration

Hopefully we have reached the point where we understand the need to work collectivity and collaboratively to solve the problems facing our public school system, but that may not make it easy to actualize, as old habits are the most difficult habits to break. If we look back over the history of education, in almost every photograph of every classroom we will see a group of students with one teacher. That is the image of school burned into our collective memories. That was what I saw for the first 20 years of my teaching career in every school where I taught. How hard might it be to change that mindset?

That mindset alone can be a roadblock to effective and productive collaboration. Other possible roadblocks are teacher perceptions, time to engage with other teachers, lack of focus, and taking the time to develop collaboration skills. First, false perceptions can destroy collaboration before it even begins. Teachers often prefer to work alone and they perceive collaboration and co-teaching as invasive. The reason can be as simple as they like to have a classroom of their "own" students. Other reasons might include mistrust of others or a concern that if they make even one, small mistake, they will be found lacking and others will publicly point out their faults. Some teachers see any critical feedback as personal criticism or an assault on their academic freedom. Secondly, finding time for collaboration is difficult. Conflicting teaching and planning schedules, as well as other duties such as bus duty, record keeping responsibilities, and grading can take up all of a teacher's non-teaching time. It may be impossible to meet before or after school as personal lives may take precedent. Thirdly, focus during collaboration meetings can be lost to personal conversations or to situations that appeared suddenly. Dealing with distractions can consume meeting time very quickly. And finally, we must understand the need for training and time to develop the skills needed for this intimate relationship. Collaboration, like a marriage, takes time to emerge into a lasting relationship.

The primary early childhood (EC) professional organizations consider a family-centered practice to be the best and most effective practice. One may assume that collaboration is critical in establishing a family-centered practice. Therefore, teacher preparation programs should include opportunities for pre-service EC educators to learn how to partner and collaborate with families. There are indications that preparation programs often do not emphasize the importance of teacher-family partnerships enough for pre-service teachers to be able to effectively include families in their teaching practice.

We may think that working with others should happen when we feel it is beneficial to us, helpful to our students, or when we feel it is necessary. However, it may be most important that we collaborate even when we do not want to work with others. We know that professionals in fields outside education are not allowed to do whatever they please or want in the workplace, and that professionals in other endeavors are required and compelled to work interdependently to achieve common goals. According to the data, the students of those teachers who do collaborate have higher achievement levels.

One way for teachers to collaborate is to co-teach classes. Most often co-teaching is seen as something teachers do to meet the needs of students with disabilities in the general education classroom. Certainly that may be how most of us think of it. However, as you read, think about other reasons for co-teaching and places where co-teaching would benefit both the teachers and the K-12 students. Co-teaching is generally thought to be when two teachers share the primary responsibility for teaching the same group of students at the same time. Teachers plan, teach, and assess the students together. But this may not be a perfect union, teachers may not agree on what to teach, how to teach it, who will teach what, or how to assess student learning.

Collaborative co-teaching can take place in many ways as the articles in this section illustrate. In addition, collaboration is used with schools and communities to help struggling children and schools. Finally, an important part of our job in schools is to help students develop life-long skills that will help them as adults; collaboration is such a skill.

Article   Prepared by: Rebecca B. Evers, *Winthrop University*

Library-Classroom Collaboration Stimulates Reading, Teaches So Much More

PATRICIA VERMILLION AND MARTY MELTON

Learning Outcomes

After reading this article, you will be able to:

- Implement new ways to work with the librarian to increase student reading.
- Increase students' research and writing skills through collaborative teaching.
- Integrate technology used by students into both the library and classroom.

Media center specialists and classroom teachers continually search for innovative ways to stimulate readers to try new genres in order to increase reading in all disciplines, be aware of the latest great novel, and locate a series or author that spurs them to read one book after another.

In order to motivate students to investigate and effectively use the media center collection, the media center specialist and social studies teacher work together to get students involved in reviewing books they like.

To kick off the year in the media center, the media center specialist or social studies teacher presents a booktalk to the class, reviewing a book new to the collection. In presenting the booktalk, the speaker uses note cards and exhibits a copy of the book along with a prop representing an idea from the text. The speaker describes a character, setting, or event in the story. If an informational text is reviewed, the speaker will explain events, procedures, or ideas from the text. A short blurb about the author may be included, along with a brief reading of the text. This early booktalk serves as an example for student presentations to come.

Another advantage of student booktalks is to facilitate the process of learning more about new students. At the beginning of the school year, it's beneficial to know more about students' particular reading interests, their strengths and struggles in reading, and materials they've previously discovered. At the Lamplighter School, an independent school of 480 students from pre-K through fourth grade in Dallas, Texas, the media specialist and fourth-grade literacy teacher have the advantage of collaborating and coteaching each week. By coplanning and carrying out lessons collectively, these two professionals provide a deeper and more compelling *curriculum* while covering the curricular goals of both the media center and the fourth-grade literacy programs. At Lamplighter, the goal is to support development of confident, well-spoken, engaging students, and therefore the children have a plethora of opportunities for public-speaking experiences, including first-person historical impersonations and biweekly video news broadcasts. Video booktalks are one in a series of planned public-speaking projects, which provide teacher and media specialist with valuable information about students and give students a public-speaking experience based on their individual interests.

In the media center, students are assigned to prepare a booktalk about a book they completed over the summer in order to encourage their peers to try something new. There are no limits as to type of book the children can review: fiction, nonfiction, one in a series, a part of the library collection (or not), or a graphic novel. Anything is possible if students read a book and want to inform their classmates about it. By enlisting students to choose the books they will review, teachers can note the interests of a particular child, the reading level of each student, and themes, authors, and genres most popular with a particular group. Additionally, no matter how well read the media center coordinator and teacher are, every year students will bring to attention new and exciting books. This is a wonderful advantage to use to continually update the media center collection with informational and literary content that supports the Common Core standards. In the SAMR (Substitution, Augmentation, Modification, Redefinition) model, this would fall under Modification. Using technology allows for significant task redesign because each booktalk is unique and the students control the camera, filming their peers. In order to read the resulting QR code video, technology must be used.

In the classroom, students are taught how to construct note cards, with title, author, and key ideas to inspire other readers. Discussion includes ways to present a booktalk by providing enough of the story or information to spark an interest in the audience without giving away the ending of a suspense novel or too much information from a text. Additionally, students plan to bring a prop to stir interest or to help a listener remember the book. Props range from a baseball to a feather duster or cherry pie, all in the interest of hooking peers to read and explore the book. Students use direct evidence of the text by reading aloud a favorite paragraph.

One to two weeks after the assignment, students present the booktalks in the media center. They bring a copy of the book, or in some cases display the cover of the book via an iPad or Mimio-Board, and individually present their booktalks using note cards and props they choose to include. During the presentations each student will be the videographer, taping another peer as his or her book review is presented. Video taping the presentations allows each child a chance to step up and make a finished presentation that can be reviewed for assessment by the student and teacher. Students can then plan for adaptations to improve the next public speaking assignment. Serving as cameraman allows students to build technology skills. Each booktalk is uploaded to YouTube by the technology teacher and assigned a QR code by the media specialist, building a resource where students, teachers, and parents can view the booktalk on an iPad or phone as they explore new books in the media center.

Children love to watch each other on video, so the collection of QR-coded book-talks is a popular feature in the media center. Not only can the students observe their own videos, but they can also enjoy videos of older students recorded in previous years, as well as their peers' videos. By watching the videos, children learn to analyze what makes a booktalk valuable and entertaining. They compare their own presentations to those of others. They learn to emulate those whose delivery style and content

they find? most compelling. Students have specific guidelines to follow, including a rubric for self-evaluation. To assess and plan for needed changes, both teacher and student review these video recordings. It is an immensely valuable learning tool used by the children at their own choosing. As students are having fun observing and critiquing delivery styles or writing techniques, they are constructing a personal understanding of public presentations, and of the value of literature. At least 95 percent of the students meet or exceed our expectations. When students play a major role in this or any learning process, everyone benefits.

The process of presenting individual book reviews is an essential part of the Lamplighter curriculum, with multiple benefits for students and professionals. One immediate and valuable result is that every student in the class and the two professionals have heard multiple enthusiastic booktalks. This helps professionals in selecting new materials to order and supports students in reading new books.

Second, the professionals develop insight into the interests and reading proficiency of students. These booktalks increase students' reading motivation and personal enjoyment in reading. The students can select their own reading from this social interaction. Reading affects all areas of the curriculum. The students' listening skills improve because they are asked to comment on the booktalk, which requires effective listening.

Third, students actively construct a booktalk and have a means to review and revise future public presentations. The students must follow an outline for their booktalk, and that requires organizational and writing skills.

Fourth, using the QR-coded collection of videos, many more students and patrons throughout the school are able to review and reuse the booktalks on iPad or iPhones for years to come. This is a popular assignment—made easy when two professionals orchestrate it together—and it pays off with big dividends. The third-grade teachers were so excited about these booktalks, the language teachers took the project, developed a unit of study, and added new QR codes to the media center collection.

Bibliography

Jones, Gwyneth. "QR codes." QR Codes in the Library. Ed. Gwyneth Jones. 2013. Web. 16 July 2013. http://www.thedaringlibrar-ian.com/.
National Governors Association Center for Best Practices, Co. Common Core Standards. 2010. Web. 17 July 2013. http://www. corestandards.org.

Critical Thinking

1. The article listed a number of positive results of this collaboration. Are there any potential drawbacks to this particular collaboration between librarians and teachers? How might those be overcome?

2. The collaboration in this article is between a librarian and a social studies teacher. Based on your curriculum and grade level, discuss two activities on which you and a librarian might collaborate.

Internet References

American Library Association
http://www.ala.org

Common Sense Media
https://www.commonsensemedia.org

School Library Monthly
http://www.schoollibrarymonthly.com

PATRICIA VERMILLION is media center coordinator at The Lamplighter School, Dallas Texas. Her first picture book, *Texas Chili, Oh My!*, was published by TCU Press in October 2013.

MARTY MELTON is a fourth grade teacher of language arts and social studies at The Lamplighter School in Dallas, Texas. She is an enthusiastic advocate for integrating subject studies and co-teaching across disciplines.

Article Prepared by: Rebecca B. Evers, *Winthrop University*

Are We Adequately Preparing Teachers to Partner with Families?

TAMARA SEWELL

Learning Outcomes

After reading this article, you will be able to:

- Describe a family-centered classroom.

- State reasons why involving parents in your classroom is important to student learning.

Introduction

Young children are the center of their family and as such their families are a wellspring of knowledge when it comes to their child's development and learning. Early childhood teachers have regular opportunities to interact with families and gather knowledge to influence their teaching practices. However, challenges arise when a teacher has not been prepared to partner effectively with families and to best serve children within the context of the family.

According to the Council for Exceptional Children's Division for Early Childhood (DEC), "practitioners in early education and intervention must be prepared to work with families whose cultural, ethnic, linguistic, and social backgrounds differ from their own" (Stayton et al. 2003, p. 11). "Class lectures, simulations, and supervised home visits with families, as well as interviews and informal conversations" (Hyson 2003, p. 140) are integral to the pre-service teachers' learning process.

The DEC's preparation program standards for early childhood professionals were developed in conjunction with the National Association for the Education of Young Children (NAEYC) and the National Board for Professional Teaching Standards (NBPTS). The DEC's program standards emphasize that the professional become involved as equal partners with families early on and that a reciprocal relationship should be maintained throughout the partnership. Additionally, because families vary in terms of priorities, resources, concerns, cultural background, views of education, and how they support their children's development and learning, training should involve families that are diverse in nature (Stayton et al. 2003). Providing comprehensive training to professionals has the potential to increase the implementation and effectiveness of family-centered practices.

Research concerning teacher preparation in the field of early childhood is limited, particularly in the area of family-centered practices. Several surveys have focused on this increasingly important topic, but results are, at best, inconsistent. However, there are two distinct issues that are repeated throughout the literature: teacher perceptions of families and the focus on family partnership in teacher preparation programs.

What Are Teachers' Perceptions of Family-Centered Practice?

Teachers and administrators struggle to partner with families due to the lack of preparation. In 2006, MetLife surveyed 1,001 public school teachers and found that "teachers consider engaging and working with parents as their greatest challenge and the area they were least prepared to manage during their first year" (Harvard Family Research Project 2006, p. 1). More specifically 31% of the teachers reported that the greatest challenge was in encouraging involvement and communicating with the family (Markow et al. 2006). The dearth of training opportunities has resulted in teachers feeling ill-prepared to work with families, which creates a multitude of challenges for the teacher, child, and family.

In-service training opportunities and topics impact practitioner perceptions and practices. Bruder et al. (2009) completed electronic surveys and phone interviews with 51 Part C coordinators and 49 coordinators of 619 programs regarding the implementation of professional development that is both systematic and sustainable. Thirty-nine of the Part C states and 35 of the 619 respondents reported offering in-service training systems that were systematic and sustainable. The training content for both Part C and 619 was based on administrative or consultant recommendations. Only 11 of the 51 Part C coordinators reported training content regarding partnering with families and none of the 619 respondents reported inclusion of family content.

Rothenberg and McDermot of the Sage College School of Education expanded on the MetLife survey by creating focus groups to gain a qualitative understanding of the nature of family-centeredness and its implementation. Teachers who were involved in the groups reported that they actually avoided working with families and found such work to be unappealing. Parents involved in the focus groups reported that they only felt comfortable working with those teachers that treated children and families with respect and high regard (Harvard Family Research Project 2006). Based on these views, it is easy to see that an unproductive cycle of teachers and families avoiding interaction is easily formed and maintained.

How Are We Preparing Teachers to Work with Families?

The Center to Inform Personnel Preparation, Policy and Practice in Early Intervention and Early Childhood Special Education (n.d.) conducted a survey of 5,659 institutions offering degree programs for all services under IDEA. Of the 1,131 respondents, 86.43% reported that they offer at least one course related to families, specifically with a focus on families with children ages three to five. Another survey, by The National Prekindergarten Center in 2004, reported a more conservative percentage of only 61% who reported that they offered at least one course dedicated to preparing professionals to work with families (Maxwell et al. 2006).

In order to establish the amount of family-centered content taught in early childhood teacher preparation programs, Rupiper and Marvin (2004) surveyed 82 institutions across the United States. Results demonstrated that family-centered content was infused across course curriculum. Twenty-eight institutions indicated that family-centered content was taught in an independent undergraduate course. Course credit hours ranged from two to eight with most respondents indicating three credit hours. Primary content of the family-centered coursework included knowledge of families, IFSP skills, respecting diversity, communication skills, and knowledge of teamwork.

Chang et al. (2005) reported on a national survey of early childhood teacher preparation programs completed in 1999 by the National Center for Early Development and Learning. One of the purposes of the study was to quantify the amount and type of coursework and practicum experiences related to families, collaboration, and home visiting required by early childhood preparation programs (Chang et al. 2005). The sample included 438 associate and bachelor level programs in 47 states that prepare individuals to work with children ranging in age from birth to four years. Participants were asked to complete a survey that included questions about required coursework and practical experiences related to families. Just under 60% of both associates and bachelor's degree programs offered at least one families course. Data also showed that students often had practical experiences with families, including home visits, without having had any in-class preparation prior to or in conjunction with the experience.

The Centre for Community Child Health in Australia (2003) convened focus groups based on common issues found in the literature on the subject of early childhood teacher preparation. One of the major issues identified by the focus groups was that students were unprepared for work with young and developing families. In particular, members of the focus group believed that although family-centered philosophies, beliefs, and practices are incorporated into course content, opportunities for students to apply and demonstrate comprehension are limited (Centre for Community Child Health 2003).

In an effort to establish how family-centered practice was taught to future teachers, Sewell (2007) conducted a critical study surveying 21 undergraduate early intervention/early childhood special education teacher preparation programs. Participants were asked to specify how family-centered practices were taught as well as how students were afforded the opportunity to articulate and apply those practices. Approximately 38% of the respondents indicated that family-centered practice was taught in an independent course. Ninety percent of the respondents indicated that more than 50% of family-centered focus was infused across course content. Eighty-one percent of respondents indicated that family-centered methods courses were linked to field experiences, however, direct contact with families during these experiences was often limited due to the nature of the placements. Echoing The Centre for Community Child Health in Australia's (2003) and Chang et al. (2005) results, participants indicated that students were taught family-centered practices and had moderate opportunities to articulate them but very little opportunity to actually apply the practices with families.

To gain a comprehensive understanding of early childhood teacher preparation program's strengths and weaknesses, Bruder and Dunst (2005) surveyed programs to determine where training emphasis was placed in regards to the following factors: family-centered practice, cross-disciplinary models, service coordination, development of IFSPs, and natural environments. Eight disciplines serving children under IDEA were examined, and a total of 449 programs completed a 30-item survey. Results indicated family-centered intervention was the only practice that constituted primary emphasis across all eight disciplines; however, none of the disciplines felt as though they were adequately prepared to work with families. The researchers recommend embedding family-centered practices into teacher preparation programs in order to prepare students to work effectively with children and families (Bruder and Dunst 2005).

Are We Influencing Preservice Teachers' Perceptions?

Teacher's perceptions of families impact their interactions with families. Murray and Mandell (2004) evaluated two pre-service programs designed to prepare graduates to provide family-centered services using the Family-Centered Pre-service Model (FCPM). The FCPM program was based on the teacher preparation professional standards developed by both NAEYC and DEC. The researchers interviewed 22 students to examine attitudes and beliefs, as well as aptitude, about issues relating to diversity. Students were also asked to report on family-centered practices that they had the opportunity to apply (Murray and Mandell 2004).

Prior to the program, approximately 70% of the participants had little experience with families and a limited understanding of family-centered practices. The FCPM program was effective in changing the students' attitudes and beliefs about working with diverse families and increasing the students understanding of families in general. In addition, didactic teaching in conjunction with experiential practice resulted in increased participant confidence to effectively utilize and apply practices (Murray and Mandell 2004).

Additional research exploring pre-service teachers' perceptions and experiences of preparedness training was conducted by Blasi (2002). Twenty-six students enrolled in a course titled "Principles of Interprofessional Collaboration," completed pre- and post-test questionnaires. At the time of the pre-test, 38% of the students felt prepared to work with children and families. Upon completion of the course, 58% of the students felt prepared. This increase is due to the fact that students "realized the importance of valuing and respecting parents as their children's first and most important teachers, and . . . saw their role in working with families as more of a 'shared power' within a 'family-first' perspective" (Blasi 2002, p. 115). The limited positive results of the course further illuminate the need to expand and increase the emphasis on family-centered learning opportunities beyond a single course.

Giallourakis et al. (2005) developed a measure to explore the specific beliefs, skills, and practices of graduate students in the field of early childhood education. The survey results indicated that a moderate level of family involvement is included in programs, but has little impact on how students perceive their education. As would be expected, frequency of contact was correlated with beliefs and practices on family-centered approaches. The two themes that evolved from the survey responses were increased empathy and awareness as well as the application of new skills in relation to family-centered practice. One student shared that the experience greatly impacted his/her perspective and work in helping him/her realize "that even the least participatory parent still holds immense knowledge regarding their child and family, and the needs and resources of the family" (Giallourakis et al. 2005, p. 4).

Students' expressive writing also gives insight into their perceptions of family-centered practice. Pang and Wert (2010) conducted a study of 87 undergraduate students enrolled in an introduction to early intervention course that introduced students to family-centered philosophy and practices. The students completed pre and post essays about their beliefs vis-à-vis the involvement of families in early intervention service delivery and how they would involve families in their practice as early interventionists. The researchers found that at both the pre and post points of the study, students recognized the importance of family involvement; however, in their post essays students placed more emphasis on actual practices, involvement of the family as a whole unit, the roles that families and professionals play, the importance of involving pre-service teachers with families early, and the challenges related to implementing family-centered practices (Pang and Wert 2010). Pre-service students involved in the study recognized family support as a critical component of early intervention services and noted that family partnerships facilitated carryover of functional skills into multiple settings. This carryover reduced the pressure on the teacher to provide the primary support, increased both family and teacher understanding of the child's development and progress, and improved functionality of team goals.

Bingham and Abernathy (2007) used concept mapping to illuminate 49 pre-service students' changing attitudes and perceptions throughout a 16 week course on the topic of partnering with families. The students completed a pre- and post-course concept map depicting their perceptions about serving individuals with disabilities and their families. Differences between pre- and post-course perceptions included the expansion of the idea of communication from "getting the job done" to "advocating for children and families" and "a more reciprocal interaction with families" with students "relinquishing the role of power broker and embracing the role of advocate" (Bingham and Abernathy 2007, p. 52). Students saw the teacher's role as more collaborative not only with families, but also the community at large. However, not all results were as encouraging. In the pre-course maps, 73% of the students positioned the teacher as the expert. The post-course maps showed only a 8% change in this perception of roles. "Regardless of the numerous activities in which they participated and the family stories they heard, they did not move away from seeing the focus of the class on the special education system and its requirements" (Bingham and Abernathy 2007, p. 55). Bingham and Abernathy hypothesize that perhaps the strong focus on the administrative aspect of working with children with special needs (the Individuals with Disabilities Education Act requirements, documentation, education plans, etc.) overwhelm the students and therefore overshadow the importance of reciprocal family partnerships.

Results from the focus groups based on the MetLife survey spurred Rothenberg and McDermot to begin implementing new strategies in coursework. Practicum students were required to hold routine conferences with parents from a strengths-based perspective. These conferences were meant to focus on positive news about children, while also allowing parents to voice the views, goals, and dreams that they have for their children. Requiring family visits provided the students with insight into the child's world within the context of the family. Seasoned supervising teachers felt that the students' work with the families would create problems, but the families were quite receptive to the extra involvement and the students reported enjoying the contact with families and found that working with families resulted in positive outcomes for the children (Harvard Family Research Project 2006).

Conclusion

Partnering with families is best and effective practice and can only enhance children's development and learning. Nevertheless, many teachers find the idea of partnering with families a daunting and unmanageable task due to lack of preparation and training. All too often preparation does not emphasize the importance of partnering with families enough to enable pre-service teachers to practically apply the knowledge.

Increased and focused student contact with families throughout their teacher training is clearly necessary. Involvement of families in the development of coursework and in-service trainings as well as the delivery of course content and fieldwork opportunities is a key to improving student comprehension of the importance of family partnership. This concept ensures that course content is realistic and offers real-life examples. Families can act as co-instructors or guest speakers and share their experiences and lives through practical field experiences.

The research demonstrates that even one course can impact pre-service teachers' perceptions regarding partnerships with families. But, one course is not sufficient to adequately prepare teachers to work reciprocally with families. Theoretically, infusing family-centeredness throughout early childhood course work is the best option. However, programs must consider that "content taught, including both emphasis and pedagogical style, varies according to each individual instructor's knowledge and experience" (Sewell 2007, p. 61). Infusion of content across coursework is ideal as long as the emphasis of content is regulated and aligned with course objectives and practical experience so that regardless of instructor, students receive consistent information. In addition, ongoing in-service training is imperative in order to not only educate practicing teachers, but to support them in their daily practice with families.

It is vital for both early childhood teacher preparation programs and in-service trainers to ensure pre-service students and practicing teachers are adequately prepared to partner with families in order to best serve the needs of the child and family.

References

Bingham, A., & Abernathy, T. V. (2007). Promoting family-centered teaching: Can one course make a difference? *Issues in Teacher Education, 16*(1), 37–60.

Blasi, M. W. (2002). An asset model: Preparing pre-service teachers to work with children and families "of promise". *Journal of Research in Childhood Education, 17*(1), 106–121.

Bruder, M. B., & Dunst, C. J. (2005). Personnel preparation in recommended early intervention practices: Degree of emphasis across disciplines. *Topics in Early Childhood Special Education, 25*(1), 25–33.

Bruder, M. B., Morgro-Wilson, C., Stayton, V. D., & Dietrich, S. L. (2009). The national status of in-service professional development systems for early intervention and early childhood special education practitioners. *Infants and Young Children, 22*(1), 13–20.

Centre for Community Child Health. (2003). *Final report on research to inform the development of a capacity building program.* Canberra, ACT: Australian Council for Children and Parenting, Commonwealth Department of Family and Community Services.

Chang, F., Early, D. M., & Winton, P. J. (2005). Early childhood teacher preparation in special education at 2- and 4-year institutions of higher education. *Journal of Early Intervention, 27*(2), 110–124.

Giallourakis, A., Pretti-Frontczak, K., & Cook, B. (2005). *Understanding family involvement in the preparation of graduate students: Measuring family-centered beliefs, skills,* systems, and practices. Cambridge, MA: Harvard Family Research Project.

Harvard Family Research Project. (2006). Is teacher preparation key to improving teacher practices with families? What are the alternatives? *FINE Network.* Retrieved from www.gse.harvard.edu/hfrp/projects/fine/memberinsights.html.

Hyson, M. (Ed.). (2003). *Preparing early childhood professionals: NAEYC's standards for programs.* Washington, DC: National Association for the Education of Young Children.

Markow, D., Moessner, C., & Horowitz, H. (Eds.). (2006). *The MetLife survey of the American teacher: Expectations and Experiences.* New York: Metropolitan Life Insurance Company.

Maxwell, K. L., Lim, C.-I., & Early, D. M. (2006). *Early childhood teacher preparation programs in the United States: National report.* Chapel Hill, NC: The University of North Carolina, FPG Child Development Institute.

Murray, M. M., & Mandell, C. J. (2004). Evaluation of a family-centered early childhood special education pre-service model by program graduates. *Topics in Early Childhood Special Education, 24*(4), 238–249.

Pang, Y., & Wert, B. (2010). Preservice teachers' attitudes towards family-centered practices in early intervention: An implication for teacher education. *Educational Research, 1*(8), 253–262.

Rupiper, M., & Marvin, C. (2004). Preparing teachers for family-centered services: A survey of pre-service curriculum content. *Teacher Education and Special Education, 27*(4), 384–395.

Sewell, T. (2007). Family-centered practice in early intervention and early childhood special education personnel preparation. (Doctoral dissertation). Retrieved from Proquest. (Publication number AAT 3273938).

Stayton, V. D., Miller, P. S., & Dinnebeil, L. A. (Eds.). (2003). *DEC Personnel preparation in early childhood special education: Implementing the DEC recommended practices.* Longmont, CO: Sopris West.

The Center to Inform Personnel Preparation, Policy and Practice in Early Intervention and Early Childhood Special Education. (n.d.). *Part C data report.* Retrieved from www.uconnucedd.org/publications/files/PPDataPartCweb.pdf.

Critical Thinking

1. Describe what your actions to create a Family-Centered classroom would include. Share your reasons.

2. Give three reasons why involving parents in your classroom is important to your teaching and student learning. Cite information from articles in this unit.

3. Why do you think that the results of the course completed in the research by Bingham and Abernathy in 2007 were not more encouraging?

4. As an administrator, you have determined that teachers need to involve parents more in the decision making and learning experiences of their children. Based on this article and others in this edition, what kind of professional development might you plan for your teachers and families?

Create Central

www.mhhe.com/createcentral

Internet References

The National Coalition for Parent Involvement in Education (NCPIE)
www.ncpie.org

TAMARA SEWELL teaches at the Bankstreet College of Education and she is the Supervised Fieldwork Advisor.

Article   Prepared by: Rebecca B. Evers, *Winthrop University*

Student-to-Student Collaboration and Coming to Consensus

GREGORY MACDOUGALL

Learning Outcomes

After reading this article, you will be able to:

- Support student collaboration during partner and small group work.

- Teach students how to come to consensus during partner and small group work.

Imagine it is a typical day in a typical middle school science classroom. Students are working in pairs on a series of problems involving Punnett squares. There is a low buzz of activity in the air. Most students are on task, discussing the problems in between talk of weekend plans and the music they think is awesome. The teacher walks around checking work and monitoring behavior. And then, as often happens, a student raises a hand and asks a typical question: "My answer is different than my partner's answer; which one is correct?"

Teachers are caring people. We like helping students learn. We like sharing our love of science with students, and we get excited when a question is asked. As such, a typical teacher response is often to point to the correct answer and explain why the answer is correct.

In another classroom, a student asks the same question, but the response from this teacher is different. In this classroom, students are expected to talk about what they think the answer is, share why they think their answer is correct, and attempt to come to a consensus on the answer before they seek mediation from their teacher. Instead of giving the student the correct answer, this teacher reinforces student-to-student collaboration by pointing to the directions for the activity and asking that the two students come to a consensus based upon credible information from their textbook, class notes, labs, or other sources.

In most classrooms, the teacher serves as giver of information and students are recipients. But this typical practice in science classrooms does not match typical science practices. Indeed, Osborne notes that "argument and debate are common in science, yet they are virtually absent from science education (2010, p. 463). Conversely, the teacher in the second scenario facilitates student thinking through orchestrating student-to-student interactions in a climate that promotes collaboration. The expectations are for students to share their thinking about science concepts, use credible evidence to justify their thinking, and reach a consensus.

With the publication of A Framework for K-12 Science Education (NRC 2012) and the Next Generation Science Standards (NGSS) (Achieve Inc. 2013), we see an intentional move in science education toward creating science classrooms where student-to-student collaboration and analysis replace a singular focus on learning "stuff." However, Schiller and Joseph note that "facilitating equitable classroom discussions is a tricky business, one that requires thought and planning" (2010). Student-to-student collaboration requires that the teacher not only plan for the cognitive demands required to learn science content, but also that the teacher make explicit plans for productive student-to-student dialogue.

The following two classroom examples come from working with nearly 100 middle school mathematics and science teachers across the state of South Carolina for the purpose of transitioning their instructional practices toward student-to-student collaboration.

The examples include the following classroom practices: Student pairs reading a text and participating in a quick activity at the start of class, often called a bell ringer. Teachers in our program, like the teacher in the second scenario, use these strategies to provide time for students to process information through student-to-student collaborations in a safe climate where teachers guide processes to ensure students both succeed in their student-to-student interactions and meet the cognitive demands of the content. Critical components of this process include a focus question to engage student thinking about science content, student-to-student communication, and coming to consensus.

Coming to Consensus through Text

The first example is a reading activity that takes place in a middle school science classroom that has been arranged so that students work in pairs. The content focus is the Moon's gravitational effects on Earth, and the teacher prepares students for the reading with an anticipatory focus question designed to provide a purpose for the reading: "A weather reporter on TV said that hurricanes are more dangerous when the Moon is full. Do you agree? Explain your answer."

Underneath the question, the teacher offers a scaffolded prompt that students may use: "I believe that hurricanes are (more/less) dangerous when the Moon is full because _____."

After all students write an individual response in their science notebook, the teacher gives them clear directions for partner talk and models appropriate behavior through a variety of methods, such as role play. The purpose of the partner talk at this point is for students to share their current thinking with a peer and allow them time to modify their answers.

Working in pairs, students are identified as Partner A and Partner B. Beginning with Partner A, each student has 30 seconds to share his or her answer and reasoning while the other partner listens without interrupting. The teacher uses a timer that all students can see, prompts Partner A to dialogue with Partner B, prompts students to switch to Partner B, and brings the student-to-student interaction to a timely close. During the partner talk, the teacher walks around the room monitoring behavior and listening to students as they talk about their thinking.

Following the focus question and partner talk, students silently read a brief section of text or other source material. Brevity is essential, as text in science is typically information dense. In the scenario described, the reading is composed of just two paragraphs. With a clear purpose for reading, students interact with the text, searching for clues that will help answer the focus question and, hopefully, resolve any differences they have identified in their initial thinking.

After silent reading, students are asked to reflect on the text by rewriting the initial response they recorded in their science notebook, this time using information from the text to support their answer. Students then engage in partner reading, where they take turns reading one paragraph of the text aloud to their partner. After the partner reading, more time is given for students to modify their answers to the focus question.

Should differences in their responses remain, the teacher may use the "silent debate" strategy. Here, students switch papers, silently read what was written by their partner, and then write a response. The teacher again offers a scaffolded prompt that students may use: "I think that your answer is (correct/ wrong) because (cite something from the text)."

Students continue to swap papers and argue through writing and citing points in the text until the pair reach a consensus. During the entire process, the teacher walks around the room to monitor behavior and listen to student-to-student dialogue. Only if pairs remain at an impasse does the teacher mediate their thinking.

Coming to Consensus Through Demonstration

Many teachers use short activities called "bell ringers" to begin a class, quick checks during class time, and exit tickets as formative assessments. The following example comes from an eighth-grade science lesson where the teacher used a quick-check question in the middle of a lesson to gauge levels of student understanding of material. The question, which asks students to predict the path of a marble as it exits a circular tube, is based on common misconceptions students have about orbital and circular motion (Hestenes, Wells, and Swackhamer 1992).

Predict the Motion of the Marble

A circular tube is placed horizontally on a table. The tube is cut so that a portion of the tube is missing. A marble is thrown into one end of the tube and exits out the other end. What would be the direction of the marble after it exits the tube?

As in the above example, the quality of the question used is essential in getting students to think about and argue their current understanding of science concepts. Common content-related misconceptions make excellent starting points for student-to-student collaboration in the science classroom, and there are many resources that a teacher can use as sources for misconceptions. However, the best questions for collaboration come when teachers conduct item analyses on their tests and quizzes to identify relevant misconceptions.

The teacher precedes the demonstration with a think-ink-pair-share (TIPS). Each student reads the question, thinks about what the answer might be, and individually commits to an answer by writing it on paper (this is the I in TIPS, for ink). In pairs, students take turns explaining and listening for a specified time period (depending on the students and question, the teacher may allow 15 to 60 seconds per person). When explaining, students must give an answer and provide their reasoning or evidence for its correctness. When listening, students pay attention to the evidence given and may not interrupt. This dialogue may change students' thinking, however, consensus is not the goal at this point.

Depending on how widespread the disagreement is between the pairs in the classroom, the teacher may orchestrate broader dialogue by using a pair-square, in which two pairs combine to form a team of four. In round-robin fashion, each student again has a specified time to present his or her answer and argue his or her point. After this structured session, time is given for team members to try to come to a consensus on the answer, though they may not yet be able to do so at this point.

Resuming the TIPS exercise, teams are asked to simultaneously share their answers to keep engagement high and prevent last-second consensus changes based on the "vote" of other teams. Teachers in our study have students use whiteboards or "finger voting" (one finger represents A, two fingers represent B, etc.) to identify their consensus response. Teams not reaching consensus may vote as individuals. In one particular classroom, students could not come to a consensus on the path of the marble via dialogue alone. They needed evidence, and they were now ready for it.

At this point, the teacher can effectively mediate their thinking and bring closure to the dialogue on the path of the marble through a purposefully planned simple demonstration. The teacher brings out a length of hollow foam insulation for pipes and a marble. The hollow insulation is placed on a table in the same configuration.

Before conducting the demonstration, the teacher again gives time and guidance for team dialogue and consensus using similar protocols from earlier in the lesson. The old adage "practice makes perfect" applies to student use of strategies in the classroom and is conducive to a classroom environment where student-to-student dialogue is the norm and student engagement is expected of all.

Although this additional time for dialogue toward consensus may appear to be redundant, it is important to note that moving from a two-dimensional drawing to a physical demonstration requires another level of thinking. During this process, some students change their answer, while others do not.

With a classroom full of students waiting to see what will happen, the teacher releases the ball. The evidence is there for all to see. With the quick check complete, the teacher continues with the lesson as planned, secure in knowing that students now have a better understanding of a science concept.

Conclusion

It is important to note that the strategies chosen at each point in, and the time frame of, the process are dependent on several factors. These teachers explicitly planned each lesson based on its placement within a coherent unit, the type of science content to be learned, and students in their classroom. Time for these processes may be reduced or lengthened depending on the level of student understanding, which the teacher can clearly see and hear. This article provided two examples of student-to-student collaboration and consensus using common classroom strategies. Most any classroom strategy can be modified to include time for student-to-student collaboration and consensus.

When considering a typical day in the middle school science classroom, we may see students working together, but we may also see that "the teacher remains at the pinnacle as the classroom leader during discussions" (Schiller and Joseph 2010, p. 57). In the Framework and NGSS, we see a shift in the role of the teacher and how students learn—they should be engaging in argument from evidence, evaluating, and communicating information. Teachers in our research project cite two roadblocks that prevent them from shifting their lessons toward student-to-student-collaboration: time and student behavior.

Osborne states that "students need to be taught the norms of social interaction and to understand that the function of their discussion is to persuade others of the validity of their arguments" (2010, p. 465). In classrooms that promote collaboration, behavior problems are minimized when students engage in productive and civil dialogue with guidance and structure provided by a well-prepared teacher.

In an era when standards and testing drive curricula, many teachers feel they do not have time for student-to-student collaboration. In both of the examples offered, much classroom time was spent adding opportunities for collaboration to promote deeper learning of specific science content. The question teachers often ask is "Do I have time to do this?" The answer, of course, is that a high degree of professional judgment must be used in planning for student-to-student collaboration in the science classroom. Yes, there are times when the pace of instruction is slow and times when it is fast, depending on the content, context, and students in the classroom. Perhaps a better question might be "What would happen to student understanding of science concepts if collaboration were a typical classroom practice?"

References

Achieve Inc. 2013. Next generation science standards. www.nextgenscience.org/next-generation-science-standards.

Hestenes, D., M. Wells, and G. Swackhamer. 1992. Force concept inventory. *Physics Teacher* 30: 141–58.

National Research Council (NRC). 2012. *A framework for K-12 science education: Practices, crosscutting concepts, and core ideas.* Washington, DC: National Academies Press.

Osborne, J. 2010. Arguing to learn in science: The role of collaborative, critical discourse. *Science* 328 (5977): 463–66.

Schiller, E., and J. Joseph. 2010. A framework for facilitating equitable discourse in science classrooms. *Science Scope* 33 (6): 56–60.

Critical Thinking

1. Theorize why teachers give information or the answer rather than encouraging students to come to consensus when they reach different conclusions?

2. In your classroom, which would you select to teach your students how to come to consensus, through text or though demonstration? Why is your selection best for your teaching situation?

3. Construct a lesson plan to teach *coming to consensus* using your chosen method from question 2.

Internet References

Center for the Collaborative Classroom
https://www.collaborativeclassroom.org

Edutopia
http://www.edutopia.org

Next Generation Science Standards
http://www.nextgenscience.org

GREGORY MACDOUGALL (gregm@usca.edu) is an educational specialist with the S2TEM Centers SC in Aiken, South Carolina.

Article

Prepared by: Rebecca B. Evers, *Winthrop University*

Using Appreciative Inquiry to Foster Intergenerational Collaboration for Positive Change in a Struggling School System

MEGAN TSCHANNEN-MORAN, BOB TSCHANNEN-MORAN, AND CYNTHIA A. LEMMERMAN

Learning Outcomes

After reading this article, you will be able to:

- Explain the five steps needed to achieve positive change through Appreciative Inquiry.

- Defend SOAR (Strengths, Observations, Aspirations, and Resources) as a more productive problem solving approach than SWOT (Strengths, Weaknesses, Opportunities, and Threats).

- Support the need for intergenerational collaboration to ensure lasting change.

I
n its heyday, Crossroads, a small city in the U.S. Rust Belt, had been a strong community with solid schools and a thriving economy. It was an attractive place for families to live and work. At one time more than 100 railroad trains stopped in and/or passed through Crossroads on a daily basis. By the start of the twenty-first century, however, Crossroads was no longer such a thriving hub. Instead, trains passed right on through the city without infusing any capital into the local economy. Combined with the erosion of its manufacturing base, this change made for a city in decline.

The Crossroads Community Schools (CCS) was no longer the well-regarded and well-supported school system it once had been. CCS had taken a hit in both performance and reputation.

This decline distinguished Crossroads as a city having more than its fair-share of troubles rather than as a desirable place for families to reside. Such negative attention became all the more pronounced when the State's Local School Report Card process documented the underperformance of CCS. In the first round of reporting, CCS received the lowest possible rating: Academic Emergency.

Initially, CCS decided to solve its problems by addressing them head on through traditional approaches to strategic planning and organizational improvement. This approach did not, however, prove to be very effective. People became disheartened and discouraged after years of hard effort and work had led to only minimal improvement in the schools' rankings. Things were looking bleak in Crossroads.

Fortunately, the Board of Education (BoE) learned about Appreciative Inquiry (AI) and decided to give it a try (Cooperrider, Whitney, & Stavros, 2008; Whitney & Trosten-Bloom, 2010; Watkins, Mohr and Kelly, 2011). The Board members first decided to experience AI for themselves at a BoE retreat. By working through the AI process on their own, the BoE saw how identifying and building upon what was right with their schools would enable them to move forward with greater confidence and enthusiasm. From this experience, the CCS leadership was able to better understand and imagine how such a process might take form in the district as a whole. Indeed, experiencing rather than just being told about AI was critical to the decision to move forward in this way.

In designing its AI process, CCS drew upon the railroad roots of its community and proclaimed "Get On Board the Celebration Express!" as the overarching theme for the process. This process helped people reclaim their pride in what the schools had been as well as their optimism in what they might yet become. The strength of the AI process in Crossroads was due, in part, to the breadth of involvement across many constituents and generations. Not only did the BoE include district leaders and teachers, they designed the process to include business and community leaders as well as the students of Crossroads' five schools. AI enabled CCS to draw its student and adult constituencies into conversation with each other on new grounds both in focus and in method. Instead of talking about how to fix what was being done wrong, with its consequent discomfort and demobilization, sessions were held across generational lines to talk with each other as to how the things that were working well could be acknowledged, expanded, built upon, and developed. Such widespread participation in the AI process—from planning through execution, by all age brackets, of each and every constituency—made the experience all the more transformative. When everyone took on and became invested in the process, things really began to change.

To kick off things, a series of eleven Define-Stage sessions were held with a variety of constituent groups within CCS, as well as in the community at large, to acquaint people of all ages with the process of AI and to enlist their support in identifying the focus of the inquiry. These sessions included the BoE, district administrators, parents and teachers, community leaders, business leaders, and students in all five of the district schools. In the case of the K-1 building, adult volunteers—including teachers, administrators, and staff members—were paired with first graders to interview them about their best experiences and wishes for their school. At the other school buildings, teachers and administrators participated in paired interviews and small-group discussions right along with the students. The pairings were then organized into small, intergenerational groups, in order to share their stories and to identify common themes.

After these 11 Define-Stage sessions were held, a group of thirty volunteers met to plan the Summit. The volunteers were divided into small groups that were each given sets of cards on which were written the 141 themes that had emerged from the Define Stage. The small groups were then asked to sort them into larger, unifying themes that would guide the AI process in CCS. When the small groups reported back to the committee as a whole, a consensus converged as to three over-arching themes that were to be explored and advanced:

- Trust and Respect
- Community Pride and Involvement
- Student Achievement and Success

A three-day Summit was planned to take place shortly after the end of the school year. The summit revolved around these themes and included the active participation of all CCS constituencies. Given the importance of maximizing diversity to AI, CCS strove to mix things up not only with the administrative, instructional, and support staff but also with the students, parents, and community leaders as well. The mayor participated and invited members of his staff to participate as part of their job responsibilities for the week. Likewise, the directors of the public libraries in town and other social service agencies participated as well. The whole community was involved with the process.

The Summit proved to be both fun and productive. Through paired interviews based upon an interview protocol structured around the three themes, as well as through small-group and large-group conversations, CCS was able to design a positive way forward. New stories and wishes were shared around the three Summit themes. Summit participants also had fun together when they played out their hopes and dreams on stage at the summit, in a variety of illustrative skits based on their positive images of the future. Provocative propositions were developed by small groups that described CCS at its very best. Creative presentations of those propositions utilizing songs, dances, and skits served as powerful expressions to the gathered community as to how that might look. Inspiring plans for implementing these propositions were subsequently developed by six, self-organized innovation teams (two for each of the Summit themes). The teams shared their plans with the whole group. Offers and requests made by members of each innovation team to bring the plans into being were recorded on planning documents.

Some of the most engaging and productive parts of the process were the times when people were able to interact with each other across institutional and generational lines. The AI process set both student and adult players in CCS in dialogue with each other to both imagine the future and to plan out ways for bringing that future to life. Doing so proved to be critical to the Summit's success. Dialogue became more welcome and real when no constituency, by process design, stood over-and-above the other. Dialogue also became more creative and productive. People were not used to hearing each other's ideas on these topics across generational lines, let alone hearing them on something of an equal footing with each other.

After the Summit, the innovation teams met over the summer to refine and to develop strategies for implementing their plans. A video presentation of the Summit was shared with the entire staff of the district during the opening convocation for the following school year, as were reports from each of the innovation teams. To support the outcomes of the Summit, CCS sought to infuse AI throughout the district. Administrators and teacher leaders were trained on appreciative approaches to supervision

Using Appreciative Inquiry to Foster Intergenerational Collaboration for Positive Change by Megan Tschannen-Moran et al.

173

and conflict resolution. The innovation work continued through the following school year, resulting in measurable improvement in each of the areas of inquiry.

Building Upon Strengths in Crossroads

AI works, in part, because it identifies, aligns with, and amplifies organizational strengths. By getting people to discover, focus on, and explore organizational strengths, AI changes the tone and character of conversations. Instead of complaining about what's not working people start celebrating what is working well. By noticing and amplifying the good things that are going on, AI turns the tables on old conversational patterns. As the search for scapegoats subsides, the safety required for innovation, risk-taking, and learning grows. People become more open, forthcoming, and confident. This is what unfolded through CCS' AI process.

By getting people to have conversations with each other about their best experiences, core values, generative conditions, and heartfelt wishes, AI created a space where new possibilities could emerge. It assisted people to generate new positive images of and propositions for the future by reconnecting them with their reason for going into education in the first place as well as with their continuing passion for working constructively with students in the here and now. Instead of attending to the wounds of what was going wrong, the process evoked new possibilities for constructive change by attending to the dimensions and nuances of what was going right. These positive, constructive conversations resulted in the planning and implementation of a number of new initiatives designed to enhance performance in the three areas of inquiry. In addition, the quality of interpersonal relationships improved in measureable ways.

Trust and Respect

Trust is foundational to learning across all stages and facets of life. That's especially true in intergenerational contexts such as schools. Whether the focus is on the learning of new academic, athletic, or social skills, the positive engagement of students with each other and with adults is essential. In the absence of trust, learning is impaired. The energy for learning is diverted into self-protective or even retributive directions. In the presence of trust, learning is enhanced (Goddard, Tschannen-Moran, & Hoy, 2001; Tschannen-Moran, 2014, 2004). The energy for learning becomes more focused on learning.

It was this recognition as well as the recognition that trust and respect at every level (adult-to-adult, adult-to-student, and student-to-student) was an area of needed growth that led CCS to make the cultivation of trust and respect a primary focus of its AI process. It utilized AI to explore the dimensions of

instances where trust and respect was higher to see what could be learned for and applied to instances where trust and respect was lower. It also reviewed the experiences of other districts to see what could be learned there as well.

One district initiative specifically designed to foster greater trust and respect involved training district employees and the Board of Education (BoE) in Nonviolent Communication (NVC), a communication process designed to facilitate the respectful understanding of people's feelings, needs, and desires (Rosenberg, 2005). NVC gives people tools for honest expression and empathetic reception of feelings, needs, and desires even when confronted with hard-to-hear messages. In preparation for a district-wide training in this process, four small-group sessions were held involving more than 50 people, including teacher-leaders, administrators, and the BoE. This was followed by a one day in-service involving all of the district employees. This training led to a follow-up Board workshop, training for the Freshman Learning Community, student initiatives, and a practice group seminar.

Community Pride and Involvement

One of the things that was clear to the participants planning CCS' AI process was that it would be difficult for the schools to improve significantly without significant improvement in the level of community support for and engagement in the schools. There was also recognition of how the community's low pride in CCS was inhibiting a robust level of community involvement. Community pride and involvement was thus selected as a second focus of CCS' AI process. Community engagement is the degree to which a school can count on involvement and support from parents and community members as well as the extent to which it provides the community with information about its activities and accomplishments. Schools with strong community engagement are responsive to the needs and concerns of parents and community members and, as a result, are better able to marshal community support when needed. Tschannen-Moran, Parish, and DiPaola (2006) found that middle school students were more likely to demonstrate success on state assessments in schools where teachers felt that parents and community members were working actively with their schools to ensure student success. By engaging their communities in positive ways, educational administrators and teachers are more likely to experience favorable results for their students.

Several new initiatives to engage parents and the community at-large grew out of CCS' AI Summit. These included:

- the founding of a Grandparents' Association that came to play an active service role within the schools and at school events,

- the founding of a district-wide Parent-Teacher Organization to facilitate communication and to support parental involvement across schools and school levels,
- the use of the school-district website to circulate electronic copies of building newsletters,
- the creation of a new staff position to serve as school-community liaison,
- the hosting of a Town Meeting by the BoE, using the AI paired-interview process, to celebrate and plan for the arts programs in the schools.

These and other initiatives enabled CCS to subsequently pass two important operating levies.

Student Achievement and Success

After launching the AI process at CCS, numerous new initiatives to improve student achievement and success were added to those that were already underway. The process worked delightfully well. It not only assisted CCS to better meet state indicators of school progress and success, it also assisted CCS to develop a system-wide climate that was much more conducive to student achievement. As schools respond to the pressures of the accountability movement to improve student achievement, attendance, and graduation rates, there is a growing recognition that the quality of interpersonal relationships, across generational lines, is a strong predictor of these outcomes. In the academic year following CCS' AI initiative, the entire district, not just one building, met AYP for the first time ever. This uplifted and encouraged people such that AI became more deeply embedded as an ongoing part of the Crossroads' culture.

The Five Principles of AI

AI is undergirded by five principles that are well illustrated by the intergenerational experiences of the people of CCS. These five principles, the positive, constructionist, simultaneity, anticipatory, and poetic principles center on the nature,

relationship, and quality of dialogue that AI enables (Cooperrider, Whitney, & Stavros, 2008). In CCS, the adult and student constituencies were in true dialogue. The way that happened revealed the underlying truth of the five principles of AI: they build effectively and essentially, one upon another.

We have represented these five principles in the image of a pyramid to show how they are related to each other and work together to generate positive actions and outcomes (Tschannen-Moran & Tschannen-Moran, 2010). See Figure 1.

The Positive Principle

Positive actions and outcomes flow naturally from the orientation and force generated by positive energy and emotions. Discouragement—the diminishment of courage—moves people in the opposite direction. It robs people of vision and power. Encouragement—the development of courage—has the opposite effect. It awakens vision and power. This certainly proved to be true at Crossroads. By working together with positive questions and foci at every stage of the process, adults and students were able to better trust and learn from each other. Awkward or even adversarial relationships became easier and mutually reinforcing. By using the AI approach, adults and students developed and diversified what was working well between them into a more productive and robust norm.

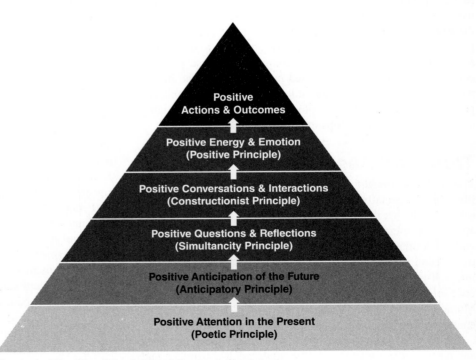

Figure 1 The Five Principles of Appreciative Inquiry
(Tschannen-Moran & Tschannen-Moran, 2010).

Using Appreciative Inquiry to Foster Intergenerational Collaboration for Positive Change by Megan Tschannen-Moran et al.

175

The Constructionist Principle

If positive energy and emotion hold so much potential for good, how do we get those? The constructionist principle asserts that positive energy and emotion are constructed through positive conversations and interactions with other people. It's not always easy to bring about those positive interactions, especially when the stakes are high and people are struggling to realize positive joint outcomes. It may seem so much easier to notice and to focus on trying to fix the squeaky wheel than on fanning the flames of positivity. That's because of the way pain tends to get our attention. Problems beg to be analyzed and fixed; in organizational or social contexts. When something isn't working right we want to find the cause and, in so doing, we too often shift into the blame game. In schools, it's especially easy for teachers and school leaders to point the finger at students and to thereby construct a negative reality of tension and resistance.

The Simultaneity Principle

When we do harm in this way we typically do so in no time at all. As soon as we ask about, focus on, and try to fix problems we can instantly amplify them into being bigger than they really are. It works the same way when it comes to asking about, focusing on, and trying to amplify strengths. The instant we turn our collective attention in that positive direction, the instant we shift to that positive approach, people and processes start shifting in positive ways as well. As the old saying goes, "Whether you think you can or think you can't, you're right." Our thinking determines our reality and it can do so in the twinkling of an eye. That's because our thinking has such a formative impact on what we say and do. By asking a new question, telling a new story, and/or making a new reflection we instantly shift the energy and direction. Focusing on problems tends to deplete available energy by leading us down a path of fault finding and blame. Focusing on the good stuff, on the other hand, tends to increase energy, renew hope, and bolster creativity. And it does all this in the twinkling of an eye. We saw this at work at CCS, as the entire system shifted its focus to the strengths of the community and its schools only to discover there were many delightful surprises and strengths.

The Anticipatory Principle

If positive questions and reflections are of such critical importance to the tenor and substance of our conversations, where do those come from? The anticipatory principle asserts that our questions and reflections flow from the things we anticipate happening in the future. By anticipating what things look like at their very best, people become more creative, resourceful, and resilient in looking for ways to make it so. In CCS, the discovery of so many positive dynamics and outcomes generated the hope that CCS could once again be a place where people were proud to say they lived or were from.

The Poetic Principle

If positive anticipation of the future sets the stage for positive questions and reflections, how do we get that? Forming the base of the pyramid upon which all the other principles are built, the poetic principle connects hope with mindfulness and intention with attention. The more we attend creatively and actively to the positive, life-giving dimensions of the present moment, the more positive will be our intentions for future moments. The engagement, excitement, and positive momentum for change generated by the AI process at CCS could certainly be described as poetry in motion.

Conclusion

This process provided evidence of how AI gave one struggling school system and community new reason to hope for better days and to invest in bringing those hopes to fruition. By celebrating the best of the present, district participants were able to dream even brighter dreams for the future. As the conversations changed, a new social reality was constructed and a cycle of positive energy was built as people encouraged one another to live from their values and to be their very best. Openness is a key ingredient when it comes to any change process. Systems cannot and do not change when key players have their brows *furled,* their arms crossed, and their toes tapping. It is much more likely to happen when they have smiling faces and open arms. Organizational change requires positive energy and excitement on the part of as many players as possible. This is a key understanding of AI in general and it is especially true of AI in schools. By not approaching its problems with a traditional SWOT (Strengths, Weaknesses, Opportunities, and Threats) approach but by utilizing a strengths-based SOAR (Strengths, Observations, Aspirations, and Resources) process, district participants were truly able to soar toward a positive future. CCS thereby evoked the willingness to, capacity for, and reality of change. CCS utilized AI to sneak up on its problems, one might say, in order to minimize resistance and maximize openness to change. Instead of focusing on what was wrong but rather on what was right, CCS was able to achieve not only established goals and objectives but to also frame and articulate new goals and objectives.

In CCS, AI proved to be a wonderfully effective way to turn things around. AI unleashed open and creative energies for change. Schools are intergenerational communities in which the key players have a common, vested interest: the energetic participation of one and all in the learning process. In intergenerational efforts such as the one that took place at CCS, strengths-based, change-oriented conversations become all the more evocative. When elementary as well as secondary students engaged with various adult players and constituencies in appreciative conversations, so as to create new visions of the future and new capacities to make it so, the likelihood of their coming to pass was enhanced.

References

Cooperrider, D. L., Whitney, D. & Stavros, J. M. (2008). *AI Handbook For Leaders of Change* (2nd Edition), Brunswick, OH: Crown Custom Publishing, Inc.

Goddard, R. D., Tschannen-Moran, M. & Hoy, W. K. (2001). A multilevel examination of the distribution and effects of teacher trust in students and parents in urban elementary schools. *Elementary School Journal, 102* (1), 3–17.

Rosenberg, M. S. (2005). *Nonviolent communication: A language of life.* Encinitas, CA: PuddleDancer Press.

Tschannen-Moran, B. & Tschannen-Moran, M. (2010). *Evocative coaching: Transforming schools one conversation at a time.* San Francisco: Jossey-Bass.

Tschannen-Moran, M. (2014). *Trust matters: Leadership for successful schools* (2nd Ed.). San Francisco: Jossey-Bass.

Tschannen-Moran, M. (2004 Nov.). *What's trust got to do with it? The role of faculty and principal trust in fostering student achievement.* Paper presented at the annual meeting of the University Council for Educational Administration, Kansas City, MO.

Tschannen-Moran, M. & Hoy, W. K. (2000). A multidisciplinary analysis of the nature, meaning, and measurement of trust. *Review of Educational Research, 71,* 547–593.

Tschannen-Moran, M., Parish, J., & DiPaola, M. F. (2006). School climate: The interplay between interpersonal relationships and student achievement. *Journal of School Leadership,* 16, 386–415.

Watkins, J. M., Mohr, B. J., & Kelly, R. (2011). *Appreciative inquiry: Change at the speed of imagination* (2nd Ed.) San Francisco, CA: Jossey-Bass/Pfeiffer.

Whitney, D. & Trosten-Bloom, A. (2010). *The power of appreciative inquiry: A practical guide to positive change* (2nd Ed.). San Francisco: Berrett-Koehler Publishers, Inc.

Critical Thinking

1. Why is intergenerational collaboration important when working to change a school system?
2. Looking at the list of new initiatives to engage parents and community members, put them in the order of importance or order of initiation. What would you add to the list of new initiatives?

Internet References

ASCD
http://www.ascd.org
Generations United
http://www.gu.org
The Center for Appreciative Inquiry
http://www.centerforappreciativeinquiry.net

Parent Perceptions and Recommendations about Homework Involving Wikis and Blogs by Christine A. Portier, et al.

177

Article

Prepared by: Rebecca B. Evers, *Winthrop University*

Parent Perceptions and Recommendations about Homework Involving Wikis and Blogs

Middle grades parents share their views of online homework assignments.

CHRISTINE A. PORTIER ET AL.

Learning Outcomes

After reading this article, you will be able to:

- Identify parent perceptions of online homework using Web 2.0 technologies.

- Describe how Web 2.0 technologies influence student learning, motivation, and collaboration skills.

- Apply implications of this study to your teaching practices.

Homework is an important way for teachers to develop relationships with their students' parents and other caregivers. The learning activities teachers assign for homework provide parents a window into the content and skills their children are learning at school. Parents have a chance to participate in their children's schooling by monitoring and assisting them with their homework. As such, homework helps to keep schools accountable to parents:

> [It] gives parents direct knowledge (albeit inevitably incomplete) about the school's educational agenda and methods. It tells them what the school is doing and lets them—to the extent of their ability, inclination, and availability—oversee and participate in the education process by assisting their children with schoolwork. (Gill & Schlossman, 2003, p. 859)

A number of researchers have found that when parents are involved in their children's homework, the learning value of the homework increases (Baker, 2003; Margolis, 2005). *This We Believe: Keys to Educating Young Adolescents* emphasizes the importance of family involvement in children's education (National Middle School Association [NMSA], 2010). Furthermore, parental involvement in student homework has been associated with higher student achievement (Cooper, Lindsay, & Nye, 2000) and the development of attitudes and behaviors associated with higher achievement (Hoover-Dempsey et al., 2001).

Much of the research on homework has involved pen and paper assignments. The limited research on online homework has most frequently examined tutoring software. For example, Mendicino, Razzaq, and Heffernan (2009) studied the outcomes of the ASSISTment system that provided grade five students with interactive scaffolding and hints, upon request, while they were completing homework, or with multi-media and self-paced learning activities. Often, the homework involved multiple-choice questions that were auto-marked so that students received immediate feedback (Lewin & Luckin, 2010).

Our research contributes something new to the conversation on parental involvement and homework by presenting parents' perspectives and recommendations related to online homework involving Web 2.0 technologies (O'Reilly, 2007). Framed by new literacies theory (Lankshear & Knobel, 2006), which views literacies as social practices that include new ways of communicating using digital and multimodal texts, our research examined the perspectives, observations, and recommendations of 19 parents whose grades five and six students contributed to wikis as part of their social studies and science homework. The two classroom teachers participating in this project had implemented an online blog for tracking and completing homework and a wiki for collaborative work in class and at home.

Two of the authors of this paper are researchers who gathered data about the teachers' writing instruction over the course of a year, carried out the survey research, and wrote the description of the parent survey results. The other two authors are grades five and six teachers who provided an authentic perspective for considering how teachers might use the survey results in their classrooms.

Using Wikis and Blogs in Class and as Homework

For three years, the teachers involved in the study used online technology to communicate with their students and with the students' parents. They began with a blogging website (www. blogger.com) and found it worked well for activities in class and at home. The teachers created an account through which they could post class assignments and inform parents and students about homework, projects, and upcoming school events. They also included a "Highlights of the Day" section to give parents a glimpse into their children's daily classroom activities. Highlights included information about classroom guests and photos and videos of students working collaboratively. Because they intended the homework blog to be used primarily as a place to post information for students, they modified the permissions so that students would not post their own comments on the parent information pages.

The teachers envisioned the homework blog as a home base for students. When they first logged on at home, students received reminders about the day's events and assignments. From the blog, they were redirected to specific subject/project blogs or wikis. Here students could post comments to each other, upload relevant research to extend their in-class learning, and include links to other resources, all of which contributed to their collaborative online assignments. For example, in social studies students were engaged in a project-based learning activity focused on current national (grade five) and global (grade six) citizenship issues. The issues were selected by the students and related to the big ideas in the provincial curriculum document. The students researched collaboratively in small groups online and then independently wrote persuasive essays about their chosen issue and social change, scripted a short public service announcement, and designed a book jacket relating images that depicted the issue and the desired social changes.

As with any other inquiry assignment, students needed to gather information to address their inquiry question. Student participation on the wiki took the form of reading comments, sharing original ideas, or responding to other students' comments. All of these forms of participation lead to active,

purposeful learning which is key to successful middle grades education (NMSA, 2010). When collaboratively working in groups of four on the wiki, students contributed one-fourth of the information independently. Later, they read and talked with the rest of their group to become informed about the remaining three-fourths of the information. The teachers conducted both formative and evaluative assessments of the students' independent work by reading and grading individual online contributions and each student's final written projects.

Research Method

Although this paper is based on the results of surveys completed by parents/guardians, this research was part of a larger year-long ethnographic study examining the ways in which middle grades teachers can use digital technology and multi-media to teach writing. As part of the larger study, the two teachers and two researchers met monthly to talk about the teachers' classroom writing practices. At one of these meetings, the teachers expressed a desire to find out parents' perspectives on the use of online homework. We developed a 21-question survey, using a combination of forced-choice and open-ended questions (see Appendix in the online version of this article at http://www.amle .org/Publications/MiddleSchoolJournal/Articles/tabid/109/ Defalt.aspx). We intended to elicit honest opinions/responses from parents, whether positive or negative, about the homework practices of their child's current teacher. To reassure parents that their responses to the survey questions would not affect their child's relationship with the teacher or any assessment or grade assigned to their child's work, we asked that the surveys be completed without mention of parents' and students' names. All grades five and six students were given the parent survey, consent forms, and blank envelopes in which to seal the completed survey. The 58 students were asked to give the surveys to their parents or guardians. If their parents completed the survey, students were asked to bring it back to school in the sealed envelope and drop it into a box in their classrooms. The teachers did not track who returned the surveys, nor did they contact any parents to suggest the survey should be completed because of the potential conflict of interest. Only the researchers saw the actual surveys. Nineteen (33%) surveys were completed and returned.

The researchers tallied the answers to the forced-choice questions and grouped themes in the written responses to identify any patterns across the completed surveys. We used the patterns and percentages to report on: (1) daily online activity of parents and their children, (2) influence of online homework on children's motivation and learning, (3) parents' homework preferences, and (4) parents' suggestions for improving online homework. A summary report was given to all parents who provided a contact address and to the two classroom teachers.

Results
Daily Online Activity of Parents and Their Children

Overall, 79% of parents rated themselves as comfortable or very comfortable using computer and online technology. All parents and students were using the computer or online tools for some purpose on a daily basis. Parents tended to use the computer for Internet searches and participating in online forums more frequently than their children, whereas children used the computer for games, socializing, and chat lines more frequently than their parents. Compared to their parents, the children used the computer more frequently for daily work and blogging, but this was likely because these activities were part of the children's homework assignments. One parent listed research as part of his or her daily computer use, and other parents additionally noted that their children used the computer for composing, drawing, communicating via Skype and MSN, and for posting videos to YouTube.

All but one of the children of participating parents could access a computer at home. Sixty-eight percent of the children were allowed to use the computer if they were supervised. Almost all the students used the computer every day for at least 30 minutes or more, with 44% of the students on the computer between one and two hours per day.

Eighty-nine percent of students spent less than an hour per day completing homework. According to parents, students who spent more time may have done so because they wanted to do more than their share or because they were distracted by other online activities and were online for extended periods of time, though not completing homework. Parents also explained that some students enjoyed the social and communicative aspect of the online homework format and simply spent more time on homework. The majority of students were reported to be spending three to four days per week on their online homework.

Thirty-nine percent of participating parents checked the homework blog frequently, either a few times per week or every day. Half the parents checked the homework blog a few times per month. Because the online blog format keeps a record of all homework and postings, parents (and students and teachers) were able to track more than one day's work at once. It is possible that parents who logged onto the homework blog a few times per month were checking not one day's homework but the entire month's work.

With the introduction of the blog and wiki, the majority of parents either did not provide their children with extra homework help (33%), or the kind of help they gave did not change with the move to an online format (33%). Many parents continued to help their children understand the homework assignments, the content of the assignments, or how to explore the research topics. A small number of parents (13%) needed to help their children with the technology—how to search the Internet to find information. A few parents noted that the only help they provided was paying for the Internet service, increasing the amount of time a child was allowed to use the computer, or freeing up a computer for the child to use.

Influence of Online Homework on Children's Motivation and Learning

Participating parents identified three areas in which they felt the online homework had either benefitted their children or, in a few cases, had made their children's learning more challenging: improved academic learning, enhanced motivation, and enhanced collaborative skills.

Improved Academic Learning

Eighty-three percent of participating parents felt the online medium had helped improve their children's learning. One parent noted that his or her child "has improved by studying harder," and another wrote, "My [child] has spent more time reading and writing, and it shows how comfortable the PC has become. All in all, I am quite happy with this technology." Other parents thought learning improved in many different academic subjects, specifying reading, writing, and social studies. A few parents observed improvements in their children's research skills, as exemplified in this comment: "Improved research skills resulted from the wiki and its inherent search and links functions compared to the 'old' library research process." Thirty-two percent of parents felt the online homework approach enabled their children to become more technologically competent. As one parent phrased it: "This method of learning will benefit the students from here to university. They will obtain knowledge that [will] last a lifetime."

Increased Motivation

Many parents (58%) noticed changes in their children's attitudes toward homework, and 63% noticed that their children were more willing to complete homework since the introduction of the blog format. One parent noted that her child "views the computer as non-threatening, compared to text," and another found that "research topics [have] become more interesting" to his child. Another parent remarked, "My child seems to voluntarily do assigned homework without being asked." These observations were echoed in many other parent responses.

As motivated as most students were to participate in the homework online, one parent observed that this motivation was more about getting online than engaging in homework. This parent observed that his child "tend[ed] to use the medium for gaming and socializing." Other parents were concerned about their children being distracted from their homework when they were working online, and 31% of the parents found it difficult to determine whether their children were working on homework or playing and socializing when they were online. A serious concern was raised by a parent whose child began posting videos without parental permission.

Improved Collaborative Skills

Many parents indicated that the wiki improved their children's group work and communication skills. Many of their children enjoyed posting comments, communicating with group members, and receiving feedback from their peers. As one parent noted: "The students no longer feel isolated." Some parents agreed that a benefit of online homework is that it "facilitates and enables group work," and students could work on group projects in class and continue when they came home. One parent appreciated that students were not expected to prepare large presentations or projects at home; rather, the research and information gathering for the large projects took place partially at home and online, and then the project presentations were worked on collaboratively in class.

One parent was concerned, however, that "while collaboration is enhanced [by the online homework] . . . typing and computer skills are not sufficiently developed."

Parents' Homework Preferences

Although this was the first year the students had used a blog at school or at home, 58% of the parents surveyed now preferred this method for tracking homework. One parent very enthusiastically endorsed using the blog and wiki "by a substantial margin." She wrote, "Homework this year has been much less stressful than last year." Twenty-six percent of parents still identified agendas as a preferred tracking method, although 11% did not prefer one method to the other. Two parents specified that they preferred to speak directly to their children about their homework.

Many parents (47%) found the online environment enhanced the homework process, explaining that it was easier for parents to check their children's work, that homework (i.e., writing) was less frustrating for their children, and that the feedback on their children's homework was more helpful and more frequent. One parent wrote: "All information [is] in one place—never forget, lose, or misunderstand assignments—can always read instructions online." This last benefit ties in with another parent's comment that the blog saves on the amount of paper traditionally used for homework.

The transition from "traditional" homework and agenda tracking to an online approach was smooth. Most parents (84%) did *not* find that their children were confused by the move to the online homework format. Two parents commented on some technical difficulties at first; but, overall, parents and children did not find the blog confusing. Only one parent identified the blog as being difficult to understand. A number of parents did

suggest that more instruction about the use of the blog would have been beneficial.

One parent observed that the new online format had changed the family dynamics in relation to homework. Previously, the family tended to discuss school and homework at the dinner table. This family pattern changed to involve discussions at the computer desk. A few parents (23%) were concerned about the new homework dynamics, which included figuring out how to manage the use of the technology and the need for the child to relocate to where the computer was located when doing homework.

Parents felt that homework should not be done exclusively online. One parent explained: "Traditional methods seem best, with the computer used as a support or research tool—not as a primary or replacement method." In agreement, another parent suggested, "The ability to learn and complete assignments need to extend to both the online and paper worlds." Four other parents supported the idea of combining traditional homework methods with new technology.

Parents' Suggestions for Improving Online Homework

Many parents encouraged the teachers to "keep up the good work" and offered suggestions to help a good practice become even better. Parent recommendations addressed two key areas: (1) training that would help parents adapt to this new online approach and (2) the equity and manageability of the homework expectations.

Recommendations included providing parents with information before the blog or wiki work is introduced and periodic reviews or updates about the blog and wiki use. Because they could not see the physical homework or the completed product, a few parents (23%) were concerned that they were unable to monitor their child's homework properly or to see the teacher's input about the homework. They were not sure about how to navigate the wiki and blog to find the information they needed about their children's participation and the teacher's feedback. These parents requested opportunities to meet with teachers to discuss ways in which they could monitor and even participate in their children's online activities. They were particularly interested in teachers' advice addressing their concerns about children posting information and setting up accounts or following non-homework related (i.e., distracting) links while working on homework.

Thirty-one percent of parents were concerned about ways to keep their children safe when online and wanted ways to ensure the posted information was kept confidential and private. As one parent noted, "Children don't understand privacy issues and can be exposed to additional dangers they are not ready for." Parents needed reassurance about the safety features the teachers had implemented to ensure student postings and identities remained confidential.

Parents appreciated the ongoing communication between school and home that was made possible by the blog. According to one parent, "Not only does it show me what assignments are due, but I can see what they [students] are talking about." Some parents, however, wished to know more about the lessons that preceded the homework assignments. One parent recommended that in-class lessons be uploaded and attached to the homework blog so that parents could better understand the particular expectations for each assignment. One parent noted that the online environment already "provides a continuous connection between school [work] and homework," so attached lessons would serve to strengthen this connection.

A few parents recommended that the amount of homework be kept manageable, in terms of both time and quantity. Some parents explained that homework could become unmanageable when some students posted less often than other group members or when some students posted too often. One parent even suggested cutting the online activity in half. A further suggestion was for the teachers to clearly distinguish (or make clear how they distinguish) between group work and individual contributions. Parents wanted to ensure that a few students were not bearing most of the work and that students were graded on their participation and individual contributions.

Discussion and Implications

Parents indicated enthusiastic support for the online homework, providing numerous examples of how their children's academic learning, collaboration and communication skills, and motivation had been enhanced. Although the generalizability of results from this small sample is limited, the results are consistent with previous research showing the value of homework (Gill & Schlossman, 2003; Hoover-Dempsey et al., 2001). The wiki enabled parents to model behaviors and attitudes associated with higher achievement as they worked with their children by seeking out information together online. Parents also read through assignments with their children and discussed what was useful for the homework assignment. The homework blog provided parents with information about what was being taught and gave them an opportunity to participate in their children's education in meaningful ways, enhancing accountability to parents (Gill & Schlossman, 2003).

The new online homework format reinforced the positive aspects of parental involvement in children's homework, as found in previous research (Baker, 2003; Margolis, 2005); although Internet security was an added concern in our study. Because online homework was new to both parents and students, parents suggested that the teachers provide more information.

Parents wanted to know more about expectations for group and independent work on the wiki and blog, about Internet security for the children, and about how parents could access and monitor the homework contributions and teacher feedback.

When introducing online tools and technology into classroom practices, teachers need to inform parents about what they are doing in the classroom while considering the range of experience and skills parents have with online tools. For many parents, the online format is an unfamiliar education environment. We want to let them know that these tools can be very useful to children and their studies and can help prepare them for their future (recognizing, of course, we cannot be certain about what the future will involve). What is emerging as a whole new teaching and learning tool is very much part of the students' lives already; we are bringing many online tools from their social and home lives into the classroom (Media Awareness Network, 2005). However, we suggest that teachers ask the children to use the technology for homework after they have learned and experienced how to use new online tools for curricular expectations. In school, the children can be taught to use the technology more safely, critically, and purposefully so that these skills may transfer when they are online outside of school.

Teachers may want to bring parents on board early in the school year. A couple of weeks into the school year, many schools offer a curriculum night for teachers and parents to talk about classroom programming, subject areas, units of study, and expectations. In response to the parent survey, the teachers included the technology and Web 2.0 aspects as part of their curriculum night. They offered a fifth and sixth grade parent meeting at the start of curriculum night to demonstrate the blog and wiki and facilitate discussion. Later in the year, the teachers plan to meet with parents again to provide an opportunity to share their suggestions for managing this new homework format and use of the family computer(s). Teachers have to find a way to inform parents about classroom online and technology practices, keeping in mind that parents vary in their knowledge of and experience with technology.

The survey responses indicated that some parents thought the students had more homework with the wiki and blog. However, the teachers did not assign any more homework after they introduced the wiki and blog; so we think that some children may have become immersed in the online tasks. The teachers found that some students wanted to go online every night, and this may have led a few parents to think it was at the teachers' insistence. However, on the blog, the teachers posted expectations about assignments and their expected amount of online participation so that parents would have easy access to this information. It is possible that some of the parents who did not return the survey were uncomfortable or inexperienced with online technology and, thus, did not share in the positive experience of the wiki and blog use.

Some of the parents surveyed commented on paying for the use of the Internet for homework. However, paying for the Internet connection was not a cost specifically associated with homework because the parents were using online tools on a daily basis. However, a concern arose when parents did not have the means to access the Internet from home. Teachers do not want to add to the pressures already facing a student's family. To access online homework, some students will need to either complete homework at school, after school, or travel to a public library or youth center. To address this concern, the teachers in this study allowed students to work on their homework after school in the classroom several days each week. This was, of course, only one possible solution, and it was contingent on a teacher remaining in the classroom after school hours. This option is not always possible with teachers frequently attending meetings, conducting enrichment or extracurricular activities, or planning and grading in other locations.

The use of a wiki and blog for homework not only facilitated student collaboration but also served to make apparent the collaborative nature of some of the classroom assignments. This finding is consistent with research showing that students' writing is more collaborative and social and that students are more highly motivated to write when using Web 2.0 technology to write, as compared to using a paper and pencil (Goldberg, Russell, & Cook, 2003; Hsu & Wang, 2011). What is less apparent is the extent of individual contributions. Although wikis and blogs allow for individual tracking, which the teachers in this study used for their own assessments, parents may not know how to navigate the site to see the frequency and quality of the contributions their child is making.

We suggest that teachers make clear the distinctions among the learning process, formative assessment, and final evaluations (Black, Harrison, Lee, Marshall, & Wiliam, 2003). For example, during the science unit on the Conservation of Energy and Resources, the teacher assigned each student to an energy form and resource research group, such as wind energy. Within this group, they read print and online texts, gathered information both individually and collaboratively, and posted it to the group wiki (learning process). The teachers met with each group to monitor their progress and discuss the quality of their contributions (formative assessment). Students collaboratively composed paragraphs about their energy form and were then assigned to a new group comprised of one student from each of the other energy groups (e.g., one student each from solar, wind, water, coal, and natural gas). In this new group, a student shared his or her own understandings from the collaborative work with other members of the group who, in turn, shared their expertise. In this way, the students practiced what they knew and learned from each other (formative assessment and learning process). Their new understandings were then applied to an individual technological problem-solving task, which involved both writing and construction (evaluation). The teachers in this study were clear about the relationships among collaborative participation, student learning, and assessments, but they realized that, with the online homework, parents may be seeing only the collaborative nature of the students' work.

Conclusion

Overall, the survey results indicated positive feelings from parents about the wiki and blog homework that was incorporated into the classroom teaching practices. We believe Web 2.0 technologies can be integrated successfully and beneficially into classrooms. These tools provide the means for students to work collaboratively both in the classroom and from home, and they allow for students' learning at school to extend into the home in meaningful ways.

References

Baker, L. (2003). The role of parents in motivating struggling readers. *Reading & Writing Quarterly: Overcoming Learning Difficulties, 19*, 87–106.

Black, P., Harrison, C., Lee, C., Marshall, B., & Wiliam, D. (2003). *Assessment for learning: Putting it into practice.* Berkshire, UK: Open University Press.

Cooper, H., Lindsay, J. J., & Nye, B. (2000). Homework in the home: How student, family, and parenting-style differences relate to the homework process. *Contemporary Educational Psychology, 25*, 464–487.

Gill, B. P., & Schlossman, S. L. (2003). Parents and the politics of homework: Some historical perspectives. *Teachers College Record, 105*, 846–871.

Goldberg, A., Russell, M., & Cook, A. (2003). The effect of computers on student writing: A meta-analysis of studies from 1992–2002. *The Journal of Technology, Learning, and Assessment, 2* (1), 1–52.

Hoover-Dempsey, K. V., Battiato, A. C., Walker, J. M. T., Reed, R. P., Dejong, J. M., & Jones, K. P. (2001). Parental involvement in homework. *Educational Psychologist, 36*, 195–209.

Hsu, H., & Wang, S. (2011). The impact of using blogs on college students' reading comprehension and learning motivation. *Literacy Research and Instruction, 50* (1), 68–88.

Lankshear, C., & Knobel, M. (2006). *New literacies: Everyday practices and classroom learning* (2nd ed.). Berkshire, UK: Open University Press.

Lewin, C., & Luckin, R. (2010). Technology to support parental engagement in elementary education: Lessons learned from the UK. *Computers & Education, 54*, 749–758.

Parent Perceptions and Recommendations about Homework Involving Wikis and Blogs by Christine A. Portier, et al.

183

Margolis, H. (2005). Resolving struggling learners' homework difficulties: Working with elementary school learners and parents. *Preventing School Failure, 50* (1), 5–12.

Media Awareness Network.(2005). *Young Canadians in a wired world.* Retrieved from http://www.media-awareness.ca/english/research/YCWW/index.cfm

Mendicino, M., Razzaq, L., & Heffernan, N. T. (2009). A comparison of traditional homework to computer-supported homework. *Journal of Research on Technology in Education, 41* (3), 331–359.

National Middle School Association. (2010). *This we believe: Keys to educating young adolescents.* Westerville, OH: Author.

O'Reilly, T. (2007). What is Web 2.0: Design patterns and business models for the next generation of software. *Communications & Strategies, 1,* 17.

Critical Thinking

1. Review parental concerns about online homework. What actions might schools/educators take to eliminate parents' concerns?

2. Describe how Web 2.0 technologies have positive effects on student learning, motivation, and collaboration skills.

3. Reflect on your opinion of online learning prior to reading this article. Did your opinion change? Provide examples from the article to support your opinion.

Create Central

www.mhhe.com/createcentral

Internet References

Go2web20
www.go2web20.net

Kahn Academy
https://www.khanacademy.org/

Open Thinking Wiki
http://couros.wikispaces.com/TechAndMediaLiteracyVids

Quest Garden
www.questgarden.com

Article   Prepared by: Rebecca B. Evers, *Winthrop University*

"I'm Not a Bystander": Developing Teacher Leadership in a Rural School-University Collaboration

Jeffrey C. Eargle

Learning Outcomes

After reading this article, you will be able to:

- Explain what constitutes a Teacher as Leader.

- Examine the benefits of school–university partnerships and collaboration.

- Summarize the implications for developing Teacher-Leaders throughout P-12 schools.

Since the early 1980s, teachers at Timberwood High School, a small rural school in the American southeast, have mentored pre-service teachers attending nearby Madison College, a small private liberal arts college.* However, in recent years the social studies teachers at the high school, feeling that they were being "used," began expressing frustration in hosting field experience students. As a result, Dr. Miller, the education department chair, and Mr. Jones, the social studies department chair, began discussing how to transform the field experience program into a professional development program for in-service social studies teachers. Babione (2010) concluded that rural teachers need professional development that is flexible ongoing and encourages collaboration and curriculum development. In addition, Warren and Peel (2005) found that collaboration between schools and colleges that creates leaders within schools is central to rural school reform. Therefore, strengthened ties between the Timberwood High School and Madison College could develop teacher leadership, encourage collaboration within the social studies department, and serve as a step toward reform.

The purpose of this article is to present a program overview examining the initial impact of the redesigned field experience program on in-service teachers. Two questions guided evaluation of the first phase of the program. First, to what extent were the social studies teachers at Timberwood High School developing a greater sense of experimentation with new instructional strategies as a result of the collaboration with Madison College? Second, in what ways was the school-university partnership between Timberwood High School and Madison College increasing the confidence of the social studies teachers to become teacher leaders? This study serves to connect the research on school-university partnerships and teacher leadership using rural teachers as the linchpin. While the goal is not to generalize the findings, this study should offer new insight into an under-researched area in teacher leadership, school-university partnerships, and rural education.

Dempsey's (1992) theory of teacher leadership images was used to conceptualize this study. Dempsey concluded that teacher leaders are characterized by four images: *Teacher as fully functioning person, teacher as reflective practitioner, teacher as scholar,* and *teacher as partner in learning.* Teacher leaders fulfill the *teacher as fully functioning person* image when they focus on professional development and growth. Likewise, teacher leaders embody the *teacher as reflective practitioner* image when they reflect for the purpose of professional

---

* All proper names are pseudonyms. This applies to institutions, stakeholders, and participants. This was done to protect the identity of the participants. The process for pseudonym assignment is discussed in the research methods section of the article.

growth. In addition, teacher leaders exemplify the *teacher as scholar* image when they engage in the learning of new knowledge and instructional methods. Finally, teacher leaders demonstrate the *teacher as partner in learning* image when they encourage collaboration among individual teachers.

Teacher Leadership

Teacher leadership, a concept that has entered academic conversations over the last three decades, is frequently used, yet has a broad range of definitions. In a review of teacher leadership, York-Barr and Duke (2004) found that it was difficult to define "teacher leadership" as researchers use many criteria in establishing the boundaries of their research. Rogus (1988) noted in an early conceptual piece that teacher leaders are those who pursue professional development, empower their peers, create a vision for education, communicate the vision to their peers, and generate trust among their peers. In a general sense, Katzanmeyer and Möller (2001) defined teacher leaders as teachers who "lead within and beyond the classroom, identify with and contribute to a community of teacher learners and leaders, and influence others toward improved educational practice" (p. 5). York-Barr and Duke (2004) observed that teacher leaders are successful practitioners, lead their peers in professional development, and participate in pre-service teacher education. Thus, defining teacher leadership is complex, yet the focus is on teachers leading the improvement of education for students by mentoring, conducting professional development, creating policy, and developing curriculum.

School University-Partnerships

Although speaking specifically of Professional Development Schools (PDS), Kirschner, Dickinson, and Blosser (1996) defined school-university partnerships as collaborations between school-based and university-based educators through which inservice teachers, pre-service teachers, and professors develop in a reciprocal relationship. To develop and sustain a reciprocal school-university partnership all stakeholders—teachers, administrators, school boards, professors, and teacher advocacy groups—must be united in implementing and sustaining a PDS (Cozza, 2007; Lefever-Davis, Johnson, & Pearman, 2007). Teacher leadership is important in this because, as York-Barr and Duke (2004) concluded, teacher leaders build relationships with college and universities. In addition, a strong school-university partnership is essential to constructing a unified and continual system of teacher development (Feiman-Nemser, 2001).

Mentoring

The mentoring of pre-service teachers by inservice teachers further connects teacher leadership and school-university partnerships. York-Barr and Duke (2004) found that teacher leaders often assume the role of mentor. The promise of a PDS is that mentor teachers grow professionally as a result of a reciprocal system. Because mentor teachers are mostly used to the advantage of universities and colleges in one-sided relationships, it is the responsibility of the teacher education programs to empower mentor teachers by increasing their involvement in the program (Hamel & Jaasko-Fisher, 2011). Russell and Russell (2011) determined that strong programs encourage mentors to conceptualize themselves as role models. It can then be decided that teachers who view themselves as role models will emerge as teacher leaders.

Although much has been written on school-university partnerships and teacher leadership, a gap exists in the research on how the two intersect in rural schools. While studies of leadership in rural schools exist, often studies focus on leadership theories among both administrators and teachers (Masumoto & Brown-Welty, 2009). Studying distributed leadership in a rural school, Anderson (2008) determined that the teacher leaders successfully transformed the school and experienced high student achievement both in the classroom and in extra-curricular activities. Anderson observed that, to accomplish such transformation, the school organizational structure focused on committees of teachers to oversee curriculum development, athletics, and community outreach. York-Barr and Duke (2004) found that teacher leaders often assume the role of mentor and forge relationships with local colleges for the purpose of professional development. Yet, research on rural education indicates that, because few opportunities exist for teachers to collaborate on curriculum, professional development should be tailored to the needs of rural teachers (Babione, 2010). In rural school-university partnerships, research focuses on developing collaborations to improve the leadership skills of administrators (Myron, Sanzo, & Clayton, 2011; Warren & Peel, 2005). However, this focus on administrators is consistent with research on the professional development needs of rural school administrators (Salazar, 2007).

Context

Timberwood High School is situated between a cow pasture and a tract of forest. Driving to the school on an autumn morning, deer stands can be seen in fields along the two-lane country roads, an indicator of the community's passion for hunting and fishing. On the same morning, the smell of pulp from a nearby plywood factory fills the air around the school. The community, which boasts a history of cotton production, remains largely agricultural as the economy has shifted to a focus on beef, poultry, eggs, and timber. Timberwood High School draws students from three communities with populations of 179,255, and 1180 respectively, and from the isolated areas in between. The communities of Timberwood High School merge into one for high school football, as barrel-sized grills hitched to pickup trucks hold hamburgers, hotdogs, and spare ribs. Designated a rural school by the National Center for Education Statistics, 727 students attend Timberwood High School. Enrollment at the time of this study was 66% white, 28% Black, 5.5% Hispanic, 0.5% American Indian and Asian, and 43% free or reduced lunch recipients.

Timberwood High School Social Studies Department

At the time of this study, the social studies department at the high school comprised six teachers. Four were female and two were male. One teacher worked part time. While there was a second-year teacher and a veteran of 34 years, the majority of the department were mid-career with seven to ten years of experience. Five of the six teachers had master's degrees. Two teachers were National Board Certified. All of the teachers served as mentors to pre-service teachers either in the current project or in the past. Only one teacher—the department chair—served the school in a formalized leadership capacity.

Methods

This case study used qualitative methodology. Data were collected by individual interviews with social studies department faculty. Although I (the researcher) am no longer on the faculty at Timberwood High School, I was a member of the social studies department at the time of the study. I interviewed the five other social studies teachers individually during a two-week timeframe near the end of the first semester in which this project was initiated. The interviews lasted between 30 and 45 minutes. Teachers were asked the same questions. However, because Ms. Allen was also the methods instructor, her interview lasted an hour and a half and she was asked an additional set of questions. At the onset of the interview, teachers were informed that, to provide anonymity, the schools and teachers would be assigned pseudonyms. The pseudonyms for the teachers were randomly selected from a list of the most common surnames in the nation (United States Census Bureau, 2000).

During the interviewing and coding process, as the researcher, I carefully considered my biases. The relationships I had with the teachers, however, allowed the teachers to feel comfortable discussing the issues related to the project. Answers to questions were recorded in field notes. At times, participants were asked to repeat answers to ensure accurate recording of their statements. After each interview session, the field notes of the interview were transcribed and coded based on the goals of the project, which centered on teacher leadership and expanding the instructional repertoire of the social studies teachers. The interview data was reexamined for additional themes. Finally,

in order to ensure that I understood the teachers' perspectives, I regularly shared my emerging findings with the teachers.

The Rationale for Initiating the School-University Social Studies Mentoring Project

Dr. Miller and Mr. Jones were professional colleagues for five years prior to developing the mentoring project. While discussing the state of the program, the two noted several areas of concern. First, the pre-service teachers enrolled in field experience were not regular in their attendance, which created inconsistency in observing and working at the placement. Second, the pre-service teachers taught two 20-minute lessons and received little if any feedback from the mentor teacher. Another concern centered on pre-service teachers having to adjust to teaching a 90-minute lesson when they entered their internship. Third, as the preservice teachers began their internships in subsequent semesters, they entered with relatively little understanding of how to use state standards and Common Core State Standards to guide instruction, creating an area of weakness in the field experience.

Likewise, Dr. Miller and Mr. Jones discussed the lack of reciprocity between the school and college and how partnership could improve the social studies department at the school. First, mentors for the preservice teachers felt that they were not truly mentoring and, thus, that the college was simply using their classroom as a "practice field." Second, the social studies department lacked a pedagogical focus and, similarly, a spirit of experimentation with new strategies. Third, recognizing the need for teacher leadership in reforming education, the purpose of working closely with the college should be to improve and develop teacher leadership among the members of the social studies department. Both parties felt that the relationship between Madison College and Timberwood High School had the potential to improve practice and leadership among in-service teachers, but the current structure did not allow for this.

The Development of the Project

Having determined the areas required for improvement, Dr. Miller and Mr. Jones created a program that would work to better develop Madison College's pre-service teachers and empower Timberwood High School's in-service teachers. Dr. Miller and Mr. Jones met with Timberwood High School's principal to explain the goals and benefits of the project. With the support of the principal, the project moved forward. While the principal was supportive, the program ran with little input from the principal beyond the initial meeting with Dr. Miller and Mr. Jones. The principal's level of involvement by design, placed the onus of leadership on the teachers.

To begin the collaboration, Dr. Miller and Mr. Jones turned to Ms. Allen, a social studies teacher at Timberwood High School. While Ms. Allen remained a full-time teacher at the high school, Madison College hired her as an adjunct instructor for the social studies methods course. Although teaching the course at the high school campus was considered, due to scheduling conflicts the course was taught at the college. The college then placed all of the social studies pre-service teachers at the high school for the field experience. However, to avoid a conflict of interest, a pre-service teacher was not placed with Ms. Allen. By this action, the pre-service teachers' professor would be on campus at all times and accessible to all of the mentor teachers. As such, the professor and mentor teachers could more easily discuss the growth of the pre-service teachers because they were colleagues at the high school. The goal was for the pre-service teachers to receive more individualized instruction based on strong and consistent feedback from the mentor teachers while the inservice teachers become empowered as mentors and collaborators with the college.

The first layer of the program involved improving the quality of the field experience at the placement. Pre-service teachers were required to teach two 45-minute lessons and one 90-minute lesson to better prepare them for their full-time student teaching internship. In addition, the mentor teachers were required to document the lesson using an observation form and provide feedback to the pre-service teachers and to Ms. Allen. In the feedback, the mentor teacher guided the field experience student in a reflective discussion about the lesson. The goal was for both the pre-service and in-service teachers to become more engaged in the field experience process and more reflective in their practice.

The second layer of the program involved using the mentor teachers as models of best practices. Each teacher received a copy of Ms. Allen's syllabus for the methods course and agreed to model the strategies that Ms. Allen would be teaching during a particular week. For example, if Ms. Allen taught about the use of role play as a strategy during the first week of October, then the teachers integrated role play into their lessons that week. Thus, the preservice teachers observed a strategy at their placement and then discussed it in class, giving them both practical and theoretical experiences using social studies strategies. The goal was to prompt the social studies teachers to integrate new strategies into their repertoire, ultimately encouraging experimentation with new methods.

The third layer of the program was that the partnership between the school and college would serve as a basis of professional development for the social studies teachers. An assignment was created in the methods course for the pre-service teachers to conduct research on their mentor teachers.

The preservice teachers generated a research question related to state standards and/or Common Core State Standards and developed a mode of evaluation based on the question, assessed the social studies teachers, and reported their findings to the social studies department. The findings determined instructional strengths and weaknesses, pointing to areas that needed improvement. For example, the field experience students found that the teachers could improve the diversity of their writing prompts. To improve, all teachers agreed to attend professional development and present their learning to the department, becoming teacher leaders in the process as they assumed the role of instructional leaders for their peers. For example, one social studies teacher attended a workshop conducted by Cris Tovoni, a literacy specialist, and demonstrated the strategies learned from the workshop to the department.

Findings

The findings of this study are divided into two parts. The first part is a narrative of Ms. Allen's experience teaching the methods course at the Madison College and tracks her growth as a teacher and teacher leader. The second part is a narrative of the Timberwood High School social studies department's participation with the field experience program and how the school-university partnership affected the department.

Ms. Allen's Growth and Development: Becoming a Methods Teacher

In June 2012, Ms. Allen was offered the opportunity to teach the social studies methods course at Madison College during the fall 2012 semester. In addition to having a master's degree in education, Ms. Allen was selected for her creativity in the classroom, her knowledge of pedagogy, and her work as a past mentor for pre-service teachers. Ms. Allen expressed a mixture of excitement and concern regarding teaching the methods course. Ms. Allen noted, *I was hesitant because of the time,* alluding to managing a schedule that would include teaching the methods course one night per week while teaching at the high school and being a mother of two young children. However, she agreed to teach the methods course because she *thought that it would be easy. I teach social studies all the time. I can teach a course on it.* Yet, while organizing the course using the previous instructor's materials as a foundation, Ms. Allen began to reflect on the responsibility of teaching pre-service teachers. As Ms. Allen wondered, *Did I know enough to teach these students? I wasn't sure. So, I started buying every methods book I could find on Amazon and reading a lot.* By questioning her existing knowledge and taking active steps to increase it, Allen was establishing a path for growth—growth for her methods students, growth for her high school students, and growth for herself. At the same time, Ms. Allen was embodying Dempsey's (1992) *teacher as fully functioning person* image as she sought to better understand the nature of schooling, instructional strategies, and the challenges teachers face.

For Ms. Allen, learning to teach the methods course can best be described as a learning curve. As Ms. Allen put it, *I thought I could plan less because . . . it would be like teaching peers. I ended up planning more than I thought. . . .* [Pre-service teachers] *are much more relatable to my high school seniors than my peers.* As a result, Ms. Allen reached out to others in the education department at the college and to her colleagues in the social studies department to help her plan for the methods course, thus exhibiting teacher leadership characteristics of collaboration and reflection (York-Barr & Duke, 2004). As she evolved as a methods instructor, she began to focus on more than teaching strategies. Teaching the pre-service teachers to understand the depth of thinking required of a teacher to plan lessons was a challenge. As Ms. Allen stated, *Getting them to understand the maturity needed as a teacher* is challenging. *They are not seeing the reason behind their work, why it is important for a classroom setting.* However, the redeveloped field experience program made this concept easier to explain and discuss as the semester progressed. *With more classroom observations,* Ms. Allen noted, *the more* [the pre-service teachers] *could relate to* real [high school student] *behavior.* Although teaching the course was a struggle at times, it was not a negative experience: *I would do it again, although it makes for longer days. I would like to change things next time.* While preconceptions about college students proved an initial challenge, they did not deter Ms. Allen from moving forward to reshape the course.

Growing as a Teacher

An important goal of the collaboration between Madison College and Timberwood High School was the growth and development of the social studies teachers at the high school. Discussing this, Ms. Allen stated that, *I've read a lot more about social studies methods . . . and the importance of literacy and inquiry. I've learned more about teaching various social studies subjects and what works for grades six through twelve.* This was important, she felt, because her daily work for the last seven years centered on teaching Government and Psychology to high school sophomores, juniors, and seniors, although mostly seniors. Ms. Allen also noted that attending the state social studies conference as part of the program's professional development requirement contributed to her growth. *I'm isolated here as the only government teacher,* Ms. Allen began. *However, talking with the guy who wrote the state standards and support documents was incredible. . . . It was eye-opening to understand the progression and flow of the standards.* When asked to explain why this was important to her growth, Ms. Allen explained, *I've sometimes thought that my class is*

terrible. But I now see what others are doing and I realize I'm doing things right. I feel more confident. In preparing to teach the methods course and attending professional development, Ms. Allen acknowledged that she had grown as a teacher in terms of knowledge, perspective, and confidence.

While discussing her growth, Ms. Allen noted how teaching the methods course prompted her to use new strategies, thus affecting her classroom instruction at the high school. At first, using new strategies was done to prepare for teaching the methods course. As Ms. Allen recalled, *I am not going to tell* [the pre-service teachers] *to do something without doing it myself.* However, as Ms. Allen continued to grow in her knowledge, trying a particular method in preparation for teaching the pre-service teachers became secondary to trying new methods to teach her high school students. Ms. Allen pointed out that, *It . . . has changed the way I do some things in my own classroom. . . . I have a binder of lesson plans. This year, I have not used it much. I am putting the focus back on my students.* While breaking out of the instructional rut was important, more significant to Ms. Allen was how her growth and development as a result of teaching the methods course prompted her to think more deeply about her government and psychology courses at Timberwood High School. *Sometimes I feel that I did things to fill time,* Ms. Allen confessed. [This experience] *has caused me to think about the over-arching, long-term goals of my classes. . . . It has made me a stronger teacher.* While developing as a methods instructor, Ms. Allen was motivated to enhance her instruction as a high school teacher, making her feel more successful. At the same time, this level of reflection is indicative of Dempsey's (1992) *teacher as reflective practitioner* image of teacher leadership.

Emerging as a Teacher Leader

Because she was connected to the college and growing instructionally, Ms. Allen began to emerge as a teacher leader in the school and district. This process began with a sense of empowerment resulting from her role as the methods instructor. Reflecting on this, Ms. Allen explained, *I am more confident in my ability to teach my students and methods students. I am a more wellrounded teacher. . . . I feel more confident talking with my peers and colleagues.* Indeed, during the 2012–2013 school year, Ms. Allen was asked by the district to organize and lead professional development sessions on adopting the Common Core State Standards. *I have never done that until this year,* Ms. Allen observed. *If we're going to be here for hours in* [school or district-based] *professional development, I want it to be useful. Now, I can pick and choose topics that can help others in our district.* Ms. Allen's confidence, combined with both the insights from developing pre-service teachers and thinking broadly about social studies instruction, developed within her the desire to use professional development to encourage reform.

As Ms. Allen explained, *As teachers, we need to discuss what is right and wrong in the district. These are important conversations for us to have if we want change in the district.*

During the project, Ms. Allen displayed characteristics of a teacher leader, such as being instructionally sound, involved in the professional development of her peers, and dedicated to curricular improvement. Indeed, Ms. Allen's actions demonstrated that she possesses "the strong intellectual underpinning required for teaching. . . that combine[s] both subject and pedagogical expertise" (Dempsey, 1992, p. 117), and, as a result, represents the *teacher as scholar* image of teacher leadership. However, when asked directly if she sees herself as a leader, she responded:

> *Maybe. I feel I have more authority now. I feel like I have something to say. But sometimes I do not feel that I have an opportunity to speak up. . . . I mean, I'm the person who is asked to plan a pep rally but not present on something.*

Ms. Allen knows she has grown, knows she has a new confidence, knows she has a voice, yet does not think of herself as a teacher leader because of how her school-level administrators continue to view her.

Social Studies Teachers Reflect on the Program: Assessing the Field Experience

The social studies department was informed of the collaboration between Timberwood High School and Madison College at the onset of the 2012–2013 school year. All department members were enthusiastic and supportive of the project. Reflecting on the initiative, Ms. Clark stated, *It is designed to be mutually beneficial for both.* While the relationship with the college has always been strong, it has also been one-side. Ms. Roberts concurred, stating, *I think it is a good plan. It is the first time incorporating the field experience into [our] school.* In addition, the critique of the social studies department by the pre-service teachers was intended to aid the in-service teachers. This was important because, as Ms. Clark pointed out, the pre-service teachers *will tell us our strengths and weaknesses. It has never been done before. It is an objective and outside view at what we are doing.* Indeed, the members of the department welcomed the idea of being assessed by the pre-service teachers from the methods course. In addition, the component of having all of the pre-service teachers in the methods course at the high school seemed to reiterate the importance of the program. Mr. Lewis observed that, *having them here is an advantage. There is always* [a pre-service teacher] *in the hallways. I do not remember that last year. They need our help. And it helps us.* From the beginning, the teachers felt that they were

taking part in a partnership that would improve them as professional educators and they embraced the new structure of the partnership.

One of the goals of the project was to increase the accountability of the pre-service teachers during their field experience. One of the new requirements in the methods course was for the pre-service teachers to teach two 45-minute lessons and one 90-minute lesson, an increase from the previous requirement of teaching two 20-minute lessons. Mr. Lewis voiced his support for this change by stating, *The number of lessons they teach is good . . . It is an improvement.* In fact the pre-service teachers were more involved in developing their lessons and taking part in the everyday tasks of teaching. As Ms. Allen observed, *They are doing more. They're not just sitting in the room. I peek in* [classrooms] *sometimes and see them working with students, passing out papers, grading work.* The consensus among the social studies teachers was that the pre-service teachers were far more engaged in the work of a teacher. This sentiment was best stated by Ms. Clark who said, *They are not passive learners. . . It is like an apprenticeship program.* The mentor teachers believed that the accountability measures of requiring greater involvement in the field experience placement through teaching more and longer lessons and becoming participants in the classroom duties were successful.

Although the teachers in the social studies department were consistent in their attitudes toward the increased requirements for the pre-service teachers, the teachers were less consistent with their views on the effectiveness of having the methods professor on campus at all times. When asked about what aspect of the project should be sustained, Ms. Roberts, whose pre-service teacher had not been to the placement by the first week of November, did not hesitate: *"Having* [Ms. Allen] *here helps a lot. I can go directly to their professor and say* [the pre-service teacher] *did not show up."* For Ms. Roberts, having direct and open contact with the methods instructor increased the accountability. Ms. Jackson took the positive support for this aspect of the project further:

> I like that the methods teacher is here. It is good for [the pre-service teachers] to see her around. It is added pressure to do well in front of an authority figure. You cannot come in shorts because your professor will see you!

Although the mentor teachers were consistent and adamant in their belief that having Ms. Allen as the methods instructor was successful, Ms. Allen herself was less positive. *I thought I would get more feedback from the department,"* stated Ms. Allen. *I was hoping the communication would be better. Like when they missed a class, I would know right away.* Though the mentors felt they were conveying adequate feedback on the performance of the methods students, Ms. Allen felt that the mentor teachers were not meeting her expectations and, consequently, not giving this component of the project its intended strength.

Despite the disagreement over the success of having the professor on campus, social studies teachers embraced and valued their role as mentors. Mr. Lewis, who was apprehensive about working with his first pre-service teacher at the beginning of the process, noted in the interview, *I am more comfortable* [being a mentor] *than I thought. . . . It just came easy to me to look over lesson plans and give feedback.* Indeed, he was enthusiastic about his experience as a mentor. *Being a mentor is rewarding and I did not realize I was being rewarded,* Mr. Lewis claimed. *I think it heightened the level of excitement in my classroom because I don't want to display* [to the pre-service teacher] *any negativity, no matter what type of day I am having.*" Although nervous about taking on a field experience early in the process, Mr. Lewis clearly saw the importance of working with a pre-service teacher. Likewise, teachers who had previous experience mentoring accepted the responsibility of nurturing pre-service teachers. Ms. Jackson said, *I've been a mentor a few times. Mostly, she* [the pre-service teacher] *stays and we talk. I want to talk to them in my planning period. We learn from conversation.* Yet, in valuing her role as a mentor, Ms. Jackson pointed to a larger issue: the professionalism of the pre-service teachers. As Ms. Jackson stated, *Yes, professionalism is often lacking, but I need to be proactive in helping* [the pre-service teacher]. *Hearing it from us* [the mentor teachers] *and Ms. Allen, they are more inclined to behave professionally.*" With this statement, it is clear that she viewed herself equally responsible for increasing the professionalism of the pre-service teachers. Thus, the obligation of professionalizing the pre-service students rests with both the college and the mentors.

Becoming a Community of Learners

Another goal of the project was to cultivate a sense of experimentation in the social studies department in terms of using new instructional strategies. One approach to accomplishing this was to provide the teachers with a copy of the syllabus for the methods course so that they could model strategies being discussed in class that week. On this issue, Ms. Allen concluded, *As far as the calendar and schedule for modeling lessons, I do not think people have gotten out of their comfort zones to do new things.* This observation resulted from discussing the strategies with the pre-service teachers in the methods course. In contrast, the mentor teachers felt that the project was prompting them to develop a more extensive repertoire or revisit dormant strategies. As Ms. Jackson noted:

> *I am a young teacher, but I forgot engaging ideas from college. I knew that* [the pre-service teachers] *were watching and I needed to show examples of creative lessons. I*

started looking up creative lessons and using some that I had not used in some time.

The trend of researching new strategies was evident in Mr. Lewis's interview. [The pre-service teachers] *are getting exposure to good teaching strategies,* he claimed. *Personally, I have been iiberprepared. . . to model what they need. They need to see it.* Both teachers felt that they were expanding their repertoires to demonstrate best practices to the pre-service teachers. While having the pre-service teachers observing and researching their practice might have spurred an immediate interest in using more strategies, the teachers acknowledged that the project itself was having an impact on their practice.

So that in-service teachers would develop a wider range of strategies for the purpose of both modeling for pre-service teachers and improving instruction in the social studies department, one goal of the project was to increase the amount of professional development to which all of the teachers in the department were exposed. Ms. Jackson, who has experience teaching in two districts, observed:

> *Usually districts send the same people out for professional development. There's no opportunity for the 'little people'—new teachers or new to the district—who have to earn their keep before going to professional development. We are trying to change that.*

Indeed there was general sense among the teachers that the approach to professional development prompted by the project was more equitable. Included in the process of attending professional development was the expectation that teachers present their learning to the department and share how they were using it with their students, giving each teacher an opportunity to be a leader within the department. As Ms. Roberts noted, *What we are doing is. . . meeting as a department to plan and brainstorm how to make ourselves better. Department meetings are more productive.* When discussing this issue, Mr. Lewis said, *It is a conscious effort to get everyone as much professional development as possible. I mean, it is November and half of the department has been out of district for professional development.* However, this sentiment was perhaps best stated by Ms. Allen: *Department meetings are now about how to become stronger teachers. Meetings are more about methods we are using and conferences we are attending and less about school policies. Department meetings are professional development meetings.* While the social studies teachers placed value in pursuing quality professional development, concern existed that the administration was not entirely supportive of the plan. Citing an inability to attend a state conference earlier in the year, Ms. Jackson said. *We have a focus on exposing all to professional development, but do not have the support from above to make it happen for all.* Given the support that administrators expressed for the school-university collaboration and for helping the social studies teachers grow professionally through conference and workshop attendance, this comment stood out. Yet, the consensus of the teachers was that they were growing as a result of the project and the new emphasis on professional development; in this case building internal capacity within the department for professional development.

Unifying as a Department

A surprising finding that emerged from the interviews was that, through the process of working with pre-service teachers and working together to grow professionally, the teachers believed that they are becoming more unified as a department. As Ms. Allen put it, *We were isolated. But now there is more discussion about what we are doing, discussions about getting better. We have a common goal for growth.* While the project gave the teachers a shared vision for improvement, it was evident from the interviews the teachers used the mentoring of pre-service teachers to reflect on their own practice and the practice of their peers. As Ms. Roberts noted, *We are now a truly collaborative group . . . In a lot of schools that does not happen . . . The more you share with one another, the more you support one another.* With this reflection, the teachers in the department represent the *teacher as partner in learning* image of teacher leadership as they felt open "to speak their own word and create their own . . . transformation" (Dempsey, 1992, p. 118) within the department. Indeed, the teachers were clear in their belief that the focus on mentoring pre-service teachers, seeking professional development, and reflecting with each other caused a greater sense of unity in the department. To this end, Mr. Lewis said:

> *It is a step up from last year. I don't recall talking about professional development last year. When we did, it was mostly about what one or two people did. . . . I think that everyone feels part of a team. We are stronger and closer as a department.*

The unity that the teachers felt was a consistent theme. The teachers felt that they were more than a department: they were, indeed, a collaborative team of educators.

Conveying Parting Thoughts

Finally, the teachers experienced an increased sense of professionalism and confidence through their involvement in the project. Aside from the sense of being involved in equitable professional development strategy, there was a sense that they experienced an increase in confidence in their abilities and pride about their profession. *It has made me feel better about being a teacher,* Mr. Lewis said. *The way* [my field experience student] *cares and listens. There is someone in the room that is learning more from me than Economics. It is inspiring.* In fact, observing

the growth of both the pre-service teachers and the discussions among the social studies teachers, Ms. Clark took a more poignant approach as she stated, *It made me wish I was teaching full time to be more a part of it.* Clearly there was a sense of pride and recognition that the work being done was significant. In addition, one teacher looked at the project as a means of generating professionalism by addressing a common stereotype about social studies teachers. Ms. Roberts stated. *We are dispelling the belief that social studies teachers are only a bunch of coaches by showing that we are professional teachers who want to teach.* Although there is no evidence in this research to indicate that this group of teachers was viewed as "a bunch of coaches," Roberts' point is clear—these teachers are engaged in deep and collaborative professional development that she believes is characteristic of professional educators. Overall, however, the entire project improved their sense of professionalism, pride, and confidence by allowing them to be a part of an innovative system for both hosting pre-service teachers in a field experience and growing as educators. As Mr. Lewis stated, *I am involved. I feel like I am contributing and, on a personal level, it is good and positive. I'm not a bystander.*

Discussion

The purpose of this article is to examine the initial impact of the collaboration between the social studies department at Timberwood High School and the education division at Madison College. Because rural schools are characterized by fewer resources (Bryant, 2007) and school university partnerships in rural areas must recognize unique needs of rural schools (Warren & Peel, 2005), the case in the present study represents how a rural school used the partnership to meet professional development needs. The first area studied in this article was the impact of the project on the social studies teachers at Timberwood High School as they experimented with new instructional strategies. All of the teachers indicated that they were focused on using new strategies. The leading cause was the knowledge that the pre-service teachers were there to learn and that the pre-service teachers would be researching the practice of the teachers. Most of the teachers mentioned breaking out of instructional ruts. Given that most of the teachers had between seven and ten years of experience, engaging in new instructional experiences is significant. According to Huberman (1989), teachers with five to nineteen years of experience tend to express doubts about careers because experimentation wanes and frustration with the school system sets in. In this case, the focus on using the field experience program as a means of professional development prompted a more cohesive pedagogical focus and resulted in improved teacher leadership. Dempsey (1992) noted that teacher leaders help create schools that are "communities of learning" (p.118) and teacher leaders must "forge these dynamic new partnerships" (p. 118) to create "open spaces for dialogue" (p.118) within schools. Also, several teachers mentioned that the goal was for all teachers to learn and experience professional development, not just one or two teachers. Lortie (1975/2002) noted that seniority is a cultural norm within schools that hinders change. Previously, in many cases, seniority has guided who received or directed professional development. However, this norm appears to be waning (Weiner, 2011); in this study, all teachers involved received professional development. The professional development in the present study, as recommended by Feiman-Nemser (2001), allowed teachers to access the wider discourses on pedagogy and to break down isolation through substantive discussion. In addition, the present study demonstrates, as other researchers have observed, the need for rural teachers to have access to a wide range of flexible and individualized professional development that includes time for collaboration (Babione, 2010; Blum, Yocom, Trent, & McLaughlin, 2005; Guenther & Weible, 1983). Through participation in this collaborative project, the in-service teachers developed a greater sense of experimentation with new instructional strategies as they worked collectively to develop pedagogical cohesion.

The second goal of this research was to observe the impact of the partnership between Timberwood High School and Madison College on the development of the social studies teachers as teacher leaders. The teacher leadership development in the program is consistent with Dempsey's (1992) images of teacher leaders as *reflective practitioners* and *partners in learning* as the social studies teachers reflected and grew together. In addition, York-Barr and Duke (2004) characterized teacher leaders, in part, as teachers offering professional development to their peers, participating in school change, creating a community of learning, and focusing on improving curriculum. Although exhibiting all of these attributes, the responses of the teachers are vague in terms of their confidence in defining themselves as leaders. This could be a result of teachers not wanting to present themselves as leaders due to the cultural norms with schools, specifically that of egalitarianism (Lortie, 1975/2002). Because of the unique challenges rural schools face, rural schools need "leadership strategies that are flexible and responsive to contextual circumstances, despite the countervailing forces that may exist in the school and broader environment" (Masumoto & Brown-Welty, 2009, p. 3). Thus, teacher leadership must be at the forefront of a rural school. In the present study, participants developed a sense of teacher leadership when they led professional development for their peers in the department, a finding consistent with research on teacher-conducted professional development in rural schools (Harris, 2005).

Though Ms. Allen felt stronger as a leader, she also felt that the school-level administration was not recognizing her growth as a teacher leader. However, Ms. Allen's frustrations are not uncommon. Because schools have a century-long tradition of having a principal as the sole instructional leader of the institution (Lortie, 1975/2002) and many principals are not prepared to relinquish authority to teachers who are underneath them in the hierarchy (Weiner, 2011), principals and teachers have conflicting views of teacher leadership. Administrators may be reluctant to cede power to teachers. In this sense, the teachers in the project were experiencing growth, but were likely held back from experiencing their growth potential by the traditional school norms and hierarchy.

However, the teachers in this study were committed to the project and its goals. As Masumoto and Brown-Welty (2009) observed, "effective rural educational leaders utilize a variety of leadership practices to develop formal and informal linkages with multiple community sources to help accomplish their mission" (p. 15). In this case, the partnership between Timberwood High School and Madison College served as a formal link to meet the challenges facing rural schools. Teachers, such as Ms. Jackson and Mr. Lewis, felt a responsibility to assist the field experience students to grow instructionally and professionally. A sense of obligation to aid teachers in their growth is a common characteristic of teacher leaders (Smylie & Brownlee-Conyers, 1992; York-Barr & Duke, 2004). In fact, the teachers in the present study spoke openly of a heightened sense of collaboration and becoming closer as a department. Given that isolation is a traditional norm that holds back change (Fullan, 1993; Lortie, 1975/2002) and that teacher leadership is a concept that is characterized by collaboration (York-Barr & Duke, 2004), it would appear that the teachers involved in the present study are beginning to dismantle school norms in the social studies department. So, while the teachers were reluctant to discuss leadership and felt that the administration was not recognizing their leadership qualities, they were also taking on the attributes of teacher leaders as part of the program by collaborating with each other. Specific to Ms. Allen, the experience of working as the methods professor changed her; yet, she felt that the perceptions school-based administrators had of her did not change at the same pace and depth. As a result the findings are mixed when it comes to inservice teachers' perceptions of the project's impact on becoming teacher leaders.

Conclusion

The initial findings of the present study generate additional questions. As the social studies teachers at Timberwood

High School continue to grow as a collaborative unit, how is their self-efficacy affected? In addition, how are high school students affected by the collaboration between the school and college? In what ways will the teachers further utilize the research conducted by the pre-service teachers in the field experience connected to the methods course? How did the pre-service teachers grow and develop as a result of the project? What further characteristics exist in this partnership that do not exist in urban or suburban partnerships? These are questions still to be answered within the project for future study. The significance of the current findings is that the voices of mentors—of rural teacher leaders—are heard. Mentoring, despite the attention it receives among professors, practitioners, and administrators, is largely overlooked (Hamel & Jaasko-Fisher, 2011). A goal of the project was to create a mentoring program that was substantive for practitioner growth, while empowering rural teachers by acknowledging and valuing their contributions.

Warren and Peel (2005) argued that rural school reform requires administrators willing to reach out to colleges and universities to form partnerships and lead their teachers into the process. However, Fullan (1993) explained that teachers, not administrative mandates, are the key to sustainable change and school reform. The mentoring program that is the focus of the present study shows the importance of involving teacher leaders in the development of rural school-university partnerships. In this study, teachers played a substantive role in the development of a field experience program for pre-service teachers. In the process, the teachers developed a stronger bond as a department, breaking out of isolation. They focused on attending and discussing professional development with the objective of implementing new strategies in their classroom. In addition, while the teachers grew as leaders, they were limited by school norms and felt little administrative support. The policy implications of the present study are best seen at the district level, where rural administrators need to allow for greater flexibility for teacher leaders to lead reform efforts in rural education.

References

Anderson, K.D. (2008). Transformational teacher leadership in rural schools. *Rural Educator, 29* (3), 8–17.

Babione, B. (2010). Rural and small community educator responses to state academic standards. *Rural Educator, 37* (3), 7–15.

Blum, H.T., Yocom, D J., Trent, A., & McLaughlin, M. (2005). Professional development: When teachers plan and deliver their own. *Rural Special Education Quarterly, 24* (2), 18–21.

Bryant, J.A. (2007). Killing Mayberry: The crisis of rural American education. *The Rural Educator, 28* (1), 7–11.

Cozza, B. (2007). Transforming teaching into a collaborative culture: An attempt to create a professional development school-university partnership. *The Educational Forum, 74* (3), 227–241.

Dempsey, R. (1992). Teachers as leaders: Towards a conceptual framework. *Teaching Education, 5* (1), 113–120.

Feiman-Nemser, S. (2001). From preparation to practice: Designing a continuum to strengthen and sustain teaching. *Teachers College Record, 103* (6), 1013–1055.

Fullan, M. (1993). *Change forces: Probing the depths of educational reform.* New York: The Falmer Press.

Guenther, J., & Weible, T. (1983). Preparing teachers for rural schools. *Rural Education, 1* (2), 59–61

Hamel, F.L., & Jaasko-Fisher, H.A. (2011). Hidden labor in the mentoring of pre-service teachers: Notes from a mentor teacher advisory council. *Teaching and Teacher Education, 27* (2), 434–442.

Harris, S. (2005). Improved professional development through teacher leadership. *The Rural Educator, 26* (2), 12–16.

Huberman, M. (1989). The professional life cycle of teachers. *Teachers College Record, 97* (1), 31–57.

Katzanmeyer, M., & Möller, G. (2001). *Awakening the sleeping giant: Helping teachers develop as leaders.* Thousand Oaks, CA: Corwin Press, Inc.

Kirschner, B.W., Dickinson, R., & Blosser, C. (1996). From cooperation to collaboration: The changing culture of a school/university partnership. *Theory into Practice, 35* (3), 205–213.

Lefever-Davis, S., Johnson, C., & Pearman, C. (2007). Two sides of a partnership: Egalitarianism and empowerment in school-university partnerships. *The Journal of Educational Research, 100* (4), 204–210.

Lortie, D. (1975/2002). *Schoolteacher: A sociological study* (2nd ed.). Chicago, IL: University of Chicago Press.

Masumoto, M, & Brown-Welty, S. (2009). Case Study of Leadership Practices and School-Community Interrelationships in High-Performing, High-Poverty, Rural California High Schools. *Journal of Research in Rural Education, 24* (1), 1–18.

Myron, S., Sanzo, K.L., & Clayton, J. (2011). Tracing the development of a rural university-district partnership: Encouraging district voice and challenging assumptions leadership. *Journal of School Leadership, 21* (5), 684–703.

Rogus, J.F. (1988). Teacher leader programming: Theoretical underpinnings. *Journal of Teacher Education, 39* (1), 46–52.

Salazar, P. (2007). The professional development needs of rural high school principals: A seven-state study. The Rural Educator, 28(3), 20–27.

Smylie, M.A., Brownlee-Conyers, J. (1992). Teacher leaders and their principals: Exploring the development of new working relationships. *Educational Administration Quarterly, 28,* 150–184.

United States Census Bureau. (2000). *Genealogy data: Frequently occurring surnames from Census 2000.* Retrieved from http://www.census.gov/genealogy/www/data/2000sumames/index.html

Warren, L.L., & Peel, H.A. (2005). Collaborative model for school reform through a rural school/university partnership. *Education, 126* (2), 346–352.

Weiner, J.M. (2011). Finding common ground: Teacher leaders and principals speak out about teacher leadership. *Journal of School Leadership, 21* (1), 7–41.

York-Barr, J., & Duke, K. (2004). What do we know about teacher leadership?: Findings from two decades of scholarship. *Review of Educational Research, 74* (3), 255–316.

Critical Thinking

1. Describe the characteristics or practices of a Teacher-Leader.

2. Explain how the university, the school, and teachers at both benefit from these partnerships.

3. While this was a study that focused on developing social studies teachers, what implications does this study have for developing all teachers as Teacher-Leaders?

Create Central

www.mhhe.com/createcentral

Internet References

American School Board Journal
www.asbj.com

Center for Comprehensive School Reform and Improvement
www.centerforcsri.org

Education Week on the Web
www.edweek.org

National Education Association
www.nea.org

JEFFREY C. EARGLE is a doctoral student at the University of South Carolina. In addition, he is a social studies teacher in the public school system in South Carolina.

Unit 8

UNIT

Prepared by: Rebecca B. Evers, *Winthrop University*

Sexual Minority Students

Over the last several years there have been widespread debates and legal actions attached to the consideration of legalizing gay marriage. At this time, 30 states have passed legislation defining marriage as only between a man and a woman, despite the numerous high-profile politicians and celebrities who have advocated for such marriages. The opponents and proponents of gay rights have engaged in very heated debates and some name-calling in public places. Persons who are in the sexual minority can often be exposed to hostility and apprehension due to their nonconformity in sexual orientation and gender identity. Our society and media may be demonstrating an increase in acceptance through positive portrayals of sexual minority persons in public venues, such as in television shows like *Modern Family* and *GLEE,* or the rise in popularity of celebrities like Ellen DeGeneres and Rachel Maddow, but we should not assume this is acceptable to everyone everywhere. Especially, we should not assume that the school experiences of students who are LGBTQ are as inclusive as the portrayals in the media or that they are accepted by all of their teachers and peers (Kim, Sheridan, & Holcomb, 2009).

Kim, Sheridan, and Holcomb (2009) note that school personnel who are LGBT face societal and legal pressures to stay "in the closet" at school and especially in front of students. This can lead to feelings of isolation and a diminished sense of safety or belonging, which in turn can hamper their efforts to teach and mentor students. School personnel, both LGBT and straight, may sometimes feel uncomfortable mentoring students because of concerns for their own personal safety and therefore, they may ignore homophobic bullying when they witness it.

Schools reflect much of the societal debate. Sexual minority adolescents challenge educators to think about the tension between competing public opinions and serving all students. Due to conflicts that may arise within the schools, many educators may not feel comfortable for political and personal reasons, or prepared for the conversation and changes in policy and practices that are necessary if sexual minority adolescents are to be successful in our schools (Kim, Sheridan, & Holcomb, 2009).

There is some mixed news reported by the Gay, Lesbian and Straight Education Network (GLSEN, 2011). There was a steady decline in the frequency of hearing homophobic remarks from 1999 to 2011. Between 2009 and 2011, student reports of hearing these types of remarks had decreased significantly. LGBTQ experiences of harassment and assault showed small but significant decreases in frequencies of verbal harassment, physical harassment, and physical assault from 2009 to 2011. The best news of this report is that there has been an increase over time in the presence of LGBTQ-related resources and supports in schools, specifically: Gay-Straight Alliances or other student clubs that address LGBTQ issues in education as well as increases in school staff who support LGBTQ students and LGBTQ-related materials in school libraries. However, if we look at the key findings noted on the website referenced below, there are still too many incidents of harassment and verbal abuse occurring in our schools. The articles in this unit will offer additional information about students who identify themselves as LGBTQ, data regarding the barriers they face in public schools, and strategies that can help you take action to remove the barriers.

In a study of sexual orientation of minority students from diverse ethnicities, researchers found that obesity in female and male bisexual youths posed serious, long term problems for their health. These findings lead to the conclusion that appropriate interventions should be offered to eliminate stressors, such as referrals for treatment and programs to promote healthful eating and life-style habits.

In this *Annual Edition: Education,* we take an in-depth look at bullying and sexual harassment in general. However, beyond stating there is a problem and it is terrible, we wanted to stress the need to provide a safe environment within schools for all students, but especially some of the most vulnerable. Looking at the suicide rates of sexual minority students who learn in protective school climates; data reveals these LGBTQ students have fewer suicidal thoughts than peers in less protective environments. That makes understanding and providing those safe school climates important.

Even if schools teach tolerance, offer safe places within the school, and have vigilant faculty and staff, bullying and harassment still may exist in some shape or form. In efforts to protect students, some school districts have open, "gay-friendly" schools. These are schools where students who are LGBTQ may self-segregate and where students are able to be who they are in a laid back, accepting environment. As one student pointed out, "We don't do drama here."

References

Kim, R., Sheridan, D., & Holcomb, S. (2009). *A Report on the Status of Gay, Lesbian, Bisexual and Transgender People in Education: Stepping Out of the Closet, into the Light.* Washington, D.C.: National Education Association. Retrieved from www.nea.org/home/Report-on-Status-of-GLBT.html

Gay, Lesbian and Straight Education Network (*2011*). *The 2011 National School Climate Survey: Key Findings on the Experiences of Lesbian, Gay, Bisexual and Transgender Youth in Our Nation's Schools.* Author. Retrieved from www.glsen.org/cgi-bin/iowa/all/news/record/2897.html

Article   Prepared by: Rebecca B. Evers, *Winthrop University*

Eating Disorder Symptoms and Obesity at the Intersections of Gender, Ethnicity, and Sexual Orientation In US High School Students

S. BRYN AUSTIN, ET AL.

Learning Outcomes

After reading this article, you will be able to:

- Explain who sexual minority students are and the major issues they face in school.
- Discuss the key findings regarding health issues of LGBT students.

The prevalence of childhood obesity has markedly increased in the past few decades, more than tripling in the last 30 years.[1] Obesity in adolescence is especially concerning because of the high risk of immediate- and long-term problems associated with the condition. Obese adolescents are at an elevated risk for high cholesterol, hypertension, prediabetes, bone and joint problems, and sleep apnea.[2–5] They are 20 times more likely to become obese adults,[6] increasing the odds of long-term health consequences secondary to obesity, such as type 2 diabetes, heart disease, stroke, cancer, and osteoarthritis.[7] Eating disorders and disordered weight-control behaviors, such as purging and diet pill use, represent the third most common chronic childhood illnesses, after obesity and asthma,[8] and are associated with a range of serious comorbidities, including disorders of the cardiovascular, gastrointestinal, and endocrine systems.[9] In addition, children and adolescents who are obese have been found to be at increased risk of eating disorder symptoms.[10–12]

These health problems affect individuals during crucial physiological and psychological developmental periods and disproportionately affect marginalized subgroups of youths. Numerous studies have highlighted disparities based on ethnicity,[13–17] sexual orientation,[18–22] and gender.[23–26] However, little is known about how these disparities intersect and the ways in which individuals who are members of multiple minority subgroups may be affected.

Minority stress theory posits that members of marginalized social populations are subject to health consequences as a result of experiences of stigma and discrimination associated with possessing a minority identity.[27] These stressors may have direct health consequences through chronic perturbations of biological systems or may cause psychological distress, influencing health behaviors (substance use, weight-control behaviors, sexual risk behaviors, etc.) and health care utilization. Multiple minority

Objectives. We examined purging for weight control, diet pill use, and obesity across sexual orientation identity and ethnicity groups.

Methods. Anonymous survey data were analyzed from 24 591 high school students of diverse ethnicities in the federal Youth Risk Behavioral Surveillance System Survey in 2005 and 2007. Self-reported data were gathered on gender, ethnicity, sexual orientation identity, height, weight, and purging and diet pill use in the past 30 days. We used multivariable logistic regression to estimate odds of purging, diet pill use, and obesity associated with sexual orientation identity in gender-stratified models and examined for the presence of interactions between ethnicity and sexual orientation.

Results. Lesbian, gay, and bisexual (LGB) identity was associated with substantially elevated odds of purging and diet pill use in both girls and boys (odds ratios [OR] range = 1.9 – 6.8). Bisexual girls and boys were also at elevated odds of obesity compared to same-gender heterosexuals (OR = 2.3 and 2.1, respectively).

Conclusions. Interventions to reduce eating disorders and obesity that are appropriate for LGB youths of diverse ethnicities are urgently needed. (*Am J Public Health.* 2013;103:e16–e22.)

Eating Disorder Symptoms and Obesity at the Intersections of Gender, Ethnicity, and Sexual Orientation   by S. Bryn Austin, et al.

199

stress theory focuses on the intersection of ethnicity, gender, and sexual orientation and proposes that lesbian, gay, and bisexual (LGB) people of color are exposed to multiple stressors that may create an additive health disadvantage.[28,29] Several population-based studies have supported the additive hypothesis, demonstrating increased prevalence of health risks among LGB people of color compared with their White LGB counterparts, including disparities in mental health disorders,[30,31] chronic health conditions,[32] adolescent suicide,[33] and obesity.[34]

The additive hypothesis of minority stress theory, however, has been scrutinized because it has not been consistently borne out. For example, other studies[35,36] found that ethnicity did not modify sexual orientation-related health disparities, and 1 study[29] found that being a member of a ethnic minority group had some protective effect on mental health among LGB individuals, specifically for adolescent girls.

We found a limited number of studies that addressed health disparities affecting LGB people of color and an even smaller number of studies that addressed adolescents and young adults.[29,33,35–37] In addition, no studies, to our knowledge, specifically examined the issue of disordered weight-control behaviors. We were aware of only 1 study that examined the prevalence of obesity among sexual minorities as associated with ethnicity; this study found that Asian Pacific Islanders had lower body mass index (BMI) and African Americans had higher BMI in a sample of lesbian and bisexual women compared with White women.[34] The aim of the present study examined how gender and ethnicity were associated with sexual orientation identity disparities in obesity and disordered weight-control behaviors in youths using data from the Youth Risk Behavior Surveillance System (YRBSS), a biennial survey conducted by the Centers for Disease Control and Prevention (CDC) in US high schools. This study was unique in its focus on disordered weight-control behaviors and obesity, 2 important adolescent health issues in LGB ethnic minority youths, who are an understudied population.

Methods

For the present study, we pooled anonymous data gathered from US high school students in 2005 and 2007 as part of the YRBSS. Four cities (Boston, Massachusetts; Chicago, Illinois; New York City, New York; and San Francisco, California) and 5 states (Delaware, Maine, Massachusetts, Vermont, and Rhode Island) administered an item on sexual orientation identity; therefore, for the present study, we analyzed data from these jurisdictions. More details about the pooling methods used and the characteristics of jurisdictions included in analyses can be found elsewhere.[38]

Measures

Students in participating high schools completed self-report surveys assessing sexual orientation identity, demographic characteristics, and health-related behaviors and exposures. An item assessing sexual orientation identity asked students to indicate which identity best described them from the options heterosexual, bisexual, lesbian or gay, or unsure.

Outcomes included purging for weight control, use of diet pills, and obesity. The YRBSS survey includes 1 item asking whether respondents engaged in self-induced vomiting or used laxatives (i.e., purging) in the past 30 days and another item asking whether they used diet pills without a doctor's orders to lose or maintain weight.[39] Each item was treated as binary. Students were asked to report their height and weight, which was then used to calculate age-and sex-specific BMI (defined as weight in kilograms divided by the square of height in meters) percentiles based on CDC guidelines; biologically implausible BMI values were also identified and set to missing per CDC guidelines.[40] Youths were then categorized as obese if their BMI was at or above the 95th percentile for their age and gender. It was shown that self-reported BMI had moderate validity in adolescents.[41]

Statistical Analysis

All descriptive analyses were carried out with SPSS (version 20; SPSS Inc, Chicago, IL), and multilevel software HLM (version 7; Scientific Software International, Lincolnwood, IL) was used to fit final multivariable models. Gender-stratified multivariable logistic regression models were used to estimate the odds of each of the 3 outcome variables (purging, diet pill use, and obesity) associated with sexual orientation identity and ethnicity, controlling for age, region, and data collection wave. Heterosexual youths served as the referent group for sexual orientation group comparisons, and White youths for ethnicity group comparisons. In additional multivariable models, we examined whether ethnicity modified associations between sexual orientation identity and the 3 outcomes by entering interaction terms into the models.

The YRBSS complex sampling design was accounted for by adjusting the relative weights and altering the effective sample size for each jurisdiction (i.e., city or state). Because data were clustered, hierarchical linear modeling was done with jurisdiction assigned at level 2 in each model. See Mustanski et al.[38] for additional information about methods used to calculate design effects and to account for intracluster correlation.

Surveys received from 28 887 youths were combined across the 9 jurisdictions and 2 waves of collection. Students were excluded if they did not provide important information for analyses (i.e., were missing covariates or outcome variables), leading to a final analytic sample of 24 591 youths (85.1% of original sample).

Results

Table 1 presents selected sociodemographic characteristics of the ethnically diverse youths included in analyses. Among girls, those identifying as a sexual minority made up more than 8% of the analytic sample, and among boys, sexual minorities made up almost 5% of the analytic sample. Mean age was 15.9 years (SD = 1.3; range = 13–18 years).

The percentage of youths engaging in purging and diet pill use are presented in Table 2 for each gender, ethnicity, and sexual orientation identity group. In general, a higher percentage of sexual minorities within each ethnicity group reported

Table 1 Sample Characteristics of US High School Students: Youth Risk Behavioral Surveillance System Survey, 2005 and 2007

Characteristics	No. (%)
Girls (n = 12 132)	
Ethnicity	
Asian-American	1357 (11.2)
African-American	3218 (26.5)
Latina	2222 (18.3)
Other ethnicity[b]	1114 (9.2)
White (Ref)	4221 (34.8)
Sexual orientation identity	
Lesbian	137 (1.1)
Bisexual	628 (5.2)
Unsure	303 (2.5)
Heterosexual (Ref)	11 064 (91.2)
Boys (n = 12 459)	
Ethnicity	
Asian-American	1714 (13.8)
African-American	2906 (23.3)
Latino	2220 (17.8)
Other ethnicity[a]	1046 (8.4)
White (Ref)	4573 (36.7)
Sexual orientation identity	
Gay	149 (1.2)
Bisexual	221 (1.8)
Unsure	268 (2.2)
Heterosexual (Ref)	11 821 (94.9)

Note. The maximum sample size was n = 24 591.

[a]Other ethnicity group includes youths who identified as Pacific Islander, American Indian, Alaskan Native, or multiple ethnicity groups.

purging and use of diet pills than did heterosexuals among both girls and boys. Within some groups, as much as a one quarter to more than one third of sexual minorities reported purging or diet pill use to control weight in the past 30 days, compared with a mean of approximately 8% of heterosexual girls and 5% of heterosexual boys across ethnicity groups. Table 2 also presents the percentages of obesity for each gender, ethnicity, and sexual orientation identity group. Among girls who were not Asian American, the percentage of obesity in heterosexuals ranged from 6% to 12% across ethnicity groups, whereas this percentage in sexual minorities ranged widely from 4% to 27%. Among boys, the percentage of obesity in bisexuals was especially elevated, ranging from 20% to 50% in Latinos, Whites, and other ethnicity groups compared with a mean of approximately 15% among heterosexuals in these groups.

Asian Americans had a lower percentage of obesity compared with other ethnicity groups among both girls and boys.

Multivariable models were fit to examine main effects for sexual orientation identity and ethnicity on eating disorder symptoms and obesity and to examine for possible interaction effects. Ethnicity did not modify sexual orientation identity associations with outcomes; therefore, results of main effects models are presented in the following and in Table 3. Sizable sexual orientation disparities in eating disorder symptoms in both girls and boys were observed. Sexual minority girls had 2 to 4 times the odds of purging and diet pill use compared with heterosexual peers, and sexual minority boys had 3 to approximately 7 times the odds of these behaviors compared with heterosexual peers. Compared with White same-gender peers, Asian American and African American girls had lower odds of purging and diet pill use, whereas African American boys had higher odds of purging, and other ethnicity boys had higher odds of both purging and diet pill use.

Sexual orientation identity disparities were also observed for obesity. Bisexual girls and boys had higher odds of obesity compared with same-gender heterosexual peers. Although Asian Americans had lower odds of obesity compared with White youths, all other youths of color, with the exception of African American boys, had higher odds of obesity than their same-gender White peers.

Discussion

Obesity and eating disorders in adolescence put young people at risk for a myriad of immediate- and long-term health problems associated with significant morbidity, disability, medical costs, and increased risk of premature death.[9,42–45] Identifying groups at elevated risk is essential to informing an effective and appropriately targeted public health response to the health burden posed by these conditions.

Findings from our study of US high school students of diverse ethnicities indicated that both female and male sexual minorities of all ethnic groups were at substantially elevated risk of disordered weight-control behaviors, in some cases as much as a 7-fold increased risk. Across ethnicity groups, as many as 1 in 3 lesbian and bisexual girls engaged in these behaviors in the past month compared with fewer than 1 in 10 heterosexual girls. Similarly, across ethnicity groups, 1 in 5 gay and bisexual boys reported disordered weight-control behaviors in the past month compared with 1 in 20 heterosexual boys. Rates of obesity were elevated in female and male bisexuals compared with their same-gender heterosexual peers.

Our findings of elevated rates of disordered weight-control behaviors among sexual minority adolescents were consistent with those from previous research.[19,21,22] Previous statewide surveys in Massachusetts and Minnesota found gay and bisexual adolescent boys had high rates of these behaviors[46,47] compared with heterosexual boys, as was also found in the Growing Up Today Study, a nationwide cohort of predominantly White youths.[19] The present study added to the literature by documenting patterns of elevated risk in sexual minority boys of diverse ethnicities living across the United States. In addition,

Eating Disorder Symptoms and Obesity at the Intersections of Gender, Ethnicity, and Sexual Orientation   by S. Bryn Austin, et al.

201

Table 2   Prevalence of Purging (Vomiting or Laxatives), Diet Pill Use, and Obesity in US High School Students: Youth Risk Behavioral Surveillance System Survey, 2005 and 2007

Characteristics	Total, No. (%)	Purge,[a] %	Diet Pills,[a] %	Obese,[b] %
Girls (n = 12 132)				
Asian-American				
Lesbian	12 (0.9)	. . .[c]	. . .[c]	0
Bisexual	33 (2.4)	13.9	11.8	0
Unsure	52 (3.8)	5.7	8.9	0
Heterosexual	1260 (92.9)	3.0	1.9	2.3
African-American				
Lesbian	52 (1.6)	15.2	1.4	19.2
Bisexual	156 (4.8)	6.3	6.7	26.9
Unsure	62 (1.9)	24.2	8.5	12.9
Heterosexual	2948 (91.6)	3.5	2.8	12.2
Latina				
Lesbian	22 (1.0)	26.7	44.7	4.5
Bisexual	124 (5.6)	15.1	9.1	16.9
Unsure	46 (2.2)	8.2	10.1	15.2
Heterosexual	2030 (91.5)	6.4	4.0	9.1
Other ethnicity[d]				
Lesbian	28 (2.5)	18.8	0	16.7
Bisexual	88 (7.9)	13.4	11.5	11.4
Unsure	50 (4.5)	22.2	3.3	14.0
Heterosexual	948 (85.1)	6.1	4.9	11.2
White				
Lesbian	23 (0.5)	15.2	18.4	13.0
Bisexual	227 (5.4)	18.6	14.2	14.5
Unsure	93 (2.2)	8.3	6.9	9.7
Heterosexual	3878 (91.9)	6.1	5.1	5.6
Boys (n = 12 459)				
Asian-American				
Gay	14 (0.8)	. . .[c]	. . .[c]	7.1
Bisexual	29 (1.7)	18.9	21.1	10.3
Unsure	9 (5.2)	9.1	1.4	5.6
Heterosexual	1582 (92.3)	2.1	2.9	9.3
African-American				
Gay	39 (1.3)	14.6	17.7	5.1
Bisexual	51 (1.8)	35.3	41.9	15.7
Unsure	52 (1.8)	7.2	6.5	13.5
Heterosexual	2764 (95.1)	4.8	3.5	14.8
Latino				
Gay	32 (1.4)	12.4	6.5	21.9
Bisexual	36 (1.6)	7.8	5.8	50.0
Unsure	24 (1.1)	17.8	29.6	25.0
Heterosexual	2128 (95.9)	2.8	4.1	18.1

(continued)

Characteristics	Total, No. (%)	Purge,[a] %	Diet Pills,[a] %	Obese,[b] %
		Girls (n = 12 132)		
Other ethnicity[d]				
Gay	21 (2.0)	22.2	23.1	23.8
Bisexual	29 (2.8)	30.4	20.0	48.3
Unsure	30 (2.9)	10.3	30.4	16.7
Heterosexual	966 (92.4)	3.7	4.2	16.6
White				
Gay	43 (0.9)	16.2	12.8	11.6
Bisexual	76 (1.7)	13.6	11.4	19.7
Unsure	73 (1.6)	11.1	9.0	22.9
Heterosexual	4381 (95.8)	2.1	2.9	3.7

Note. The maximum sample size was n = 24 591.

[a]Purging defined as any vomiting or use of laxatives in the past month to control weight; diet pill use defined as use of diet pills to control weight without a doctor's prescription in the past month.

[b]Obesity defined as body mass index three quarters of 95th percentile for age and sex as per percentile definitions based on guidelines from the US Centers for Disease Control and Prevention.

[c]Fewer than 10 participants responded in this category; therefore, data are not presented.

[d]Other ethnicity group includes youths who identified as Pacific Islander, American Indian, Alaskan Native, or multiple ethnicity groups.

the present study added to previous studies on adolescent girls,[19,22] by providing clear evidence that purging for weight control and diet pill use were highly prevalent among sexual minority girls of diverse ethnicities.

In relation to ethnicity, our study suggested that African American female adolescents might have some protection against engaging in vomiting or abuse of laxatives or diet pills to control weight. Previous studies showed mixed results on this point, with some finding a similar protective effect,[17,48] whereas others did not find reduced risk.[15,21,49] Our study also suggested that Asian American girls might be at decreased risk for disordered weight-control behaviors compared with Whites, consistent with previous findings from the National Latino and Asian American Study.[50] Among ethnic minority boys, our findings were consistent with previous research that showed Latino and African American boys had higher rates of disordered weight-control behaviors compared with White boys.[16,49] This trend was not found among Asian American boys, which was consistent with previous literature.[50]

Few studies have examined associations of sexual orientation with obesity in adolescents. One previous study with youths participating in the Growing Up Today Study, a cohort made up predominantly of White youths, demonstrated that sexual orientation minority girls had a higher BMI than heterosexual girls, whereas among boys the reverse was found, with heterosexual boys having higher BMI than gay boys.[18] For girls, the present findings differed from the previous study, in that elevated odds of obesity were found only for bisexuals and not lesbians. For boys, results from the present study also differed from previous findings, in that gay boys did not differ from heterosexuals, whereas bisexual boys had 2 times the odds of obesity compared with heterosexual peers.

A number of studies have shown elevated rates of obesity among ethnic minority adolescents,[13–17] especially in African American and Latina girls compared with their White same-gender peers. Our findings were consistent with these studies, demonstrating an increased notable risk of obesity among African American and Latina girls. Our results were also consistent with those of previous research, which found Asian American youths were at lower risk of obesity compared with White youths.[14,51]

The present study did not find support for the additive hypothesis of multiple minority stress theory, as sexual orientation-by-ethnicity interactions were not found to be significant in multivariable regression models. This null finding might have been because of insufficient statistical power; however, prevalence estimates for outcomes presented in Table 2 did not suggest any consistent patterns of additivity. Contemporary approaches to intersectionality research recommend studying the risk associated with the unique experiences of being LGB people of color (e.g., the experience of being Asian American, bisexual, and female), rather than assuming that the experience was merely the sum of the risk of being a sexual minority in addition to an ethnic minority.[52–54] Such research requires collecting data on the processes and contexts that generate unique risks and protections for individuals with LGB people of color identities. For example, a few studies found that gay and bisexual males who were an ethnic minority, especially Latino, might be at particularly elevated risk for mental health problems because of family rejection.[28,37,55]

Limitations

Our study had several limitations that should be considered. Although our analytic sample was very large, we still might

Eating Disorder Symptoms and Obesity at the Intersections of Gender, Ethnicity, and Sexual Orientation   by S. Bryn Austin, et al.

203

Table 3   Odds of Purging, Diet Pill Use, and Obesity Associated With Ethnicity and Sexual Orientation Identity in US High School Students: Youth Risk Behavioral Surveillance System Survey, 2005 and 2007

	Purging,[a] OR (95% CI)	Diet Pill Use,[a] OR (95% CI)	Obese,[b] OR (95% CI)
	Girls		
Age, y	1.02 (0.96, 1.10)	1.16* (1.07, 1.26)	0.99 (0.93, 1.05)
Ethnicity			
Asian-American	0.42* (0.27, 0.65)	0.46* (0.27, 0.79)	0.45* (0.29, 0.68)
African-American	0.59* (0.45, 0.77)	0.58* (0.43, 0.80)	2.59* (2.14, 3.14)
Latina	0.92 (0.79, 1.20)	0.89 (0.65, 1.22)	1.90* (1.51, 2.41)
Other ethnicity[c]	0.93 (0.72, 1.21)	0.94 (0.67, 1.32)	2.16* (1.73, 2.70)
White (Ref)	1.0	1.0	1.0
Sexual orientation identity			
Lesbian	3.95* (2.26, 6.89)	4.00* (2.11, 7.58)	1.50 (0.81, 2.76)
Bisexual	3.23* (2.52, 4.16)	3.06* (2.29, 4.11)	2.25* (1.75, 2.88)
Unsure	2.55* (1.77, 3.73)	1.91* (1.09, 3.35)	1.41 (0.88, 2.24)
Heterosexual (Ref)	1.0	1.0	1.0
	Boys		
Age, y	1.04 (0.97, 1.11)	1.15 (1.05, 1.27)	0.97 (0.93, 1.01)
Ethnicity			
Asian-American	0.77 (0.52, 1.14)	0.84 (0.51, 1.39)	0.66* (0.53, 0.83)
African-American	1.60* (1.26, 2.03)	1.16 (0.84, 1.61)	1.16 (0.98, 1.36)
Latino	1.28 (0.96, 1.70)	1.21 (0.84, 1.75)	1.61* (1.35, 1.91)
Other ethnicity[c]	1.54* (1.19, 2.01)	1.49* (1.06, 2.09)	1.41* (1.18, 1.68)
White (Ref)	1.0	1.0	1.0
Sexual orientation identity			
Gay	5.21* (3.47, 7.82)	4.33* (2.72, 6.91)	0.87 (0.53, 1.41)
Bisexual	6.16* (4.09, 9.26)	6.77* (4.20, 10.91)	2.10* (1.43, 3.07)
Unsure	3.76* (2.51, 5.65)	3.00* (1.71, 5.29)	1.21 (0.84, 1.74)
Heterosexual (Ref)	1.0	1.0	1.0

Note. CI = confidence interval; OR = odds ratio. Models are gender-stratified and control for age, ethnicity, sexual orientation, region, and data collection wave. The maximum sample size was n = 24 591.

[a] Purging defined as any vomiting or use of laxatives in the past month to control weight; diet pill use defined as use of diet pills to control weight without a doctor's prescription in the past month.

[b] Obese defined as body mass index of three quarters of 95th percentile for age and sex based on guidelines from the US Centers for Disease Control and Prevention.

[c] Other ethnicity group includes youths who identified as Pacific Islander, American Indian, Alaskan Native, or multiple ethnicity groups.
*P < .05.

not have had sufficient statistical power to detect sexual-orientation- by-ethnicity interactions or to detect a possible modest increased odds of obesity for lesbians compared with heterosexual peers. Generalizability of findings was limited to the jurisdictions across the country that provided data. Our findings relied on self-reported height and weight. Studies showed that although self-reported height and weight are highly correlated with measured height and weight, adolescents tend to overreport their height and underreport their weight. In particular, some studies found that males and non-Hispanic Whites were more likely to overreport height and females were more likely to underreport weight.[39,56,57] Importantly, another study of adolescents and young adults found no evidence that sexual orientation modified bias in self-reported BMI among females, although gay males were found to underreport BMI to a greater degree than were heterosexual males.[58] The YRBSS provided little information on important factors that might help to explain disparities in disordered weight-control behaviors and obesity, such as socioeconomic status, harassment and violence victimization, respondents' family and social environment, and psychological health.[8,59,60] The use of identity to classify sexual orientation hindered our ability to examine the subset of sexual minorities who had same- or both-gender attractions or sexual partners but did not identify as bisexual, gay, or lesbian. The YRBSS did not assess several important indicators of eating disorders, such as fasting and psychological symptoms; therefore, our analyses likely underestimated the prevalence of eating disorder symptoms in the population. Our dichotomous measures of any purging and diet pill use in the past 30 days did not allow us to examine symptom severity, which also might differ by sexual orientation identity and ethnicity.

Conclusions

Eating disorders and obesity are serious conditions with short- and long-term implications for comorbid disease risk, medical and psychiatric treatment costs, quality of life, and longevity.[9,42–45] In the present study, sizable disparities in disordered weight control behaviors adversely affecting all sexual minority groups of both genders were found for self-induced vomiting and abuse of laxatives and diet pills. Because of minimal regulation on the sale of laxatives and diet pills in the United States,[61] vulnerable and marginalized youths, such as sexual minorities and others, have largely unfettered access to purchase these products, which are then too often abused in dangerous attempts to control weight. As done with regard to other abused substances, such as alcohol and tobacco, public health professionals and policymakers need to step up efforts to protect minors from industries that currently profit from the abuse of their products by vulnerable youths.[61] The findings of the present study also highlighted the serious issue of obesity in female and male bisexual youths. Obesity in adolescence is strongly associated with a myriad immediate- and long-term adverse consequences.[6,7] Health and other professionals working with sexual minority youths need to establish mechanisms to screen for symptoms of eating disorders so that affected youths can be referred for treatment and need to develop programs to promote healthful weight-control behaviors in sexual minorities of all ethnicities and in both girls and boys. In addition, interventions that are appropriate for sexual orientation minority youths of diverse ethnicities are urgently needed to eliminate stressors and other factors contributing to these disparities.

References

1. Ogden CL, Carroll MD, Kit BK, Flegal KM. Prevalence of obesity and trends in body mass index among US children and adolescents, 1999–2010. *JAMA*. 2012;307 (5):483–490.
2. Freedman DS, Zuguo M, Srinivasan SR, Berenson GS, Dietz WH. Cardiovascular risk factors and excess adiposity among overweight children and adolescents: the Bogalusa Heart Study. *J Pediatr*. 2007;150(1):12–17.
3. Li C, Ford ES, Zhao G, Mokdad AH. Prevalence of pre-diabetes and its association with clustering of cardiometabolic risk factors and hyperinsulinemia among US adolescents: NHANES 2005–2006. *Diabetes Care*. 2009;32(2):342–347.
4. Daniels SR, Arnett DK, Eckel RH, et al. Overweight in children and adolescents: pathophysiology, consequences, prevention, and treatment. *Circulation*. 2005; 111(15):1999–2012.
5. Dietz WH. Overweight in childhood and adolescence. *N Engl J Med*. 2004;350(9):855–857.
6. Whitaker RC, Wright JA, Pepe MS, et al. Predicting obesity in young adulthood from childhood and parental obesity. *N Engl J Med*. 1997;337(13):869–873.
7. Office of the Surgeon General. *The Surgeon General's Vision for a Healthy and Fit Nation*. Rockville, MD: U.S. Department of Health and Human Services; 2010.
8. Croll J, Neumark-Sztainer D, Story M, Ireland M. Prevalence and risk and protective factors related to disordered eating behaviors among adolescents: relationship to gender and ethnicity. *J Adolesc Health*. 2002;31(2):166–175.
9. Crow S. Medical complications of eating disorders. In: Wonderlich S, Mitchell J, de Zwaan M, Steiger H, eds *Eating Disorders Review, Part 1*. Abingdon, UK: Radcliffe Publishing Ltd.; 2005:127–136.
10. Haines J, Kleinman KP, Rifas-Shiman S, Field AE, Austin SB. Examination of shared risk and protective factors for weight-related disorders in adolescents. *Arch Pediatr Adolesc Med*. 2010;164(4):336–343.
11. Neumark-Sztainer DR, Wall MM, Haines JI, Story MT, Sherwood NE, van den Berg PA. Shared risk and protective factors for overweight and disordered eating in adolescents. *Am J Prev Med*. 2007;33(5):359–369.
12. Goldschmidt AB, Aspen VP, Sinton MM, Tanofsky-Kraff M, Wilfley DE. Disordered eating attitudes and behaviors in overweight youth. *Obesity (Silver Spring)*. 2008;16(2):257–264.
13. Scharoun-Lee M, Kaufman JS, Popkin BM, Gordon-Larsen P. Obesity, race/ethnicity and life course socioeconomic status across the transition from adolescence to adulthood. *J Epidemiol Community Health*. 2009;63(2):133–139.
14. Yates A, Edman J, Aruguete M. Ethnic differences in BMI and body/self-dissatisfaction among Whites, Asian subgroups, Pacific Islanders, and African-Americans. *J Adolesc Health*. 2004;34(4):300–307.
15. Austin SB, Spadano-Gasbarro J, Greaney ML, et al. Disordered weight control behaviors in early adolescent boys and girls of color: an under-recognized factor in the epidemic of childhood overweight. *J Adolesc Health*. 2011;48(1):109–112.
16. Johnson WG, Rohan KJ, Kirk AA. Prevalence and correlates of binge eating in white and African American adolescents. *Eat Behav*. 2002;3(2):179–189.
17. Neumark-Sztainer D, Croll J, Story M, Hannan PJ, French SA, Perry C. Ethnic/racial differences in weight-related concerns and behaviors among adolescent girls and boys: findings from Project EAT. *J Psychosom Res*. 2002;53(5):963–974.
18. Austin SB, Ziyadeh NJ, Corliss HL, et al. Sexual orientation disparities in weight status in adolescence: findings from a prospective study. *Obesity (Silver Spring)*. 2009;17(9):1776–1782.
19. Austin SB, Ziyadeh NJ, Corliss HL, et al. Sexual orientation disparities in purging and binge eating from early to late adolescence. *J Adolesc Health*. 2009;45(3): 238–245.
20. Austin SB, Ziyadeh N, Kahn JA, Camargo CA Jr, Colditz GA, Field AE. Sexual orientation, weight concerns, and eating-disordered behaviors in adolescent girls and boys. *J Am Acad Child Adolesc Psychiatry*. 2004;43(9):1115–1123.
21. French SA, Story M, Remafedi G, Resnick MD, Blum RW. Sexual orientation and prevalence of body dissatisfaction and eating disordered behaviors: a population-based study of adolescents. *Int J Eat Disord*. 1996;19(2):119–126.
22. Wichstrøm L. Sexual orientation as a risk factor for bulimic symptoms. *Int J Eat Disord*. 2006;39(6):448–453.
23. Darcy AM, Doyle AC, Lock J, Peebles R, Doyle P, Le Grange D. The eating disorders examination in adolescent males with

Eating Disorder Symptoms and Obesity at the Intersections of Gender, Ethnicity, and Sexual Orientation by S. Bryn Austin, et al.

205

anorexia nervosa: how does it compare to adolescent females? *Int J Eat Disord.* 2012;45(1):110–114.

24. Dominé F, Berchtold A, Akré C, Michaud PA, Suris JC. Disordered eating behaviors: what about boys? *J Adolesc Health.* 2009;44(2):111–117.

25. Farrow JA. The adolescent male with an eating disorder. *Pediatr Ann.* 1992;21(11):769–774.

26. Saewyc EM, Bearinger LH, Heinz PA, Blum RW, Resnick MD. Gender differences in health and risk behaviors among bisexual and homosexual adolescents. *J Adolesc Health.* 1998;23(3):181–188.

27. Meyer IH. Prejudice, social stress, and mental health in lesbian, gay, and bisexual populations: conceptual issues and research evidence. *Psychol Bull.* 2003;129 (5):674–697.

28. Balsam KF, Molina Y, Beadnell B, Simoni J, Walters K. Measuring multiple minority stress: the LGBT People of Color Microaggressions Scale. *Cultur Divers Ethnic Minor Psychol.* 2011;17(2):163–174.

29. Consolacion TB, Russell ST, Sue S. Sex, race/ethnicity, and romantic attractions: multiple minority status adolescents and mental health. *Cultur Divers Ethnic Minor Psychol.* 2004;10(3):200–214.

30. Kim H-J, Fredriksen-Goldsen KI. Hispanic lesbians and bisexual women at heightened risk of health disparities. *Am J Public Health.* 2012;102(1):e9–e15.

31. Cochran SD, Mays VM, Ortega AN, Alegria M, Takeuchi D. Mental health and substance use disorders among Latino and Asian American lesbian, gay, and bisexual adults. *J Consult Clin Psychol.* 2007;75(5):785–794.

32. Mays VM, Yancey AK, Cochran SD, Weber M, Fielding JE. Heterogeneity of health disparities among African American, Hispanic, and Asian American women: unrecognized influences of sexual orientation. *Am J Public Health.* 2002;92(4):632–639.

33. O'Donnell S, Meyer IH, Schwartz S. Increased risk of suicide attempts among Black and Latino lesbians, gay men, and bisexuals. *Am J Public Health.* 2011;101 (6):1055–1059.

34. Yancey AK, Cochran SD, Corliss HL, Mays VM. Correlates of overweight and obesity among lesbian and bisexual women. *Prev Med.* 2003;36(6):676–683.

35. Kertzner RM, Meyer IH, Frost DM, Stirratt MJ. Social and psychological well-being in lesbians, gay men, and bisexuals: the effects of race, gender, age, and sexual identity. *Am J Orthopsychiatry.* 2009;79(4):500–510.

36. Mustanski BS, Garofalo R, Emerson EM. Mental health disorders, psychological distress, and suicidality in a diverse sample of lesbian, gay, bisexual, and transgender youths. *Am J Public Health.* 2010;100(12):2426–2432.

37. Ryan C, Huebner D, Diaz RM, Sanchez J. Family rejection as a predictor of negative health outcomes in white and Latino lesbian, gay, and bisexual young adults. *Pediatrics.* 2009;123(1):346–352.

38. Mustanski B, Van Wagenen A, Birkett M, Eyster S, Corliss H. Identifying sexual orientation health disparities in adolescents:methodological approach for analysis of a pooled YRBS dataset. *Am J Public Health.* 2012.

39. Brener ND, Mcmanus T, Galuska DA, Lowry R, Wechsler H. Reliability and validity of self-reported height and weight among high school students. *J Adolesc Health.* 2003;32(4):281–287.

40. Centers for Disease Control and Prevention. Growth charts. Available at: www.cdc.gov/growthcharts. Accessed on December 3, 2012.

41. Sherry B, Jefferds ME, Grummer-Strawn LM. Accuracy of adolescent self-report of height and weight in assessing overweight status: a literature review. *Arch Pediatr Adolesc Med.* 2007;161(12):1154–1161.

42. Crow S, Peterson CB. The economic and social burden of eating disorders: a review. In: Maj M, Halmi K, Lopez-Ibor JJ, Sartorius N, eds *Eating Disorders.* Hoboken, NJ: John Wiley & Sons, Ltd; 2003:383–396.

43. Franko DL, Keel PK. Suicidality in eating disorders: occurrence, correlates, and clinical implications. *Clin Psychol Rev.* 2006;26(6):769–782.

44. Jia H, Lubetkin EI. The impact of obesity on health-related quality-of-life in the general adult U.S. population. *J Public Health.* 2005;27(2):156–164.

45. Mokdad AH, Ford ES, Bowman BA, et al. Prevalence of obesity, diabetes, and obesity-related health risk factors, 2001. *JAMA.* 2003;289(1):76–79.

46. Ackard DM, Fedio G, Neumark-Sztainer D, Britt HR. Factors associated with disordered eating among sexually active adolescent males: gender and number of sexual partners. *Psychosom Med.* 2008;70(2):232–238.

47. Massachusetts Department of Education. *1999 Youth Risk Behavior Survey.* Malden, MA: Massachusetts Department of Education; 2000.

48. Chao YM, Pisetsky EM, Dierker LC, et al. Ethnic differences in weight control practices among U.S. adolescents from 1995 to 2005. *Int J Eat Disord.* 2008;41(2):124–133.

49. Field AE, Colditz GA, Peterson KE. Racial/ethnic and gender differences in concern with weight and in bulimic behaviors among adolescents. *Obes Res.* 1997;5 (5):447–454.

50. Nicdao EG, Hong S, Takeuchi DT. Prevalence and correlates of eating disorders among Asian Americans: results from the National Latino and Asian American Study. *Int J Eat Disord.* 2007;40(suppl):S22–S26.

51. Shabbir S, Swan D, Wang MC, Shih M, Simon PA. Asians and Pacific Islanders and the growing childhood obesity epidemic. *Ethn Dis.* 2010;20(2):129–135.

52. Bowleg L. When black + lesbian + woman ≠ black lesbian woman: the methodological challenges of qualitative and quantitative intersectionality research. *Sex Roles.* 2008;59(5–6):312–325.

53. Collins PH. It's all in the family: intersections of gender, race, and nation. *Hypatia.* 1998;13(3):62–82.

54. Weber L, Parra-Medina D. Intersectionality and women's health: charting a path to eliminating health disparities. *Advances Gend Res.* 2003;7:181–230.

55. Díaz RM, Ayala G, Bein E, Henne J, Marin BV. The impact of homophobia, poverty, and racism on the mental health of gay and bisexual Latino men: findings from 3 US cities. *Am J Public Health.* 2001;91(6): 927–932.

56. Elgar FJ, Roberts C, Tudor-Smith C, Moore L. Validity of self-reported height and weight and predictors of bias in adolescents. *J Adolesc Health.* 2005;37(5): 371–375.

57. Himes JH, Hannan P, Wall M, Newmark-Sztainer D. Factors associated with errors in self-reports of stature, weight, and body mass index in Minnesota adolescents. *Ann Epidemiol.* 2005;15(4):272–278.

58. Richmond TK, Walls CE, Austin SB. Sexual orientation and bias in self-reported body mass index. *Obesity (Silver Spring).* 2012;20(8):1703–1709.

59. Gordon-Larsen P, Nelson M, Page P, Popkin BM. Inequality in the built environment underlies key health disparities in physical activity and obesity. *Pediatrics.* 2006;117(2):417–424.

60. Swanson SA, Crow SJ, Le Grange D, Swendsen J, Merikangas KR. Prevalence and correlates of eating disorders in adolescents. *Arch Gen Psychiatry.* 2011;68 (7):714–723.

61. Pomeranz JL, Taylor L, Austin SB. Over-the-counter and out-of-control: legal strategies to protect youth from abusing products for weight control. *Am J Public Health.* 2012 (Epub ahead of print).

Critical Thinking

1. Explain why this information is important to educational professionals?

2. Design two interventions that could be implemented in a school setting to alleviate or eliminate eating disorders or obesity for sexually minority students.

Create Central

www.mhhe.com/createcentral

Internet References

Safe Schools
www.safeschoolscoalition.org/
LGTB Youth Organizations
http://brandonshire.com/lgbt-youth-organizations/

S. BRYN AUSTIN and **JEREL P. CABO** are with the Division of Adolescent and Young Adult Medicine at Boston Children's Hospital, Boston, MA, and the Department of Pediatrics of Harvard Medical School, BOSTON. **S. BRYN AUSTIN** is also with the Department of Society, Human Development, and Health, Harvard School of Public Health, Boston. Lauren A. Nelson is with Department of Pediatrics, University of California San Francisco Medical Center, San Francisco, Michelle A. Birkett is with Department of Medical Social Sciences, Northwestern University, Chicago, IL. Bethany Everett is with Department of Sociology, University of Illinois at Chicago.

Correspondence should be sent to **S. BRYN AUSTIN**, ScD, Division of Adolescent and Young Adult Medicine, Boston Children's Hospital, 300 Longwood Ave., Boston, MA 02115 (e-mail: bryn.austin@childrens .harvard.edu). Reprints can be ordered at www.ajph.org by clicking the "Reprints" link. This article was accepted November 8, 2012.

Contributors—S. B. Austin was responsible for study conceptualization, data analysis and interpretation, and article preparation. M. A. Birkett was responsible for data analysis and interpretation, and article preparation. L. A. Nelson, J. P. Calzo, and B. Everett were responsible for data interpretation and article preparation.

Acknowledgments—This project was supported by the Eunice Kennedy Shriver National Institute of Child Health and Human Development (Award Number R21HD051178) and by the IMPACT LGBT Health and Development Program at Northwestern University. Assistance from the Centers for Disease Control and Prevention (CDC) Division of Adolescent and School Health and the work of the state and local health and education departments who conduct the Youth Risk Behavior Surveys made the project possible. S. B. Austin is supported by the Leadership Education in Adolescent Health project, Maternal and Child Health Bureau (HRSA grant 6T71-MC00009). J. P. Calzo is supported by National Research Service Award F32HD066792, and B. Everett is supported by grant R03 HD062597, both from the Eunice Kennedy Shriver National Institute of Child Health and Human Development.

The authors would like to thank Annabel Chang for her help with preparing the article, and the thousands of students and school staff across the country who made this study possible.

Note—The content is solely the responsibility of the authors and does not necessarily represent the official views of the National Institutes of Health, the CDC, or any agencies involved in collecting the data.

Human Participant Protection—Protocol approval was not necessary because de-identified data were obtained from secondary sources. Data use agreements were obtained from Vermont Department of Health and the Rhode Island Department of Health, which were the only 2 state departments of health that required these agreements for access to Youth Risk Behavior Surveillance System data.

Protective School Climates and Reduced Risk for Suicide Ideation in Sexual Minority Youths by Mark L. Hatzenbuehler, et al.

207

Article

Prepared by: Rebecca B. Evers, *Winthrop University*

Protective School Climates and Reduced Risk for Suicide Ideation in Sexual Minority Youths

MARK L. HATZENBUEHLER ET AL.

Objectives. We examined whether sexual minority students living in states and cities with more protective school climates were at lower risk of suicidal thoughts, plans, and attempts.

Methods. Data on sexual orientation and past-year suicidal thoughts, plans, and attempts were from the pooled 2005 and 2007 Youth Risk Behavior Surveillance Surveys from 8 states and cities. We derived data on school climates that protected sexual minority students (e.g., percentage of schools with safe spaces and Gay–Straight Alliances) from the 2010 School Health Profile Survey, compiled by the Centers for Disease Control and Prevention.

Results. Lesbian, gay, and bisexual students living in states and cities with more protective school climates reported fewer past-year suicidal thoughts than those living in states and cities with less protective climates (lesbians and gays: odds ratio [OR] = 0.68; 95% confidence interval [CI] = 0.47, 0.99; bisexuals: OR = 0.81; 95% CI = 0.66, 0.99). Results were robust to adjustment for potential state-level confounders. Sexual orientation disparities in suicidal thoughts were nearly eliminated in states and cities with the most protective school climates.

Conclusions. School climates that protect sexual minority students may reduce their risk of suicidal thoughts. (*Am J Public Health.* 2014;104:279–286. doi:10.2105/AJPH.2013.301508)

Learning Outcomes

After reading this article, you will be able to:

- Explain the link between school climates and suicide risk levels for sexual minority students.

- Describe what constitutes a supportive school climate for LGBTQ youth.

- Explore possible barriers to creating protective school climates.

Suicide is the third leading cause of death among youths aged 15 to 24 years.[1] Decades of research have identified multiple risk factors for adolescent suicide ideation and attempts.[2] One of the most consistent findings is that lesbian, gay, and bisexual (LGB, or sexual minority) adolescents are more likely than heterosexual adolescents to endorse suicidal thoughts[3,4] and to report having a suicide plan.[5] Additionally, a recent review of the epidemiological literature found that LGB youths are between 2 and 7 times more likely to attempt suicide than their heterosexual peers.[6]

Given the elevated risk of suicidal ideation, plans, and attempts among sexual minority youths, researchers have focused on identifying factors that explain these marked disparities. Theories of minority stress[7] and stigma[8] have highlighted the important roles that social-structural contexts as well as institutional practices and policies play in contributing to mental health disparities. Consistent with these theories, LGB adults who live in states with fewer protective social policies have higher rates of psychiatric and substance use disorders than

LGB adults living in states with more protective policies.[9,10] For instance, LGB adults in states that passed constitutional amendments banning same-sex marriage experienced a 37% increase in mood disorders, a 40% increase in alcohol use disorders, and nearly a 250% increase in generalized anxiety disorders in the year following the enactment of the amendments.[10] These and other studies[11] have shown that the broader social contexts surrounding LGB adults shape their mental health.

Among adolescents, schools are an important social context that contributes to developmental and health outcomes.[12] For sexual and gender minority youths in particular, the social context of schools can promote both vulnerability and resilience.[13–16] A variety of methodological approaches have been used to evaluate the mental health consequences of school climates for LGB students. The predominant approach is to ask LGB adolescents to report on the supportiveness of their schools.[17–19] Studies using this approach have indicated that LGB youths who report greater school connectedness and school safety also report lower suicidal ideation and fewer suicide attempts.[18] Although informative, this research may introduce bias because information is self-reported for both the exposure and the outcome.[20] Studies using alternative methodologies may therefore improve the validity of the inferences on the relationship between the social environment and individual health outcomes.

An alternative methodological approach has been to develop indicators of school climate that do not rely on self-report, such as geographic location of the school (i.e., urban vs rural)[21] and the presence of Gay—Straight Alliances in the school.[22] Although this approach has received comparatively less attention in the literature, recent studies have documented associations between these more objective measures of school climate and sexual minority mental health. For example, lesbian and gay adolescents are at lower risk for attempting suicide if they live in counties where a greater proportion of school districts have antibullying policies that include sexual orientation.[23] Although they provide important initial insights, existing studies have been limited by examining only 1 aspect of school climate (e.g., antibullying policies or presence of Gay—Straight Alliances),[16,22,23] relying on nonprobability samples,[16,22] and using a single location,[16,22,23] all of which can restrict generalizability.

We built on this previous research by using data on multiple school climate variables relevant to LGB students that we obtained from the 2010 School Health Profile Survey, compiled by the Centers for Disease Control and Prevention (CDC).[24] We then linked this information on school climate to population-based data of adolescents living in 8 states and cities across the United States. We hypothesized that LGB adolescents living in states and cities with school climates that are more protective of sexual minority youths would be less likely to report past-year suicidal thoughts, plans, and attempts than LGB youths living in areas with less protective school climates.

Methods

The study analyzed a data set that pooled 2005 and 2007 Youth Risk Behavior Surveillance Surveys (YRBSs) from several jurisdictions that included 1 or more measures of sexual orientation. The general approach to pooling the data and analyzing the pooled data set, along with the sexual orientation items and characteristics of the sample by jurisdiction, are described in detail elsewhere in this issue.[25] The current study analyzed data from the 9 jurisdictions that measured sexual orientation identity (i.e., as heterosexual, lesbian or gay, bisexual, or unsure), including Boston, Massachusetts; Chicago, Illinois; Delaware; Maine; Massachusetts; New York City, New York; San Francisco, California; Vermont; and Rhode Island. Because Boston did not have data on the school climate measures (see "Measures"), we dropped it from the analyses. Consequently, we analyzed data from 8 states and cities. Table 1 presents the

Table 1 Sexual Orientation by 8 US Jurisdictions: Youth Risk Behavior Surveillance Surveys, United States, 2005 and 2007

Jurisdiction	Heterosexual, No. (%)	Lesbian or Gay, No. (%)	Bisexual, No. (%)	Unsure, No. (%)
Chicago, IL	1697 (90.9)	45 (2.3)	66 (3.6)	57 (3.3)
Delaware	4890 (94.2)	56 (1.1)	189 (3.4)	67 (1.3)
Maine	1241 (94.5)	11 (0.8)	36 (3.0)	32 (1.7)
Massachusetts	6095 (93.8)	89 (1.3)	225 (3.2)	117 (1.7)
New York City, NY	15117 (92.0)	222 (1.1)	648 (3.7)	459 (3.1)
Rhode Island	1954 (90.1)	47 (1.9)	123 (5.4)	55 (2.7)
San Francisco, CA	4357 (89.9)	80 (1.5)	176 (3.7)	229 (4.9)
Vermont	16293 (93.3)	185 (0.9)	584 (3.1)	516 (2.7)
Total	51644 (92.8)	735 (1.3)	2047 (3.5)	1532 (2.4)

number of respondents by sexual orientation and by the 8 jurisdictions used in the analyses. We focused on sexual orientation identity given that school climates and policies are likely to be most salient to youths who self-identify as LGB.

Measures

Measures for demographic characteristics (gender, age, race/ethnicity) and sexual orientation were assessed via self-report. The measurement and pooling of sexual orientation and race/ethnicity items are described elsewhere in this issue.[25] We excluded from the analysis those who did not respond to the sexual orientation items. The final sample size was 55599.

School Climate

We obtained data on school climate from the 2010 School Health Profile (SHP) survey, which is compiled biennially by the CDC. The SHP survey employs probability sampling to create a representative sample of public schools serving students in grades 6 through 12. Of the 8 items used in the current study, 7 were completed by the principal of the school; 1 item was completed by the lead health education teacher. Participation in the survey was voluntary and confidential. Across the 5 states and 3 cities in our pooled sample that were participating in the 2010 SHP, the sample sizes of the

principal surveys ranged from 33 to 613, and the response rates ranged from 71% to 86%. Sample sizes and response rates were similar for the lead health education teacher surveys. Further information on the SHP survey is provided elsewhere.[24]

We chose the 8 items from the SHP that assess multiple dimensions of schools that are particularly relevant for LGB students, including the presence of protective environments (e.g., Gay—Straight Alliances and safe spaces) as well as curricula and services that address the unique concerns of sexual minority youths. (Table 2). Importantly, significant variation exists across these 8 jurisdictions. For instance, the lowest percentage of schools that provided curricula or supplementary materials concerning lesbian, gay, bisexual, transgender, and questioning (LGBTQ) students was 31.6%, whereas the highest was 83.7%.

We conducted a factor analysis on the 8 items, using principal axis factoring. A single factor emerged, explaining 81.7% of the variance. Factor loadings ranged from 0.69 to 0.99, and the Cronbach α for the 8 items was 0.97, providing support for a single underlying factor. To create a total score, we standardized each of the 8 items and then averaged and summed them. Scores ranged from -1.059 (Delaware) to 2.015 (San Francisco). A score of 0 indicates an average school climate across the 8 localities. Negative scores indicate a less-than-average school

Table 2   School Climates in 8 US Jurisdictions Affecting Sexual Minority Youths: 2010 School Health Profile Survey

Variable	%, Range (Mean)
Percentage of schools that had a Gay–Straight Alliance or similar club	27.8–90.8 (45.3)
Percentage of schools that provided curricula or supplementary materials that included HIV, STD, or pregnancy prevention information relevant to LGBTQ youths	31.6–83.7 (45.3)
Percentage of schools that identified safe spaces where LGBTQ youths could receive support from staff	39.8–100 (66.24)
Percentage of schools that prohibited harassment based on a student's perceived or actual sexual orientation or gender identity	75.1–100 (89.8)
Percentage of schools that encouraged staff to attend professional development on safe and supportive school environments for all students regardless of sexual orientation or gender identity	48.1–100 (73.29)
Percentage of schools that facilitated access to providers not on school property who had experience in providing health services to LGBTQ youths	44.8–100 (62.4)
Percentage of schools that facilitated access to providers not on school property who had experience in providing social and psychological services to LGBTQ youths	40.8–100 (62.4)
Percentage of schools that provided curricula or supplementary materials that included HIV, STD, or pregnancy prevention information relevant to LGBTQ youths and engaged in all 5 practices regarding LGBTQ youths[a]	8.7–81.6 (25.2)

Note. LGBTQ = lesbian, gay, bisexual, transgender, and questioning; STD = sexually transmitted disease. The 8 study jurisdictions were Chicago, IL; Delaware; Maine; Massachusetts; New York City, NY; San Francisco, CA; Vermont; and Rhode Island.
[a]These 5 practices refer to the responses from the third through seventh items listed in this column.

climate—the lower the score, the worse the school environment for LGBTQ youths; conversely, positive scores indicate a better-than-average school environment—the larger the score, the better the school environment for LGBTQ youths. Collectively, more supportive school climates are those that

1. have a Gay—Straight Alliance and safe spaces for LGBTQ youths,
2. provide curricula on health matters relevant to LGBTQ youths (e.g., HIV),
3. prohibit harassment based on sexual orientation or gender identity,
4. encourage staff to attend trainings on creating supportive environments for LGBTQ youths, and
5. facilitate access to providers off school property that provide health and other services specifically targeted to LGBTQ youths.

Suicide Outcomes

Participants were asked the following question regarding suicidal thoughts: "During the past 12 months, did you ever seriously consider attempting suicide?" Suicide plans were assessed by asking respondents, "During the past 12 months, did you make a plan about how you would attempt suicide?" Response options for suicide thoughts and plans were dichotomous (yes or no). Suicide attempts were assessed via 1 item: "During the past 12 months, how many times did you actually attempt suicide?" Given the nonnormal distribution of this variable, we coded the responses dichotomously. The suicidal thought ($\kappa = 83.8$), plan ($\kappa = 77.0$), and attempt ($\kappa = 76.4$) variables have demonstrated excellent test–retest reliability.[26] Table 3 depicts the prevalence of suicide outcomes by sexual orientation group.

Table 3 Prevalence of Suicide Outcomes by Sexual Orientation Group and Other Demographic Variables: Youth Risk Behavior Surveillance Surveys, United States, 2005 and 2007

Variable	Suicide Thoughts, % (95% CI)	Suicide Plan, % (95% CI)	Suicide Attempt, % (95% CI)
Total sample	13.2 (12.7, 13.6)	11.2 (10.9, 11.6)	7.8 (7.4, 8.2)
Sexual orientation			
Heterosexual	11.6 (11.2, 12.0)	9.9 (9.5, 10.2)	6.5 (6.1, 6.9)
Lesbian or gay	29.7 (25.1, 34.8)	26.6 (22.7, 30.9)	24.7 (20.4, 29.4)
Bisexual	39.6 (36.8, 42.5)	32.2 (29.5, 34.9)	28.8 (26.1, 31.6)
Not sure	25.3 (22.2, 28.6)	22.2 (19.0, 25.7)	17.3 (14.7, 20.2)
Race/ethnicity			
White	12.3 (11.5, 13.2)	10.2 (9.7, 10.8)	5.4 (5.0, 5.9)
African American	11.7 (11.0, 12.5)	10.8 (10.0, 11.6)	8.0 (7.3, 8.9)
Hispanic	13.2 (12.2, 14.2)	10.9 (10.1, 11.8)	9.9 (9.0, 10.8)
Asian	13.0 (11.8, 14.3)	11.5 (10.2, 12.9)	6.7 (5.6, 8.0)
Other	17.0 (15.9, 18.0)	14.6 (13.6, 15.6)	11.3 (10.3, 12.4)
Gender			
Male	9.2 (8.7, 9.7)	8.6 (8.2, 9.1)	5.8 (5.3, 6.3)
Female	16.8 (16.1, 17.5)	13.5 (13.0, 14.2)	9.5 (8.9, 10.1)
Age, y			
13	20.4 (12.3, 31.8)	10.0 (8.2, 12.1)	6.8 (5.4, 8.5)
14	14.4 (13.1, 15.8)	12.0 (11.0, 12.9)	8.6 (7.7, 9.7)
15	14.1 (13.3, 14.9)	11.6 (10.8, 12.3)	8.5 (7.7, 9.4)
16	12.9 (12.1, 13.8)	11.4 (10.7, 12.2)	7.3 (6.7, 8.0)
17	11.8 (11.0, 12.7)	10.2 (9.5, 11.0)	6.6 (5.9, 7.4)
18	13.2 (12.0, 14.5)	11.1 (10.0, 12.3)	8.7 (7.7, 9.7)

Note. CI = confidence interval. Numbers are unweighted.

Protective School Climates and Reduced Risk for Suicide Ideation in Sexual Minority Youths by Mark L. Hatzenbuehler, et al.

211

Covariates

To minimize spurious contextual influences on our results, we controlled for 2 covariates: (1) density of same-sex couples (per 1000) living in the cities or states (mean = 9.55; SD = 6.54; range = 4.03–30.25); and (2) median household income (mean = \$61 604.03; SD = \$11 737.11; range = \$45 775.00–\$90 931.41). We obtained data for both covariates from the 2010 US Census. Preliminary analyses indicated that these 2 variables were strongly associated with the school climate variable (for density of same-sex couples, $r = 0.75$; $P < .01$; for median household income, $r = 0.50$; $P = .06$), indicating the importance of their inclusion as potential confounders of the relationship between school climate and suicide outcomes.

Statistical Analysis

We conducted descriptive analyses for creating the school climate variable using SPSS versions 20 and 21 (SPSS Inc, Chicago, IL). Furthermore, we used the SPSS (version 21) Complex Samples software package to conduct descriptive analyses on prevalence of sexual orientation and suicide outcomes (Tables 1 and 3) to account for the complex sample design of the YRBS. We fit models examining the relationship between school climate and suicide outcomes using the multilevel software HLM version 7 (Scientific Software International, Lincolnwood, IL). Hierarchical linear modeling accounted for the complex sampling design of the pooled YRBS data set by adjusting the relative weights and altering the effective sample size using design effects calculated for each jurisdiction. The approach to calculating design effects and accounting for the clustering of the data are described in detail elsewhere in this issue.[25]

Hierarchical linear modeling analyses proceeded in several steps. First, we examined an unconditional model to determine whether there were significant between-group (i.e., between-jurisdiction) differences in the suicide outcomes. Second, we added level 1 covariates, including sexual orientation (dummy coded gay or lesbian, bisexual, and not sure, with heterosexual as the reference group), gender (male or female), race/ethnicity (dummy coded African American, Hispanic, Asian, and other, with White as the reference group), and age (continuous). Third, we added level 2 variables, including school climate and the 2 covariates (density of same-sex couples and median household income). In the final model, we allowed the slopes for sexual orientation to vary (i.e., we treated them as a random effect), and we included school climate as a predictor of the variance of the sexual orientation slopes. This approach, similar to testing a cross-level interaction between school climate and sexual orientation, permitted an evaluation of the primary research question: does school climate modify the relationship between sexual orientation and suicidal thoughts, plans, and attempts? We ran analyses separately for the 3 suicide outcomes (thoughts, plans, and attempts).

Given the small amount of missing data on covariates (age: 0.5%; gender: 0.8%; race: 2.6%), we handled missing data for covariates using listwise deletion. Nonrandom missing data were also present for suicidal thoughts, as Vermont did not include that survey item. We therefore excluded Vermont from the suicidal thoughts analysis but included it for the analysis of suicidal plans and attempts. Statistical significance was set at $P < .05$.

Results

In the unconditional model, the variance components (VCs) indicated that there was significant variation across states and cities in suicidal thoughts (VC = 0.02; $\chi^2 = 133.17$; $P < .001$), plans (VC = 0.03; $\chi^2 = 177.81$; $P < .001$), and attempts (VC = 0.07; $\chi^2 = 266.15$; $P < .001$), supporting the inclusion of additional variables to explain between-group variance in these outcomes.

Suicidal Thoughts

In the first model, we added all level 1 sociodemographic covariates to the unconditional model (Table 4). Compared with their heterosexual peers, lesbian and gay youths (odds ratio [OR] = 3.28; 95% confidence interval [CI] = 2.40, 4.47), bisexual youths (OR = 4.52; 95% CI = 3.79, 5.40), and youths who were unsure of their sexual orientation (OR = 2.08; 95% CI = 1.62, 2.65) were significantly more likely to report suicidal thoughts in the past year. Male gender was significantly associated with reduced odds of reporting suicidal thoughts (OR = 0.54; 95% CI = 0.49, 0.60), whereas "other" race/ethnicity was significantly associated with increased odds of suicidal thoughts (OR = 1.23; 95% CI = 1.01, 1.42).

In the second model, we entered the level 2 variables (school climate, density of same-sex couples, and median household income) as predictors of suicidal thoughts. When we controlled for level 1 variables, none of the level 2 variables were associated with the intercept for suicidal thoughts (i.e., the average student in the sample).

In the third and final model, we examined cross-level interactions between the slopes of sexual orientation and school climate. This model indicated that lesbian and gay youths (OR = 0.68; 95% CI = 0.47, 0.99) and bisexual youths (OR = 0.81; 95% CI = 0.66, 0.99) living in jurisdictions with more protective school climates were significantly less likely to report suicidal thoughts than lesbian and gay adolescents living in jurisdictions with less supportive school climates, with control for sociodemographics and the level 2 covariates. Results were not statistically significant for the unsure group (OR = 0.83; 95% CI = 0.64, 1.09).

Figure 1 depicts the results for suicidal ideation, showing an incremental reduction in the odds of reporting suicidal thoughts

Table 4 Associations Between School Climate and Suicidality: Youth Risk Behavior Surveillance Surveys, United States, 2005 and 2007

Variable	Suicidal Thoughts, OR (95% CI)			Suicide Plan, OR (95% CI)			Suicide Attempt, OR (95% CI)		
	Model 1	Model 2	Model 3	Model 1	Model 2	Model 3	Model 1	Model 2	Model 3
Intercept	0.17 (0.15, 0.19)	0.17 (0.14, 0.19)	0.16 (0.14, 0.19)	0.13 (0.11, 0.15)	0.13 (0.11, 0.14)	0.13 (0.11, 0.14)	0.06 (0.05, 0.07)	0.06 (0.05, 0.07)	0.06 (0.05, 0.07)
Sexual orientation				**Level 1 covariates**					
Heterosexual (Ref)	1.00	1.00	1.00	1.00	1.00	1.00	1.00	1.00	1.00
Lesbian or gay	3.28 (2.40, 4.47)	3.27 (2.39, 4.46)	3.50 (2.31, 5.30)	2.98 (2.20, 4.03)	2.97 (2.20, 4.03)	3.13 (2.13, 4.60)	3.87 (2.67, 5.63)	3.88 (2.67, 5.65)	4.12 (2.50, 6.80)
Bisexual	4.52 (3.79, 5.40)	4.52 (3.78, 5.39)	4.77 (3.77, 6.04)	4.37 (3.69, 5.16)	4.36 (3.69, 5.15)	4.46 (3.58, 5.55)	5.72 (4.72, 6.94)	5.71 (4.71, 6.93)	6.07 (4.64, 7.95)
Not sure	2.08 (1.62, 2.65)	2.07 (1.62, 2.65)	2.35 (1.64, 3.35)	2.10 (1.67, 2.65)	2.09 (1.66, 2.64)	2.32 (1.69, 3.19)	2.44 (1.82, 3.27)	2.43 (1.82, 3.26)	2.66 (1.78, 3.99)
Race/ethnicity									
White (Ref)	1.00	1.00	1.00	1.00	1.00	1.00	1.00	1.00	1.00
African American	0.89 (0.78, 1.02)	0.89 (0.77, 1.02)	0.89 (0.77, 1.02)	0.93 (0.89, 1.07)	0.93 (0.81, 1.08)	0.93 (0.80, 1.08)	1.45 (1.21, 1.73)	1.39 (1.16, 1.67)	1.42 (1.8, 1.70)
Hispanic	1.01 (0.87, 1.17)	1.01 (0.87, 1.17)	1.00 (0.86, 1.16)	1.01 (0.87, 1.19)	1.01 (0.87, 1.18)	1.01 (0.86, 1.18)	1.78 (1.48, 2.13)	1.70 (1.41, 2.05)	1.71 (1.42, 2.07)
Asian	1.04 (0.90, 1.22)	1.03 (0.87, 1.22)	1.03 (0.87, 1.22)	1.11 (0.95, 1.31)	1.09 (0.92, 1.29)	1.08 (0.91, 1.28)	1.24 (1.02, 1.52)	1.18 (0.94, 1.49)	1.19 (0.94, 1.50)
Other	1.23 (1.01, 1.42)	1.22 (1.06, 1.41)	1.22 (1.05, 1.41)	1.42 (1.23, 1.63)	1.41 (1.23, 1.63)	1.40 (1.22, 1.62)	1.81 (1.51, 2.16)	1.75 (1.46, 2.10)	1.76 (1.46, 2.11)
Gender									
Female (Ref)	1.00	1.00	1.00	1.00	1.00	1.00	1.00	1.00	1.00
Male	0.54 (0.49, 0.60)	0.54 (0.49, 0.60)	0.54 (0.49, 0.60)	0.67 (0.61, 0.74)	0.67 (0.61, 0.74)	0.67 (0.61, 0.74)	0.65 (0.58, 0.75)	0.66 (0.58, 0.75)	0.66 (0.58, 0.75)
Age	0.96 (0.93, 1.00)	0.96 (0.93, 1.00)	0.96 (0.93, 1.00)	0.97 (0.93, 1.01)	0.97 (0.93, 1.01)	0.97 (0.93, 1.01)	0.94 (0.90, 0.99)	0.94 (0.90, 0.99)	0.94 (0.90, 0.99)
				Level 2 covariates					
School climate	...	1.05 (0.88, 1.26)	1.07 (0.89, 1.30)	...	1.09 (0.94, 1.27)	1.13 (0.96 1.33)	...	1.05 (0.89, 1.25)	1.08 (0.89, 1.30)
Same-sex couples	...	0.98 (0.95, 1.02)	0.98 (0.95, 1.02)	...	1.00 (0.98, 1.03)	1.01 (0.98, 1.03)	...	0.98 (0.96, 1.01)	0.98 (0.95, 1.01)
Median household income	...	1.00 (1.00, 1.00)	1.00 (1.00, 1.00)	...	0.99 (1.00, 1.00)	0.99 (1.00, 1.00)	...	1.00 (1.00, 1.00)	1.00 (1.00, 1.00)
				Cross-level Interactions					
Lesbian or gay × school climate	...	...	0.68 (0.47, 0.99)	...	...	0.73 (0.51, 1.06)	...	...	0.80 (0.49, 1.30)
Bisexual × school climate	...	...	0.81 (0.66, 0.99)	...	...	0.82 (0.66, 1.02)	...	...	0.80 (0.61, 1.05)
Not sure × school climate	...	...	0.83 (0.64, 1.09)	...	...	0.80 (0.62, 1.02)	...	...	0.80 (0.57, 1.12)

Note. CI = confidence interval; OR = odds ratio.

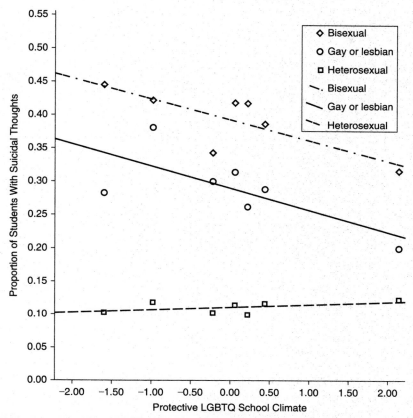

LGBTQ = lesbian, gay, bisexual, transgender, and questioning. The x-axis depicts protective school climates for sexual minority youths. Values represent standardized z scores for the 8 items from the School Health Profile Survey. A score of 0 indicates an average school climate across the 8 localities. Negative scores indicate school climates that are less protective for LGBTQ youths; conversely, positive scores indicate more protective school climates for LGBTQ youths. The figure depicts both raw values as well as the regression lines fit by sexual orientation groups.

Figure 1   Relationship between suicidal thoughts and protective school climates, by sexual orientation status: Youth Risk Behavior Surveillance Surveys, United States, 2005 and 2007.

(y-axis) among lesbian or gay and bisexual youths relative to increasing protectiveness of school climates (x-axis). As can also be seen in Figure 1, this pattern was not observed among heterosexual youths, whose odds of suicidal thoughts did not differ across the protectiveness of school climates. Notably, in jurisdictions with the highest score on the school climate measure (depicted on the far right side of the x-axis in Figure 1), sexual orientation disparities in suicidal thoughts were sharply reduced, particularly for the lesbian and gay adolescents.

Suicide Plans

Lesbian and gay youths (OR = 2.98; 95% CI = 2.20, 4.03), bisexual youths (OR = 4.37; 95% CI = 3.69, 5.16), and youths who were unsure of their sexual orientation (OR = 2.10; 95% CI = 1.67, 2.65) were significantly more likely than heterosexual youths to report a suicide plan in the past 12 months. (model 1, Table 4). Male gender was significantly associated

with reduced odds of reporting a suicide plan (OR = 0.67; 95% CI = 0.61, 0.74), whereas "other" race/ethnicity was significantly associated with increased odds of reporting a suicide plan (OR = 1.42; 95% CI = 1.23, 1.63). None of the level 2 variables were associated with the intercept for suicide plan in the full sample (model 2).

In the final model (model 3), lesbian and gay youths (OR = 0.73; 95% CI = 0.51, 1.06; P =.083), bisexual youths (OR = 0.82; 95% CI = 0.66, 1.02; P = .066), and youths unsure of their sexual orientation (OR = 0.80; 95% CI = 0.62, 1.02; P = .067) who were living in jurisdictions with more protective school climates were less likely to report a suicide plan than sexual minority adolescents living in jurisdictions with less supportive school climates. Although the magnitude and direction of these associations were nearly identical to those of suicidal thoughts, the results for suicide plan did not achieve statistical significance at the .05 level.

Suicide Attempts

Lesbian and gay youths (OR = 3.87; 95% CI = 2.67, 5.63), bisexual youths (OR = 5.72; 95% CI = 4.72, 6.94), and youths unsure of their sexual orientation (OR = 2.44; 95% CI = 1.82, 3.27) were more likely to report a past-year suicide attempt (model 1, Table 4). Each racial/ethnic group was significantly more likely than Whites to report a suicide attempt in the past year; male gender and older age were both significantly associated with decreased odds of reporting a past-year suicide attempt. None of the level 2 variables were associated with the intercept for suicide attempts in the full sample (model 2). Finally, results for the cross-level interaction (model 3) indicated that sexual minority youths were less likely to report a suicide attempt if they lived in jurisdictions with more supportive climates. Although the magnitude and direction of these associations were similar to those of suicide thoughts, none reached statistical significance at the .05 level (gay and lesbian youths: $P = .298$; bisexual youths: $P = .09$; unsure youths: $P = .157$).

Discussion

The 2011 report on LGBT health disparities from the Institute of Medicine noted the need for research on social ecological determinants of adverse health outcomes in this population, and named social influences on the lives of LGBT people as 1 of 5 priority research areas for advancing the field.[27] With the current study, we address this research priority by focusing on school climate as a key social developmental context for sexual minority adolescents. We evaluate the extent to which the prevalence of suicide ideation, plans, and attempts among LGB youths are reduced in regions with school climates that protect sexual minority students.

Our results demonstrate that LGB youths living in states and cities with more protective school climates were significantly less likely to report past-year suicidal thoughts than LGB youths living in states and cities with less protective school climates. Associations between positive school climates and reduced risk for suicidal thoughts remained significant after we controlled for potential confounders. We documented that these effects were specific to LGB adolescents; LGB supportive school climates were not associated with suicidal thoughts among heterosexual youths. Importantly, we found that higher levels of protectiveness of school climates for sexual minority students substantially reduced sexual orientation disparities in suicidal thoughts. The magnitude and direction of the results were similar for suicide plans and attempts, but these outcomes did not reach statistical significance at the .05 level.

Limitations

This study has several limitations. Our data on school climate came from the 2010 SHP survey, the first year for which data on LGBTQ school climates were available, whereas the outcome data are from 2005 to 2007, the most recently available data to have been pooled for examination of sexual orientation disparities. Thus, we take the 2010 climate data to be a good proxy of the school climate in 2005 through 2007. The assumption is based on the idea that schools are more likely to progress gradually in improving school climate, rather than shifting drastically over years. If that is so, then our measure correctly captures variability among the localities even if it is not perfectly accurate with regard to how the specific items that comprise the measure would have been rated in 2005 through 2007. To assess the assumption of continuity, we selected 2 items (percentage of schools that had a safe-passage-to-school program and percentage of schools that had a program to prevent bullying) from the SHP survey principal report, from which the 8 items in our scale were taken. Unlike the items that comprise our LGBTQ school climate scale, these 2 items had been assessed over a longer period (2004–2010) in the same 8 jurisdictions as our sample. Although these 2 items measure school safety and antibullying contexts aimed at all students, we selected them because we believe they are particularly relevant for the LGB students in our sample and thus may be used to approximate the unmeasured LGBTQ school climate variables in 2005 through 2007. Consistent with our assumption, measures of these 2 items were consistent and positively correlated between 2004 and 2006 and between 2006 and 2010 (r's for safe passage were 0.9 and 0.8, respectively, and r's for bullying prevention were 0.7 and 0.4, respectively). This indicates that each of the earlier measures provided a good approximation of the later measure. This in turn suggests that despite the discrepancy in time between exposure and outcome measures, our school climate construct properly estimated the school climate in 2005 through 2007, when outcome measures were collected. To the extent that this assumption is wrong, and the 2010 measure is not a good proxy for the 2005–2007 climate, our analyses would have suffered from the incorporation of measurement error. Introducing measurement error, which is random, would have reduced our ability to find significant findings rather than bias our results in the hypothesized direction (that is, leading us to conclude that positive school climate is protective when in fact it is not). Thus, although questions remain about the accuracy of the later measure as a proxy for earlier years, which we cannot answer, we are satisfied that inaccuracy, to the extent that it exists, has not led us to report our positive findings. (On the other hand, it is plausible that measurement error would lead to null findings regarding suicide plan and attempt.)

An additional limitation is that no psychometric properties of the LGBTQ school climate items in the 2010 SHP exist. The school climate measure relies on principals' and teachers' reports; to the extent that such results are unreliable, the validity and reliability of the measure may be compromised.

However, we are confident that principals and teachers are familiar with school, district, and state policies, which they are charged with enforcing, suggesting that reporting biases are likely to be minimal. Another limitation of the school climate variable is that it is aggregated to the city and state level and may not represent the climate for the individual school that the respondent attended. However, both this and the reliance on principals' and teachers' observations would introduce random error into the school climate variable because it is unlikely that such misclassification will be systematically related to the proportion of students with suicidal thoughts, plans, and attempts. Thus, these limitations would bias results toward the null, suggesting that the results are conservative estimates of the association between school climates and suicidal thoughts among sexual minority youths.

We take the selected items of school climate to represent greater underlying concern for the well-being of LGBTQ students on the part of school authorities. Such concern may have been manifested in other measures that generally improve protections to LGBTQ students in the localities. Thus, the items that were available to us were used as a proxy to the more general construct of affirmative school climate. We attempted to create a global measure that captures the extent to which a particular jurisdiction has a positive LGBTQ school climate. Because the specific items are to be interpreted as representing a more general construct, they do not comprise a simple index. The cost of this approach is that the measure is not intuitively interpretable.

Although we obtained data on school climates from 8 states and cities, which is an improvement over existing studies,[16,22,23] the locales for which data were available represent a restricted range for this variable. For example, across the 49 states and 19 cities that participated in the 2010 SHP survey, the range for the variable "provides curricula or supplementary materials that include HIV, STD, or pregnancy prevention information relevant to LGBTQ youth" was 6.1% to 100.0%, whereas for the 8 jurisdictions in the current study, it was only 31.6% to 83.7%. Related to this, the regions for which data were available to us were more liberal socially and they had more protective social climates. The restricted range most likely is related to an underestimate of the effect of school climates on suicide risk. Consequently, our results should be interpreted as providing a conservative estimate of the true size of the effect of school climate on suicidal thoughts in sexual minority adolescents.

Additionally, external validity of the study may be limited because this selective data set is not generalizable to the regions not included in the study. Future studies would benefit from greater diversity in the jurisdictions sampled to evaluate the magnitude of the effects and the generalizability of the results across different social milieu. Further limiting generalization

is that although the YRBS is a representative sample of youths in public schools, it excludes youths in private and parochial schools, as well as runaway and homeless youths. Also, the YRBS does not include measures of transgender identity or gender nonconformity, thereby preventing us from evaluating the effect of LGBTQ supportive environments on risk of suicide outcomes among transgender adolescents.

Finally, despite the large sample size, the outcomes (especially suicide attempts) were relatively rare. This restricted our statistical power to examine effect modification by certain characteristics (e.g., gender, race/ethnicity), which may have masked important subgroup differences. Additionally, as in all cross-sectional studies, we infer about but cannot test causal relationships between school climate and suicidal thoughts, plans, and attempts.

Strengths

The current study has several methodological strengths, including the use of a representative sample of public school youths with a large enough sample size to permit disaggregation of sexual orientation groups. In addition, the study sample came from 8 states and cities across the United States, increasing the generalizability of the findings. Finally, previous studies have identified schools as 1 social context that can have significant consequences for the mental health of sexual minority students.[4,13–16,19,22] With some notable exceptions,[21,23] however, existing work has tended to use self-report measures of sexual minority youths' perceptions of their school environments.[17–19] These measures capture important appraisal processes, but they are measured with the same method as the outcome (i.e., self-report), which may lead to biased estimates of the relationship between school climate and mental health.[20] The current study overcame many of these limitations by using ecological measures of the exposure (i.e., school climates and policies) that did not rely on self-report and therefore were not confounded with the outcome of interest.

Conclusions

The results of this study should be assessed within the context of existing knowledge. Our study expands on the contributions from previous research on social determinants of sexual minority health that demonstrate the positive impact of supportive interventions on LGB health and well-being.[7,9,10,28,29] The findings point to potential targets for public health interventions aimed at reducing sexual orientation disparities in suicide risk. In particular, comprehensive suicide prevention and interventions for sexual minority adolescents should address not only individual-level[3,4] and family-level[14,30,31] factors but also broader social-contextual influences, including school climate.

Acknowledgments

This project was supported by grants from the Eunice Kennedy Shriver National Institute of Child Health and Human Development (R21 HD051178) and the National Institute of Drug Abuse (to M. L. H.; K01 DA032558), and by the IMPACT LGBT Health and Development Program at Northwestern University.

Assistance from the Centers for Disease Control and Prevention (CDC) Division of Adolescent and School Health and the work of the state and local health and education departments who conduct the Youth Risk Behavior Surveillance Survey made the project possible.

Note. The contents of this article are solely the responsibility of the authors and do not necessarily represent the official views of the National Institutes of Health, the CDC, or any agencies involved in collecting the data.

Human Participant Protection

Protocol approval was not necessary because deidentified data were obtained from secondary sources. Data use agreements were obtained from the Vermont and Rhode Island departments of health.

References

1. Centers for Disease Control and Prevention, National Center for Injury Prevention and Control. Web-based Injury Statistics Query and Reporting System (WISQUARS). Available at: http://www.cdc.gov/ncipc/wisqars. Accessed October 27, 2013.
2. Gould MS, Greenberg T, Velting DM, Shaffer D. Youth suicide risk and preventive interventions: a review of the past 10 years. *J Am Acad Child Adolesc Psychiatry.* 2003;42(4):386–405.
3. Garofalo R, Wolf RC, Wissow LS, Woods ER, Goodman E. Sexual orientation and risk of suicide attempts among a representative sample of youth. *Arch Pediatr Adolesc Med.* 1999;153(5):487–493.
4. Russell ST, Joyner K. Adolescent sexual orientation and suicide risk: evidence from a national study. *Am J Public Health.* 2001;91(8):1276–1281.
5. Marshal MP, Dietz LJ, Friedman MS, et al. Suicidality and depression disparities between sexual minority and heterosexual youth: a meta-analytic review. *J Adolesc Health.* 2011;49(2):115–123.
6. Haas AP, Eliason M, Mays VM, et al. Suicide and suicide risk in lesbian, gay, bisexual, and transgender populations: review and recommendations. *J Homosex.* 2011;58(1):10–51.
7. Meyer IH. Prejudice, social stress, and mental health in lesbian, gay, and bisexual populations: conceptual issues and research evidence. *Psychol Bull.* 2003;129(5): 674–697.
8. Link BG, Phelan JC. Conceptualizing stigma. *Annu Rev Sociol.* 2001;27:363–385.
9. Hatzenbuehler ML, Keyes KM, Hasin DS. State-level policies and psychiatric morbidity in lesbian, gay, and bisexual populations. *Am J Public Health.* 2009;99 (12):2275–2281.
10. Hatzenbuehler ML, McLaughlin KA, Keyes KM, Hasin DS. The impact of institutional discrimination on psychiatric disorders in lesbian, gay, and bisexual populations: a prospective study. *Am J Public Health.* 2010;100(3):452–459.
11. Rostosky SS, Riggle ED, Horne SG, Denton FN, Huellemeier JD. Lesbian, gay, and bisexual individuals' psychological reactions to amendments denying access to civil marriage. *Am J Orthopsychiatry.* 2010;80(3): 302–310.
12. Eccles JS, Roeser RW. School and community influences on human development. In: Bornstein MH, Lamb ME, eds. *Developmental Science: An Advanced Textbook.* 6th ed. New York, NY: Psychology Press; 2011:571–643.
13. Russell ST, Muraco A, Subramaniam A, Laub C. Youth empowerment and high school gay-straight alliances. *J Youth Adolesc.* 2009;38(7):891–903.
14. Russell ST, Ryan C, Toomey RB, Diaz RM, Sanchez J. Lesbian, gay, bisexual, and transgender adolescent school victimization: implications for young adult health and adjustment. *J Sch Health.* 2011;81(5):223–230.
15. Toomey RB, Ryan C, Diaz RM, Card NA, Russell ST. Gender-nonconforming lesbian, gay, bisexual, and trans-gender youth: school victimization and young adult psychosocial adjustment. *Dev Psychol.* 2010;46(6): 1580–1589.
16. Toomey RB, Ryan C, Diaz RM, Russell ST. High school gay-straight alliances (GSAs) and young adult well-being: an examination of GSA presence, participation, and perceived effectiveness. *Appl Dev Sci.* 2011;15 (4):175–185.
17. Birkett M, Espelage DL, Koenig B. LGB and questioning students in schools: the moderating effects of homophobic bullying and school climate on negative outcomes. *J Youth Adolesc.* 2009;38(7):989–1000.
18. Eisenberg ME, Resnick MD. Suicidality among gay, lesbian and bisexual youth: the role of protective factors. *J Adolesc Health.* 2006;39(5):662–668.
19. McGuire JK, Anderson CR, Toomey RB, Russell ST. School climate for transgender youth: a mixed method investigation of student experiences and school responses. *J Youth Adolesc.* 2010;39(10):1175–1188.
20. Diez Roux AV. Neighborhoods and health: where are we and where do we go from here? *Rev Epidemiol Sante Publique.* 2007;55(1):13–21.
21. Kosciw JG, Greytak EA, Diaz EM. Who, what, where, when, and why: demographic and ecological factors contributing to hostile school climate for lesbian, gay, bisexual, and transgender youth. *J Youth Adolesc.* 2009;38(7):976–988.
22. Walls NE, Freedenthal S, Wisneski H. Suicidal ideation and attempts among sexual minority youths receiving social services. *Soc Work.* 2008;53(1):21–29.
23. Hatzenbuehler ML, Keyes KM. Inclusive anti-bullying policies reduce suicide attempts in lesbian and gay youth. *J Adolesc Health.* 2013; 53(1 suppl):S21–S26.
24. Brener ND, Demissie Z, Foti K, et al. *School Health Profiles 2010: Characteristics of Health Programs Among Secondary Schools in Selected US Cities.* Atlanta, GA: Centers for Disease Control and Prevention; 2011.

Protective School Climates and Reduced Risk for Suicide Ideation in Sexual Minority Youths by Mark L. Hatzenbuehler, et al.

217

25. Mustanski B, Van Wagenen A, Birkett M, Eyster S, Corliss HL. Identifying sexual orientation health disparities in adolescents: analysis of pooled data from the Youth Risk Behavior Survey, 2005 and 2007. *Am J Public Health.* 2014;104(2):211–217.

26. Brener ND, Collins JL, Kann L, Warren CW, Williams BI. Reliability of the Youth Risk Behavior Survey Questionnaire. *Am J Epidemiol.* 1995;141(6): 575–580.

27. National Academy of Sciences for the Institute of Medicine. *The Health of Lesbian, Gay, Bisexual and Transgender People: Building a Foundation for Better Understanding.* Washington, DC: National Academies Press; 2011.

28. Hatzenbuehler ML. The social environment and suicide attempts in lesbian, gay, and bisexual youth. *Pediatrics.* 2011;127(5):896–903.

29. Hatzenbuehler ML, O'Cleirigh C, Grasso C, Mayer K, Safren S, Bradford J. Effect of same-sex marriage laws on health care use and expenditures in sexual minority men: a quasi-natural experiment. *Am J Public Health.* 2012; 102(2):285–291.

30. Diamond GM, Diamond GS, Levy S, Closs C, Ladipo T, Siqueland L. Attachment-based family therapy for suicidal lesbian, gay, and bisexual adolescents: a treatment development study and open trial with preliminary findings. *Psychotherapy.* 2012;49(1):62–71.

31. Ryan C, Huebner D, Diaz RM, Sanchez J. Family rejection as a predictor of negative health outcomes in white and Latino lesbian, gay, and bisexual young adults. *Pediatrics.* 2009;123(1):346–352.

Critical Thinking

1. Looking at the results section of this article, did you find data that surprised you? Explain your answer.

2. Think back to your own high school experience and school climate. Would you consider that school to be a protective school? What did educators do to be protective? Or what experiences led you to believe they were not protective?

3. Suggest reasons why schools may not be protective of all students? Include all the barriers you know of or can imagine.

Create Central

www.mhhe.com/createcentral

Internet References

GLSEN: Gay, Lesbian and Straight Education Network
http://www.glsen.org/cgi-bin/iowa/all/home/index.html

LGTB Youth Organizations
http://brandonshire.com/lgbt-youth-organizations/

Safe Schools
http://www.safeschoolscoalition.org/

MARK L. HATZENBUEHLER is with the Department of Socio-medical Sciences, Mailman School of Public Health, Columbia University, New York, NY. Michelle Birkett is with the Feinberg School of Medicine, Northwestern University, Chicago, IL. Aimee Van Wagenen is with the Center for Population Research in LGBT Health, Fenway Institute, Boston, MA. Ilan H. Meyer is with the Williams Institute, School of Law, University of California, Los Angeles.

Correspondence should be sent to Mark L. Hatzenbuehler, PhD, Department of Sociomedical Sciences, Mailman School of Public Health, Columbia University, 722 West 168th St, Room 549.B, New York, NY 10032 (e-mail: mlh2101@columbia.edu). Reprints can be ordered at http://www.ajph.org by clicking the "Reprints" link.

This article was accepted June 7, 2013.

M. L. Hatzenbuehler initiated the study idea, led the research and writing, and supervised the data analysis. M. Birkett conducted the statistical analyses. A. Van Wagenen obtained the data from the SHP Survey. I. H. Meyer supervised the data analyses. All authors contributed original ideas and edited drafts of the article.

Article   Prepared by: Rebecca B. Evers, *Winthrop University.*

Having Allies Makes a Difference

One of the nation's only schools created specifically to be gay-friendly has made the difficult teenage years easier for a population of students who often struggle.

PRISCILLA PARDINI

Learning Outcomes

After reading this article, you will be able to:

- Explain why having allies in a gay-friendly school is important for the well-being and support of students who are LGBT.

Walk in the front door of Milwaukee's gay-friendly Alliance School and at first it doesn't seem all that different from many big-city high schools. Metal lockers line the hallways of the old cinderblock building, once home to a city recreation program. Interspersed with the lockers are colorful student artwork and fliers taped to the walls and classroom doors. Before and after school and during passing periods, students crowd the hallways, jostling and calling out loudly to each other, even as others make little to no eye contact. Teachers threading their way through answer questions about homework and order kids to class. Students drift into the office asking for bus passes. Lockers, one after another, slam shut.

But, look and listen more closely, and the unique characteristics of Alliance emerge. Its vibe: laid-back but edgy. No bells signal the beginning and end of class periods. Students talk freely on their cell phones and address teachers by their first names. But many of the flyers and wall posters carry messages urging "peace" and "respect." Some students seem wary of a visitor in the building, with more than one asking, "Are you a sub?" And even by the almost anything goes sartorial standard of today's high school, many Alliance students stand out for their wildly flamboyant, unconventional style. To be sure, plenty of boys are wearing jeans, some carrying skateboards or basketballs under their arms. But it's not unusual to see them talking to other males wearing multiple earrings and dramatic, perfectly applied eye makeup. Some girls are dressed as if for a fashion show runway, wearing three-inch heels and glittery tops. Others express themselves through rainbow-hued hair, multiple body piercings, or a long, black trench coat.

Teachers eventually clear the halls, curbing off-color and rude comments. And students know that once they get to class, cell phones must be silenced and used only to take emergency calls. Yes, there are rules. But, on a day last fall when a substitute teacher ordered a student out of her classroom for refusing to take off his hat, regular staff members rolled their eyes at what was clearly viewed as an overreaction. "Why would I waste my time worrying about students wearing hats in class given the problems they're facing, the issues they're dealing with?" asked English teacher Paul Moore, one of the school's founding teachers. "What we need to be doing is establishing relationships with these kids and making sure they feel safe and accepted. Only then can we can expect them to be in a position to learn."

> **What they need is a place to be safe from physical abuse and psychological trauma while they explore who they think they are, and get a chance to grow, in peace, at their own rate.**
> — Paul Moore, English and social studies teacher

A Safe Haven

Moore and his colleagues at Alliance face the daunting task of meeting the social/emotional *and* academic needs of a group of students whose sexual orientation puts them in what some say is society's last unprotected class. The school opened in 2005 as a teacher-led charter school operating under the auspices of the Milwaukee Public Schools. The school's lead teacher is Tina Owen, a former MPS instructor whose vision shaped Alliance as a safe haven for students who had been bullied or discriminated against not only because of their sexual orientation, but also their beliefs, abilities, or appearance.

Several students transferred to Alliance after being bullied at their neighborhood schools for their conservative Christian views, and some academically oriented students taunted for being nerdy enrolled at Alliance seeking the chance to study in peace. Still other students say they were driven out of their neighborhood schools by unrelenting criticism of their weight, clothing choices, or body odor.

When it opened, Alliance was one of only two high schools in the country (the other, New York City's Harvey Milk High School) explicitly designated as gay-friendly. Four years later, it was expanded to include grades six through eight, making it the first and only such school in the country to serve middle school students.

Alliance is small—it has 172 students, 12 full-time, and six part-time faculty and staff. Last year's graduating class was made up of just 21 students. Like most urban schools, Alliance also is diverse in terms of race, family income, and special education eligibility. About 40% of its students are black, 31% are white, 24% are Hispanic, and 5% are Asian. Almost 77% are eligible for free- or reduced-priced lunch, 25% are homeless or in foster care, and close to one-third qualify for special education.

Still, Alliance is primarily known as Milwaukee's "gay school," with about half of the student body identifying as gay, lesbian, bisexual, or transgender. They come to Alliance from all over the city, its suburbs, and from rural communities as far as 50 miles away.

"Once you're explicitly gay-friendly and say that, it sets up a certain level of expectation," Owen said.

But she points out that the school's mission is broader. "We're not looking only through the lens of gender," she said. "That's just one piece of who we are as humans. At other schools, if you don't fit in this box or that box, you're harassed, kicked around, pushed out. Here, it doesn't matter. We promise all our students the same level of safety and acceptance we promise the LGBT students."

To that end, Alliance's curriculum is designed to address the issue of bullying with restorative justice practices and community-building activities. Its Restorative Justice class, a popular elective course for upperclassmen taught by Heather Sattler, trains students to participate in Peacemaking Circles, a technique derived from Native American traditions and steeped in ritual, that are used to resolve conflicts, promote honest communication, and develop positive relationships. During an intense circle session convened by Sattler and Beth Wellinghoff last fall in an English class they coteach, they asked each student to tell of a significant change in his or her life. They shared experiences that were overwhelmingly personal and often tragic. One girl revealed that at the age of six she had been blamed by family members for the accidental death of her baby sister. Another, who admitted that for years she had considered committing suicide, said she now felt she had to go on living in order to care for her cancer-stricken mother. "It's a nonjudgmental way to tap into what the kids are about and to begin to develop trust," said Sattler of the circle process.

Culture of Acceptance

Jasmin Price, 16, is one of several dozen students who on most days end up eating lunch in Moore's classroom, a huge space dominated at one end by an elevated stage. Some join Moore for a round of the card game Magic; others play Dungeons & Dragons. A third group of kids settles in on the old couch and easy chairs scattered around the stage to play a video game.

Jasmin, a relative newcomer, sits nearby watching, a book open on her lap. Her path to Alliance, which began in 5th grade, is heartbreakingly typical of that reported by many of her peers. Raised in a mostly upscale Milwaukee suburb 20 miles from the city, she loved elementary school.

"But middle school was horrible," she said. "If you didn't have a lot of money and weren't a real girly girl, you'd get picked on. It was constant. And I'd get so anxious I'd make myself sick, which meant I'd miss school, which would make me even more anxious."

Jasmin, whose mother is gay, describes herself as bisexual. She begged to be homeschooled, but, because that wasn't an option, she bounced around to a few other traditional schools before happily landing at Alliance last September.

"After just four weeks here, I'm already more comfortable than I've been since 5th grade," she said. "It's really different, in a good way. Everyone here knows what it's like to be bullied or harassed just for being yourself. So we don't pick on each other. We may not all be best friends, but we treat each other like human beings."

Sommer Kersten, 17, describes herself as pansexual. She said she has a "boyfriend" who is a girl. "I don't care about people's gender," Sommer said. "I have my own taste, but I accept that there are many gender options." At her former school she was routinely called a "dyke"—when she wasn't being ignored. "Here, I felt real comfortable right away. I noticed there were some people who liked the same things as me—like the piercings. And I wasn't the only one with exotic hair."

According to Domonic Exum, 19, the culture at Alliance is based on the premise that "You get along with everyone, and everyone gets along with you." At his former high school, he said, "Kids would start out arguing about petty stuff. There would be a lot of 'He said . . . ' and 'She said . . . ' By the end of the day, it would have escalated to the point where the police were called, and the school was put on lockdown. Here, we're more mellow. New kids sometimes come with an attitude, but by the time they're four weeks in, they get the message: We don't do the drama stuff here."

An At-Risk Population

Because so many of Alliance's students are considered at risk of dropping out of school before graduating, the school operates on a four-days-a-week, year-round schedule. The block schedule enables students to take just four, 100-minute classes each day.

Going to school year round not only helps combat the so-called summer brain drain that affects many low-income and minority students, but also aims to counteract an even more alarming reality: higher-than-average national suicide rates for students who are homeless, in foster care, or who identify as transgender. "Many of them don't have the ongoing support they need outside of school," Owen said.

As a charter school, Alliance also has the flexibility to set aside Tuesdays for staff professional development; students don't report to school, but instead are expected to spend the day working to complete a 60-hour community service requirement for which they receive one-half course credit, and a required online course. Among the students' online class options: credit recovery classes, remedial education classes designed to boost math or English skills, Advanced Placement classes, or electives such as Art History or Digital Art. Some students also spend Tuesdays working at part-time jobs. Giving students so much flexibility in their schedule, Owen said, helps them learn how to manage "freedom with responsibility."

Students say the culture at Alliance and the way classes are structured make it easier for them to concentrate on their schoolwork. "I remember I used to try to buckle down in my classes, but there was so much stress, and I was so depressed or angry that I ended up cutting school a lot," Sommer said. "Here, I go every day, the teachers are easygoing, and I only have four classes to deal with at a time."

Meeting Academic Needs

Yet, despite such accolades, huge challenges persist. Owen is so concerned about the 10% of Alliance students who are transgender that she's made their academic needs one of the issues she's focusing on this year. Although she says transgender students are well accepted, many of them struggle to achieve. The transgender community, she wrote in her annual mission statement, is "particularly vulnerable to street crime, homelessness, sexual assault, and discrimination. The sense of hopelessness that many of these young people feel is devastating, and this has a measurable effect on their achievement."

But teachers also struggle to meet the academic needs of the school's less emotionally vulnerable students. Due to Alliance's small size, the number of course offerings is limited. With the exception of 9th-grade English and math, classes are taught in mixed grade-level settings where student ability varies widely. In fact, because Alliance offers a full-inclusion special education program, some students are reading at only the 4th- or 5th-grade level. Beyond that, many average or above-average students come to Alliance after spending years in hostile environments where they languished academically, severely underachieving and developing bad habits.

One day last fall in teacher Chris Gruntzel's Advanced Algebra class, Gruntzel had a group of eager students in the palm of his hand as he taught a lesson on root-mean-square error. Yet as he explained how the concept measures differences between values predicted by a mathematical model, Gruntzel was interrupted by students arriving late to class and later was forced to slow the pace of the lesson to attend to several students who clearly were lost.

Asked if psychological support trumped intellectual rigor, Sattler said that while social justice issues permeate her teaching, and that teacher-student relationships are critical to Alliance's mission, "I don't coddle students when it comes to academics." Indeed, the first of "The Six Agreements" drawn up by Alliance's inaugural class and posted on a bulletin board in Sattler's classroom states that "Schoolwork comes first."

Owen, who teaches online Spanish and physical education classes, said that's the norm. "I don't think academics take a backseat here," she said. "We're tough. You don't do the work, you're going to fail." Nonetheless, she conceded, "It does sometimes take awhile to get students where we want them to be. But we're patient. We don't give up. We don't get angry. We just keep pulling them forward."

But, said Moore, "It's especially challenging to find ways to offer the smart kids the level of rigor they need." He routinely supplements their required reading lists, asks them in-class discussion questions designed to promote higher-level thinking, and sets increasingly higher standards when it comes to their written work. Gruntzel is in the process of building a sequence of math courses designed to offer Alliance's brightest students more rigor.

Standardized test data, at first glance, is not encouraging. Last year, according to the Wisconsin Department of Public Instruction, only 33% of Alliance 10th graders scored at the proficient or advanced level in reading; 25% did so in math. In both cases, that was lower than the district average, landing Alliance on the list of Schools Identified for Improvement for the second time in three years. But Owen points out that only 24 10th graders took the test last year, including eight special education students. "Given the sample's small size and its makeup, it's hard to see the scores as meaningful," she said.

Owen prefers to look for evidence of success in other measures, such as Alliance's mobility rate, which has decreased from 60% in 2005 to 17% this year, and its attendance rate, which over the same period has jumped from 66% to 91%. And she points with special pride to the fact that 15 of the 21 students in the 2012 graduating class are now in college or other postsecondary schools.

Ana Jimenez, 19, is one of those students. A freshman at Milwaukee's Alverno College, she vividly recalls years of bullying, family problems, and depression that nearly derailed her. At Alliance, she "became part of a family," she said, and transitioned from "a girl who looked and felt angry all the time" to the school's prom queen and talent show winner. She also won Alliance's Toccara Wilson Award, named in memory of one of the school's founders and awarded to the student who best represents, over four years, the ideals to which Alliance aspires. "I still can't believe it. This school saved my life," Ana said.

Spreading the Word

A spate of positive national publicity, not to mention several awards, have helped boost Alliance's reputation. *Time, U.S. News & World Report,* and *People* magazines, as well as ABC News, all have showcased its program. The school also was honored with the Wisconsin Charter Schools Association's 2011 Charter School of the Year Platinum Award and, last January, the Fair Wisconsin Organization of the Year Award.

In August, Owen learned that the school had received a $125,000 grant from Wisconsin's Department of Public Instruction.

Owen said the grant money will be used to underwrite anti-bullying workshops and restorative justice training sessions that Alliance staff and students will put on at other area secondary schools, universities, and community agencies. Plans also call for creating a video and summer training programs, and developing visitation days when the school will be opened to those interested in learning more about how to replicate the Alliance model.

Yet even the positive press, the awards, and the grant money couldn't stop state budget cuts that have forced Alliance to begin phasing out its middle school program. This year, its 6th grade was eliminated; by the 2014–15 school year, it will serve only high schoolers. "It's a shame," Owen said. "There are so many middle school kids who really need to be in this kind of an environment."

Despite the setback, Owen and her staff know Alliance continues to meet the profound needs of a subset of students whose very lives, in some cases, depend on its continued existence. They have become adept at responding to the often-heard criticism that Alliance's model provides nothing more than a temporary respite, a Band-Aid for students who would be better served by learning how to stand up and face—rather than be sheltered from—the abuse bound to be heaped on those living on what many still consider the fringe of society.

"What they need," Moore said, "is a place to be safe from physical abuse and psychological trauma while they explore who they think they are, and get a chance to grow, in peace, at their own rate. Sure, they'll face discrimination, but it's a whole different ballgame once you're 17 or 18 and a more confident person than it is when you're just 13 or 14."

Sommer said she's contemplated the hard reality of taking her place in the real world. "Sure, I'll have to deal with it. And I will. But for now, here, I can just be myself."

Critical Thinking

1. Overtly gay-friendly schools are controversial, even in the gay rights community. Pick a side, either for or opposing. Prepare to debate the issue. Use information from the other articles in this unit and information from the websites at the beginning of the unit for more information.

2. Do you know of gay-friendly schools in your area? If so, research the local response to the school. Perhaps you could interview someone at the school, such as a teacher, administrator, or student. Other persons to consider could be a parent, a neighbor who lives near the school, or a local school district official.

Create Central

www.mhhe.com/createcentral

Internet References

Parents, Families, and Friends of Lesbians and Gays (PFLAG)
www.pflag.org

PRISCILLA PARDINI is a freelance education writer in suburban Milwaukee, Wisc.

Pardini, Priscilla. From *Phi Delta Kappan*, vol. 94, no. 5, February 2013, pp. 14–20. Reprinted with permission of Phi Delta Kappa International. All rights reserved. www.pdkintl.org

Article   Prepared by: Rebecca B. Evers, *Winthrop University*

Hostile Hallways

It's not as common as run-of-the-mill bullying, but sexual harassment in schools may have worse long-term effects, research suggests.

CHRISTOPHER MUNSEY

Learning Outcomes

After reading this article, you will be able to:

- Hypothesize why bullying is so difficult to stop.
- Conduct a survey to learn how much bullying and/or sexual harassment is present in your school.

Bullying has received intense national attention in recent years. But psychologists say there's an equally serious problem in schools that's not drawing nearly as much attention: sexual harassment.

A troubling 44% of female and 27% of male middle and high school students report experiencing unwanted sexual touching from another student, according to a 2009 Center for Research on Women report. What's more, only 16% of students who had been harassed by a fellow student reported it, says report author, psychologist Lynda Sagrestano, PhD, of the University of Memphis.

It may not be as common as bullying, but school-based sexual harassment may be even worse for students' health and school outcomes, according to a study published in 2008 in the journal *Sex Roles*.

"Sexual harassment, more so than bullying, diminishes students' trust of teachers. . . . Sexually harassed students are much more alienated from school than bullied students in terms of thinking about quitting or transferring schools or skipping school," says James Gruber, PhD, a sociology professor at the University of Michigan-Dearborn.

Yet, despite the seriousness of school-based sexual harassment, most schools do not have an administrator trained to investigate sexual harassment complaints and educate teachers and students about how to intervene, says Dorothy Espelage, PhD, a professor of psychology with the department of educational psychology at the University of Illinois at Urbana-Champaign.

"We need more research, we need a better curriculum, and we need to start talking to kids about sexual harassment," she says.

A Toxic Environment

Sexual harassment in the school environment can lead to a constellation of ill effects for students, says Linda L. Collinsworth, PhD, an associate professor of psychology at Millikin University in Decatur, Ill. In a 2008 study of 569 students from seven Midwestern high schools that appeared in *Psychology of Women Quarterly,* Collinsworth and her colleagues found that girls who had been upset by one or more incidents of sexual harassment across a wide range of harassing behaviors reported signs of depression and anxiety.

Both boys and girls who perceived their school as tolerating sexual harassment reported more symptoms of depression, Collinsworth says.

"It's like second-hand smoke," says Collinsworth. "If you're in this environment where there's this tolerance of sexual harassment, it has this effect on you, even if you're not harassed."

Lesbian, gay, bisexual and questioning students are especially at risk for sexual harassment, according to the survey of 522 middle school and high school students published by Gruber in 2008. He and co-author Susan Fineran, PhD, of the University of Southern Maine, found that 71% of LGBQ students had experienced sexual harassment in the last year, compared with 35% of students overall. "Maybe the real victims are LGBQ students," Gruber says. "They not only report much higher levels of bullying and sexual harassment, but the harm is significantly greater, both in terms of health outcomes and school outcomes."

What Can Be Done

Psychologists and other researchers who study sexual harassment in schools say that key steps to address it include:

- **Educating educators.** Teachers and school administrators need more training on how to respond to sexual harassment and its negative consequences, says Nan Stein, EdD, a senior research scientist at the Wellesley Centers for Women.

Preventing Sexual Assault in College

In April 2011, when Vice President Joseph Biden and Secretary of Education Arne Duncan announced the release of federal guidance on preventing sexual violence on college campuses, they cited a prevention program designed by psychologist Victoria Banyard, PhD, and her colleagues at the University of New Hampshire as a model for other colleges and universities across the country.

Banyard's "Bringing in the Bystander" program teaches both men and women how to prevent sexual violence through an hourlong skill-building educational session that covers how to intervene in scenarios that could culminate in sexual assault. The effort includes a campus-based social marketing campaign to build community awareness.

On a college campus, that might mean noticing if someone who's had too much to drink is being led away from the party by a fellow party-goer. In that case, steering the pair back to the party and making sure the woman's friends are watching out for her could help prevent a possible assault, Banyard says.

In more extreme situations, concerned bystanders might need to request assistance from a resident adviser or the campus police, she says.

"We're trying to teach people safe tools that might make them more likely to step in and help out, in situations across the continuum of sexual violence," Banyard says.

The program also teaches students how to support a friend who reports being assaulted. It helps victims heal if they hear "It's not your fault" and "I believe you" instead of the blame they often receive from family and friends, Banyard says.

About one in three women and one in five men will have a friend tell them about an unwanted sexual experience, she says.

—C. MUNSEY

- **Teaching students.** Educators should add class modules teaching students how to spot harassment and the steps for filing a complaint. Schools also need to encourage students to report sexual harassment to a trusted network of specially trained school officials, and stress that they will not face negative repercussions or retribution, Stein says.
- **Enforcing consequences for offenders and supporting victims.** Some school systems, such as the Austin Independent School District in Texas, allow students to file for a "stay away" order that requires an offender to avoid contact with the victim on school grounds. And through a program called Expect Respect, victims of sexual harassment are offered individual counseling and an invitation to a school-sponsored support group.

Critical Thinking

1. What is the difference between bullying and sexual harassment? If you are not clear on the difference, visit the website (provided at the beginning of this unit) for the American Association of University Women's research report, *Crossing the Line*.

2. Check with a local school or district official for information on bullying and sexual harassment. Do they collect data for both or just for bullying with no differential for harassment?

3. The *Bringing in the Bystander* program at the University of New Hampshire addresses harassment at the college level. Which of their activities might be used to address harassment in middle and high schools?

Create Central

www.mhhe.com/createcentral

Internet References

Olweus Bullying Prevention Program
  www.violencepreventionworks.org/
American Association of University Women
  www.aauw.org/learn/research/crossingtheline.cfm

CHRISTOPHER MUNSEY is a staff writer for *Monitor on Psychology*.

Article   Prepared by: Rebecca B. Evers, *Winthrop University*

Building LGBTQ Awareness and Allies in Our Teacher Education Community and Beyond

Laura-Lee Kearns, Jennifer Mitton Kukner, and Joanne Tompkins

Learning Outcomes

After reading this article, you will be able to:

- Summarize the need for building awareness among teacher candidates in higher education teacher education programs.

- Interrupt and respond to instances of bullying and harassment in schools and elsewhere.

- Discuss issues faced by pre-service teachers who want to do the right thing, but have concerns when mentor teachers oppose such actions.

Introduction

Research has demonstrated that over 75% of Lesbian, Gay and Bi-sexual youth and 95% of Transgendered students do not feel safe at school compared to 20% of heterosexual students (Taylor et al., 2011, 47). The current bullying discourse does not often highlight the vulnerability of sexual minority youth. According to the *First National Climate Survey on Homophobia in Canadian Schools* (Taylor et al., 2009) "homophobic and transphobic bullying are neither rare nor harmless but major problems that schools need to address" (p. 2). The Canadian Charter of Human Rights and Freedoms, provincial equity policies, school and school board policies and curricula emphasize "human rights and diversity" however, "LGBTQ students feel unsafe, insulted or harassed," on a daily basis (Taylor as cited in Petz 2011). Compounding this issue is the reality that LGBTQ youth hear and see a lot of homophobia and transphobia in schools, and they don't see adults in leadership positions interrupting this type of discrimination (Goldstein et al., 2007; Kumashiro 2002; Taylor et al., 2011). This is particularly regrettable as research also shows that "the climate is significantly better in the schools that have taken even modest steps to combat homophobia" (Taylor, 2011, para 4). To that end, we are trying to promote anti-oppressive pedagogy as part of our approach to teaching and learning in our faculty of education.

Here we share the impact of a training program, Positive Space I (PSI) and Positive Space II (PSII), two three-hour workshops, that have been integrated into mandatory education classes, Sociology of Education and Inclusion I, which help to promote pre-service teachers' understandings of and abilities to create safe spaces for LGBTQ youth. The purpose of our study is to explore the impact of this training program, and to consider challenges and best practices to build awareness and allies in our own higher-education context, as well as to help create better learning communities for LGBTQ youth and allies in schools. Our Positive Space Training program is also critical as many future teachers are not prepared to address "issues of homophobia and heterosexism in the classroom" (Stiegler, 2008, p. 117). By honouring our students and helping them become "activists" who may help advance "academics and social justice" (Kumashiro, 2002, p. 13), we hope to better inform not only our own practice but also that of the field of higher education.

Our teacher education faculty is situated within St. Francis Xavier University in rural Atlantic Canada. Our Bachelor of Education is a two-year program, with approximately 240 students. Prior to 2009, PS I & PS II were voluntary. Since 2009 it has been institutionalized as part of our B.Ed program in courses that discuss issues around power and privilege, and interlocking forms of oppressions. Positive Space I features awareness building with a focus on language and terminology and Positive Space II focuses on becoming an ally, which gives the opportunity for preservice educators to witness and role play educators interrupting heteronormativity. Recognizing that "a lack of a solid Canadian evidence base has been a major impediment faced by educators who need to understand the situation of . . . LGBTQ students in order to respond appropriately" (Taylor et al., 2009, p. 2), sharing our work is timely and necessary. As a further impetus, we also recognize that in addition to feeling unsafe, rural LGBTQ youth have been shown to experience more hostile climates than their urban counterparts compounded by fewer resources and supports, including a lower prevalence of Gay Straight Alliances (GSAs), supportive staff, inclusive curricula, and comprehensive anti-bullying policies (GLSEN Report, 2012).

Data Collection

This paper describes the Positive Space training program and its relationship to our teacher education program. It highlights findings from workshop evaluations of Positive Space I and II provided by participants 2010–2012, incorporates findings from pre- and post-training on-line surveys in 2011–2012, and follow-up interviews with individuals and a small focus group in 2013.

Themes Arising from the Data
On the Need to Create LGBTQ Awareness

There is a broad range of awareness and understanding of LGBTQ realities among our pre-service teachers. In the pre-survey at the very beginning of their B.Ed in September, in response to the question, *"Have you ever had any previous training in LGBTQ issues?"* 84% of respondents said "No". Of the 16% who said "Yes", some said they had friends or parents who identified as LGBTQ. And others had taken Positive Space training as part of women's studies programs. In response to the question, *"When you were in school, was there a Gay Straight Alliance (GSA)?"* 13% said "Yes", 74% said "No" and 16% wrote that they were unsure. In response to *"Have you ever had the experience of participating in any LGBTQ event?"* 24% said "Yes", and 76% said "No" (Pre-Training Electronic responses Fall 2011). For those who said "Yes", the events listed included mostly Pride parades and same sex weddings. Although workshop feedback and pre-survey data showed that some pre-service educators self-identified as allies who wanted

more critical discussions on these issues, we found it surprising that a majority of pre-service teachers would not have had the opportunity to engage with the LGBTQ community. All of this information is insightful, as it indicates that both formally and informally pre-service educators need support and explicit LGBTQ training to engage with anti-oppressive pedagogy.

Positive Impact of the Training

The training proved to be important on multiple levels. Many participants said it helped with their confidence in terms of awareness about the challenges some LGBTQ individuals face. As one participant shared, the training "opened my eyes to issues I hadn't thought of before . . . [I didn't] recognize the severity and impact [homophobia] might have [on LGBTQ youth]" (Interviewee 7). The training not only created more understanding about the challenges LGBTQ individuals face, it clarified language and terminology, and also helped people recognize and examine the privilege of heterosexuals. It created a way to discuss complex issues and also showed the importance of interrupting homophobia. One participant shared "my awareness of LGBTQ issues and comfort intervening when I witness a homophobic act is much greater since taking these Positive Space Training sessions" (Postsurvey electronic response—Winter 2012). Further, we learned that without this specific training, some pre-service educators may not have seen responding to the needs of LGBTQ or human rights advocacy as part of their professional responsibilities. As one interviewee shared, prior to the training "sexuality wasn't big on my radar for school because I was so worried about . . . [having] a good lesson" (Interviewee 8). The interviewees also shared that since many had not participated in GSAs in their own schools, they said the training was critical to understanding what they were and that everyone was welcome to be an ally. Certainly, pre-service educators found it is important to consciously name discrimination and weave ways to address homophobia in our program.

Lack of Understanding of What It Meant to Interrupt

Although the pre-service teachers we worked with emphasized the importance of learning more about how to create and sustain positive spaces for LGBTQ youth and allies in schools, a common thread emerging from follow-up focus group interviews was their lack of understanding of what it meant to interrupt situations of a discriminatory nature. For example, one pre-service teacher, in describing his action of crossing out the word 'gay' that had been negatively written over a Positive Space sticker in a school washroom, commented, "I don't know if that was appropriate but at least they [LGBTQ youth] don't have to see it . . . I guess that's a step in the positive direction."

Some of the pre-service teachers' uncertainty about interruptions and their seeming lack of understanding about the power of small actions, as seen in our previous example, may be connected to their prior experiences as learners in schools, or imagining that anti-discrimination actions need to be extraordinary, or their field placement experiences in which they witnessed few examples of anti-oppressive pedagogy. For us, these discussions helped us recognize that we need to highlight the power of small, ongoing interruptions as part of pre-service teachers' understanding of anti-oppressive pedagogy and the ways it might inform their work in schools.

Power Imbalance

Our follow-up interviews also showed that issues of power impact the sense of agency our pre-service teachers feel as they attempt to interrupt homophobia and transphobia. On one level there is a power imbalance between pre-service teachers and their cooperating teachers. They are student interns working alongside mentor teachers. The relationship is meant to be of mutual benefit. Though there is an imbalance the opinions of the licensed teacher hold some weight in the student's evaluation and potentially future employment prospects. It is a power relationship of which our pre-service teachers are highly aware: "the power structure is against us in a variety of ways. We want to have good references and . . . do a good job . . . all those things conflict depending on who your CT is. . . . my career is at stake" (Interviewee 4). This power dynamic can also be a problem for some pre-service teachers who want to interrupt homophobia when the cooperating teacher does not. One student explains: ". . . I had a student pass a note to another student and it had faggot written on it . . . And I couldn't think of a way to approach the class about it and my CT didn't want to deal with it . . ." (Interviewee 1). Reflecting back on the incident, the student teacher said "it's hard being a student teacher" and asked ". . . how do I make this work"? Though several pre-service teachers felt supported to act as an ally, others worried that their attempts to challenge homophobia and heteronormativity could be viewed negatively and felt limited to act as an ally.

The Gender Binary: Responding and Interrupting

It was clear that the gender binary, a system of overtly and covertly naming and stereotyping differences between boys and girls is learned and reproduced by schools. Our follow-up interviews showed our pre-service teachers grappling with just how *profound* this binary is instilled and trying to find ways to disrupt or work within it. For example, one interviewee in our focus group shared that she would try to show the grade primary class "non-gendered pictures" and the 5 and 6 year

olds "would ask is this a boy or a girl and how can you tell" (Interviewee 3). The pre-service teacher would think to herself, "it doesn't matter it's just a [picture]". Yet she understood that "it was all the systems that they grew up with and what they were used to . . . boys wear pants and shirts . . . and . . . [to] try and break an entire system . . . It's really difficult." The boy and girl codes though deeply entrenched, were recognized by this pre-service teacher, who at least wanted to start doing "small things" to open up more possibilities. In her context, she "started asking 'are you a boy or are you a girl? It's your choice, I'll put down whatever you tell me you are.'" At the secondary level the importance of gender was also at the fore. One interviewee shared that in the social studies classroom there were more opportunities to discuss human rights, but in the physical education classroom, where there was still a lot of "boys vs girls" it was more challenging. This one student teacher had a transgender student in his class, so in order to respond, he asked the student which team s/he preferred to play on: "I'd let [James] play on the girls team if he wanted to" (Interviewee 8). Pre-service teachers are engaged in the gender binary in schools daily, some are trying to complicate it, disrupt it or simply adhere to it in different ways.

Implications: Continuing Our Work in Higher Education

Our study has substantiated some of what we know about the importance of including LGBTQ in higher education programs (Goldstein et al., 2007; Kitchen & Bellini, 2012; Taylor et al., 2009, 2011). Our research also shows that by taking part in the training, pre-service teachers felt they were more capable at supporting LGBTQ youth, colleagues, people and/or participating in GSAs. Key themes that emerged in our data and which we note as different from other studies is the lack of understanding that pre-service teachers had about small interruptions as being an important part of their anti-oppressive pedagogy. We also note how they were able to identify the gender binary as a presence in schools and curriculum, and the choices they made in such situations with actions that they felt enabled students to have broader choices about who they felt themselves to be. While we emphasize the positive impact of the training, we also note that participants expressed concerns about how much they were able to do in schools in relation to LGBTQ work, putting particular emphasis on a power imbalance between themselves and their cooperating teachers. Several participants also mentioned that they wanted more training opportunities, and in response we are planning a Positive Space III and IV. Our efforts will continue to focus on ways to support opportunities for future, early career, and experienced teachers to create inclusive spaces in schools.

Conclusion

As a result of positive space training teacher, candidates' awareness of LGBTQ issues has increased and they are developing a vocabulary to name heterosexism and identify instances in which they should intervene to interrupt homophobia and transphobia. Importantly they are developing the skills to proactively create inclusive environments. Results also indicate areas for further growth, particularly in pre-service teachers' sense of efficacy to act as allies. The opportunity for teacher candidates to understand how to incorporate anti-discrimination work in their teaching practice is a key component of school and education reform. Social justice policies and procedures exist in many school settings, but unless new teachers have the opportunity to explore and apply their grounded knowledge from professional development, these well-meaning policies are often neglected or ignored. We suggest that this particular program is an example of how to work towards the development of a pedagogy that does not oppress; one that truly embraces, celebrates, and honours all learners.

References

GLSEN (2007). *Gay-straight alliances; creating safer schools for LGBTQ students and their allies (GLSEN research brief).* New York: Gay, Lesbian and Straight Education Network.

Goldstein, T., Russell, V., & Daley, A. (2007). Safe positive and queering moments in teaching education and schooling: A conceptual framework. *Teaching Education, 18*(3), 183–199.

Kitchen J. & Bellini, C. (2012). Addressing lesbian, gay, bisexual, transgender, and queer (lgbtq) issues in teacher education: Teacher candidates' perceptions. *Alberta Journal of Educational Research, 58*(3), 444–460.

Kumashiro, K. (2002). *Troubling education: "Queer" activism and anti-Oppressive pedagogy.* New York, NY: Routledge.

Stiegler, S. (2008). Queer youth as teachers: Dismantling silence of queer issues in a teacher preparation program committed to social justice. *Journal of LGBTQ Youth, 5*(4), 116–123.

Taylor, C., Peter, T., Schachter, K., Paquin, S., Beldom, S., Gross, Z., & McMinn, T. L. (2009). *Youth speak up about homophobia and transphobia: The first national climate survey on homophobia in Canadian Schools. Phase one report.* Toronto, Canada: Egale Canada Human Rights Trust.

Taylor, C., & Peter, T., with McMinn, T.L., Elliott, T., Beldom, S., Ferry, A., Gross, Z., Paquin, S., & Schachter, K. (2011). *Every class in every school: The first national climate survey on homophobia, biphobia, and transphobia in Canadian schools. Final report.* Toronto, ON: Egale Canada Human Rights Trust. Available from http://www.egale.ca/index .asp?lang=E&menu=1&item=1489

Taylor, C. (2011). Homophobia creates hostile world for Canadian students [Press release]. University of Winnipeg. Retrieved from http://www.uwinnipeg.ca/index/uw-news-action/story.572/title .homophobiacreates-hostile-world-for-canadian-students

Critical Thinking

1. If you do not have an opportunity to discuss LGBTQ issues in your program, would you feel free to request that this information be provided?

2. Based on this article, what suggestions would you give professors who are considering introducing the topic in a class? What format should be used, online, face-to-face, or small group workshops? What specific topics should be discussed?

3. Write a scenario in which you tried to help a student who is being bullied, but your mentor teacher told you to stop intervening. What would you tell your mentor teacher and how would you respond to rejection of your ideas?

Internet References

American Civil Liberties Union-LGBT Youth
   https://www.aclu.org/issues/lgbt-rights/lgbt-youth
Gay-Straight Alliance Network
   https://www.gsanetwork.org
National Resource Center for Youth Development
   http://www.nrcyd.ou.edu/lgbtq-youth
StopBullying.gov
   http://www.stopbullying.gov
Welcoming Schools
   http://www.welcomingschools.org